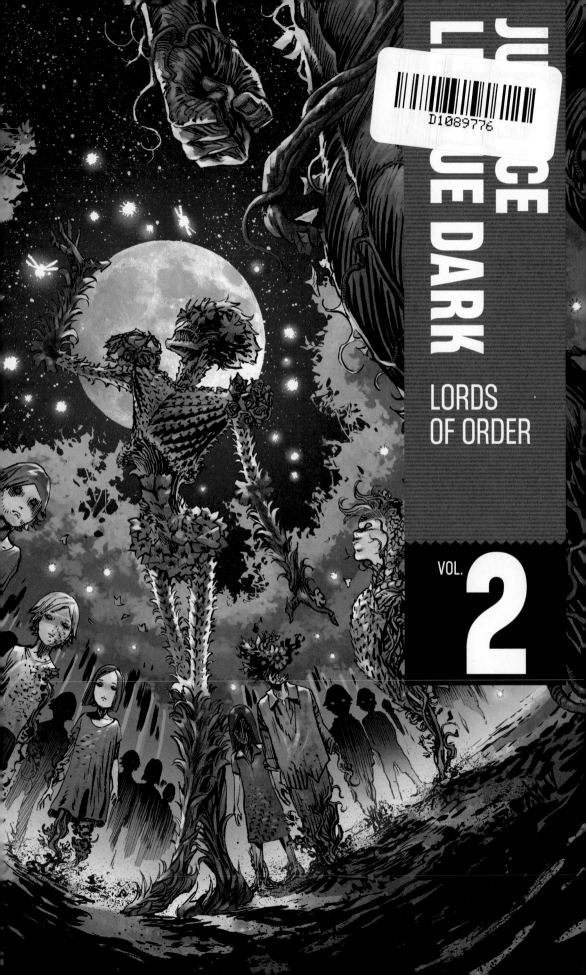

JUSTICE LEAGUE DARK

LORDS
OF ORDER

VOL. 2

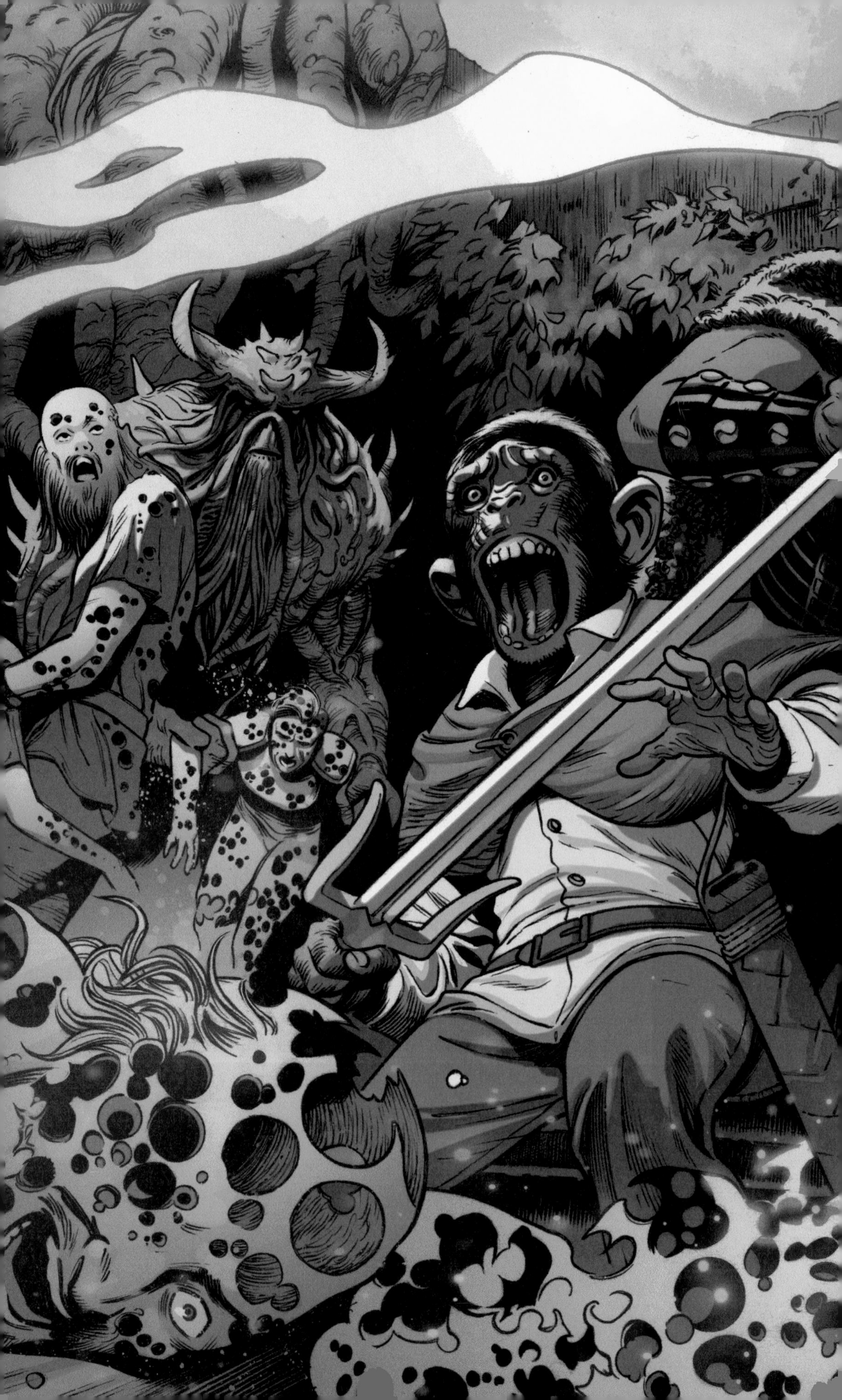

JUSTICE LEAGUE DARK

LORDS OF ORDER

writers

JAMES TYNION IV
RAM V

pencillers

ALVARO MARTÍNEZ BUENO
GUILLEM MARCH
DANIEL SAMPERE
MARK BUCKINGHAM
MIGUEL MENDONÇA

inkers

RAUL FERNANDEZ
GUILLEM MARCH
JUAN ALBARRAN
MICK GRAY
MIGUEL MENDONÇA

colorists

BRAD ANDERSON
ARIF PRIANTO
ADRIANO LUCAS

letterer

ROB LEIGH

collection cover artist

CLAYTON CRAIN

SUPERMAN created by
JERRY SIEGEL and JOE SHUSTER
By special arrangement with the
JERRY SIEGEL family

VOL.

2

MARIE JAVINS ANDREW MARINO BRITTANY HOLZHERR Editors – Original Series
JEB WOODARD Group Editor – Collected Editions
ROBIN WILDMAN Editor – Collected Edition
STEVE COOK Design Director – Books
MEGEN BELLERSEN Publication Design
ERIN VANOVER Publication Production

BOB HARRAS Senior VP – Editor-in-Chief, DC Comics
PAT McCALLUM Executive Editor, DC Comics

DAN DiDIO Publisher
JIM LEE Publisher & Chief Creative Officer
BOBBIE CHASE VP – New Publishing Initiatives & Talent Development
DON FALLETTI VP – Manufacturing Operations & Workflow Management
LAWRENCE GANEM VP – Talent Services
ALISON GILL Senior VP – Manufacturing & Operations
HANK KANALZ Senior VP – Publishing Strategy & Support Services
DAN MIRON VP – Publishing Operations
NICK J. NAPOLITANO VP – Manufacturing Administration & Design
NANCY SPEARS VP – Sales
MICHELE R. WELLS VP & Executive Editor, Young Reader

JUSTICE LEAGUE DARK VOL. 2: LORDS OF ORDER

DC Comics, 2900 West Alameda Ave., Burbank, CA 91505
Printed by LSC Communications, Kendallville, IN, USA. 9/13/19. First Printing.
ISBN: 978-1-4012-9460-1

Library of Congress Cataloging-in-Publication Data is available.

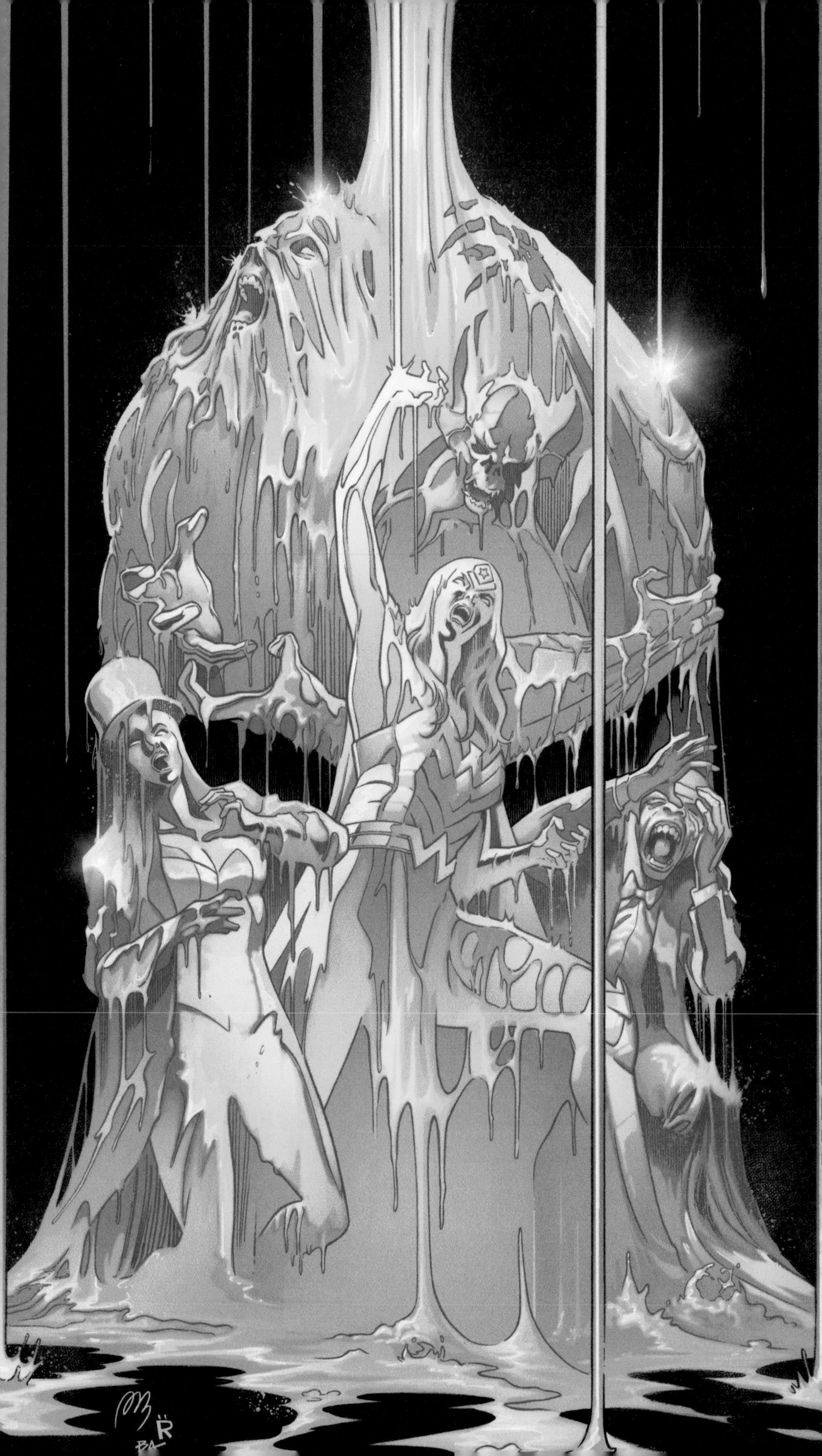

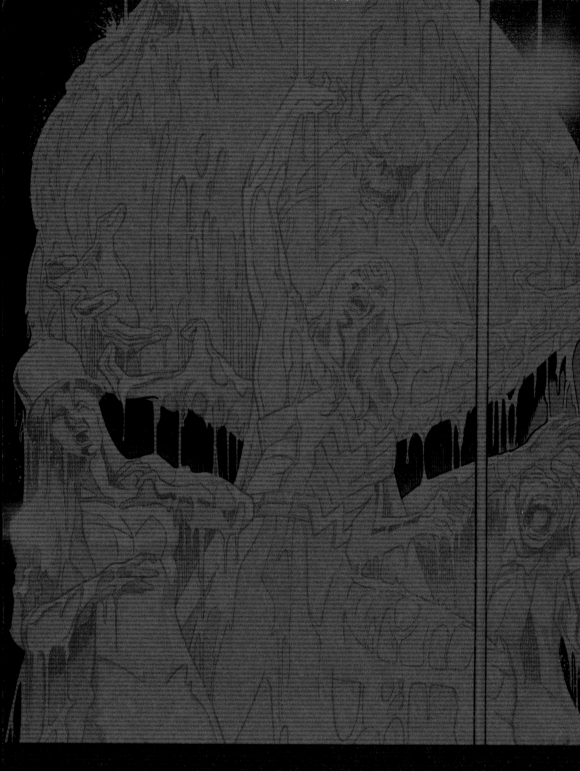

JUSTICE LEAGUE DARK
#8

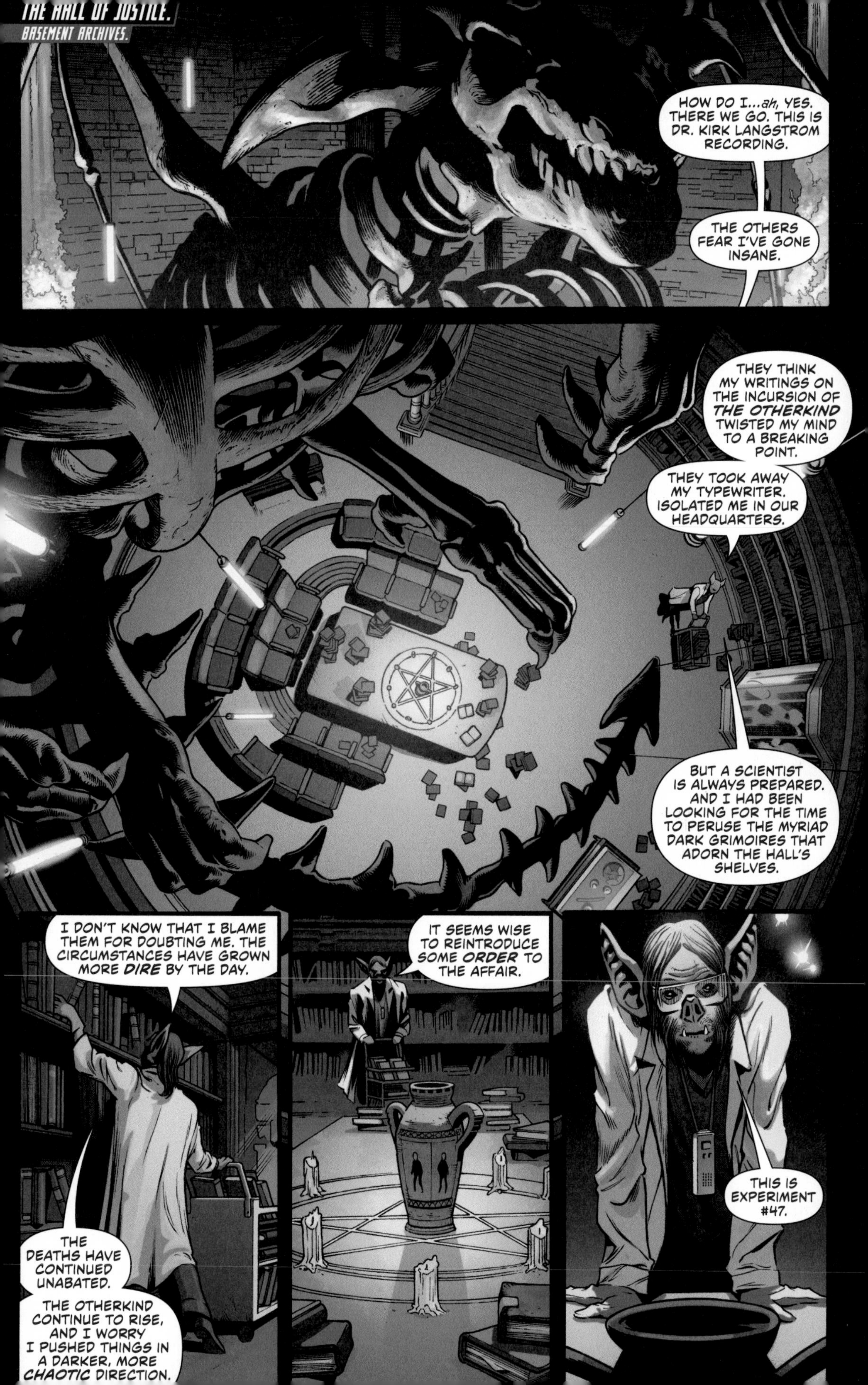
THE HALL OF JUSTICE.
BASEMENT ARCHIVES.
HOW DO I...*ah*, YES. THERE WE GO. THIS IS DR. KIRK LANGSTROM RECORDING.
THE OTHERS FEAR I'VE GONE INSANE.
THEY THINK MY WRITINGS ON THE INCURSION OF ***THE OTHERKIND*** TWISTED MY MIND TO A BREAKING POINT.
THEY TOOK AWAY MY TYPEWRITER. ISOLATED ME IN OUR HEADQUARTERS.
BUT A SCIENTIST IS ALWAYS PREPARED. AND I HAD BEEN LOOKING FOR THE TIME TO PERUSE THE MYRIAD DARK GRIMOIRES THAT ADORN THE HALL'S SHELVES.
I DON'T KNOW THAT I BLAME THEM FOR DOUBTING ME. THE CIRCUMSTANCES HAVE GROWN MORE ***DIRE*** BY THE DAY.
THE DEATHS HAVE CONTINUED UNABATED.
THE OTHERKIND CONTINUE TO RISE, AND I WORRY I PUSHED THINGS IN A DARKER, MORE ***CHAOTIC*** DIRECTION.
IT SEEMS WISE TO REINTRODUCE SOME ***ORDER*** TO THE AFFAIR.
THIS IS EXPERIMENT #47.

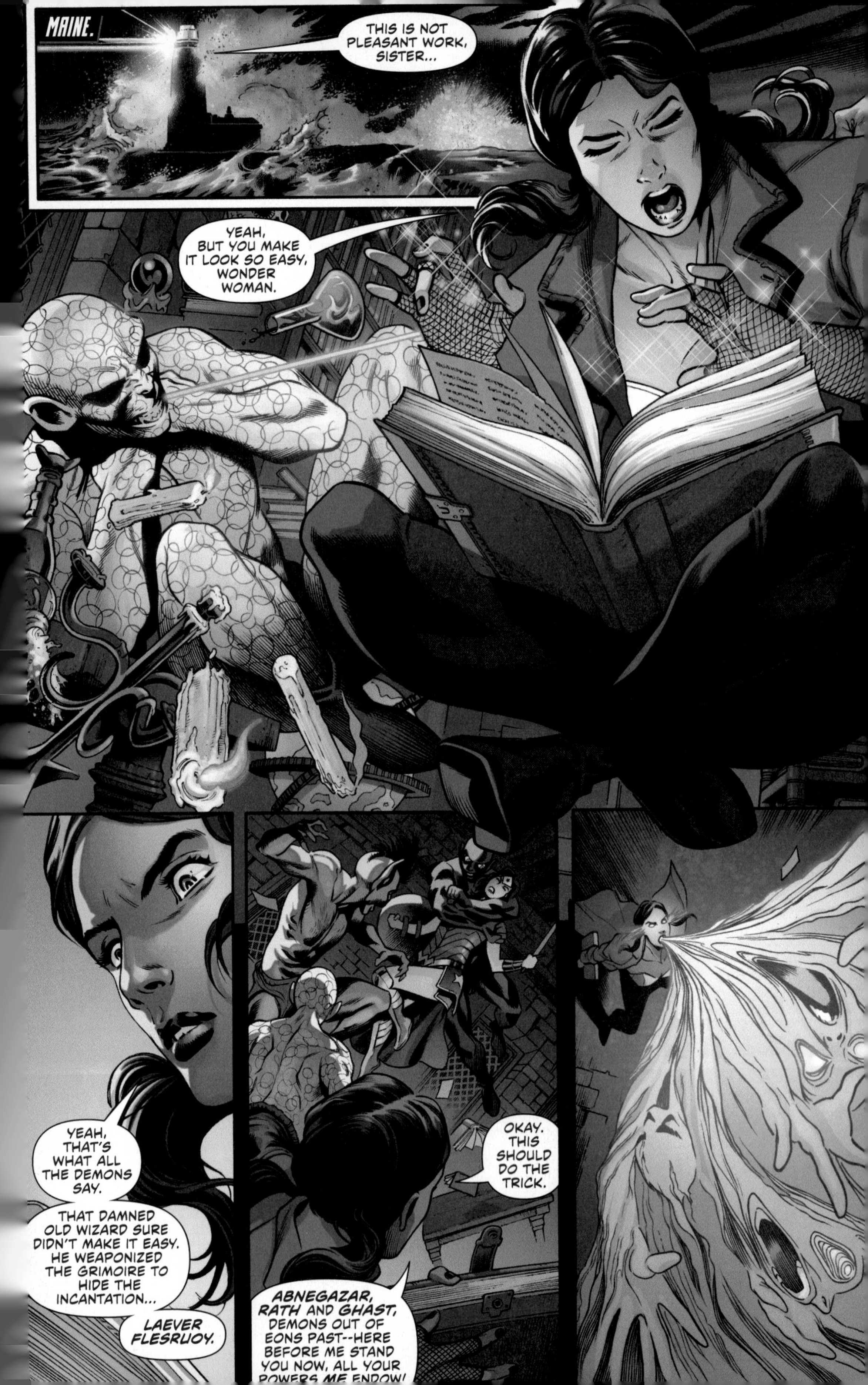
MAINE.
THIS IS NOT PLEASANT WORK, SISTER...
YEAH, BUT YOU MAKE IT LOOK SO EASY, WONDER WOMAN.
YEAH, THAT'S WHAT ALL THE DEMONS SAY.
THAT DAMNED OLD WIZARD SURE DIDN'T MAKE IT EASY. HE WEAPONIZED THE GRIMOIRE TO HIDE THE INCANTATION...
LAEVER FLESRUOY.
OKAY. THIS SHOULD DO THE TRICK.
ABNEGAZAR, RATH AND GHAST, DEMONS OUT OF EONS PAST--HERE BEFORE ME STAND YOU NOW, ALL YOUR POWERS ME ENDOW!

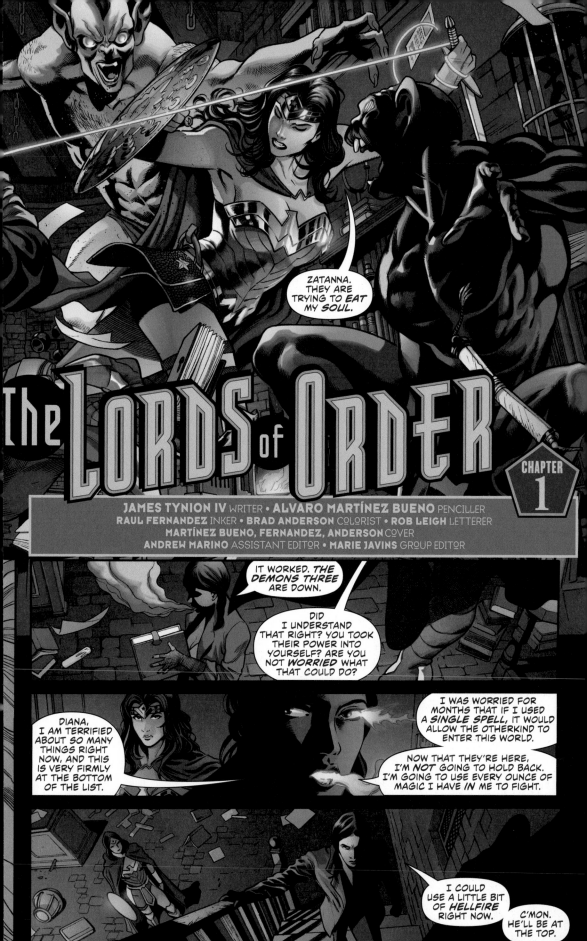

ZATANNA. THEY ARE TRYING TO *EAT* MY SOUL.

The Lords of Order

CHAPTER 1

JAMES TYNION IV WRITER • ALVARO MARTÍNEZ BUENO PENCILLER
RAUL FERNANDEZ INKER • BRAD ANDERSON COLORIST • ROB LEIGH LETTERER
MARTÍNEZ BUENO, FERNANDEZ, ANDERSON COVER
ANDREW MARINO ASSISTANT EDITOR • MARIE JAVINS GROUP EDITOR

IT WORKED. *THE DEMONS THREE* ARE DOWN.

DID I UNDERSTAND THAT RIGHT? YOU TOOK THEIR POWER INTO YOURSELF? ARE YOU NOT *WORRIED* WHAT THAT COULD DO?

DIANA, I AM TERRIFIED ABOUT SO MANY THINGS RIGHT NOW, AND THIS IS VERY FIRMLY AT THE BOTTOM OF THE LIST.

I WAS WORRIED FOR MONTHS THAT IF I USED A *SINGLE SPELL*, IT WOULD ALLOW THE OTHERKIND TO ENTER THIS WORLD.

NOW THAT THEY'RE HERE, I'M *NOT* GOING TO HOLD BACK. I'M GOING TO USE EVERY OUNCE OF MAGIC I HAVE *IN* ME TO FIGHT.

I COULD USE A LITTLE BIT OF *HELLFIRE* RIGHT NOW.

C'MON. HE'LL BE AT THE TOP.

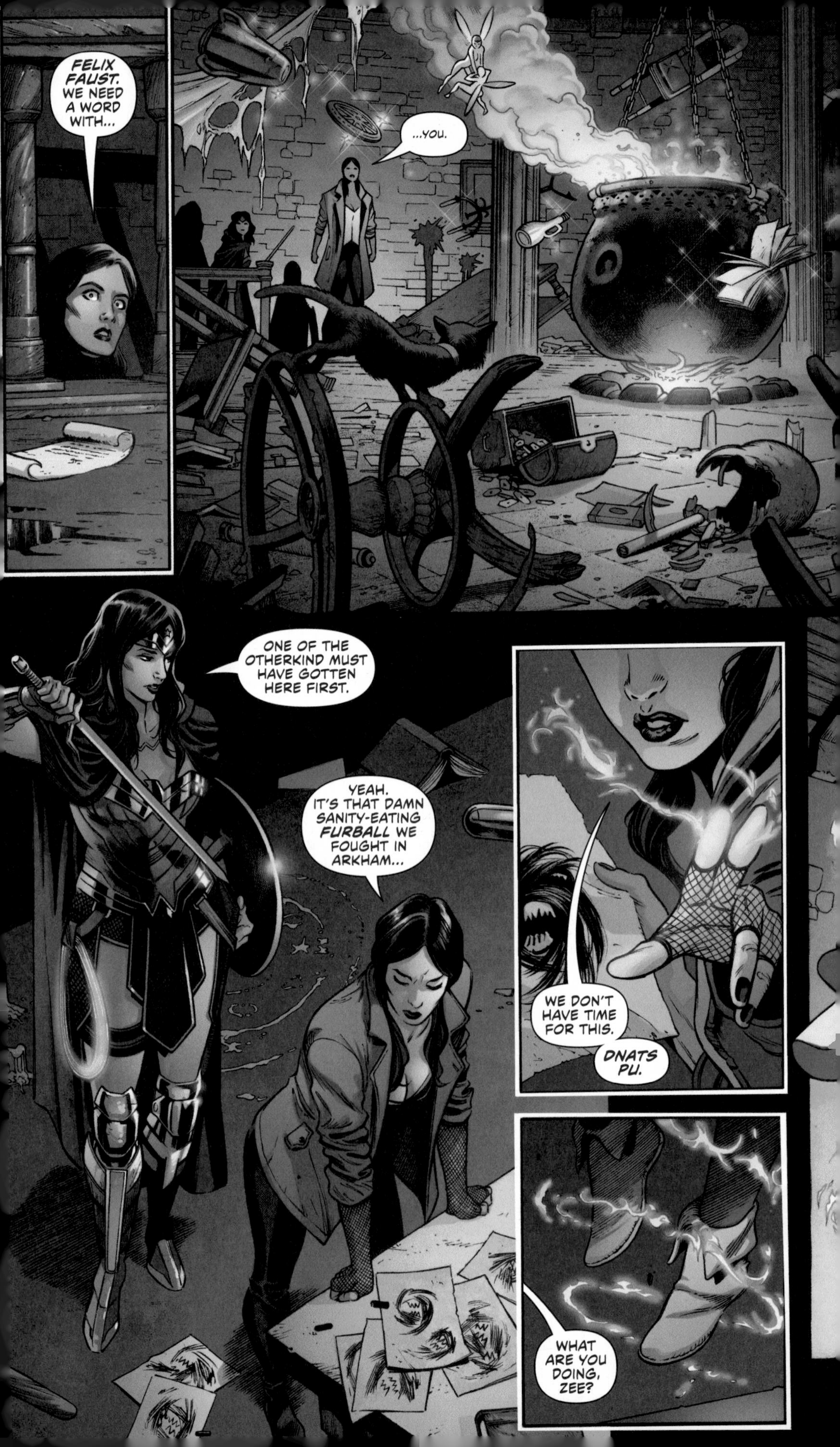
FELIX FAUST. WE NEED A WORD WITH...
...YOU.
ONE OF THE OTHERKIND MUST HAVE GOTTEN HERE FIRST.
YEAH. IT'S THAT DAMN SANITY-EATING FURBALL WE FOUGHT IN ARKHAM...
WE DON'T HAVE TIME FOR THIS.
DNATS PU.
WHAT ARE YOU DOING, ZEE?

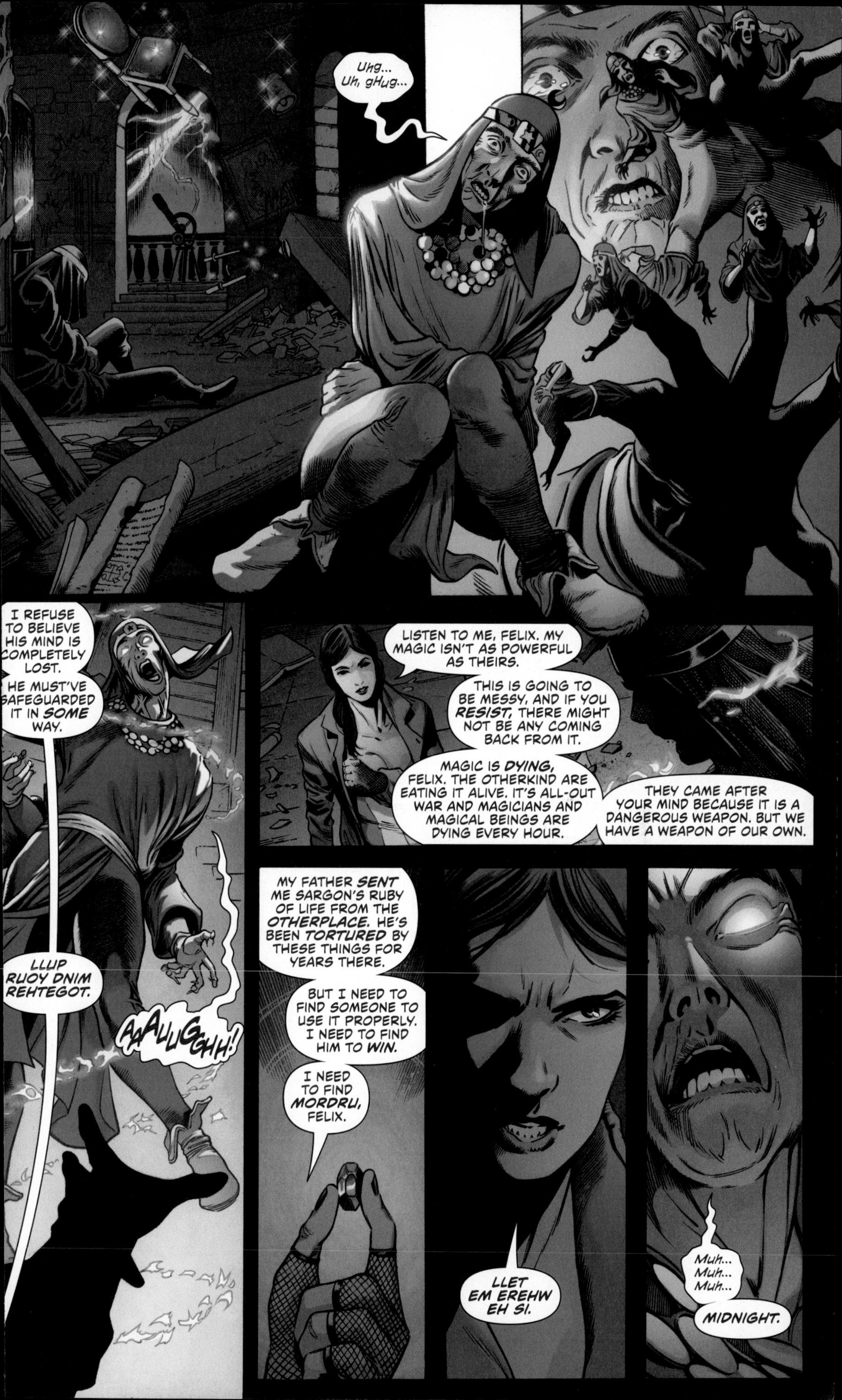

Uhg...
Uh, gHug...
I REFUSE TO BELIEVE HIS MIND IS COMPLETELY LOST.
HE MUST'VE SAFEGUARDED IT IN SOME WAY.
LLUP RUOY DNIM REHTEGOT.
AAAUUGGHH!
LISTEN TO ME, FELIX. MY MAGIC ISN'T AS POWERFUL AS THEIRS.
THIS IS GOING TO BE MESSY, AND IF YOU RESIST, THERE MIGHT NOT BE ANY COMING BACK FROM IT.
MAGIC IS DYING, FELIX. THE OTHERKIND ARE EATING IT ALIVE. IT'S ALL-OUT WAR AND MAGICIANS AND MAGICAL BEINGS ARE DYING EVERY HOUR.
THEY CAME AFTER YOUR MIND BECAUSE IT IS A DANGEROUS WEAPON. BUT WE HAVE A WEAPON OF OUR OWN.
MY FATHER SENT ME SARGON'S RUBY OF LIFE FROM THE OTHERPLACE. HE'S BEEN TORTURED BY THESE THINGS FOR YEARS THERE.
BUT I NEED TO FIND SOMEONE TO USE IT PROPERLY. I NEED TO FIND HIM TO WIN.
I NEED TO FIND MORDRU, FELIX.
LLET EM EREHW EH SI.
Muh... Muh... Muh...
MIDNIGHT.

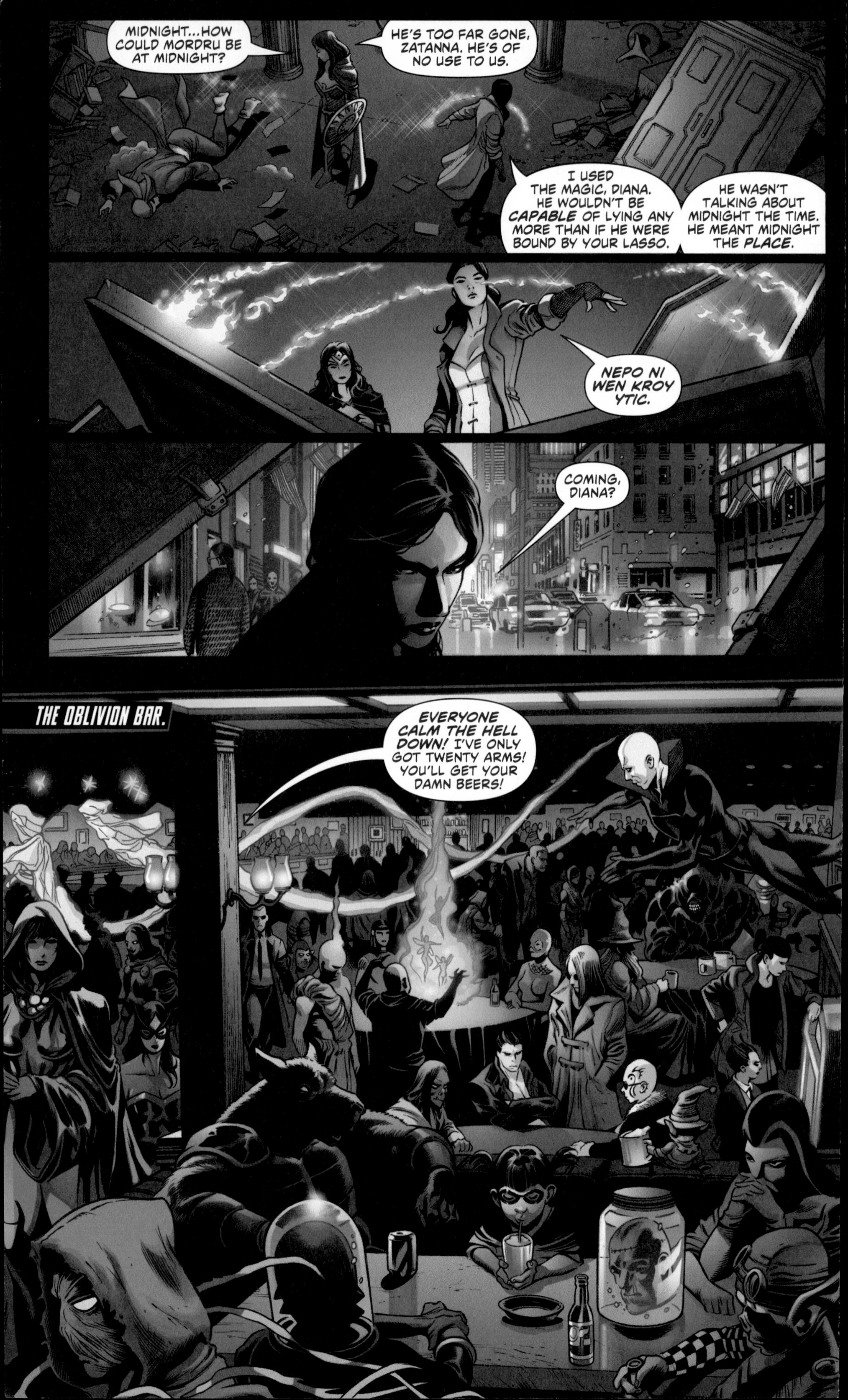
MIDNIGHT...HOW COULD MORDRU BE AT MIDNIGHT?
HE'S TOO FAR GONE, ZATANNA. HE'S OF NO USE TO US.
I USED THE MAGIC, DIANA. HE WOULDN'T BE CAPABLE OF LYING ANY MORE THAN IF HE WERE BOUND BY YOUR LASSO.
HE WASN'T TALKING ABOUT MIDNIGHT THE TIME. HE MEANT MIDNIGHT THE PLACE.
NEPO NI WEN KROY YTIC.
COMING, DIANA?
THE OBLIVION BAR.
EVERYONE CALM THE HELL DOWN! I'VE ONLY GOT TWENTY ARMS! YOU'LL GET YOUR DAMN BEERS!

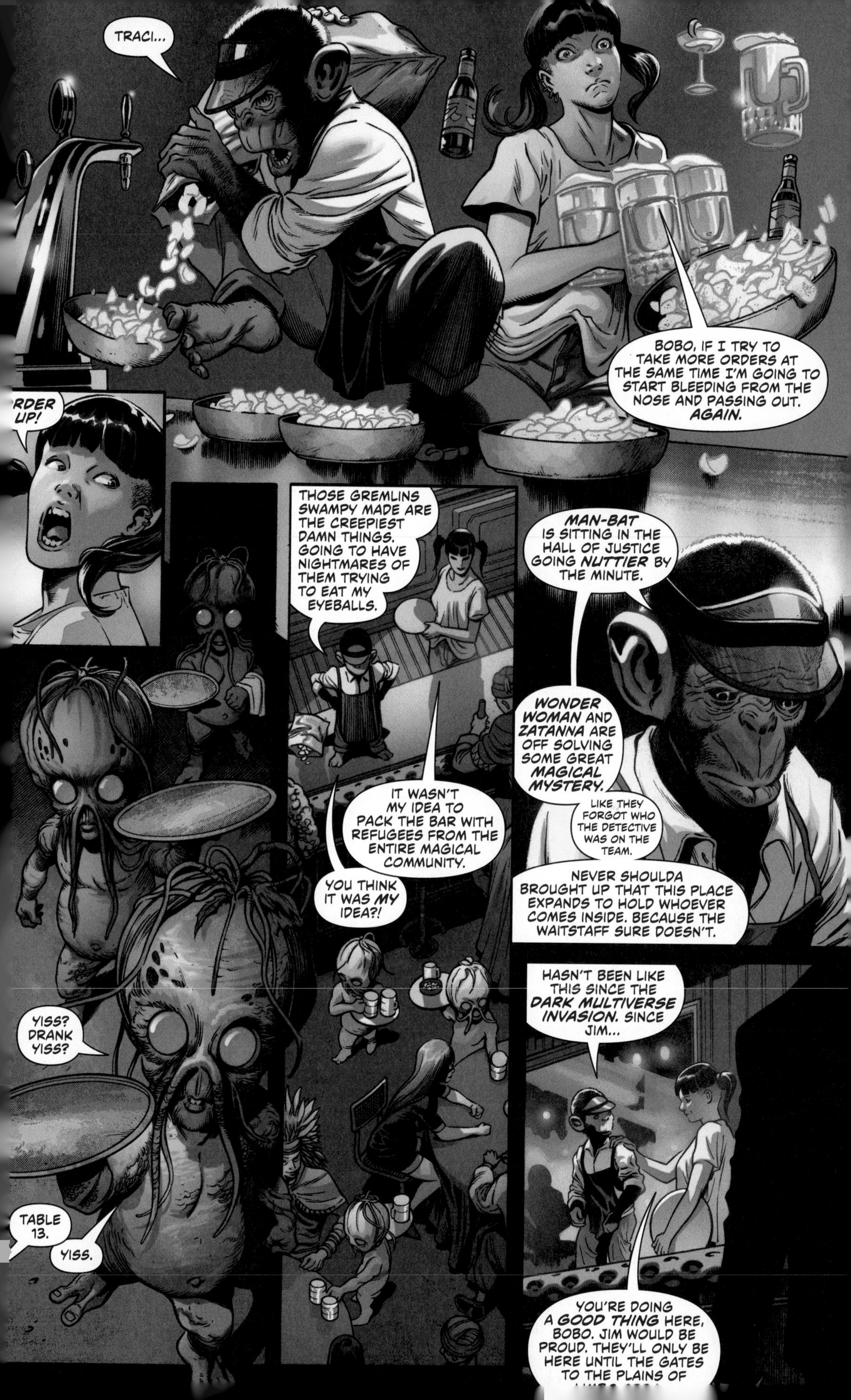
TRACI...
BOBO, IF I TRY TO TAKE MORE ORDERS AT THE SAME TIME I'M GOING TO START BLEEDING FROM THE NOSE AND PASSING OUT. AGAIN.
RDER UP!
THOSE GREMLINS SWAMPY MADE ARE THE CREEPIEST DAMN THINGS. GOING TO HAVE NIGHTMARES OF THEM TRYING TO EAT MY EYEBALLS.
IT WASN'T MY IDEA TO PACK THE BAR WITH REFUGEES FROM THE ENTIRE MAGICAL COMMUNITY.
YOU THINK IT WAS MY IDEA?!
MAN-BAT IS SITTING IN THE HALL OF JUSTICE GOING NUTTIER BY THE MINUTE.
WONDER WOMAN AND ZATANNA ARE OFF SOLVING SOME GREAT MAGICAL MYSTERY.
LIKE THEY FORGOT WHO THE DETECTIVE WAS ON THE TEAM.
NEVER SHOULDA BROUGHT UP THAT THIS PLACE EXPANDS TO HOLD WHOEVER COMES INSIDE. BECAUSE THE WAITSTAFF SURE DOESN'T.
YISS? DRANK YISS?
TABLE 13.
YISS.
HASN'T BEEN LIKE THIS SINCE THE DARK MULTIVERSE INVASION. SINCE JIM...
YOU'RE DOING A GOOD THING HERE, BOBO. JIM WOULD BE PROUD. THEY'LL ONLY BE HERE UNTIL THE GATES TO THE PLAINS OF

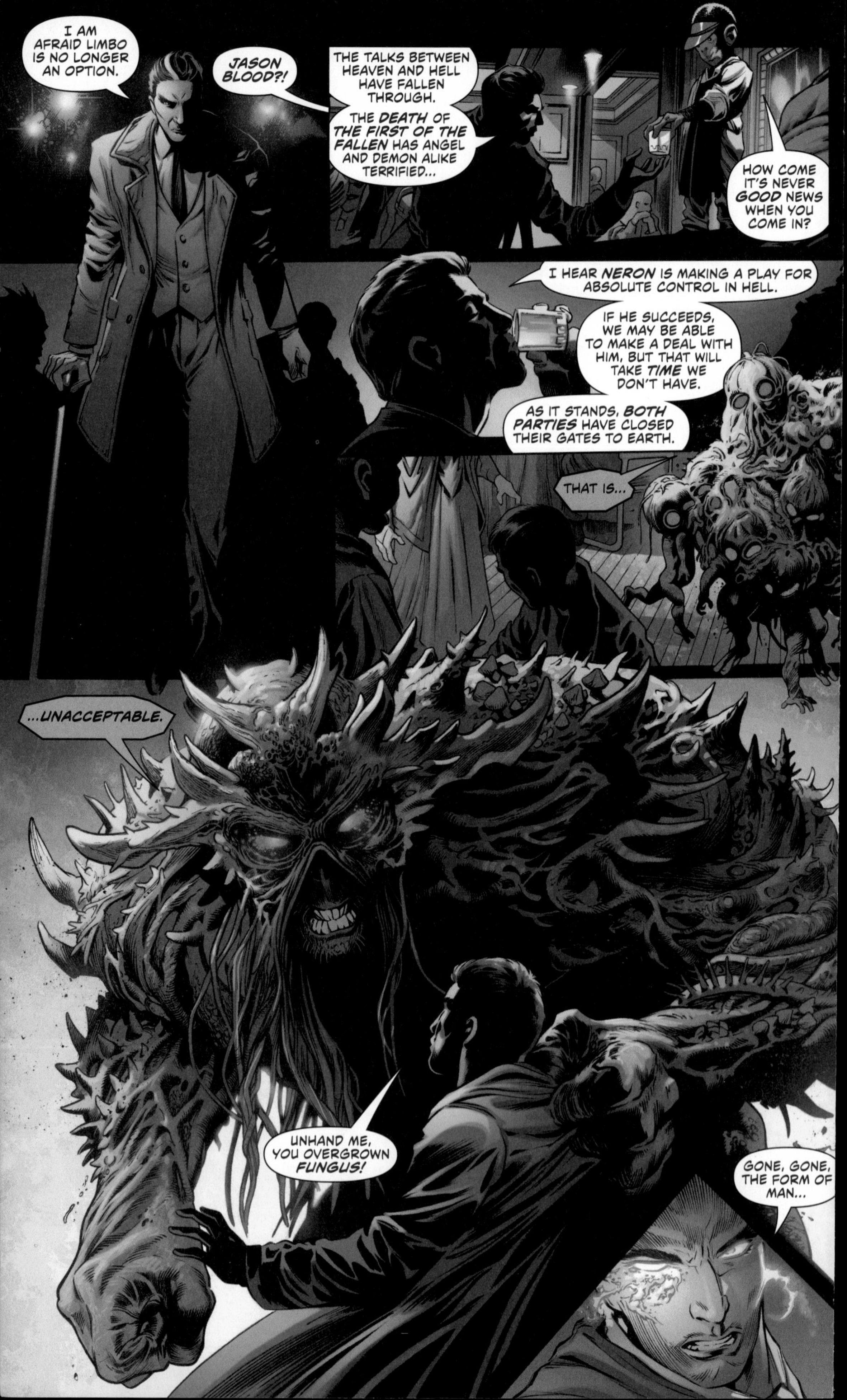
I AM AFRAID LIMBO IS NO LONGER AN OPTION.
JASON BLOOD?!
THE TALKS BETWEEN HEAVEN AND HELL HAVE FALLEN THROUGH.
THE DEATH OF THE FIRST OF THE FALLEN HAS ANGEL AND DEMON ALIKE TERRIFIED...
HOW COME IT'S NEVER GOOD NEWS WHEN YOU COME IN?
I HEAR NERON IS MAKING A PLAY FOR ABSOLUTE CONTROL IN HELL.
IF HE SUCCEEDS, WE MAY BE ABLE TO MAKE A DEAL WITH HIM, BUT THAT WILL TAKE TIME WE DON'T HAVE.
AS IT STANDS, BOTH PARTIES HAVE CLOSED THEIR GATES TO EARTH.
THAT IS...
...UNACCEPTABLE.
UNHAND ME, YOU OVERGROWN FUNGUS!
GONE, GONE, THE FORM OF MAN...

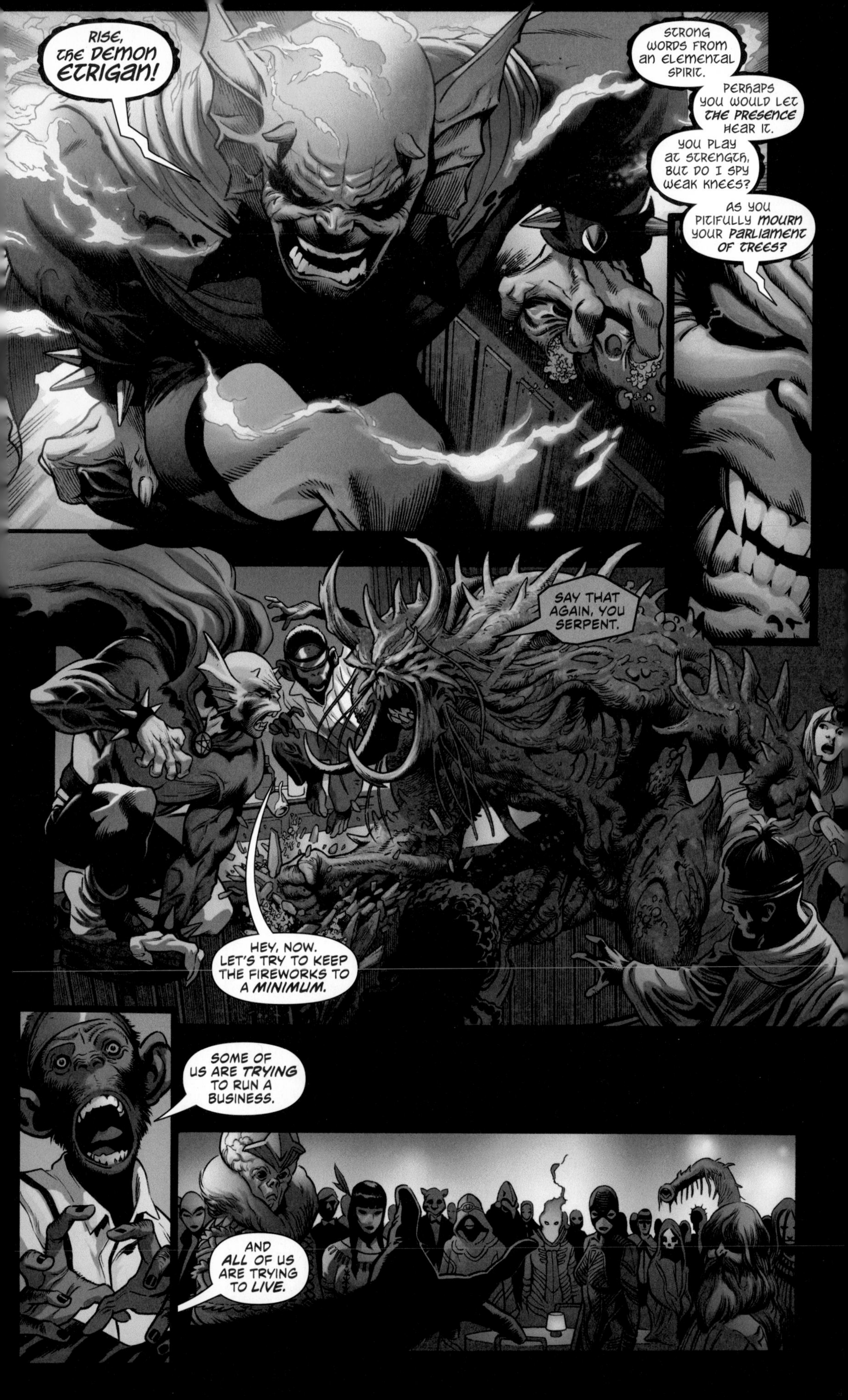
RISE, THE DEMON ETRIGAN!
STRONG WORDS FROM AN ELEMENTAL SPIRIT.
PERHAPS YOU WOULD LET THE PRESENCE HEAR IT.
YOU PLAY AT STRENGTH, BUT DO I SPY WEAK KNEES?
AS YOU PITIFULLY MOURN YOUR PARLIAMENT OF TREES?
SAY THAT AGAIN, YOU SERPENT.
HEY, NOW. LET'S TRY TO KEEP THE FIREWORKS TO A MINIMUM.
SOME OF US ARE TRYING TO RUN A BUSINESS.
AND ALL OF US ARE TRYING TO LIVE.

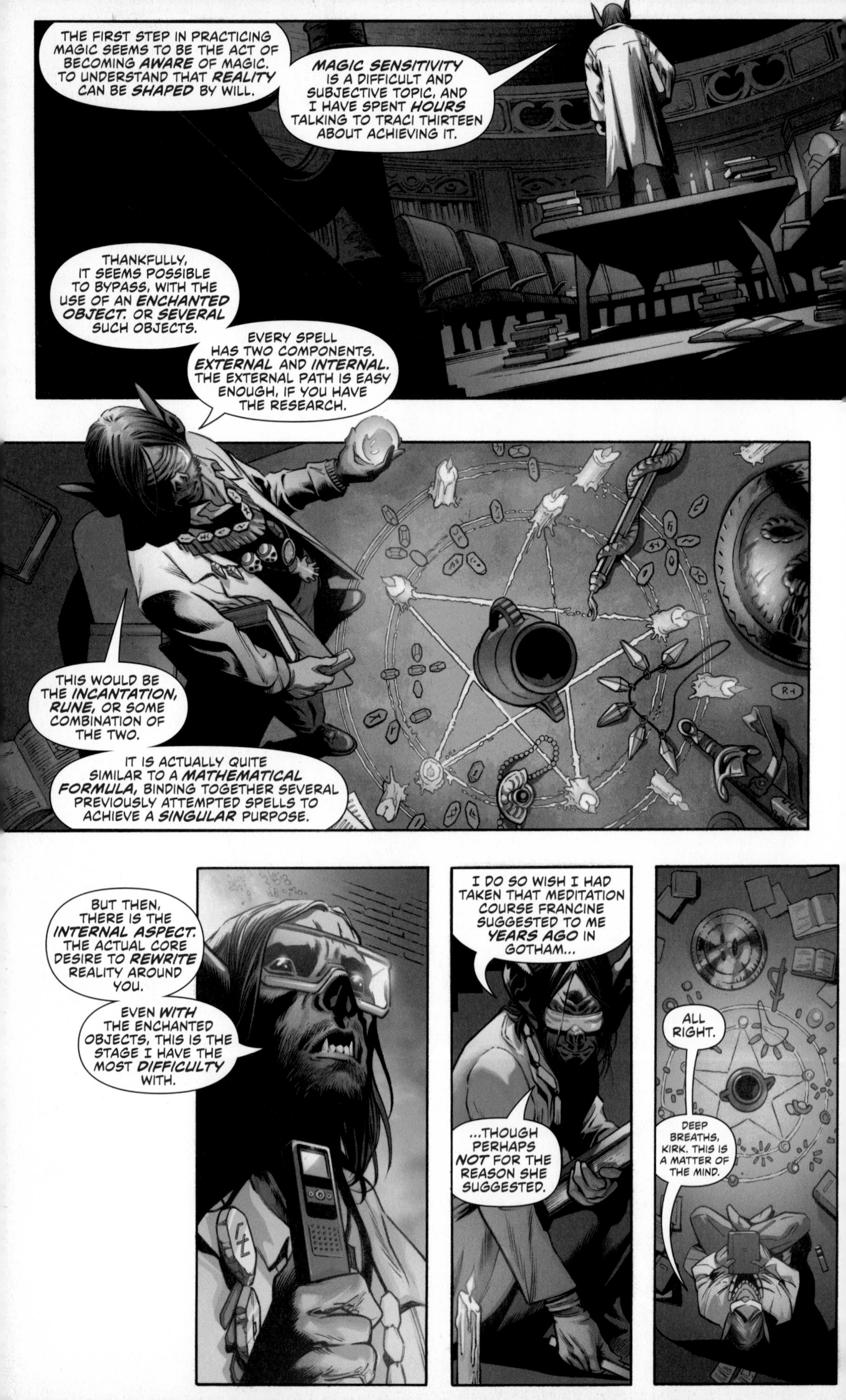
THE FIRST STEP IN PRACTICING MAGIC SEEMS TO BE THE ACT OF BECOMING AWARE OF MAGIC. TO UNDERSTAND THAT REALITY CAN BE SHAPED BY WILL.
MAGIC SENSITIVITY IS A DIFFICULT AND SUBJECTIVE TOPIC, AND I HAVE SPENT HOURS TALKING TO TRACI THIRTEEN ABOUT ACHIEVING IT.
THANKFULLY, IT SEEMS POSSIBLE TO BYPASS, WITH THE USE OF AN ENCHANTED OBJECT, OR SEVERAL SUCH OBJECTS.
EVERY SPELL HAS TWO COMPONENTS. EXTERNAL AND INTERNAL. THE EXTERNAL PATH IS EASY ENOUGH, IF YOU HAVE THE RESEARCH.
THIS WOULD BE THE INCANTATION, RUNE, OR SOME COMBINATION OF THE TWO.
IT IS ACTUALLY QUITE SIMILAR TO A MATHEMATICAL FORMULA, BINDING TOGETHER SEVERAL PREVIOUSLY ATTEMPTED SPELLS TO ACHIEVE A SINGULAR PURPOSE.
BUT THEN, THERE IS THE INTERNAL ASPECT. THE ACTUAL CORE DESIRE TO REWRITE REALITY AROUND YOU.
EVEN WITH THE ENCHANTED OBJECTS, THIS IS THE STAGE I HAVE THE MOST DIFFICULTY WITH.
I DO SO WISH I HAD TAKEN THAT MEDITATION COURSE FRANCINE SUGGESTED TO ME YEARS AGO IN GOTHAM...
...THOUGH PERHAPS NOT FOR THE REASON SHE SUGGESTED.
ALL RIGHT.
DEEP BREATHS, KIRK. THIS IS A MATTER OF THE MIND.

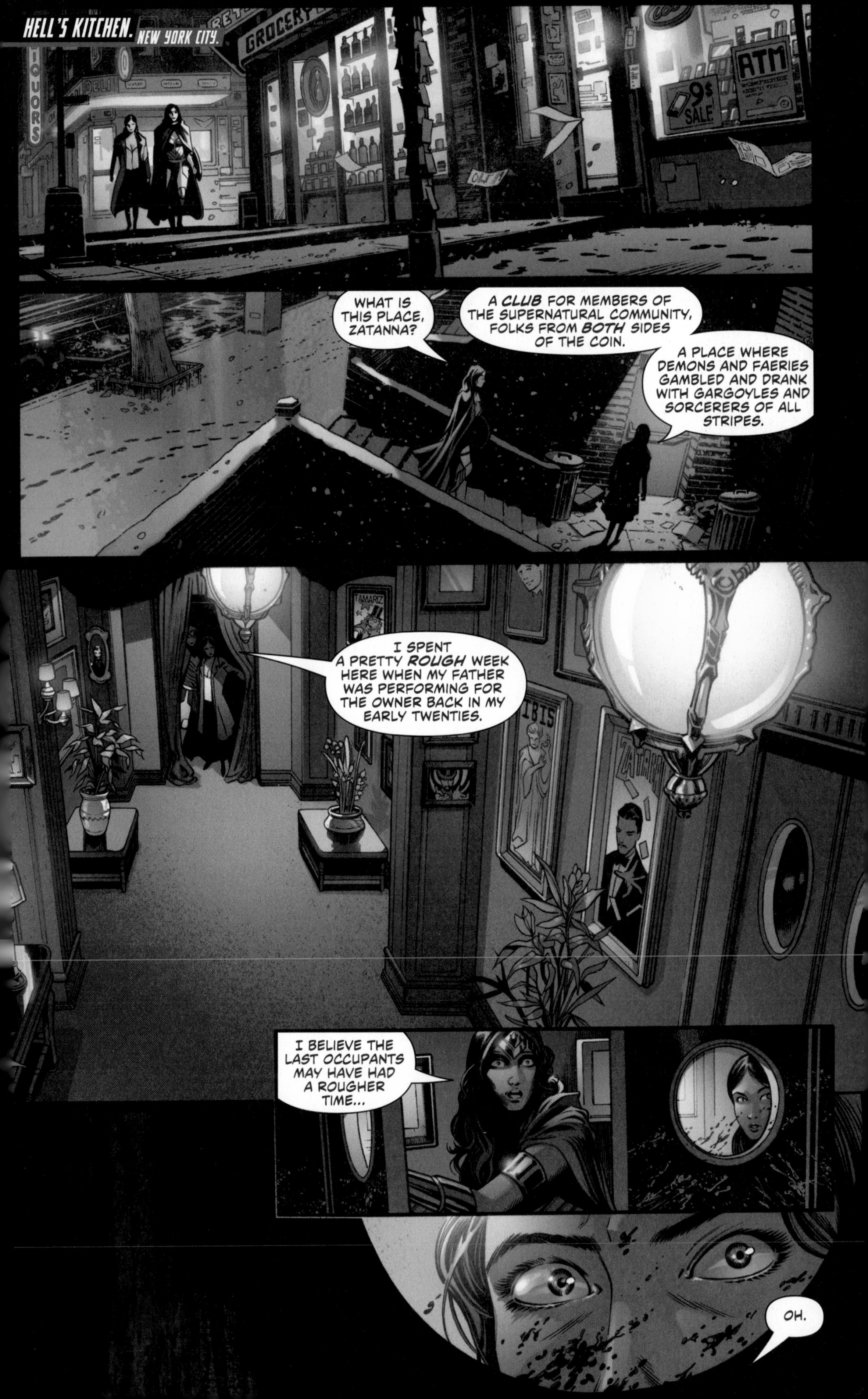
HELL'S KITCHEN. NEW YORK CITY.
WHAT IS THIS PLACE, ZATANNA?
A CLUB FOR MEMBERS OF THE SUPERNATURAL COMMUNITY, FOLKS FROM BOTH SIDES OF THE COIN.
A PLACE WHERE DEMONS AND FAERIES GAMBLED AND DRANK WITH GARGOYLES AND SORCERERS OF ALL STRIPES.
I SPENT A PRETTY ROUGH WEEK HERE WHEN MY FATHER WAS PERFORMING FOR THE OWNER BACK IN MY EARLY TWENTIES.
I BELIEVE THE LAST OCCUPANTS MAY HAVE HAD A ROUGHER TIME...
OH.

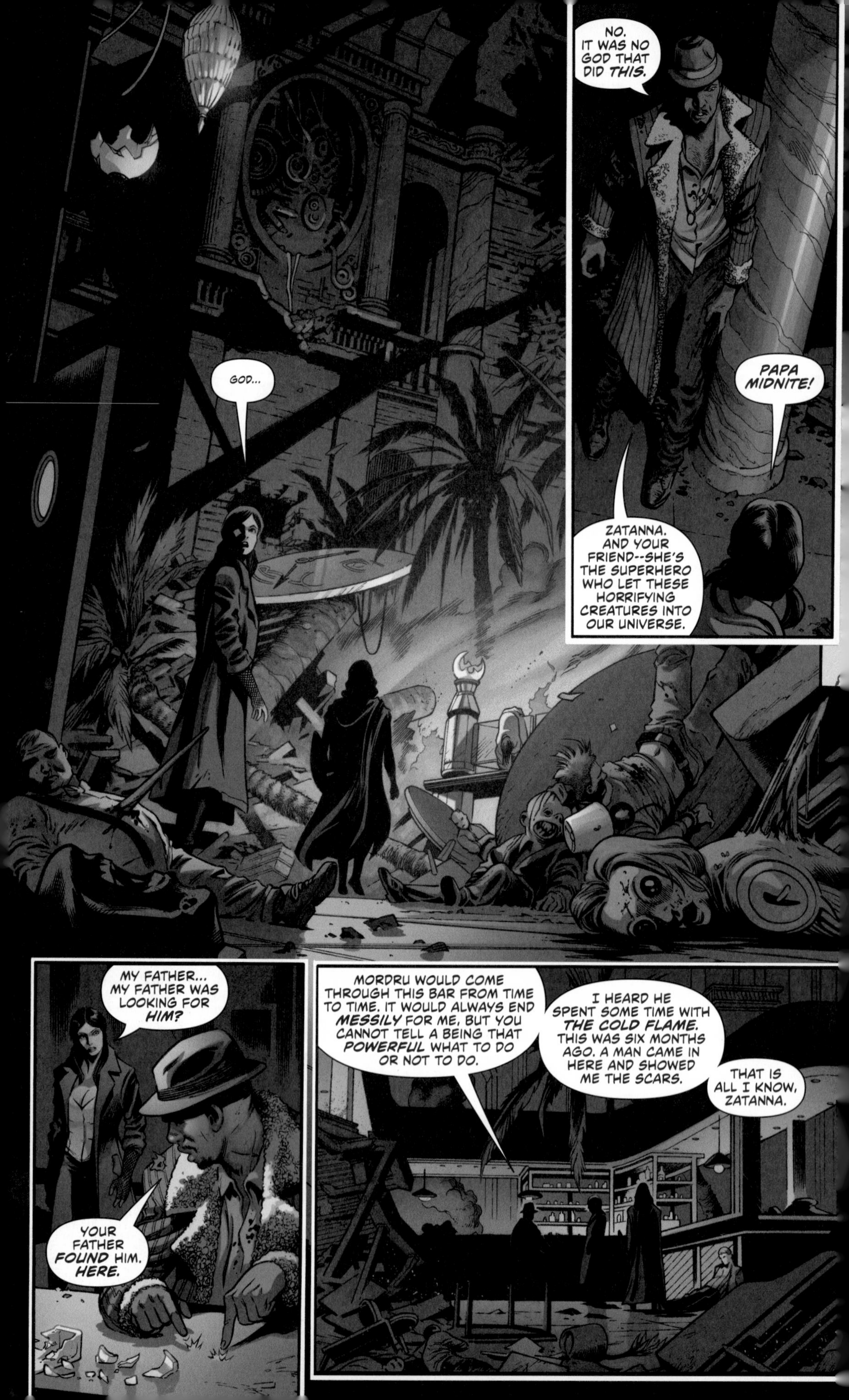
GOD...
NO. IT WAS NO GOD THAT DID THIS.
PAPA MIDNITE!
ZATANNA. AND YOUR FRIEND--SHE'S THE SUPERHERO WHO LET THESE HORRIFYING CREATURES INTO OUR UNIVERSE.
MY FATHER... MY FATHER WAS LOOKING FOR HIM?
YOUR FATHER FOUND HIM. HERE.
MORDRU WOULD COME THROUGH THIS BAR FROM TIME TO TIME. IT WOULD ALWAYS END MESSILY FOR ME, BUT YOU CANNOT TELL A BEING THAT POWERFUL WHAT TO DO OR NOT TO DO.
I HEARD HE SPENT SOME TIME WITH THE COLD FLAME. THIS WAS SIX MONTHS AGO. A MAN CAME IN HERE AND SHOWED ME THE SCARS.
THAT IS ALL I KNOW, ZATANNA.

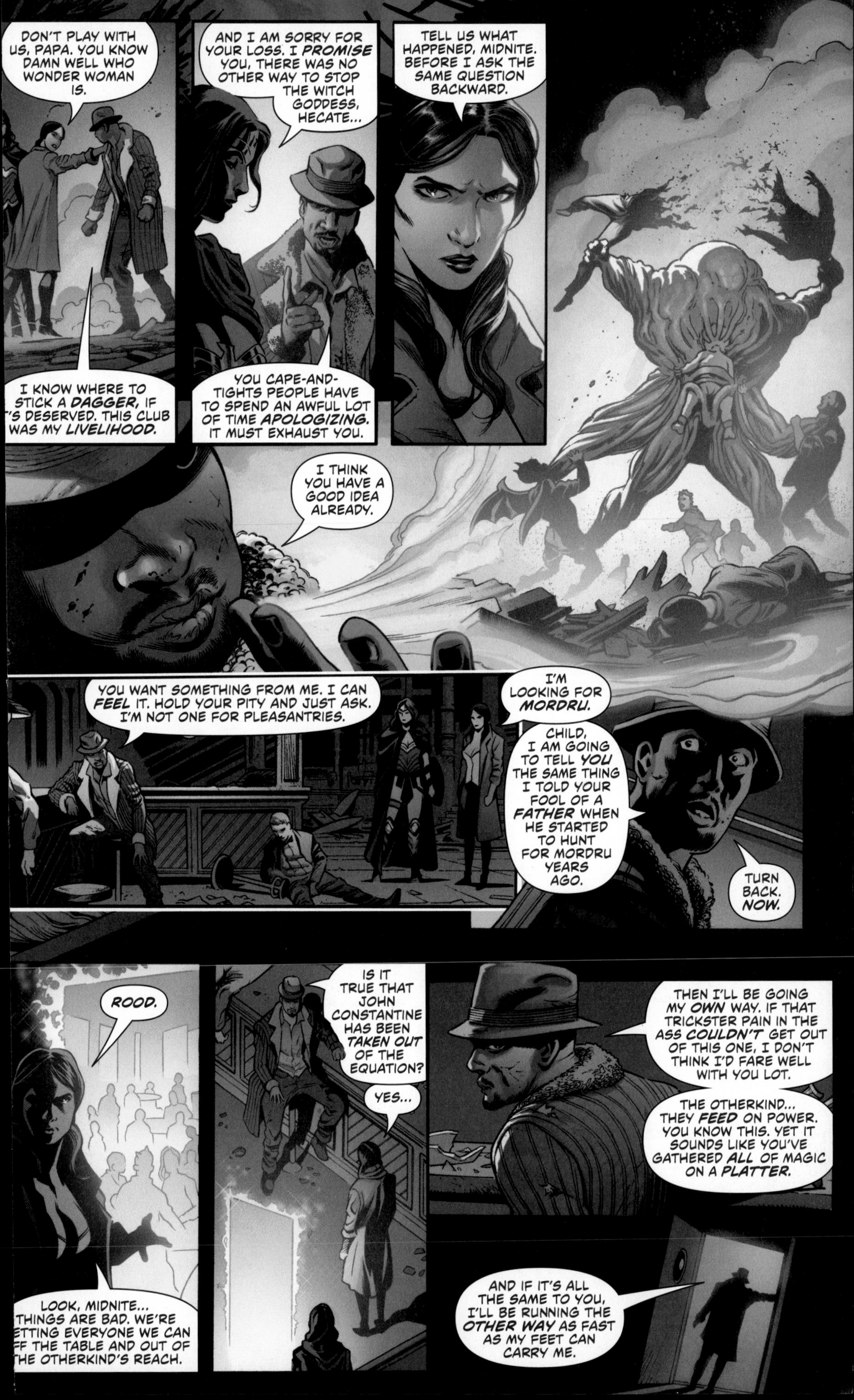
DON'T PLAY WITH US, PAPA. YOU KNOW DAMN WELL WHO WONDER WOMAN IS.
I KNOW WHERE TO STICK A DAGGER, IF IT'S DESERVED. THIS CLUB WAS MY LIVELIHOOD.
AND I AM SORRY FOR YOUR LOSS. I PROMISE YOU, THERE WAS NO OTHER WAY TO STOP THE WITCH GODDESS, HECATE...
YOU CAPE-AND-TIGHTS PEOPLE HAVE TO SPEND AN AWFUL LOT OF TIME APOLOGIZING. IT MUST EXHAUST YOU.
TELL US WHAT HAPPENED, MIDNITE. BEFORE I ASK THE SAME QUESTION BACKWARD.
I THINK YOU HAVE A GOOD IDEA ALREADY.
YOU WANT SOMETHING FROM ME. I CAN FEEL IT. HOLD YOUR PITY AND JUST ASK. I'M NOT ONE FOR PLEASANTRIES.
I'M LOOKING FOR MORDRU.
CHILD, I AM GOING TO TELL YOU THE SAME THING I TOLD YOUR FOOL OF A FATHER WHEN HE STARTED TO HUNT FOR MORDRU YEARS AGO.
TURN BACK. NOW.
ROOD.
LOOK, MIDNITE... THINGS ARE BAD. WE'RE GETTING EVERYONE WE CAN OFF THE TABLE AND OUT OF THE OTHERKIND'S REACH.
IS IT TRUE THAT JOHN CONSTANTINE HAS BEEN TAKEN OUT OF THE EQUATION?
YES...
THEN I'LL BE GOING MY OWN WAY. IF THAT TRICKSTER PAIN IN THE ASS COULDN'T GET OUT OF THIS ONE, I DON'T THINK I'D FARE WELL WITH YOU LOT.
THE OTHERKIND... THEY FEED ON POWER. YOU KNOW THIS. YET IT SOUNDS LIKE YOU'VE GATHERED ALL OF MAGIC ON A PLATTER.
AND IF IT'S ALL THE SAME TO YOU, I'LL BE RUNNING THE OTHER WAY AS FAST AS MY FEET CAN CARRY ME.

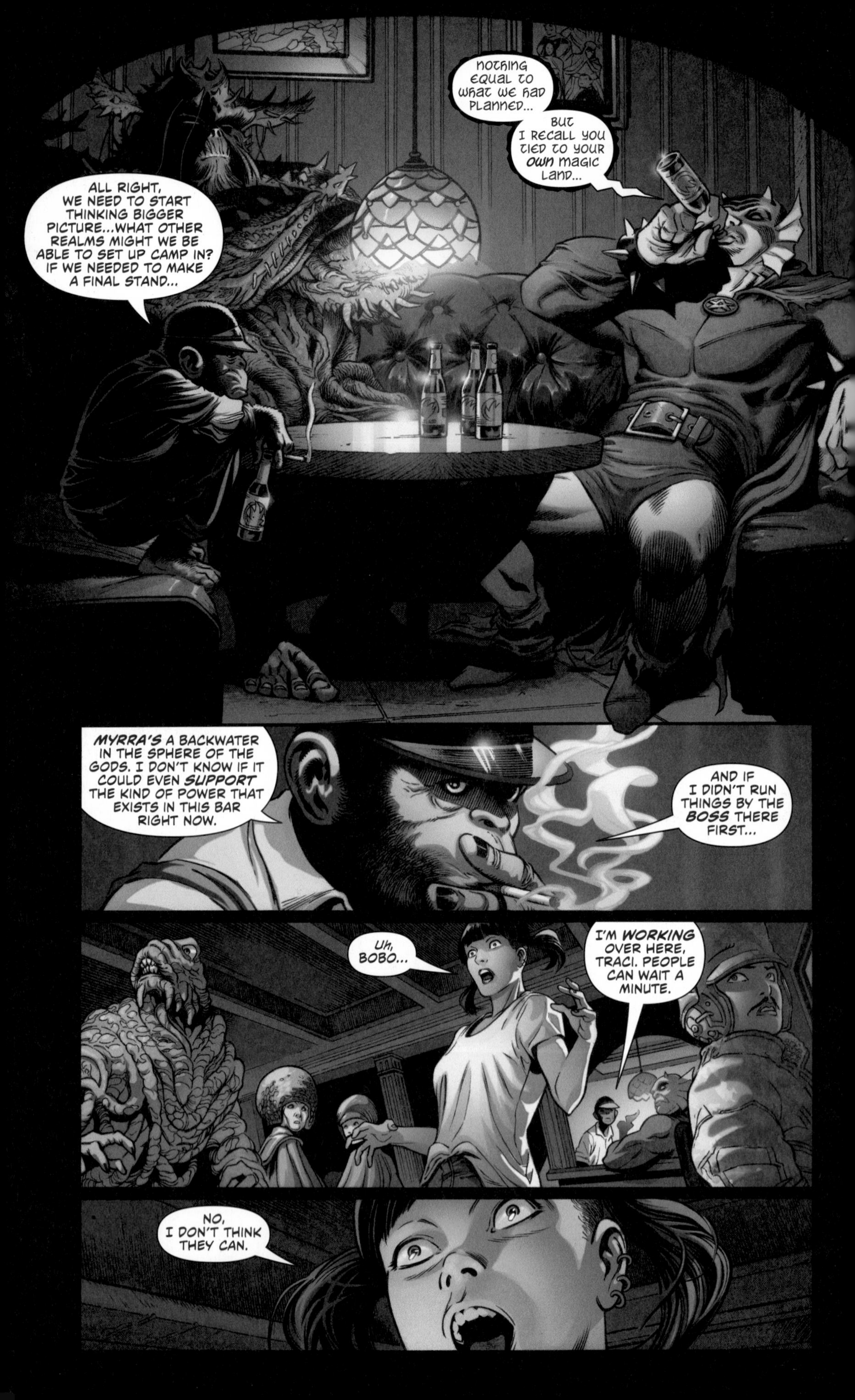
ALL RIGHT, WE NEED TO START THINKING BIGGER PICTURE...WHAT OTHER REALMS MIGHT WE BE ABLE TO SET UP CAMP IN? IF WE NEEDED TO MAKE A FINAL STAND...
NOTHING EQUAL TO WHAT WE HAD PLANNED...
BUT I RECALL YOU TIED TO YOUR OWN MAGIC LAND...
MYRRA'S A BACKWATER IN THE SPHERE OF THE GODS. I DON'T KNOW IF IT COULD EVEN SUPPORT THE KIND OF POWER THAT EXISTS IN THIS BAR RIGHT NOW.
AND IF I DIDN'T RUN THINGS BY THE BOSS THERE FIRST...
Uh, BOBO...
I'M WORKING OVER HERE, TRACI. PEOPLE CAN WAIT A MINUTE.
NO, I DON'T THINK THEY CAN.

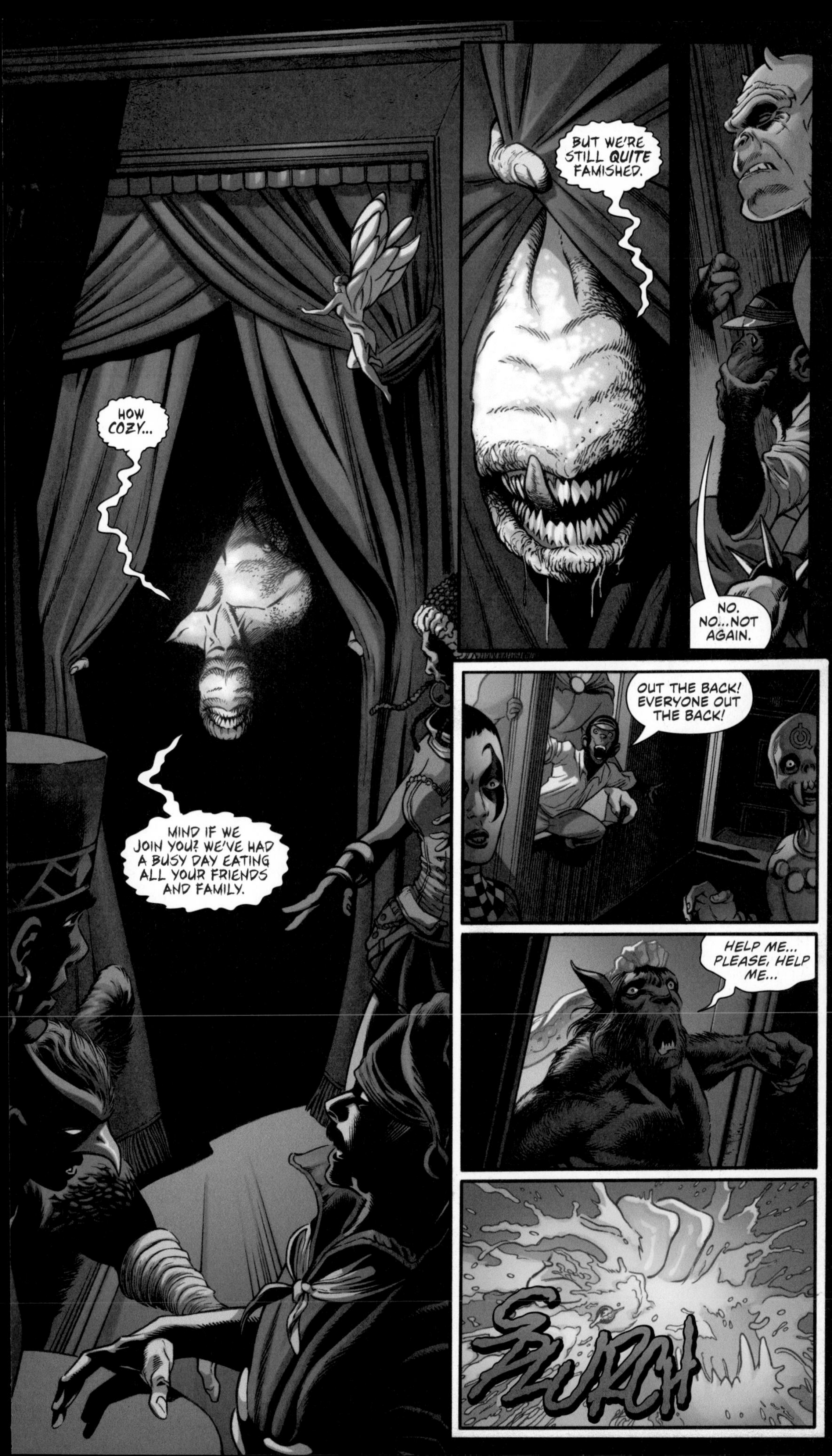
HOW COZY...
MIND IF WE JOIN YOU? WE'VE HAD A BUSY DAY EATING ALL YOUR FRIENDS AND FAMILY.
BUT WE'RE STILL QUITE FAMISHED.
NO. NO...NOT AGAIN.
OUT THE BACK! EVERYONE OUT THE BACK!
HELP ME... PLEASE, HELP ME...
SPLURCH

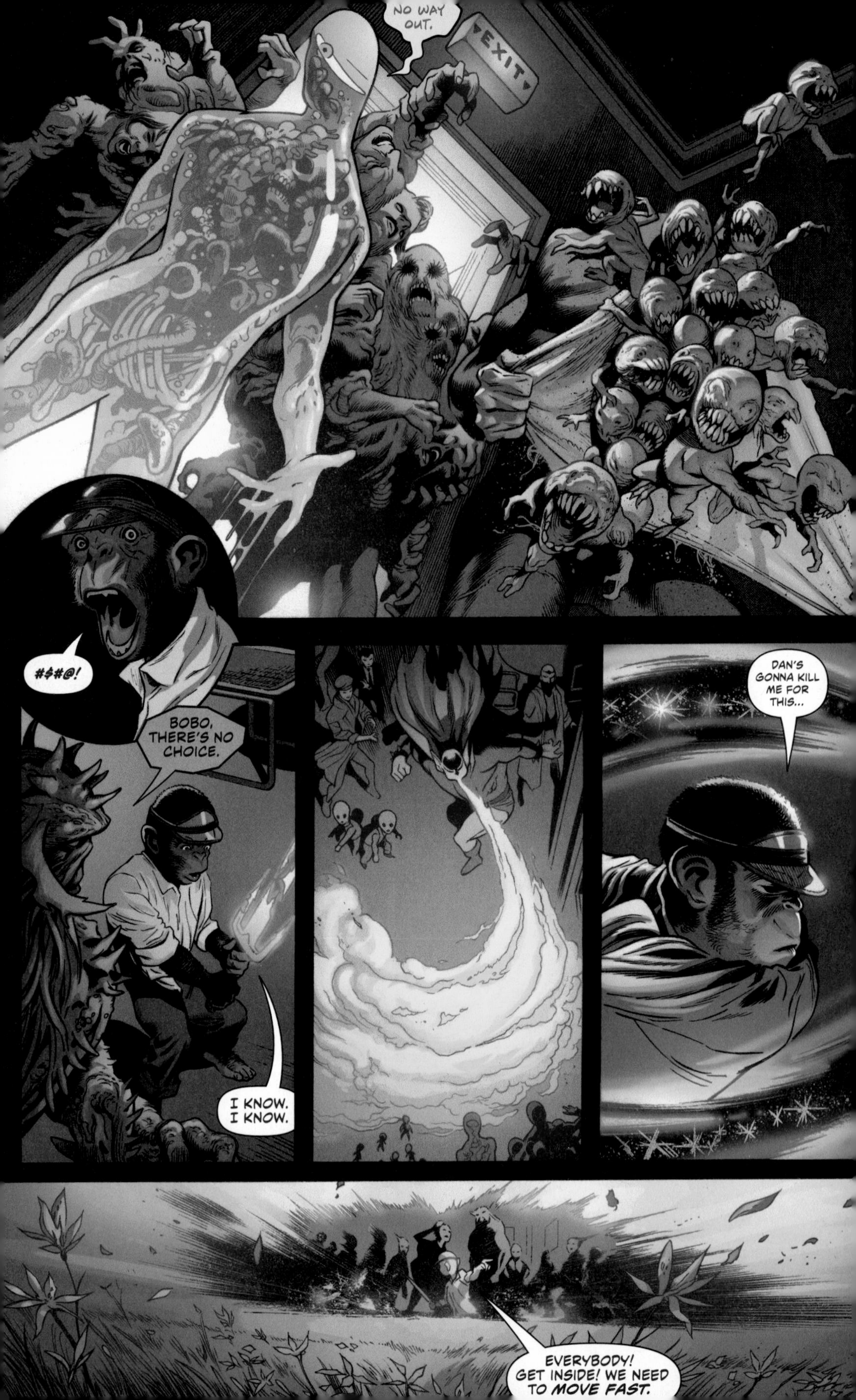
NO WAY OUT.
EXIT
#$#@!
BOBO, THERE'S NO CHOICE.
I KNOW. I KNOW.
DAN'S GONNA KILL ME FOR THIS...
EVERYBODY! GET INSIDE! WE NEED TO MOVE FAST.

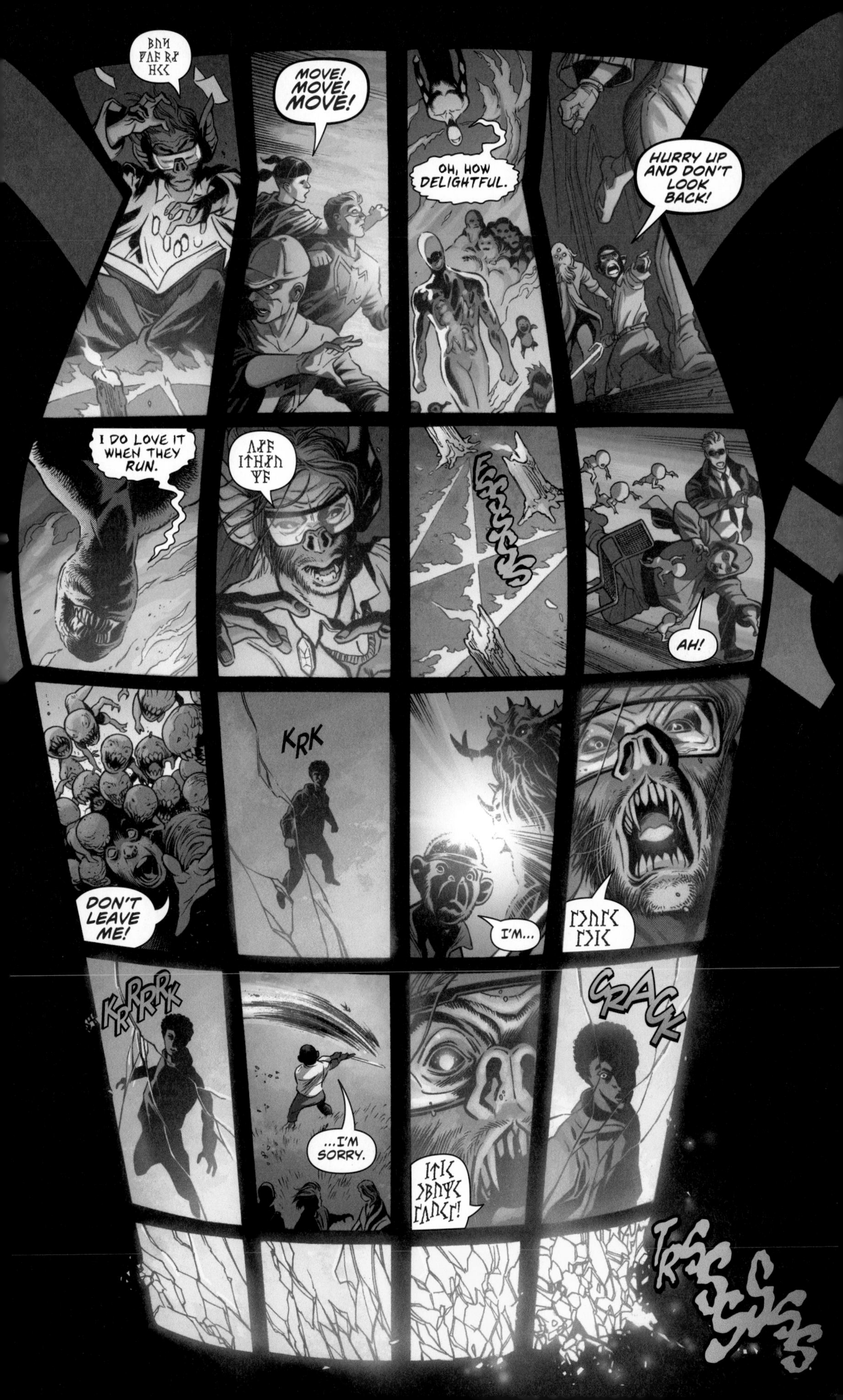
MOVE! MOVE! MOVE!
OH, HOW DELIGHTFUL.
HURRY UP AND DON'T LOOK BACK!
I DO LOVE IT WHEN THEY RUN.
AH!
DON'T LEAVE ME!
KRK
I'M...
KRRRRK
...I'M SORRY.
CRACK

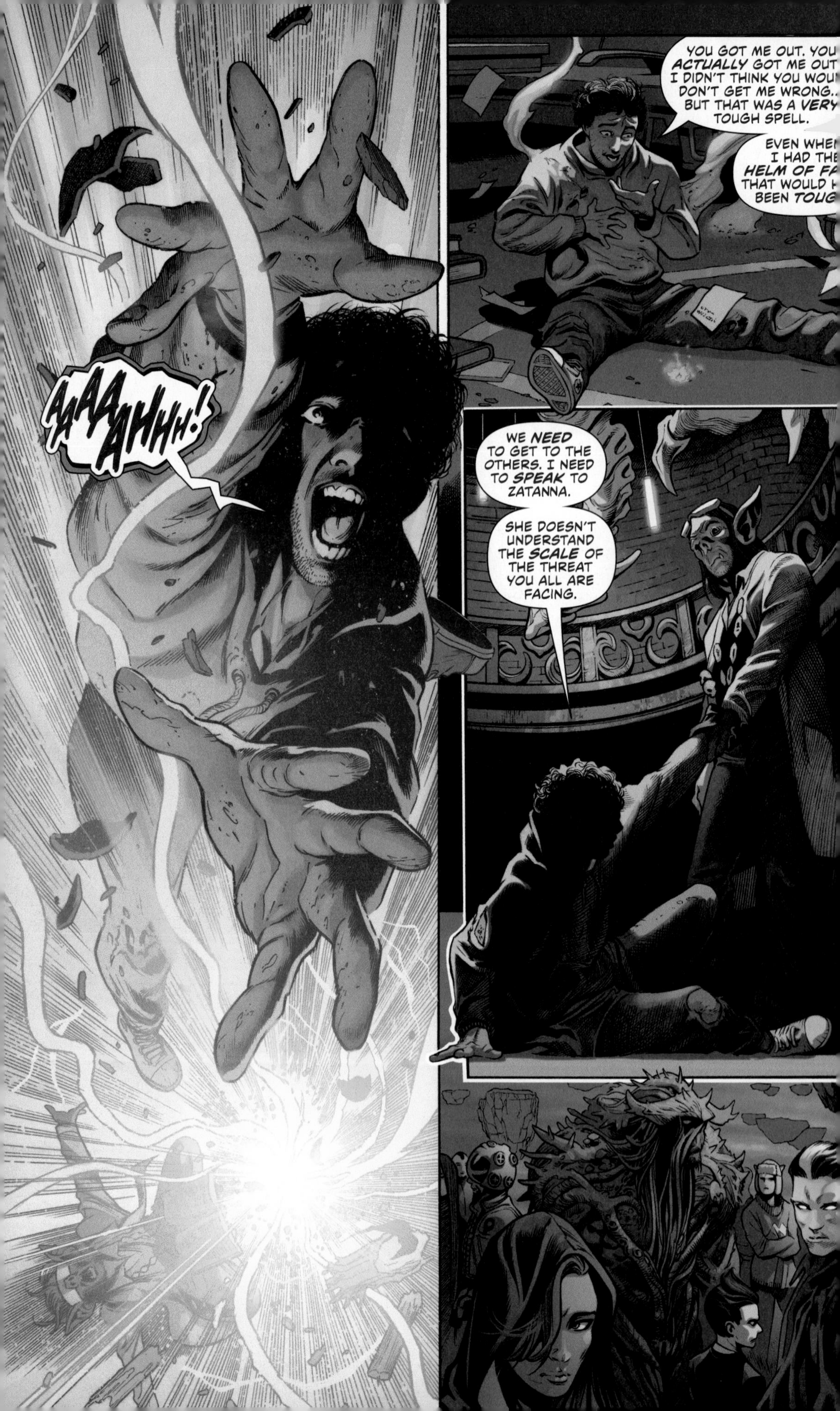

AAAAAAHHH!
YOU GOT ME OUT. YOU ACTUALLY GOT ME OUT. I DIDN'T THINK YOU WOU DON'T GET ME WRONG.. BUT THAT WAS A VERY TOUGH SPELL.
EVEN WHE I HAD THE HELM OF FA THAT WOULD BEEN TOUG
WE NEED TO GET TO THE OTHERS. I NEED TO SPEAK TO ZATANNA.
SHE DOESN'T UNDERSTAND THE SCALE OF THE THREAT YOU ALL ARE FACING.

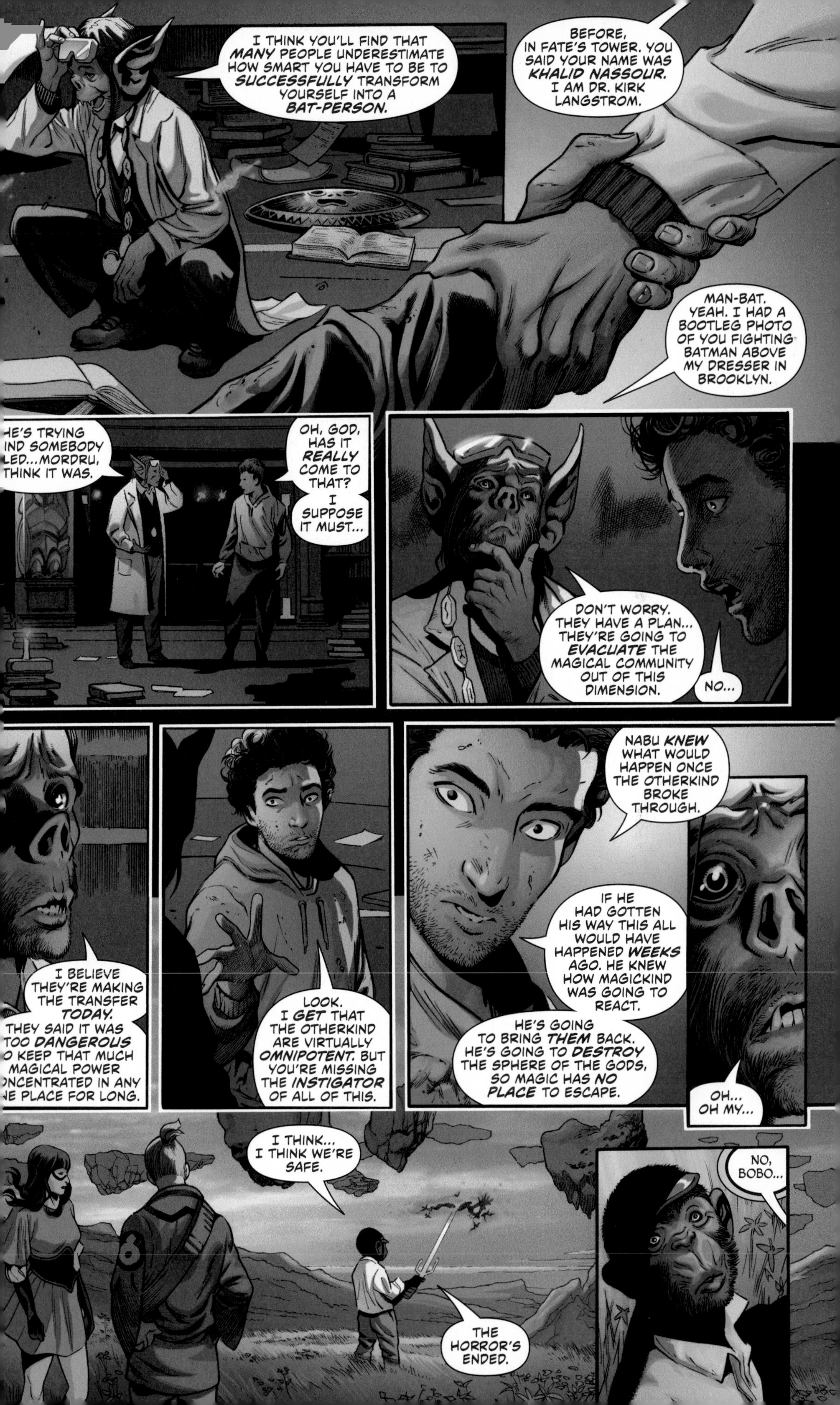

I THINK YOU'LL FIND THAT MANY PEOPLE UNDERESTIMATE HOW SMART YOU HAVE TO BE TO SUCCESSFULLY TRANSFORM YOURSELF INTO A BAT-PERSON.
BEFORE, IN FATE'S TOWER. YOU SAID YOUR NAME WAS KHALID NASSOUR. I AM DR. KIRK LANGSTROM.
MAN-BAT. YEAH. I HAD A BOOTLEG PHOTO OF YOU FIGHTING BATMAN ABOVE MY DRESSER IN BROOKLYN.
HE'S TRYING IND SOMEBODY LED...MORDRU, THINK IT WAS.
OH, GOD, HAS IT REALLY COME TO THAT?
I SUPPOSE IT MUST...
DON'T WORRY. THEY HAVE A PLAN... THEY'RE GOING TO EVACUATE THE MAGICAL COMMUNITY OUT OF THIS DIMENSION.
NO...
I BELIEVE THEY'RE MAKING THE TRANSFER TODAY.
THEY SAID IT WAS TOO DANGEROUS O KEEP THAT MUCH MAGICAL POWER ONCENTRATED IN ANY NE PLACE FOR LONG.
LOOK. I GET THAT THE OTHERKIND ARE VIRTUALLY OMNIPOTENT. BUT YOU'RE MISSING THE INSTIGATOR OF ALL OF THIS.
NABU KNEW WHAT WOULD HAPPEN ONCE THE OTHERKIND BROKE THROUGH.
IF HE HAD GOTTEN HIS WAY THIS ALL WOULD HAVE HAPPENED WEEKS AGO. HE KNEW HOW MAGICKIND WAS GOING TO REACT.
HE'S GOING TO BRING THEM BACK. HE'S GOING TO DESTROY THE SPHERE OF THE GODS, SO MAGIC HAS NO PLACE TO ESCAPE.
OH... OH MY...
I THINK... I THINK WE'RE SAFE.
THE HORROR'S ENDED.
NO, BOBO...

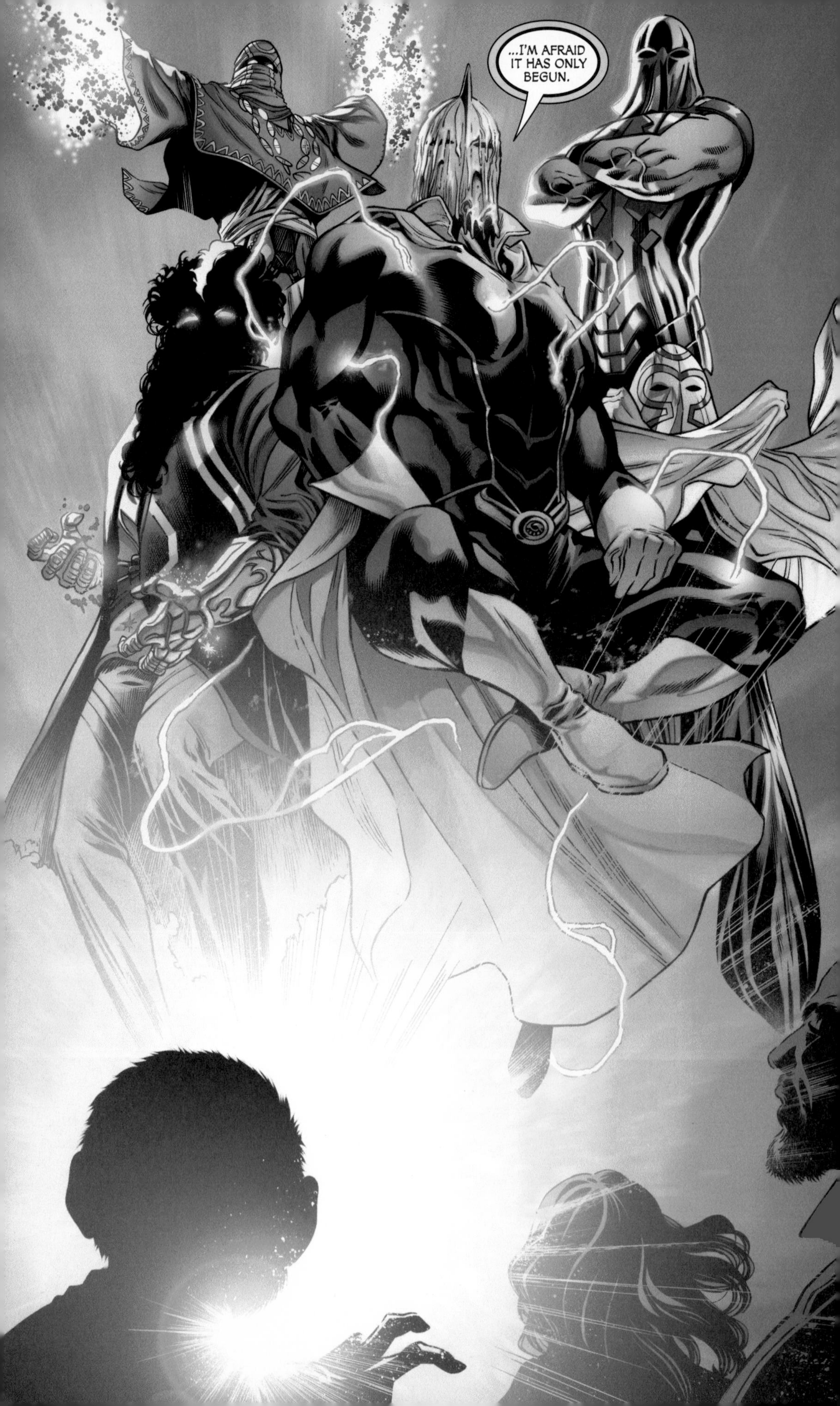
...I'M AFRAID IT HAS ONLY BEGUN.

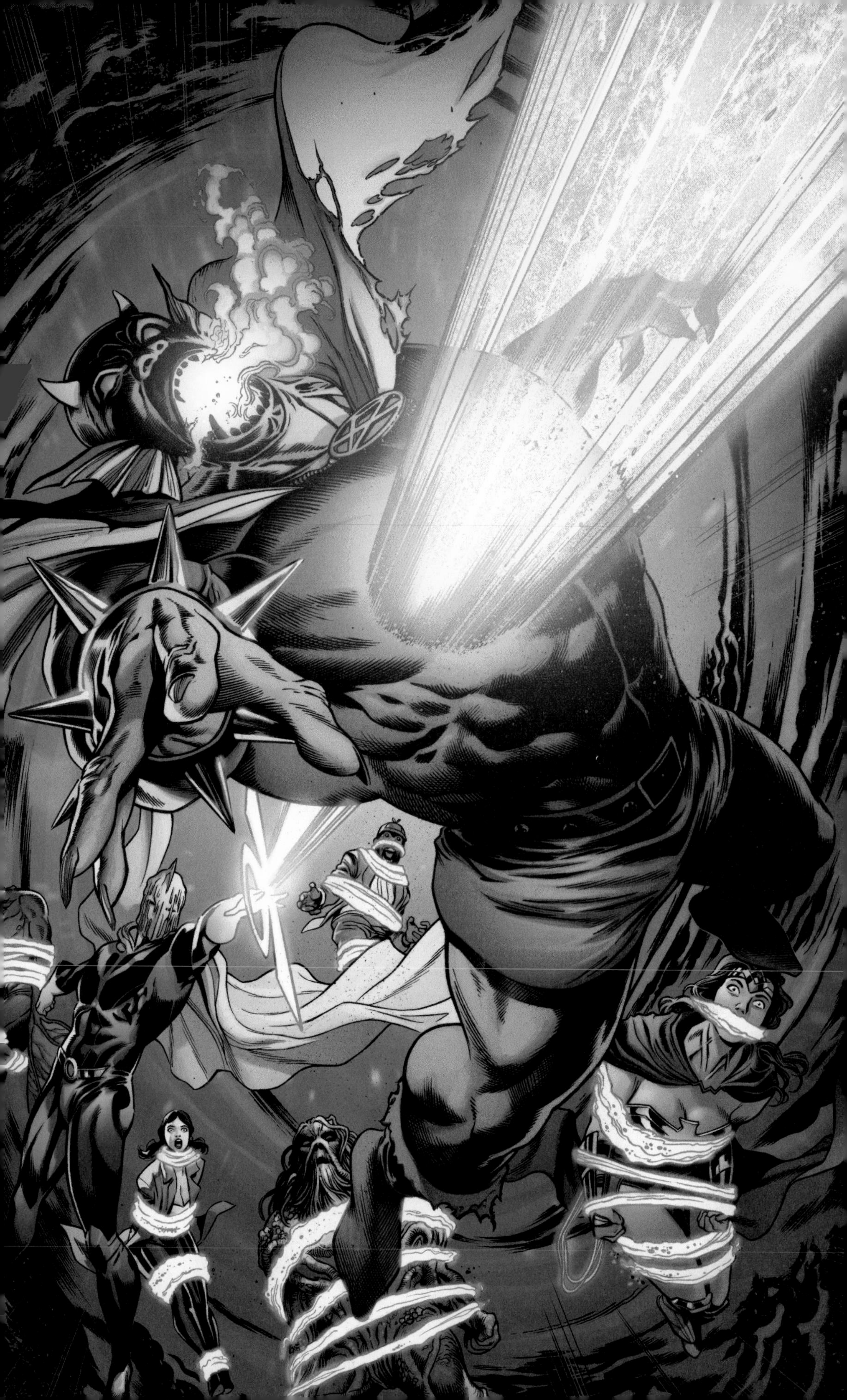

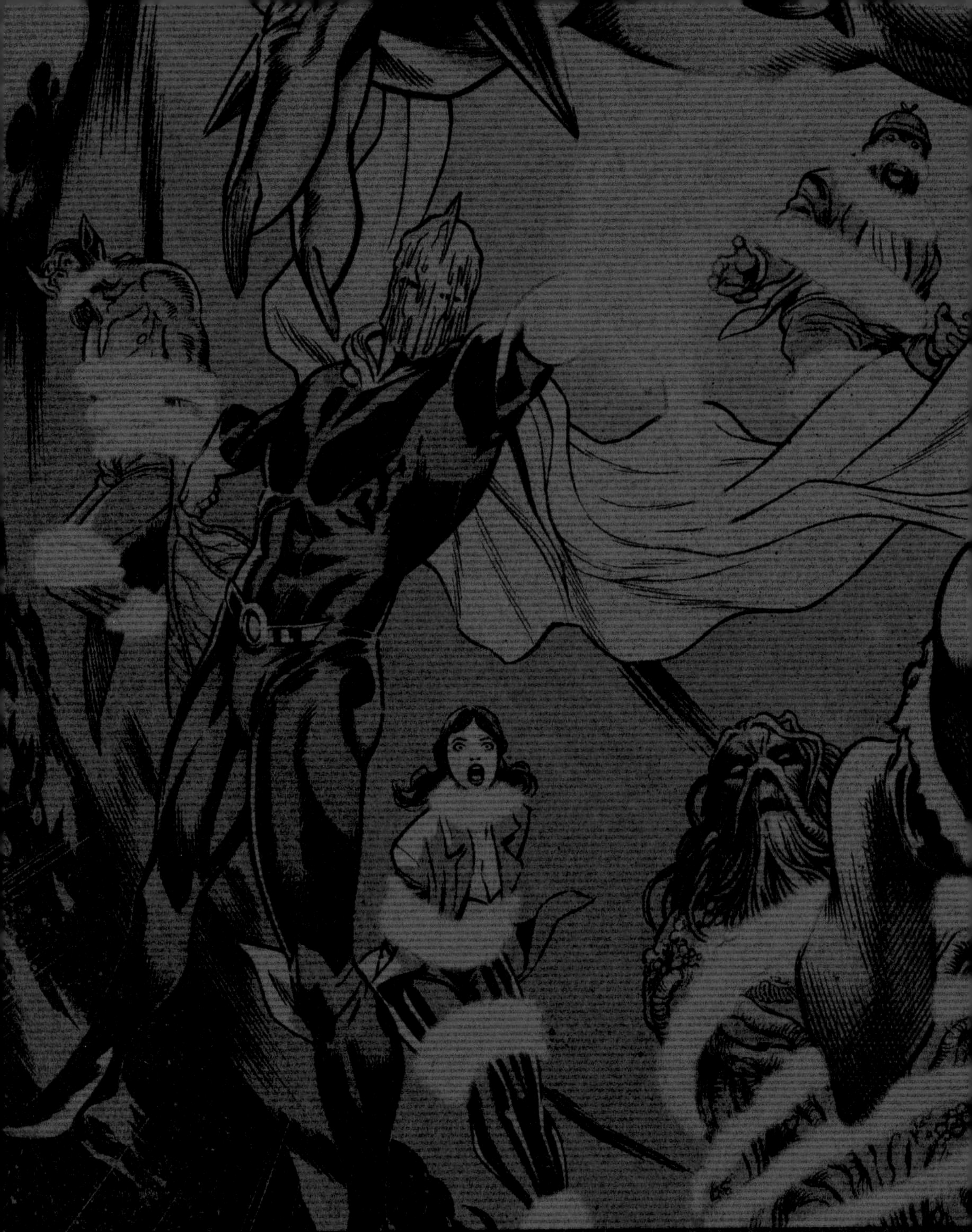

JUSTICE LEAGUE DARK

#9

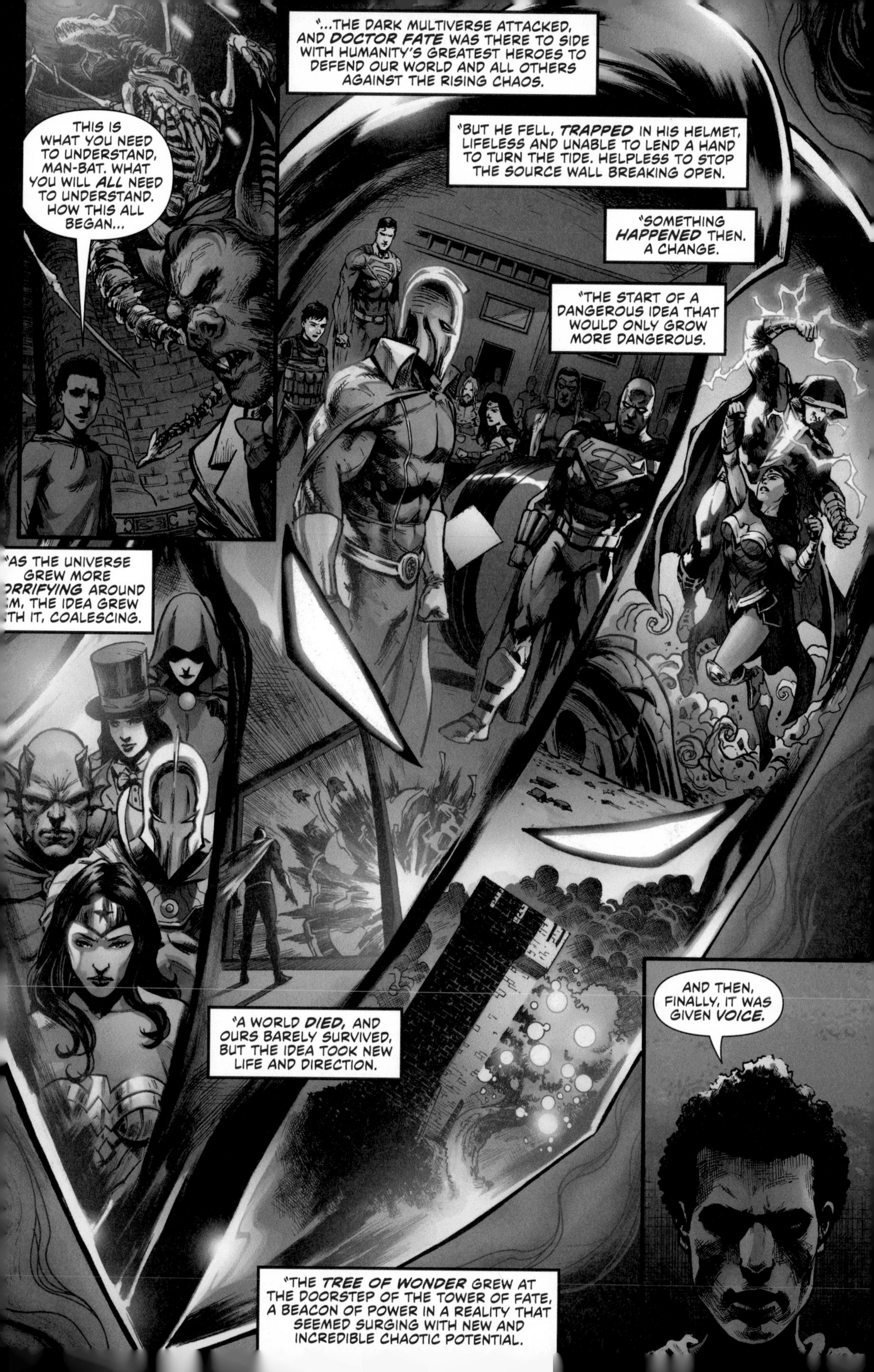
THIS IS WHAT YOU NEED TO UNDERSTAND, MAN-BAT. WHAT YOU WILL ALL NEED TO UNDERSTAND. HOW THIS ALL BEGAN...
"...THE DARK MULTIVERSE ATTACKED, AND DOCTOR FATE WAS THERE TO SIDE WITH HUMANITY'S GREATEST HEROES TO DEFEND OUR WORLD AND ALL OTHERS AGAINST THE RISING CHAOS.
"BUT HE FELL, TRAPPED IN HIS HELMET, LIFELESS AND UNABLE TO LEND A HAND TO TURN THE TIDE. HELPLESS TO STOP THE SOURCE WALL BREAKING OPEN.
"SOMETHING HAPPENED THEN. A CHANGE.
"THE START OF A DANGEROUS IDEA THAT WOULD ONLY GROW MORE DANGEROUS.
"AS THE UNIVERSE GREW MORE ORRIFYING AROUND EM, THE IDEA GREW TH IT, COALESCING.
"A WORLD DIED, AND OURS BARELY SURVIVED, BUT THE IDEA TOOK NEW LIFE AND DIRECTION.
"THE TREE OF WONDER GREW AT THE DOORSTEP OF THE TOWER OF FATE, A BEACON OF POWER IN A REALITY THAT SEEMED SURGING WITH NEW AND INCREDIBLE CHAOTIC POTENTIAL.
AND THEN, FINALLY, IT WAS GIVEN VOICE.

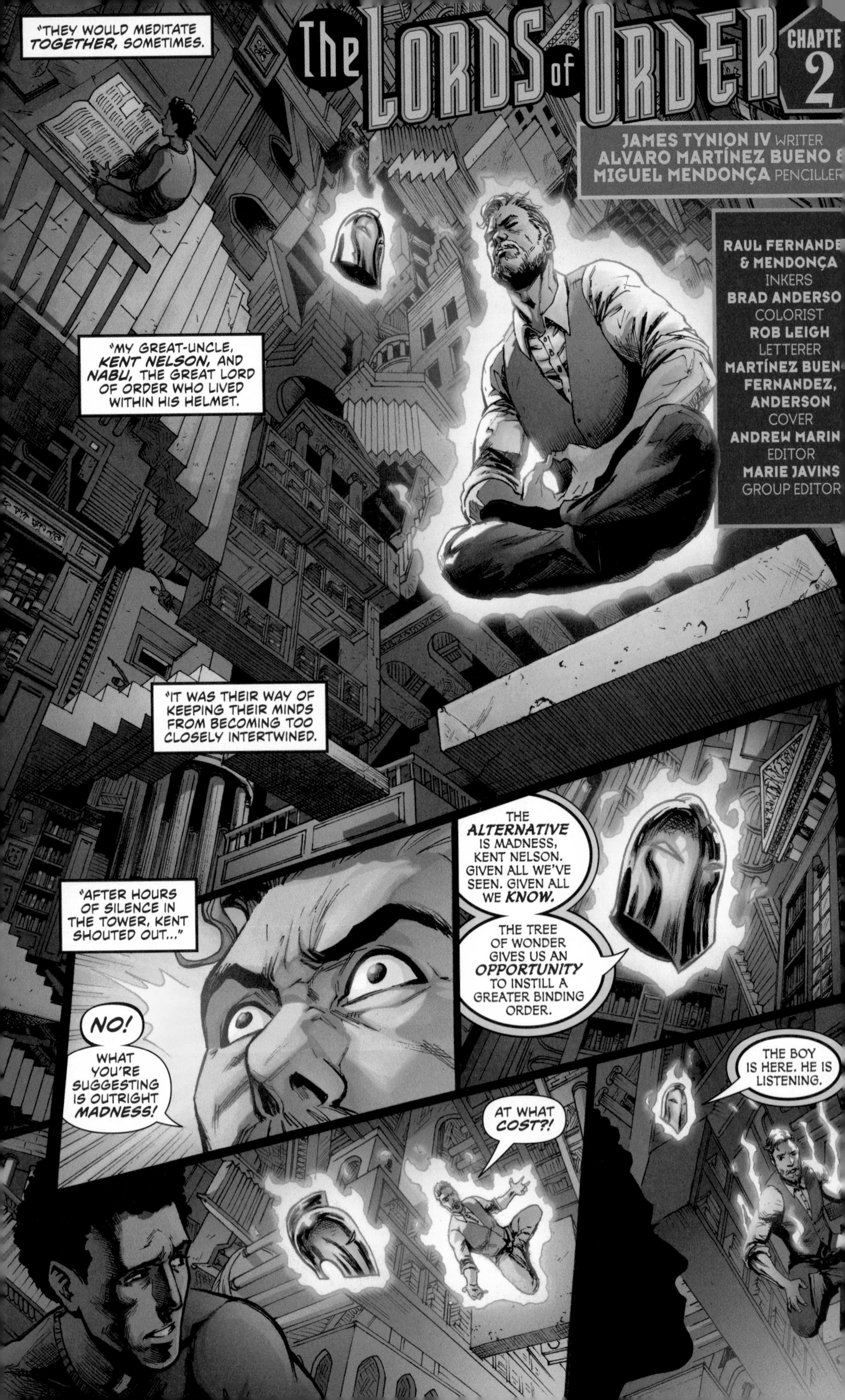
"THEY WOULD MEDITATE TOGETHER, SOMETIMES.
The LORDS of ORDER
CHAPTE 2
JAMES TYNION IV WRITER
ALVARO MARTÍNEZ BUENO &
MIGUEL MENDONÇA PENCILLER
RAUL FERNANDE & MENDONÇA INKERS
BRAD ANDERSO COLORIST
ROB LEIGH LETTERER
MARTÍNEZ BUEN FERNANDEZ, ANDERSON COVER
ANDREW MARIN EDITOR
MARIE JAVINS GROUP EDITOR
"MY GREAT-UNCLE, KENT NELSON, AND NABU, THE GREAT LORD OF ORDER WHO LIVED WITHIN HIS HELMET.
"IT WAS THEIR WAY OF KEEPING THEIR MINDS FROM BECOMING TOO CLOSELY INTERTWINED.
"AFTER HOURS OF SILENCE IN THE TOWER, KENT SHOUTED OUT..."
NO!
WHAT YOU'RE SUGGESTING IS OUTRIGHT MADNESS!
THE ALTERNATIVE IS MADNESS, KENT NELSON. GIVEN ALL WE'VE SEEN. GIVEN ALL WE KNOW.
THE TREE OF WONDER GIVES US AN OPPORTUNITY TO INSTILL A GREATER BINDING ORDER.
AT WHAT COST?!
THE BOY IS HERE. HE IS LISTENING.

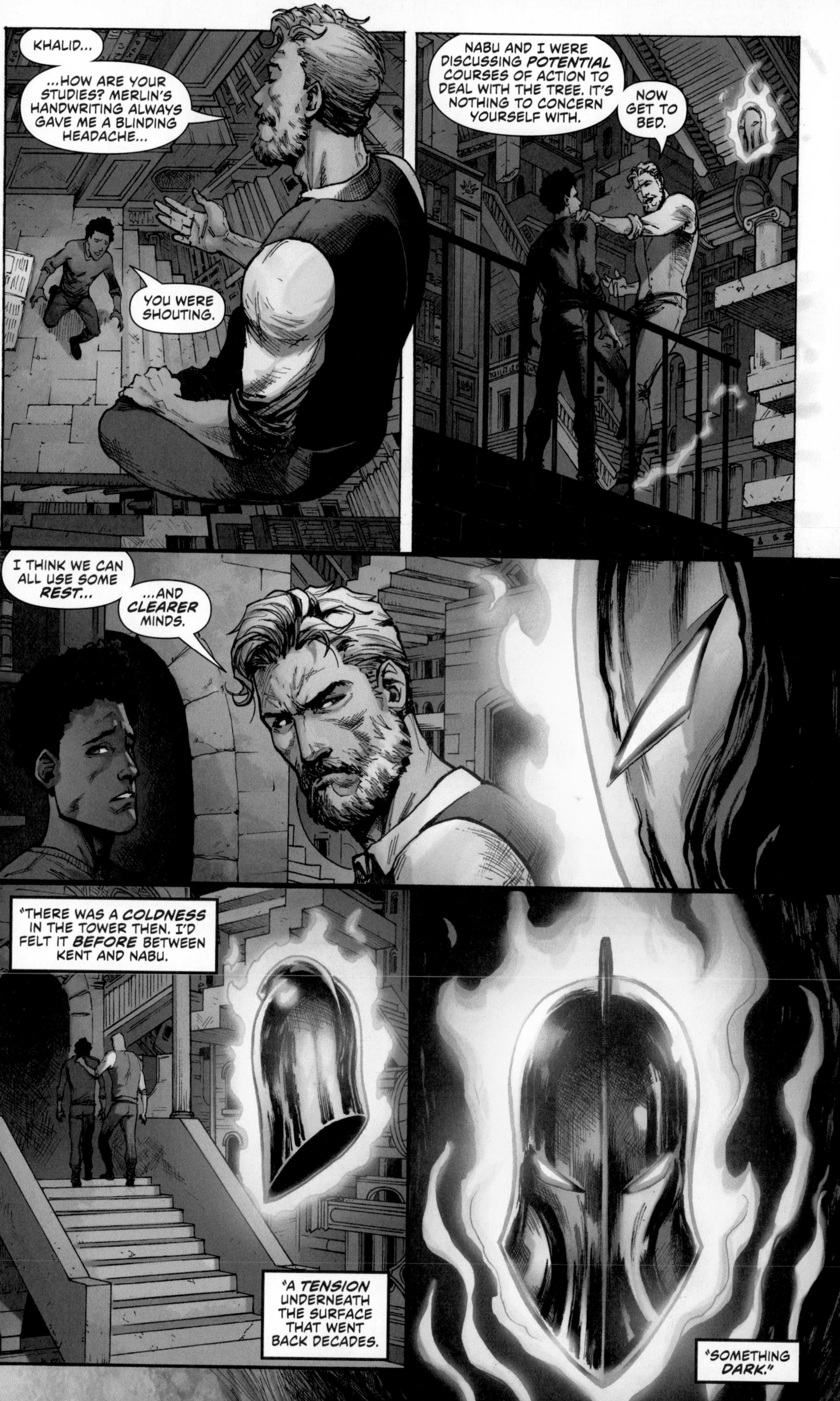
KHALID...
...HOW ARE YOUR STUDIES? MERLIN'S HANDWRITING ALWAYS GAVE ME A BLINDING HEADACHE...
YOU WERE SHOUTING.
NABU AND I WERE DISCUSSING POTENTIAL COURSES OF ACTION TO DEAL WITH THE TREE. IT'S NOTHING TO CONCERN YOURSELF WITH.
NOW GET TO BED.
I THINK WE CAN ALL USE SOME REST...
...AND CLEARER MINDS.
"THERE WAS A COLDNESS IN THE TOWER THEN. I'D FELT IT BEFORE BETWEEN KENT AND NABU.
"A TENSION UNDERNEATH THE SURFACE THAT WENT BACK DECADES.
"SOMETHING DARK."

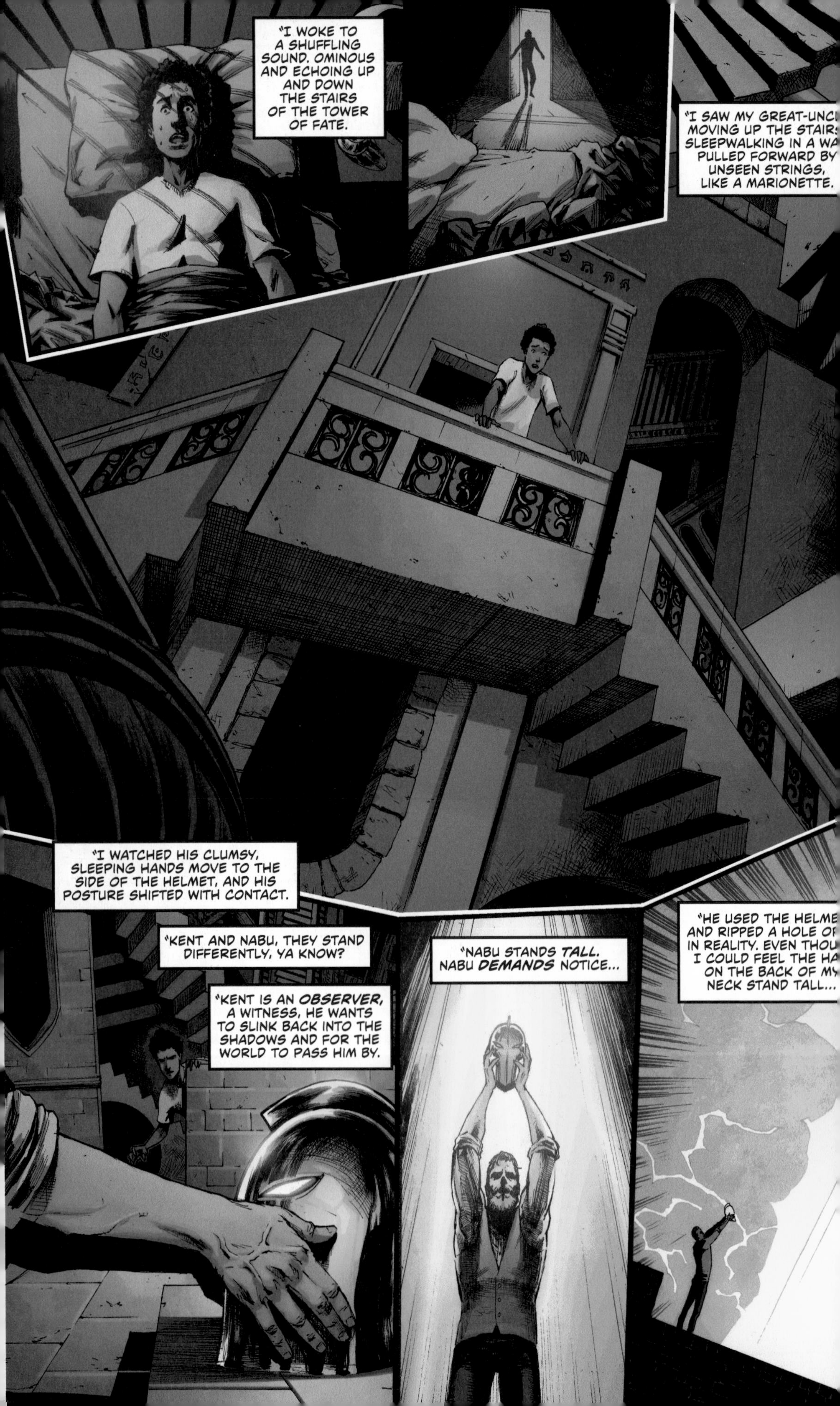
"I WOKE TO A SHUFFLING SOUND. OMINOUS AND ECHOING UP AND DOWN THE STAIRS OF THE TOWER OF FATE.
"I SAW MY GREAT-UNC MOVING UP THE STAIR SLEEPWALKING IN A WA PULLED FORWARD BY UNSEEN STRINGS, LIKE A MARIONETTE.
"I WATCHED HIS CLUMSY, SLEEPING HANDS MOVE TO THE SIDE OF THE HELMET, AND HIS POSTURE SHIFTED WITH CONTACT.
"KENT AND NABU, THEY STAND DIFFERENTLY, YA KNOW?
"KENT IS AN OBSERVER, A WITNESS, HE WANTS TO SLINK BACK INTO THE SHADOWS AND FOR THE WORLD TO PASS HIM BY.
"NABU STANDS TALL. NABU DEMANDS NOTICE...
"HE USED THE HELME AND RIPPED A HOLE O IN REALITY. EVEN THOU I COULD FEEL THE HA ON THE BACK OF M NECK STAND TALL...

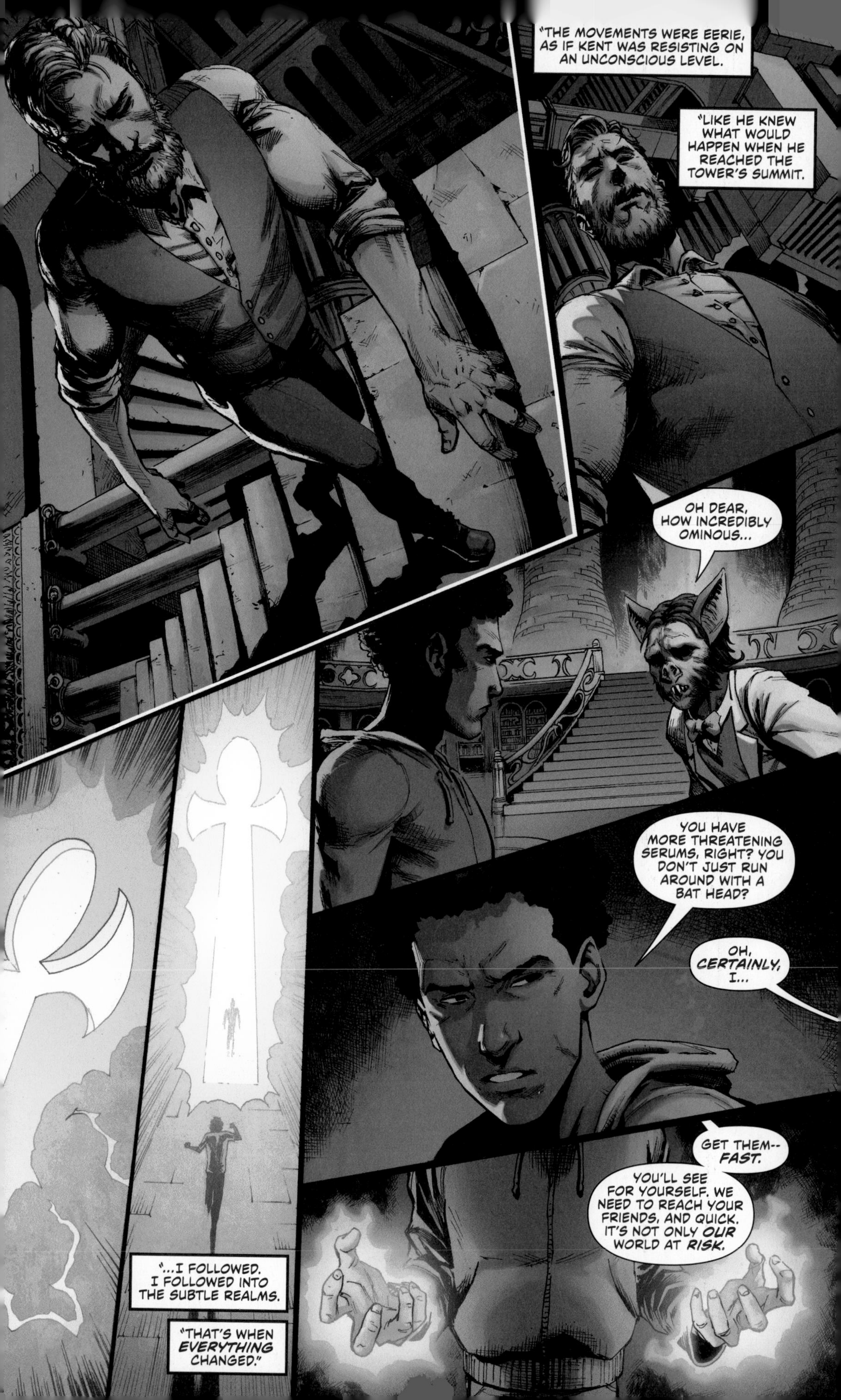
"THE MOVEMENTS WERE EERIE, AS IF KENT WAS RESISTING ON AN UNCONSCIOUS LEVEL.
"LIKE HE KNEW WHAT WOULD HAPPEN WHEN HE REACHED THE TOWER'S SUMMIT.
OH DEAR, HOW INCREDIBLY OMINOUS...
YOU HAVE MORE THREATENING SERUMS, RIGHT? YOU DON'T JUST RUN AROUND WITH A BAT HEAD?
OH, *CERTAINLY*, I...
GET THEM-- *FAST.*
YOU'LL SEE FOR YOURSELF. WE NEED TO REACH YOUR FRIENDS, AND QUICK. IT'S NOT ONLY *OUR* WORLD AT *RISK*.
"...I FOLLOWED. I FOLLOWED INTO THE SUBTLE REALMS.
"THAT'S WHEN *EVERYTHING* CHANGED."

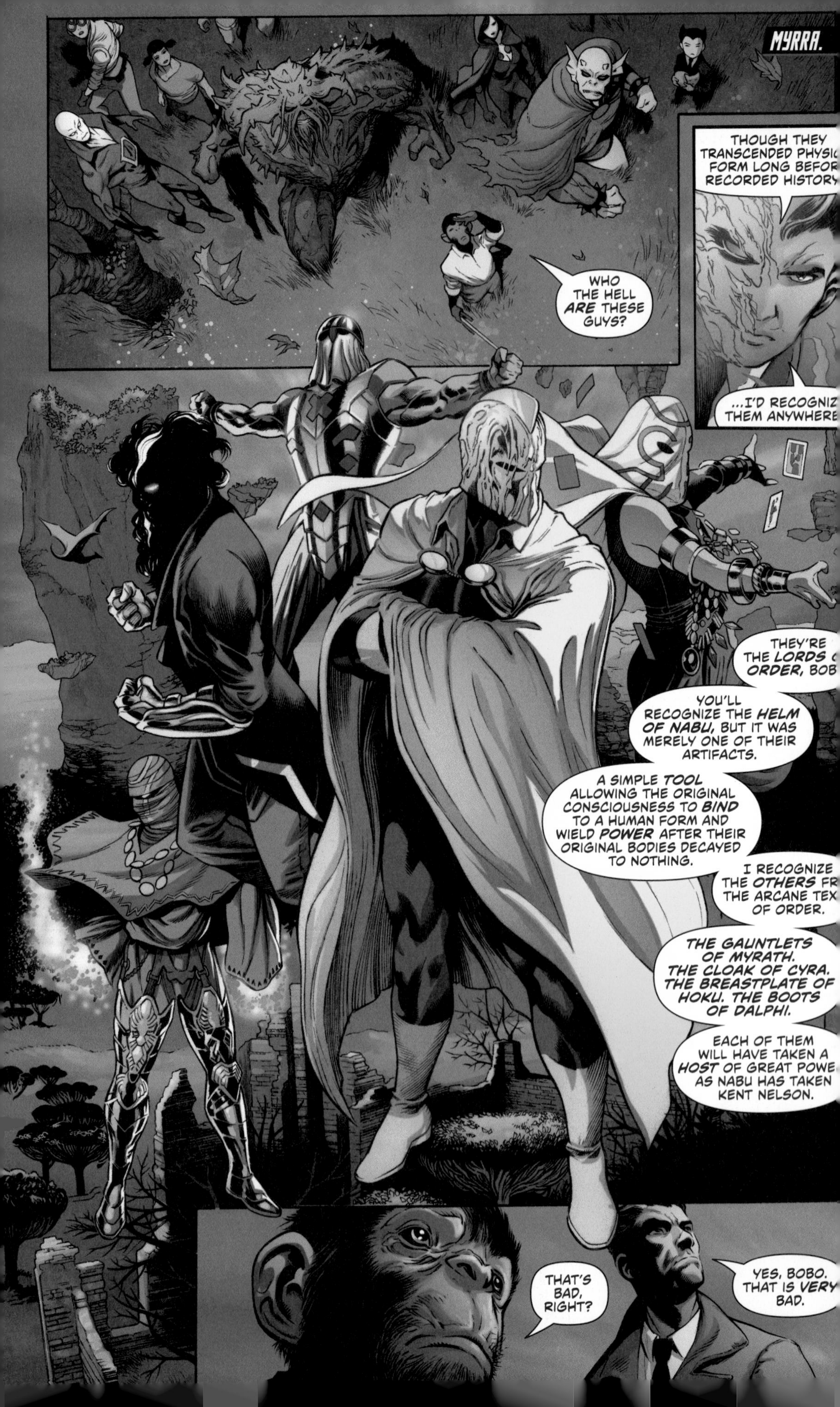
MYRRA.
WHO THE HELL ARE THESE GUYS?
THOUGH THEY TRANSCENDED PHYSIC FORM LONG BEFOR RECORDED HISTORY
...I'D RECOGNIZ THEM ANYWHERE
THEY'RE THE LORDS ORDER, BOB
YOU'LL RECOGNIZE THE HELM OF NABU, BUT IT WAS MERELY ONE OF THEIR ARTIFACTS.
A SIMPLE TOOL ALLOWING THE ORIGINAL CONSCIOUSNESS TO BIND TO A HUMAN FORM AND WIELD POWER AFTER THEIR ORIGINAL BODIES DECAYED TO NOTHING.
I RECOGNIZE THE OTHERS FR THE ARCANE TEX OF ORDER.
THE GAUNTLETS OF MYRATH. THE CLOAK OF CYRA. THE BREASTPLATE OF HOKU. THE BOOTS OF DALPHI.
EACH OF THEM WILL HAVE TAKEN A HOST OF GREAT POWE AS NABU HAS TAKEN KENT NELSON.
THAT'S BAD, RIGHT?
YES, BOBO. THAT IS VERY BAD.

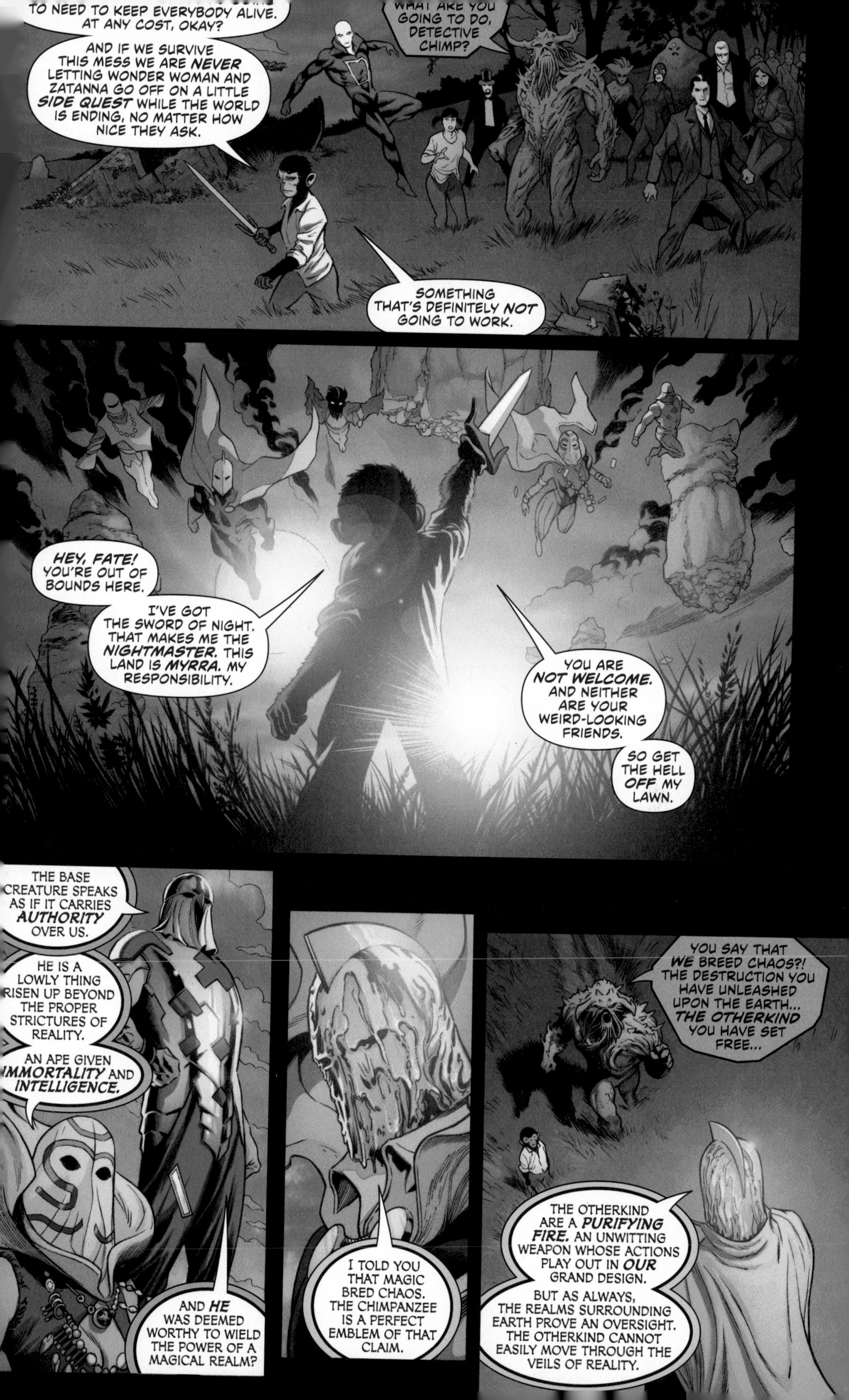
TO NEED TO KEEP EVERYBODY ALIVE. AT ANY COST, OKAY?
AND IF WE SURVIVE THIS MESS WE ARE NEVER LETTING WONDER WOMAN AND ZATANNA GO OFF ON A LITTLE SIDE QUEST WHILE THE WORLD IS ENDING, NO MATTER HOW NICE THEY ASK.
WHAT ARE YOU GOING TO DO, DETECTIVE CHIMP?
SOMETHING THAT'S DEFINITELY NOT GOING TO WORK.
HEY, FATE! YOU'RE OUT OF BOUNDS HERE.
I'VE GOT THE SWORD OF NIGHT. THAT MAKES ME THE NIGHTMASTER. THIS LAND IS MYRRA. MY RESPONSIBILITY.
YOU ARE NOT WELCOME. AND NEITHER ARE YOUR WEIRD-LOOKING FRIENDS.
SO GET THE HELL OFF MY LAWN.
THE BASE CREATURE SPEAKS AS IF IT CARRIES AUTHORITY OVER US.
HE IS A LOWLY THING RISEN UP BEYOND THE PROPER STRICTURES OF REALITY.
AN APE GIVEN IMMORTALITY AND INTELLIGENCE.
AND HE WAS DEEMED WORTHY TO WIELD THE POWER OF A MAGICAL REALM?
I TOLD YOU THAT MAGIC BRED CHAOS. THE CHIMPANZEE IS A PERFECT EMBLEM OF THAT CLAIM.
YOU SAY THAT WE BREED CHAOS?! THE DESTRUCTION YOU HAVE UNLEASHED UPON THE EARTH... THE OTHERKIND YOU HAVE SET FREE...
THE OTHERKIND ARE A PURIFYING FIRE. AN UNWITTING WEAPON WHOSE ACTIONS PLAY OUT IN OUR GRAND DESIGN.
BUT AS ALWAYS, THE REALMS SURROUNDING EARTH PROVE AN OVERSIGHT. THE OTHERKIND CANNOT EASILY MOVE THROUGH THE VEILS OF REALITY.

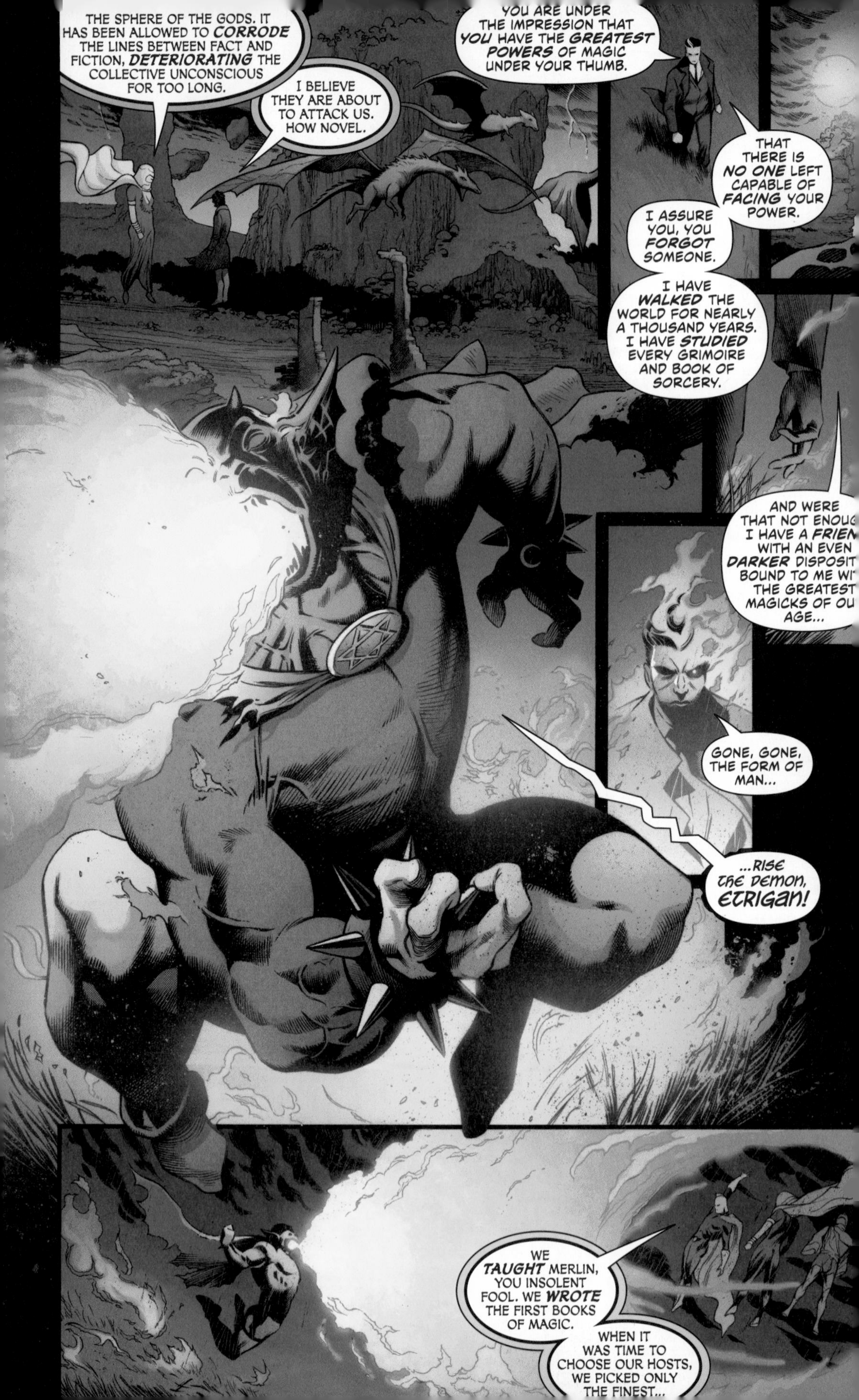

THE SPHERE OF THE GODS. IT HAS BEEN ALLOWED TO CORRODE THE LINES BETWEEN FACT AND FICTION, DETERIORATING THE COLLECTIVE UNCONSCIOUS FOR TOO LONG.
I BELIEVE THEY ARE ABOUT TO ATTACK US. HOW NOVEL.
YOU ARE UNDER THE IMPRESSION THAT YOU HAVE THE GREATEST POWERS OF MAGIC UNDER YOUR THUMB.
THAT THERE IS NO ONE LEFT CAPABLE OF FACING YOUR POWER.
I ASSURE YOU, YOU FORGOT SOMEONE.
I HAVE WALKED THE WORLD FOR NEARLY A THOUSAND YEARS. I HAVE STUDIED EVERY GRIMOIRE AND BOOK OF SORCERY.
AND WERE THAT NOT ENOUG I HAVE A FRIEN WITH AN EVEN DARKER DISPOSIT BOUND TO ME WI THE GREATEST MAGICKS OF OU AGE...
GONE, GONE, THE FORM OF MAN...
...RISE THE DEMON, ETRIGAN!
WE TAUGHT MERLIN, YOU INSOLENT FOOL. WE WROTE THE FIRST BOOKS OF MAGIC.
WHEN IT WAS TIME TO CHOOSE OUR HOSTS, WE PICKED ONLY THE FINEST...

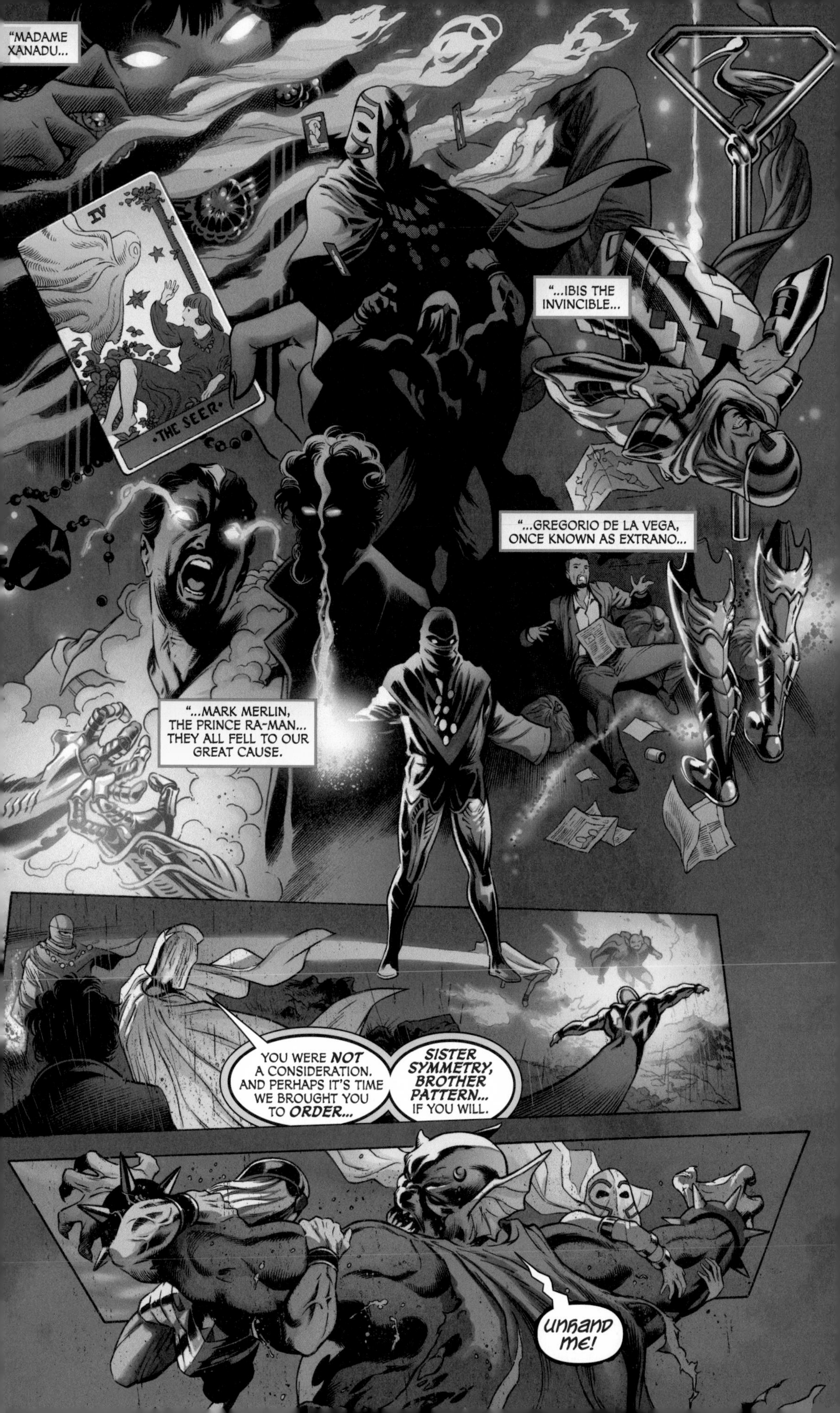
"MADAME XANADU...
THE SEER
"...IBIS THE INVINCIBLE...
"...GREGORIO DE LA VEGA, ONCE KNOWN AS EXTRANO...
"...MARK MERLIN, THE PRINCE RA-MAN... THEY ALL FELL TO OUR GREAT CAUSE.
YOU WERE NOT A CONSIDERATION. AND PERHAPS IT'S TIME WE BROUGHT YOU TO ORDER...
SISTER SYMMETRY, BROTHER PATTERN... IF YOU WILL.
UNHAND ME!

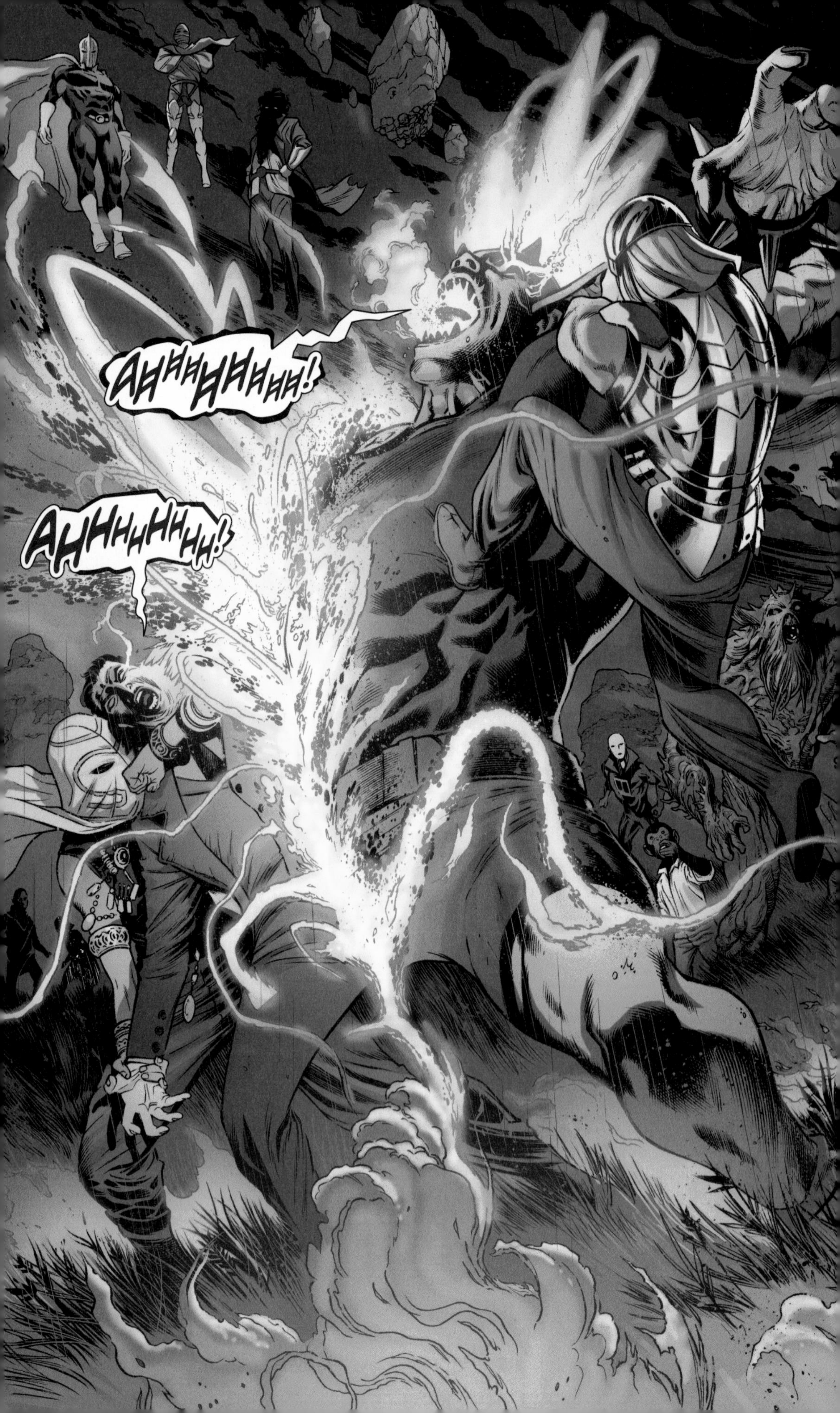
AHHHHHHHHHH!
AHHHHHHHHH!

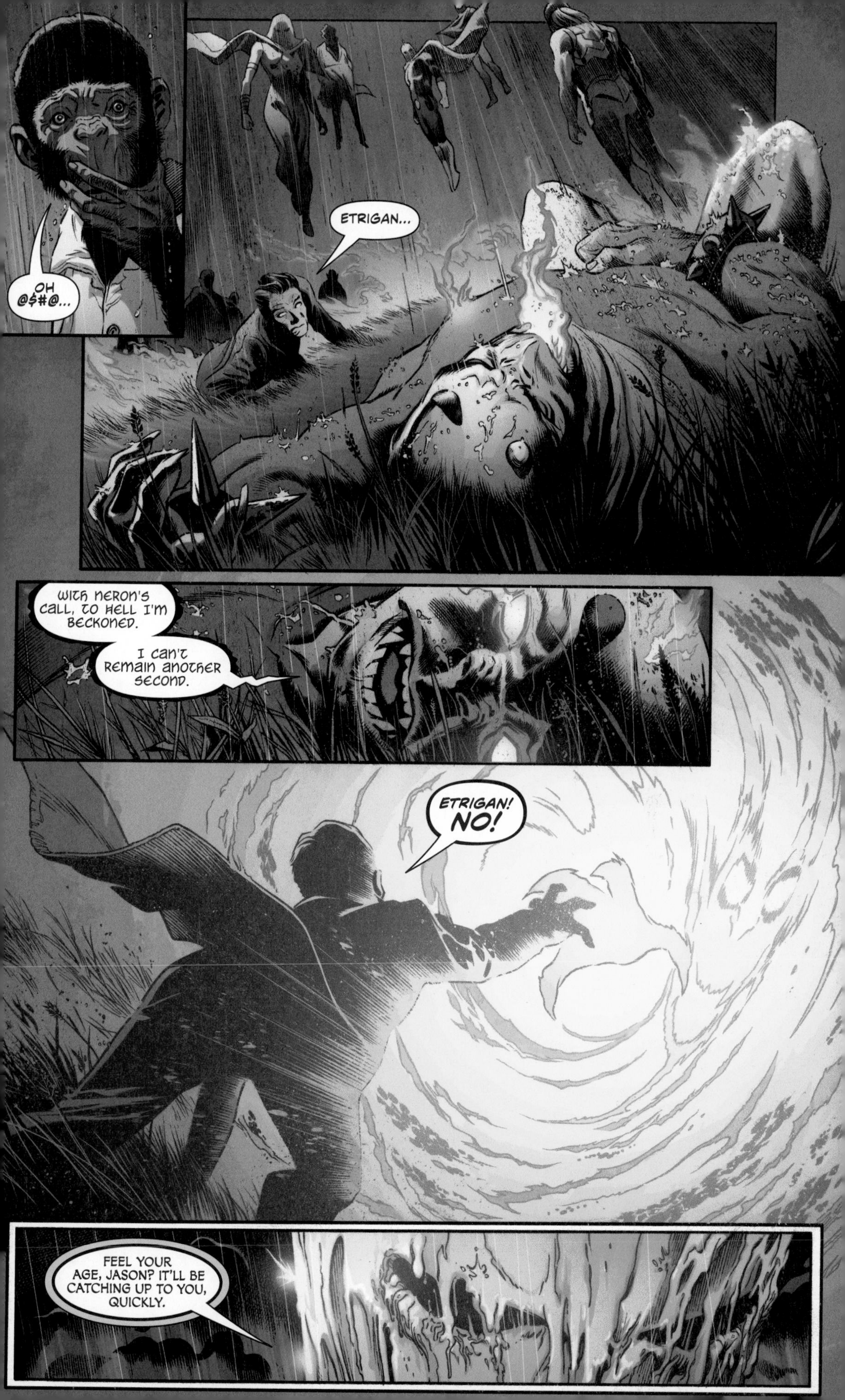
OH @$#@...
ETRIGAN...
WITH NERON'S CALL, TO HELL I'M BECKONED.
I CAN'T REMAIN ANOTHER SECOND.
ETRIGAN! NO!
FEEL YOUR AGE, JASON? IT'LL BE CATCHING UP TO YOU, QUICKLY.

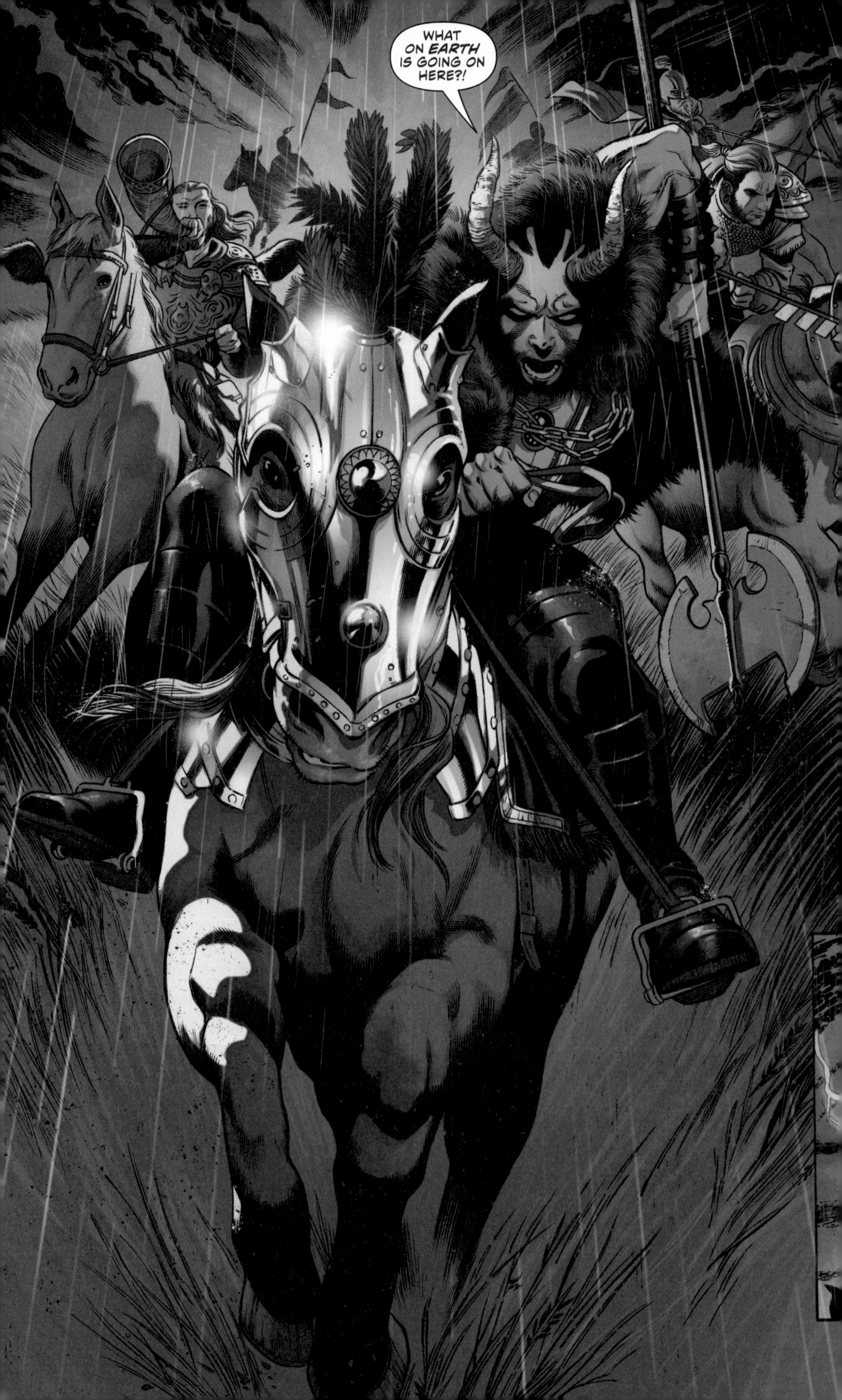
WHAT ON *EARTH* IS GOING ON HERE?!

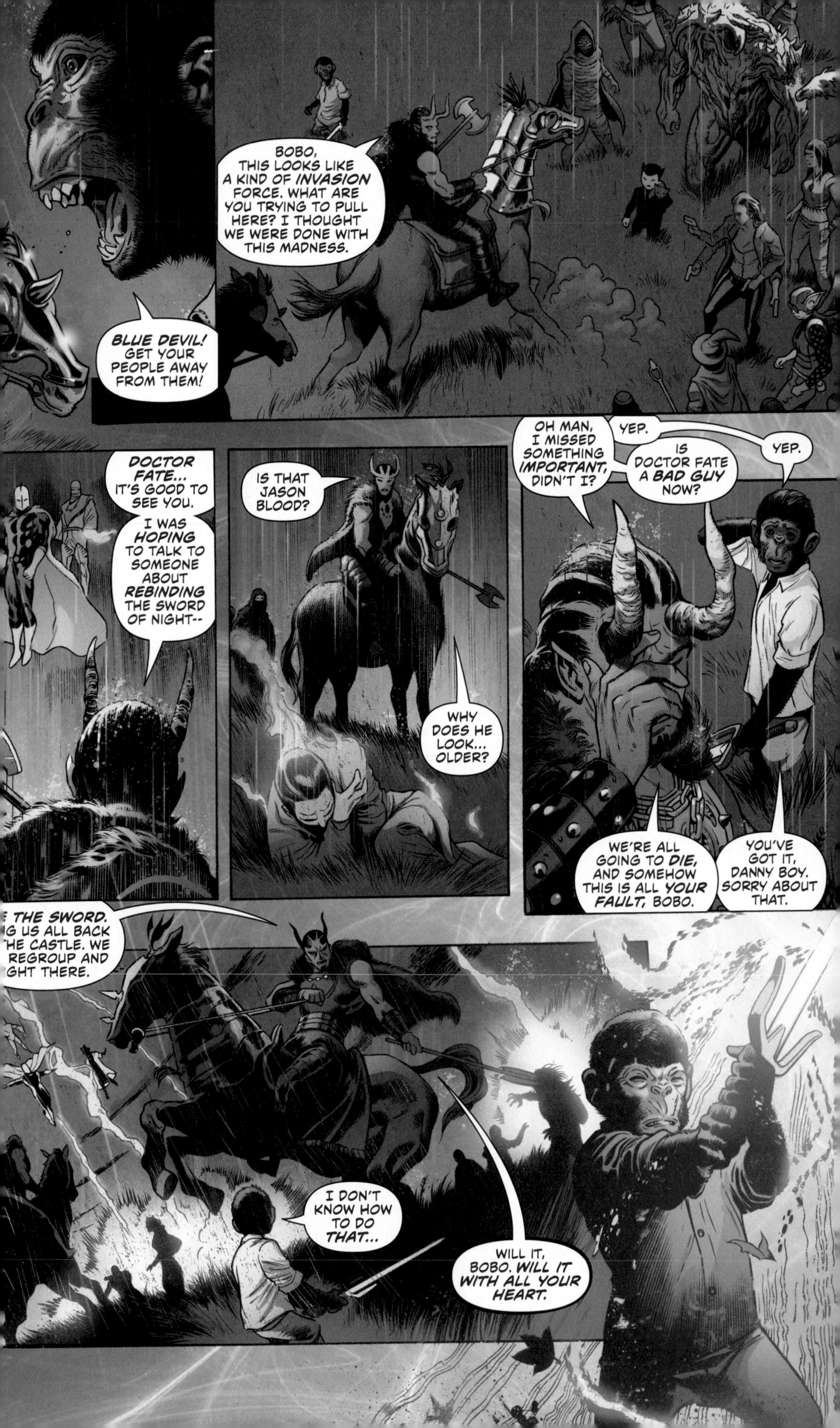
BOBO, THIS LOOKS LIKE A KIND OF *INVASION* FORCE. WHAT ARE YOU TRYING TO PULL HERE? I THOUGHT WE WERE DONE WITH THIS MADNESS.
BLUE DEVIL! GET YOUR PEOPLE AWAY FROM THEM!
DOCTOR FATE... IT'S GOOD TO SEE YOU.
I WAS *HOPING* TO TALK TO SOMEONE ABOUT *REBINDING* THE SWORD OF NIGHT--
IS THAT JASON BLOOD?
WHY DOES HE LOOK... OLDER?
OH MAN, I MISSED SOMETHING *IMPORTANT,* DIDN'T I?
YEP.
IS DOCTOR FATE A *BAD GUY* NOW?
YEP.
WE'RE ALL GOING TO *DIE,* AND SOMEHOW THIS IS ALL *YOUR FAULT,* BOBO.
YOU'VE GOT IT, DANNY BOY. SORRY ABOUT THAT.
E *THE SWORD.* G US ALL BACK HE CASTLE. WE REGROUP AND GHT THERE.
I DON'T KNOW HOW TO DO *THAT...*
WILL IT, BOBO. *WILL IT WITH ALL YOUR HEART.*

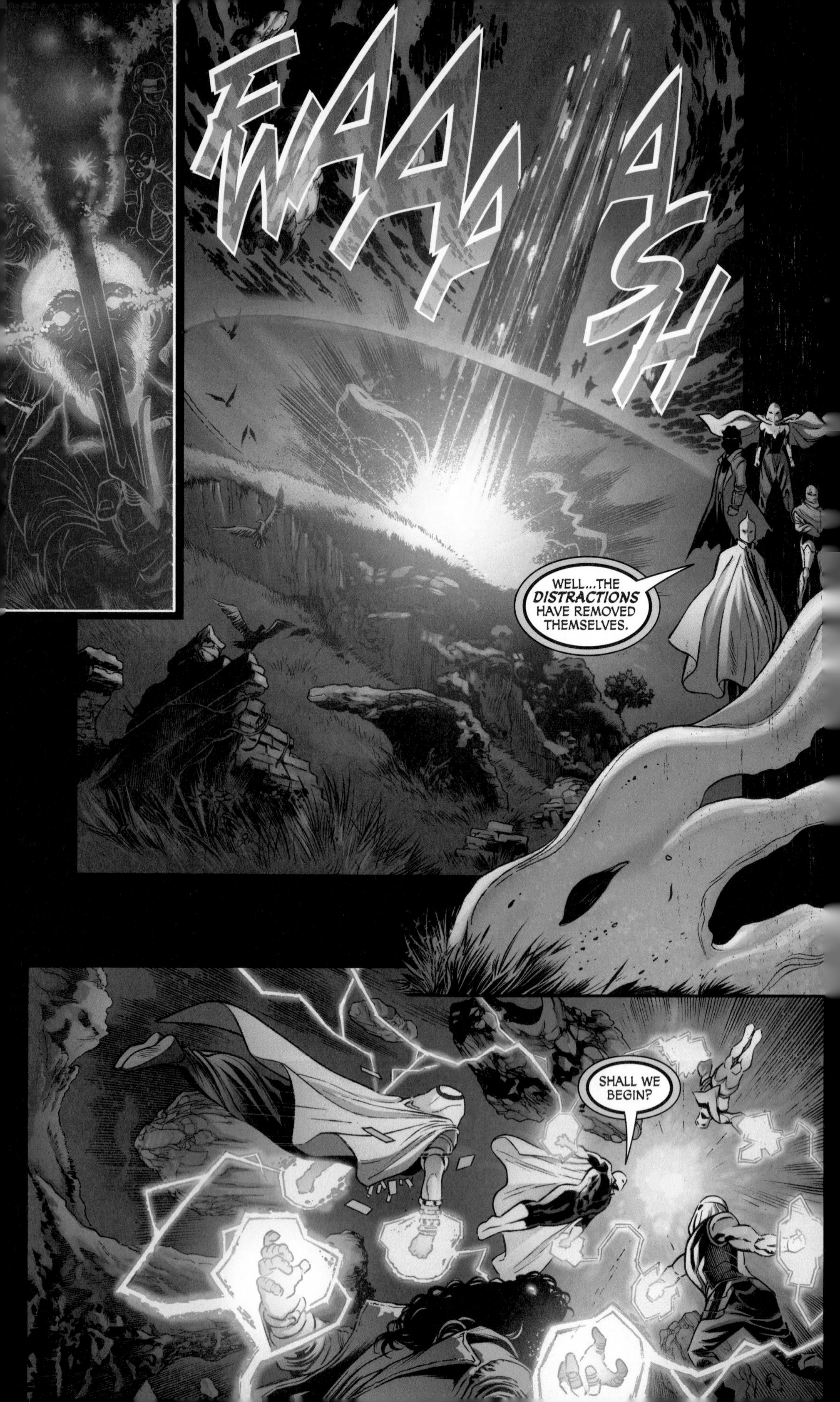
FWAAAASH
WELL...THE DISTRACTIONS HAVE REMOVED THEMSELVES.
SHALL WE BEGIN?

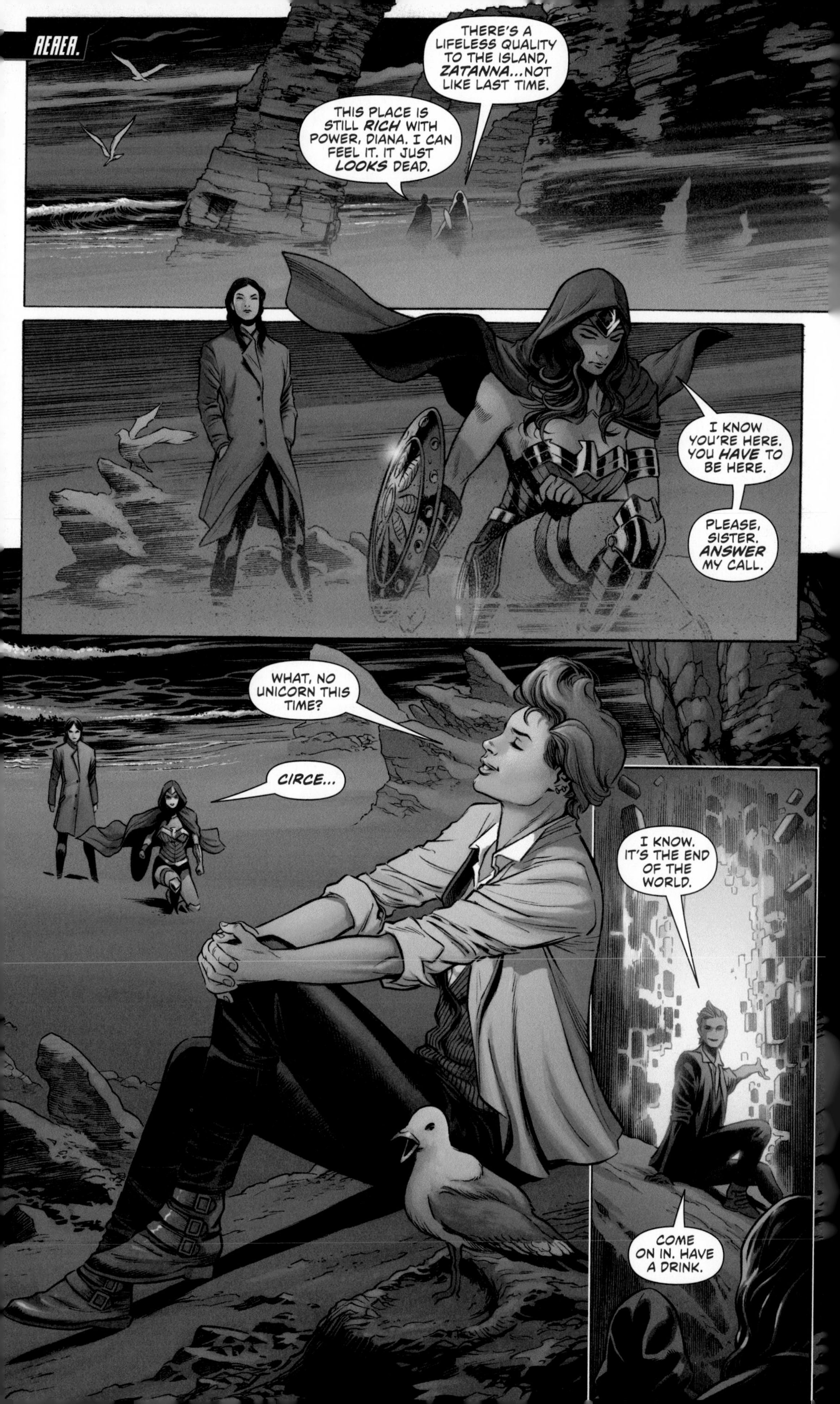
AEAEA.
THERE'S A LIFELESS QUALITY TO THE ISLAND, ZATANNA...NOT LIKE LAST TIME.
THIS PLACE IS STILL RICH WITH POWER, DIANA. I CAN FEEL IT. IT JUST LOOKS DEAD.
I KNOW YOU'RE HERE. YOU HAVE TO BE HERE.
PLEASE, SISTER. ANSWER MY CALL.
WHAT, NO UNICORN THIS TIME?
CIRCE...
I KNOW. IT'S THE END OF THE WORLD.
COME ON IN. HAVE A DRINK.

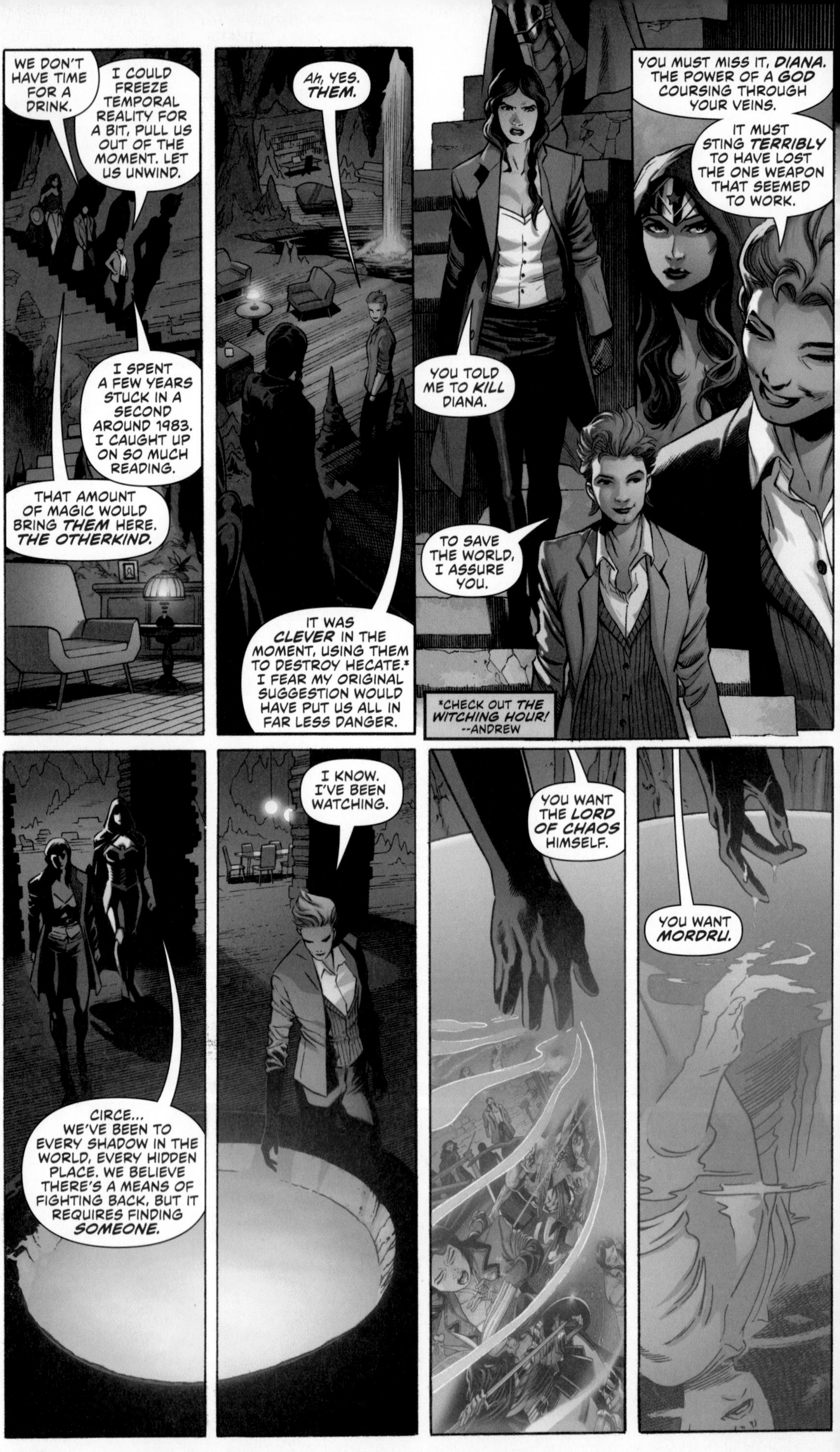

WE DON'T HAVE TIME FOR A DRINK.
I COULD FREEZE TEMPORAL REALITY FOR A BIT, PULL US OUT OF THE MOMENT. LET US UNWIND.
I SPENT A FEW YEARS STUCK IN A SECOND AROUND 1983. I CAUGHT UP ON SO MUCH READING.
THAT AMOUNT OF MAGIC WOULD BRING *THEM* HERE. *THE OTHERKIND.*
Ah, YES. *THEM.*
IT WAS *CLEVER* IN THE MOMENT, USING THEM TO DESTROY HECATE.* I FEAR MY ORIGINAL SUGGESTION WOULD HAVE PUT US ALL IN FAR LESS DANGER.
YOU MUST MISS IT, *DIANA*. THE POWER OF A *GOD* COURSING THROUGH YOUR VEINS.
IT MUST STING *TERRIBLY* TO HAVE LOST THE ONE WEAPON THAT SEEMED TO WORK.
YOU TOLD ME TO *KILL* DIANA.
TO SAVE THE WORLD, I ASSURE YOU.
*CHECK OUT *THE WITCHING HOUR!* --ANDREW
CIRCE... WE'VE BEEN TO EVERY SHADOW IN THE WORLD, EVERY HIDDEN PLACE. WE BELIEVE THERE'S A MEANS OF FIGHTING BACK, BUT IT REQUIRES FINDING *SOMEONE.*
I KNOW. I'VE BEEN WATCHING.
YOU WANT THE *LORD OF CHAOS* HIMSELF.
YOU WANT *MORDRU.*

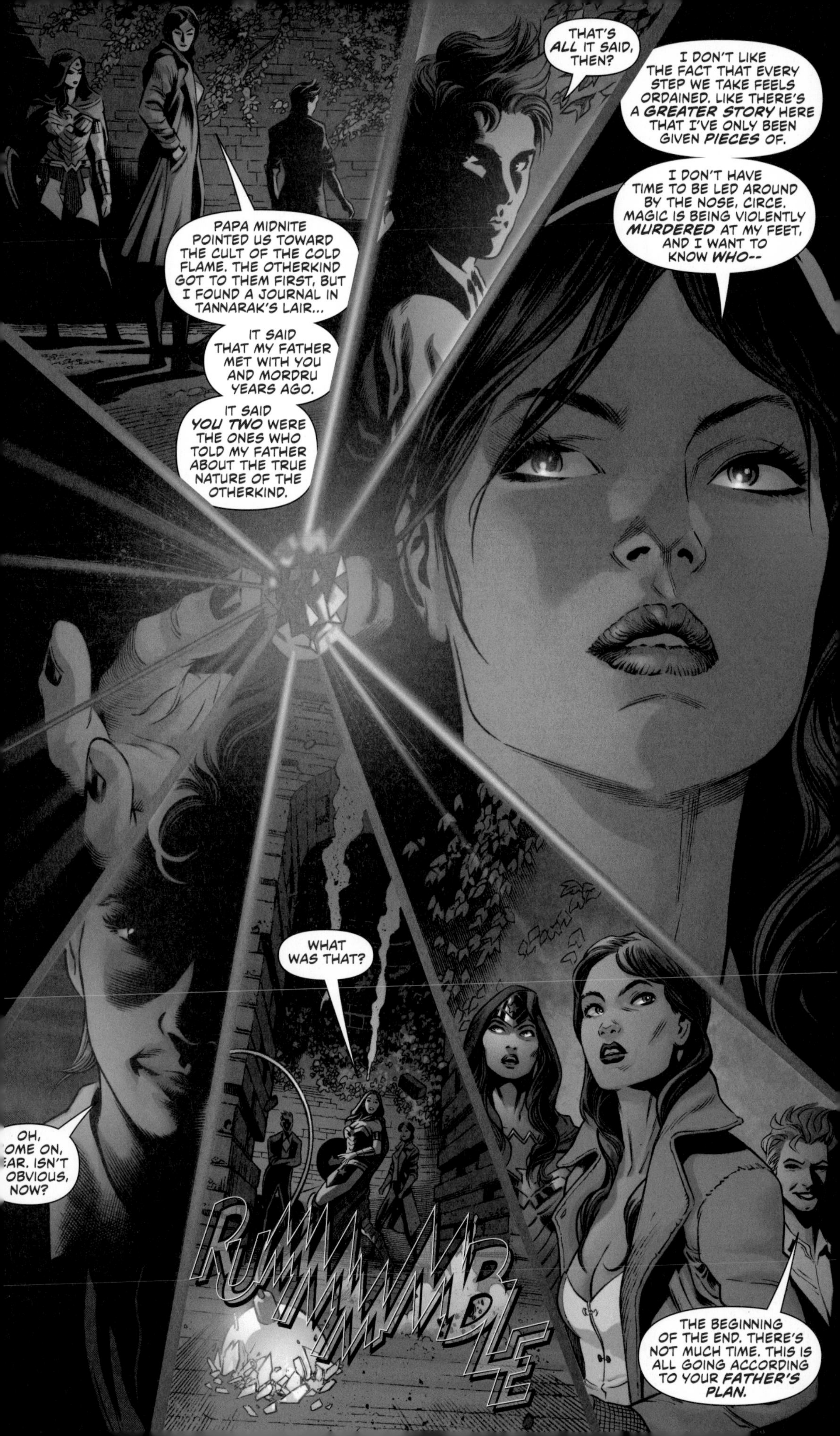
PAPA MIDNITE POINTED US TOWARD THE CULT OF THE COLD FLAME. THE OTHERKIND GOT TO THEM FIRST, BUT I FOUND A JOURNAL IN TANNARAK'S LAIR...
IT SAID THAT MY FATHER MET WITH YOU AND MORDRU YEARS AGO.
IT SAID YOU TWO WERE THE ONES WHO TOLD MY FATHER ABOUT THE TRUE NATURE OF THE OTHERKIND.
THAT'S ALL IT SAID, THEN?
I DON'T LIKE THE FACT THAT EVERY STEP WE TAKE FEELS ORDAINED. LIKE THERE'S A GREATER STORY HERE THAT I'VE ONLY BEEN GIVEN PIECES OF.
I DON'T HAVE TIME TO BE LED AROUND BY THE NOSE, CIRCE. MAGIC IS BEING VIOLENTLY MURDERED AT MY FEET, AND I WANT TO KNOW WHO--
OH, OME ON, EAR. ISN'T OBVIOUS, NOW?
WHAT WAS THAT?
RUMMMMBLE
THE BEGINNING OF THE END. THERE'S NOT MUCH TIME. THIS IS ALL GOING ACCORDING TO YOUR FATHER'S PLAN.

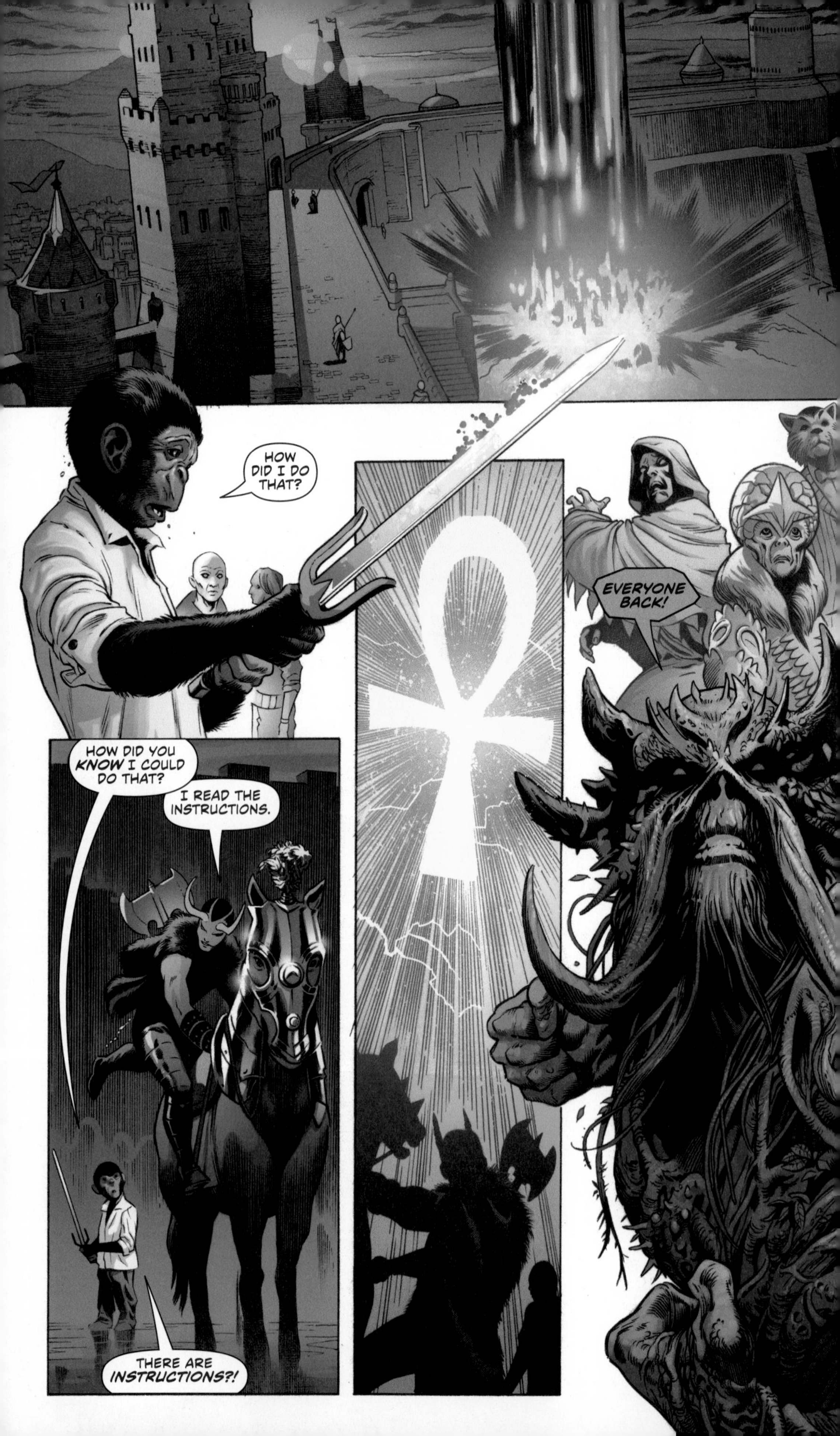
HOW DID I DO THAT?
EVERYONE BACK!
HOW DID YOU KNOW I COULD DO THAT?
I READ THE INSTRUCTIONS.
THERE ARE INSTRUCTIONS?!

WHO ARE YOU?

MY NAME IS *KHALID NASSOUR.* I WAS DOCTOR FATE ONCE. A PUPIL OF KENT NELSON AND NABU...

...BEFORE NABU WENT DOWN THIS DARK ROAD.

Ah! WONDERFUL, WE'VE FOUND THEM!

GOOD. GOOD. THEN THERE'S STILL TIME.

WASN'T HE *TRAPPED* IN A VASE?

I GOT HIM OUT!

WHO LET THE CRAZY MAD SCIENTIST LEARN MAGIC?! HAVEN'T YOU GOTTEN US ALL IN ENOUGH TROUBLE AS IT IS, MAN-BAT?

BOBO, PERHAPS YOU *SHOULDN'T* TALK.

THAT'S A DAMN FINE IDEA.

OK, THIS PLACE HELD ITS OWN AGAINST A HORDE OF THE UNDEAD FOR MONTHS.

IF WE START FIGURING OUT WHO OUR STRONGEST POWER PLAYERS ARE, WE SHOULD BE ABLE TO MOUNT A DEFENSE.

NO...I'M TERRIBLY SORRY. IF WE ACT FAST, WE *STILL* MIGHT BE ABLE TO SAVE THE SPHERE OF THE GODS AS A WHOLE...

...BUT *MYRRA...*

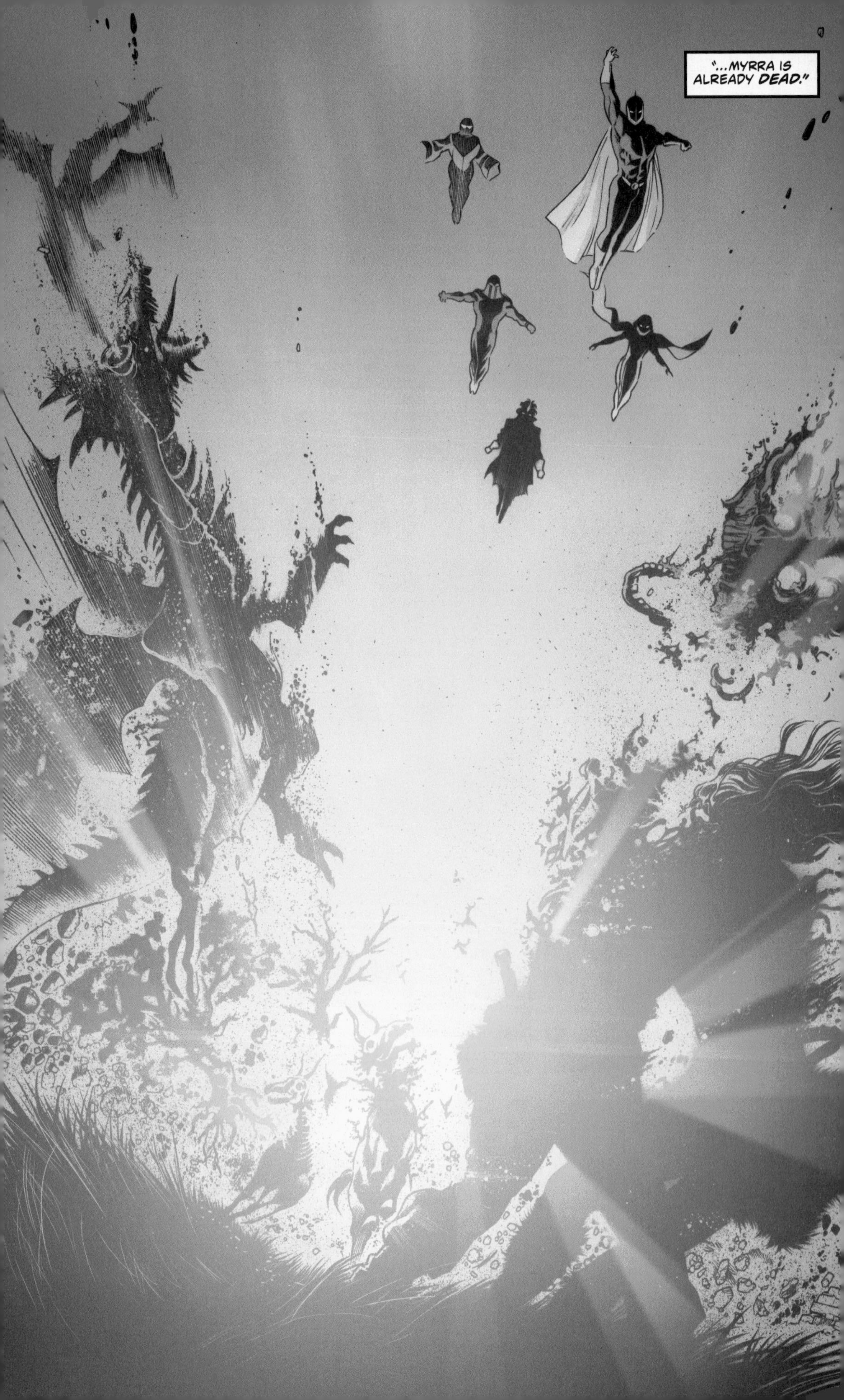
"...MYRRA IS ALREADY DEAD."

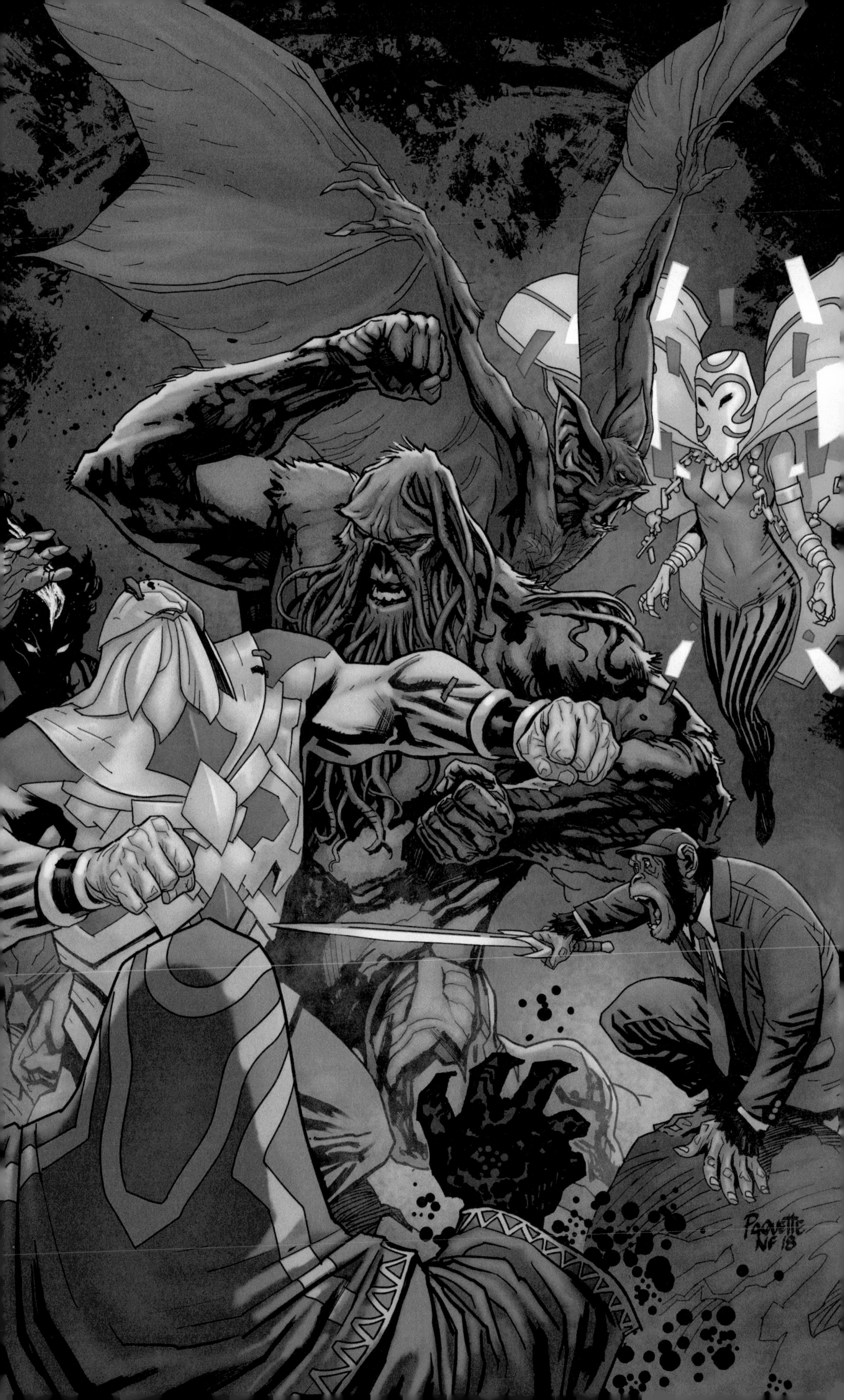
PAQUETTE
NF 18

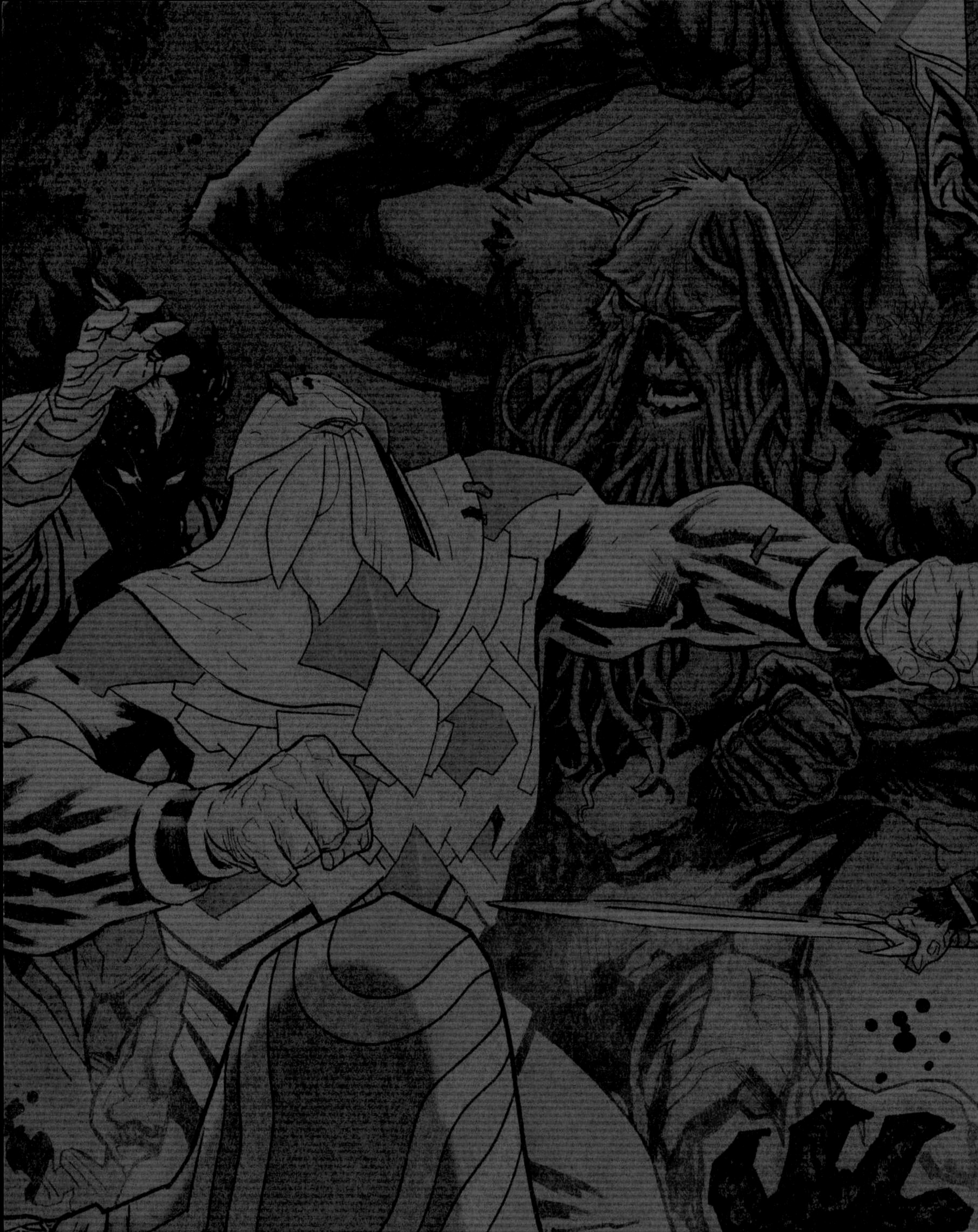

JUSTICE LEAGUE DARK
#10

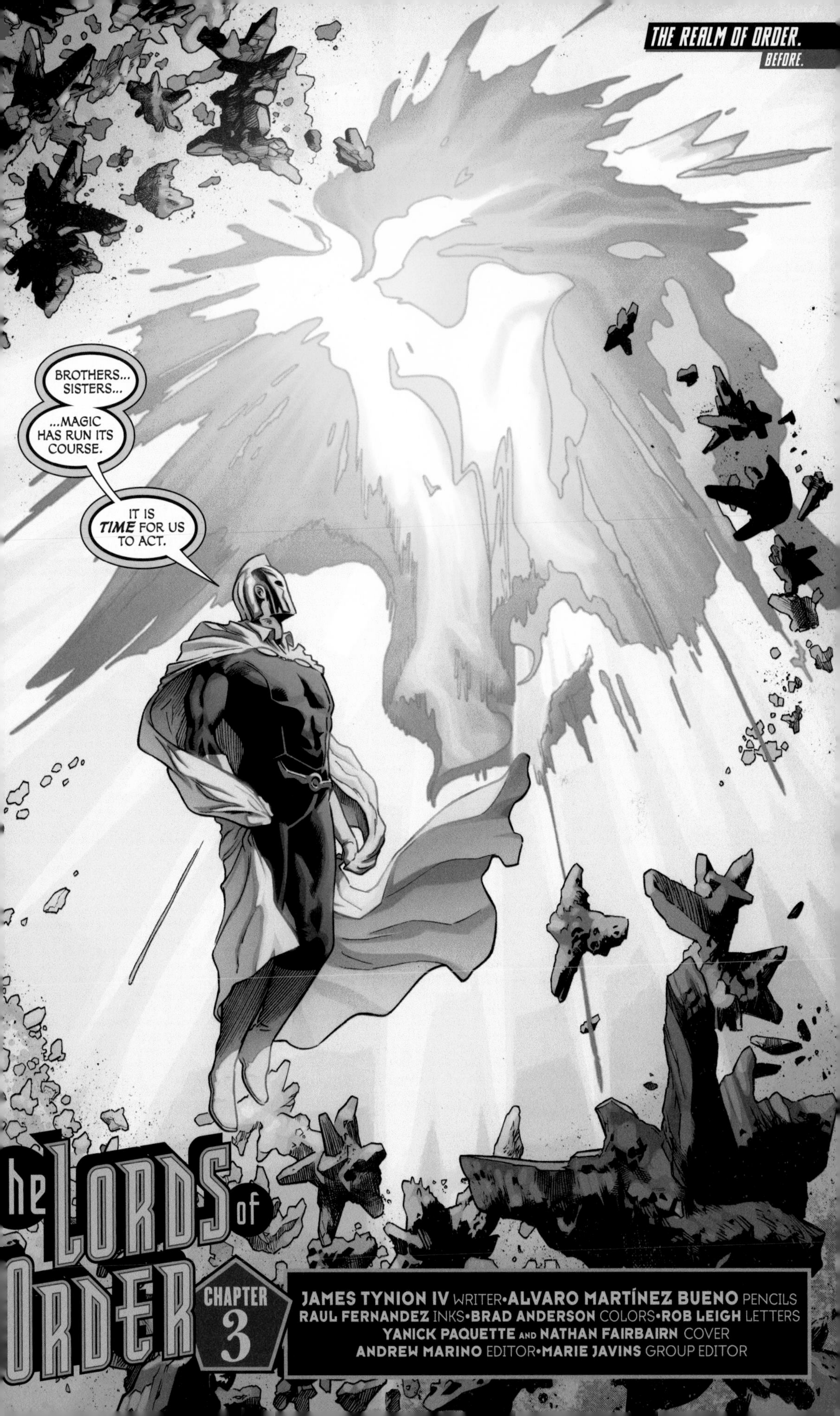
THE REALM OF ORDER.
BEFORE.
BROTHERS... SISTERS...
...MAGIC HAS RUN ITS COURSE.
IT IS TIME FOR US TO ACT.
The LORDS of ORDER
CHAPTER 3
JAMES TYNION IV WRITER•ALVARO MARTÍNEZ BUENO PENCILS
RAUL FERNANDEZ INKS•BRAD ANDERSON COLORS•ROB LEIGH LETTERS
YANICK PAQUETTE AND NATHAN FAIRBAIRN COVER
ANDREW MARINO EDITOR•MARIE JAVINS GROUP EDITOR

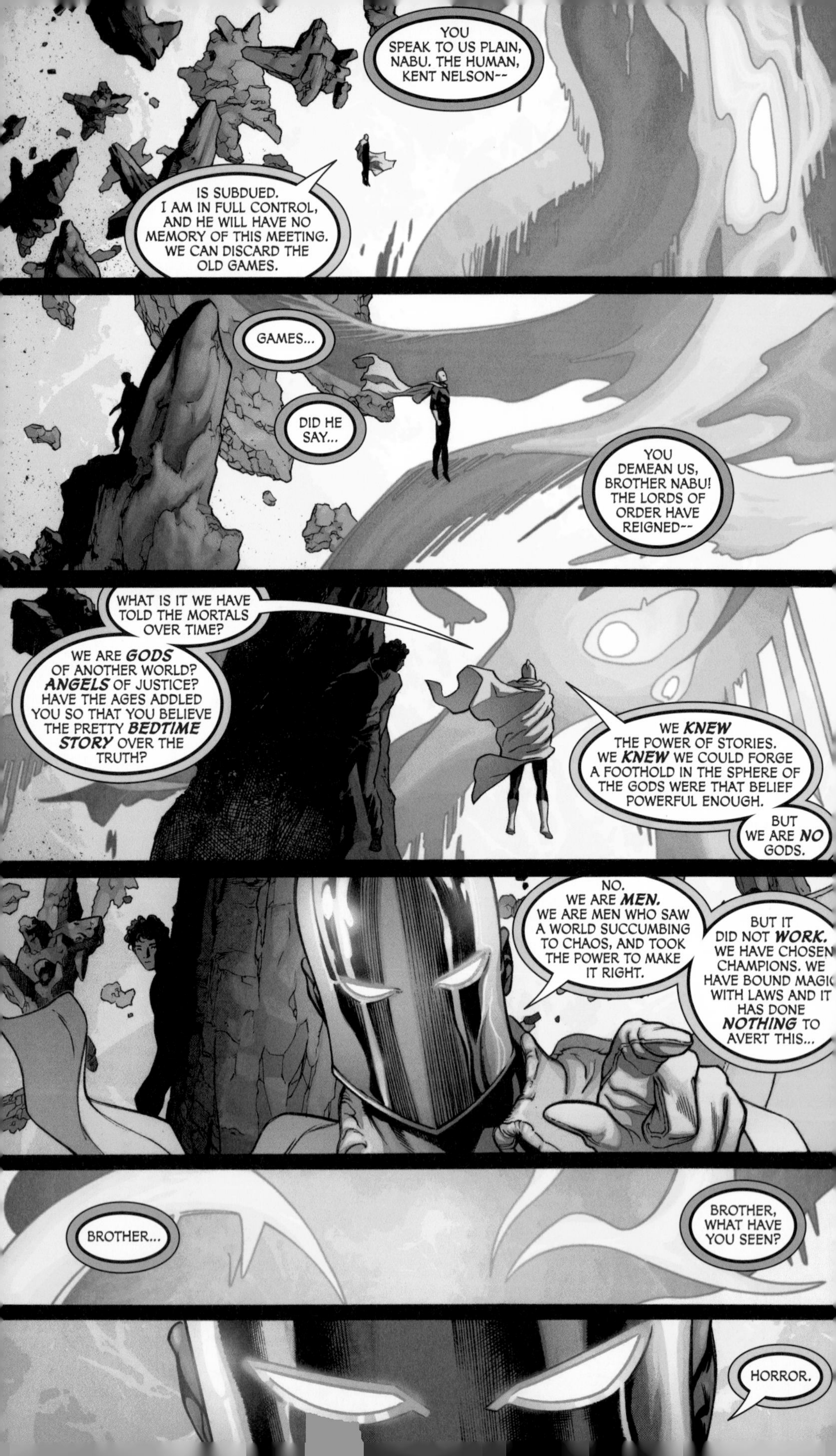

YOU SPEAK TO US PLAIN, NABU. THE HUMAN, KENT NELSON--
IS SUBDUED. I AM IN FULL CONTROL, AND HE WILL HAVE NO MEMORY OF THIS MEETING. WE CAN DISCARD THE OLD GAMES.
GAMES...
DID HE SAY...
YOU DEMEAN US, BROTHER NABU! THE LORDS OF ORDER HAVE REIGNED--
WHAT IS IT WE HAVE TOLD THE MORTALS OVER TIME?
WE ARE **GODS** OF ANOTHER WORLD? **ANGELS** OF JUSTICE? HAVE THE AGES ADDLED YOU SO THAT YOU BELIEVE THE PRETTY **BEDTIME STORY** OVER THE TRUTH?
WE **KNEW** THE POWER OF STORIES. WE **KNEW** WE COULD FORGE A FOOTHOLD IN THE SPHERE OF THE GODS WERE THAT BELIEF POWERFUL ENOUGH.
BUT WE ARE **NO** GODS.
NO. WE ARE **MEN.** WE ARE MEN WHO SAW A WORLD SUCCUMBING TO CHAOS, AND TOOK THE POWER TO MAKE IT RIGHT.
BUT IT DID NOT **WORK.** WE HAVE CHOSEN CHAMPIONS. WE HAVE BOUND MAGIC WITH LAWS AND IT HAS DONE **NOTHING** TO AVERT THIS...
BROTHER...
BROTHER, WHAT HAVE YOU SEEN?
HORROR.

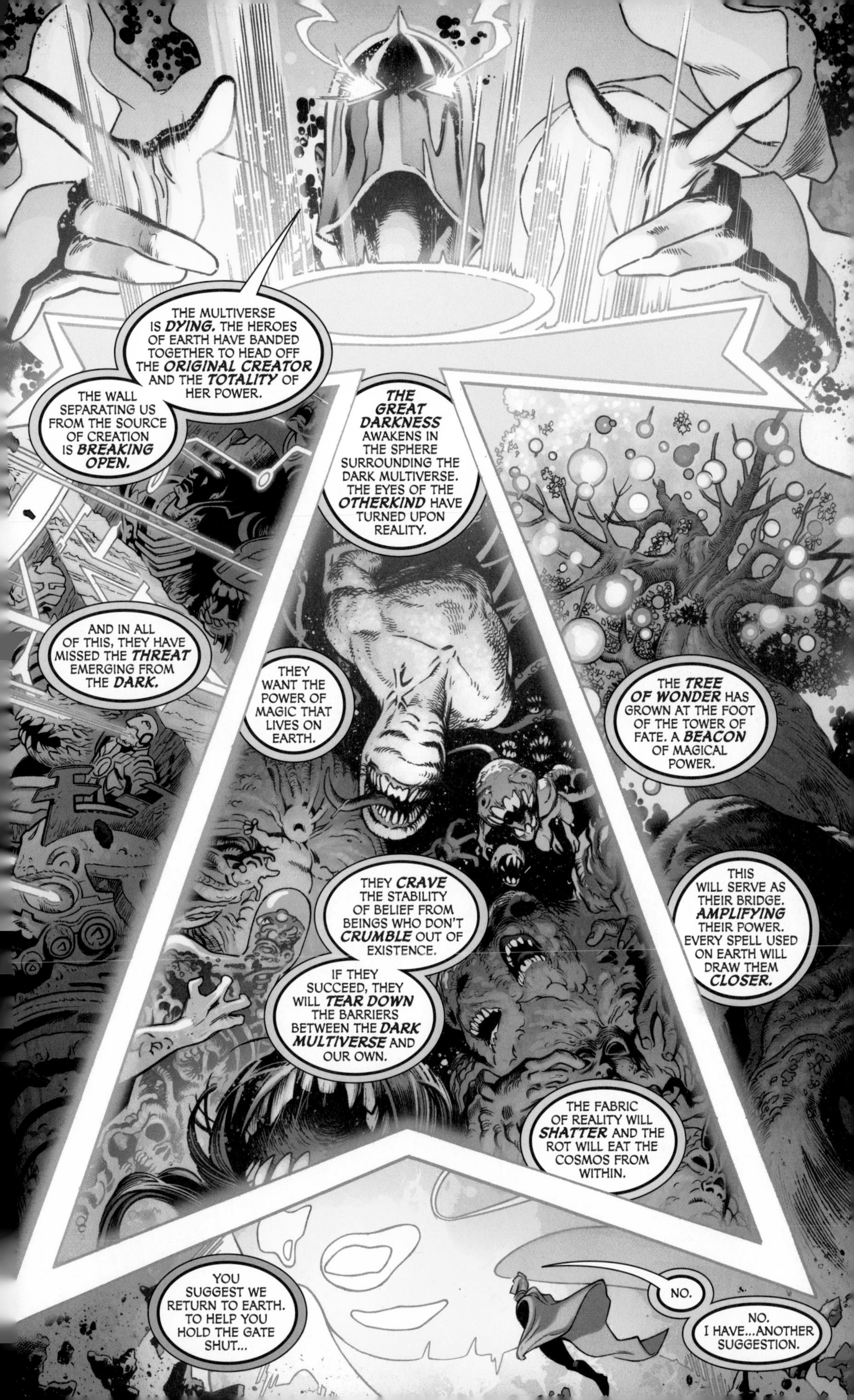
THE MULTIVERSE IS DYING. THE HEROES OF EARTH HAVE BANDED TOGETHER TO HEAD OFF THE ORIGINAL CREATOR AND THE TOTALITY OF HER POWER.
THE WALL SEPARATING US FROM THE SOURCE OF CREATION IS BREAKING OPEN.
AND IN ALL OF THIS, THEY HAVE MISSED THE THREAT EMERGING FROM THE DARK.
THE GREAT DARKNESS AWAKENS IN THE SPHERE SURROUNDING THE DARK MULTIVERSE. THE EYES OF THE OTHERKIND HAVE TURNED UPON REALITY.
THEY WANT THE POWER OF MAGIC THAT LIVES ON EARTH.
THEY CRAVE THE STABILITY OF BELIEF FROM BEINGS WHO DON'T CRUMBLE OUT OF EXISTENCE.
IF THEY SUCCEED, THEY WILL TEAR DOWN THE BARRIERS BETWEEN THE DARK MULTIVERSE AND OUR OWN.
THE TREE OF WONDER HAS GROWN AT THE FOOT OF THE TOWER OF FATE. A BEACON OF MAGICAL POWER.
THIS WILL SERVE AS THEIR BRIDGE. AMPLIFYING THEIR POWER. EVERY SPELL USED ON EARTH WILL DRAW THEM CLOSER.
THE FABRIC OF REALITY WILL SHATTER AND THE ROT WILL EAT THE COSMOS FROM WITHIN.
YOU SUGGEST WE RETURN TO EARTH. TO HELP YOU HOLD THE GATE SHUT...
NO.
NO. I HAVE...ANOTHER SUGGESTION.

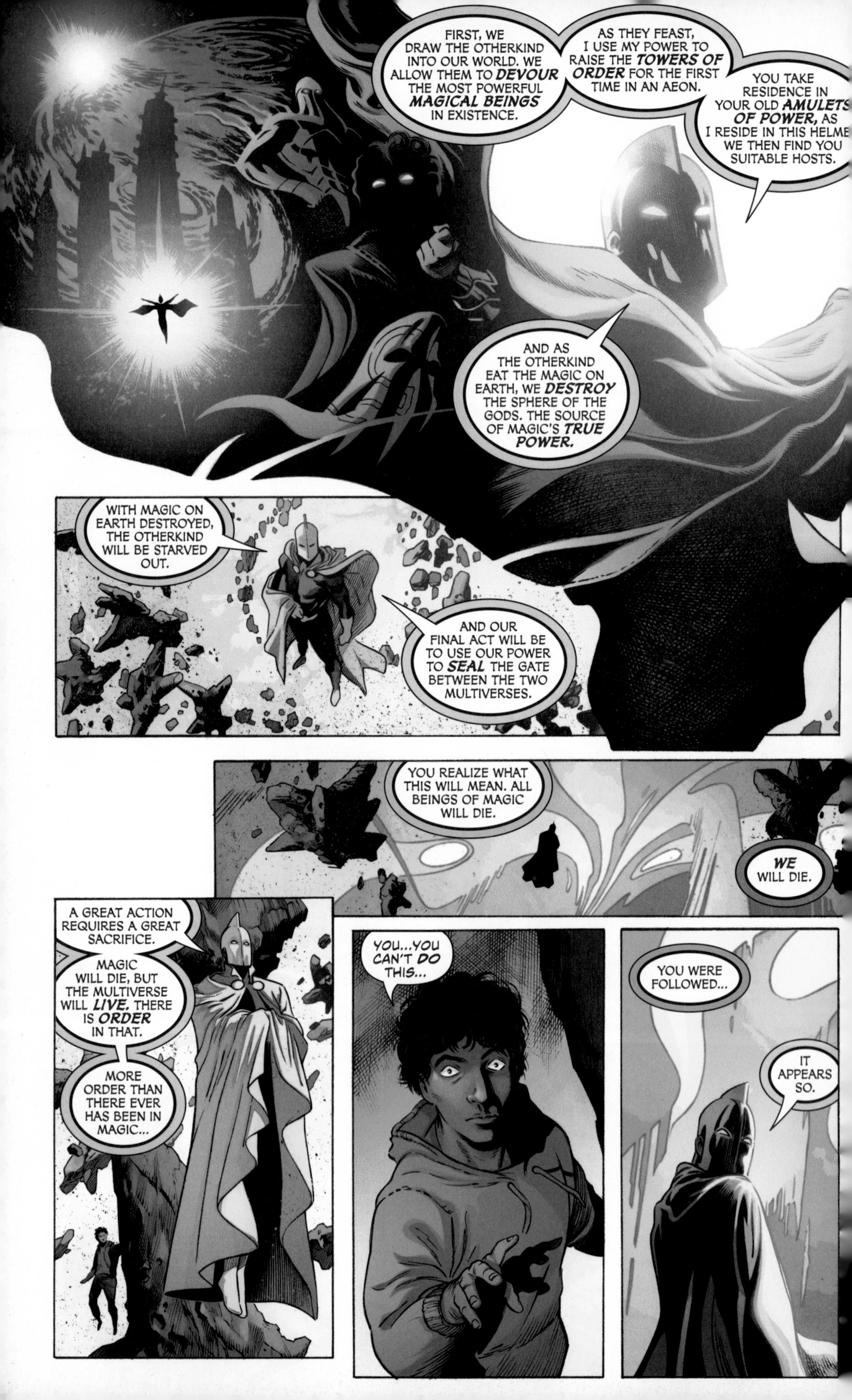
FIRST, WE DRAW THE OTHERKIND INTO OUR WORLD. WE ALLOW THEM TO *DEVOUR* THE MOST POWERFUL *MAGICAL BEINGS* IN EXISTENCE.
AS THEY FEAST, I USE MY POWER TO RAISE THE *TOWERS OF ORDER* FOR THE FIRST TIME IN AN AEON.
YOU TAKE RESIDENCE IN YOUR OLD *AMULETS OF POWER,* AS I RESIDE IN THIS HELME WE THEN FIND YOU SUITABLE HOSTS.
AND AS THE OTHERKIND EAT THE MAGIC ON EARTH, WE *DESTROY* THE SPHERE OF THE GODS. THE SOURCE OF MAGIC'S *TRUE POWER.*
WITH MAGIC ON EARTH DESTROYED, THE OTHERKIND WILL BE STARVED OUT.
AND OUR FINAL ACT WILL BE TO USE OUR POWER TO *SEAL* THE GATE BETWEEN THE TWO MULTIVERSES.
YOU REALIZE WHAT THIS WILL MEAN. ALL BEINGS OF MAGIC WILL DIE.
WE WILL DIE.
A GREAT ACTION REQUIRES A GREAT SACRIFICE.
MAGIC WILL DIE, BUT THE MULTIVERSE WILL *LIVE.* THERE IS *ORDER* IN THAT.
MORE ORDER THAN THERE EVER HAS BEEN IN MAGIC...
YOU...YOU CAN'T *DO* THIS...
YOU WERE FOLLOWED...
IT APPEARS SO.

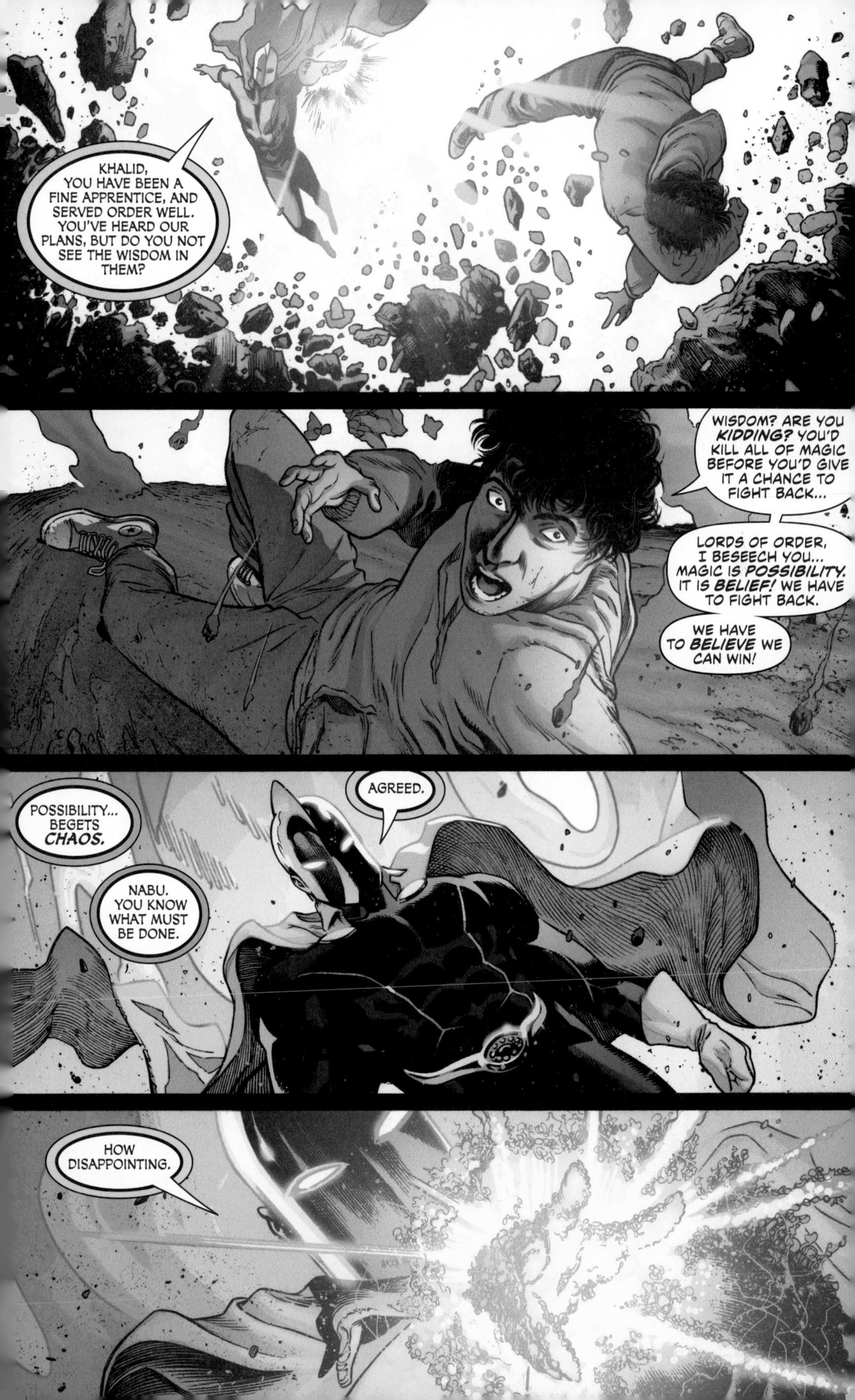
KHALID, YOU HAVE BEEN A FINE APPRENTICE, AND SERVED ORDER WELL. YOU'VE HEARD OUR PLANS, BUT DO YOU NOT SEE THE WISDOM IN THEM?
WISDOM? ARE YOU *KIDDING?* YOU'D KILL ALL OF MAGIC BEFORE YOU'D GIVE IT A CHANCE TO FIGHT BACK...
LORDS OF ORDER, I BESEECH YOU... MAGIC IS *POSSIBILITY.* IT IS *BELIEF!* WE HAVE TO FIGHT BACK.
WE HAVE TO *BELIEVE* WE CAN WIN!
POSSIBILITY... BEGETS *CHAOS.*
AGREED.
NABU. YOU KNOW WHAT MUST BE DONE.
HOW DISAPPOINTING.

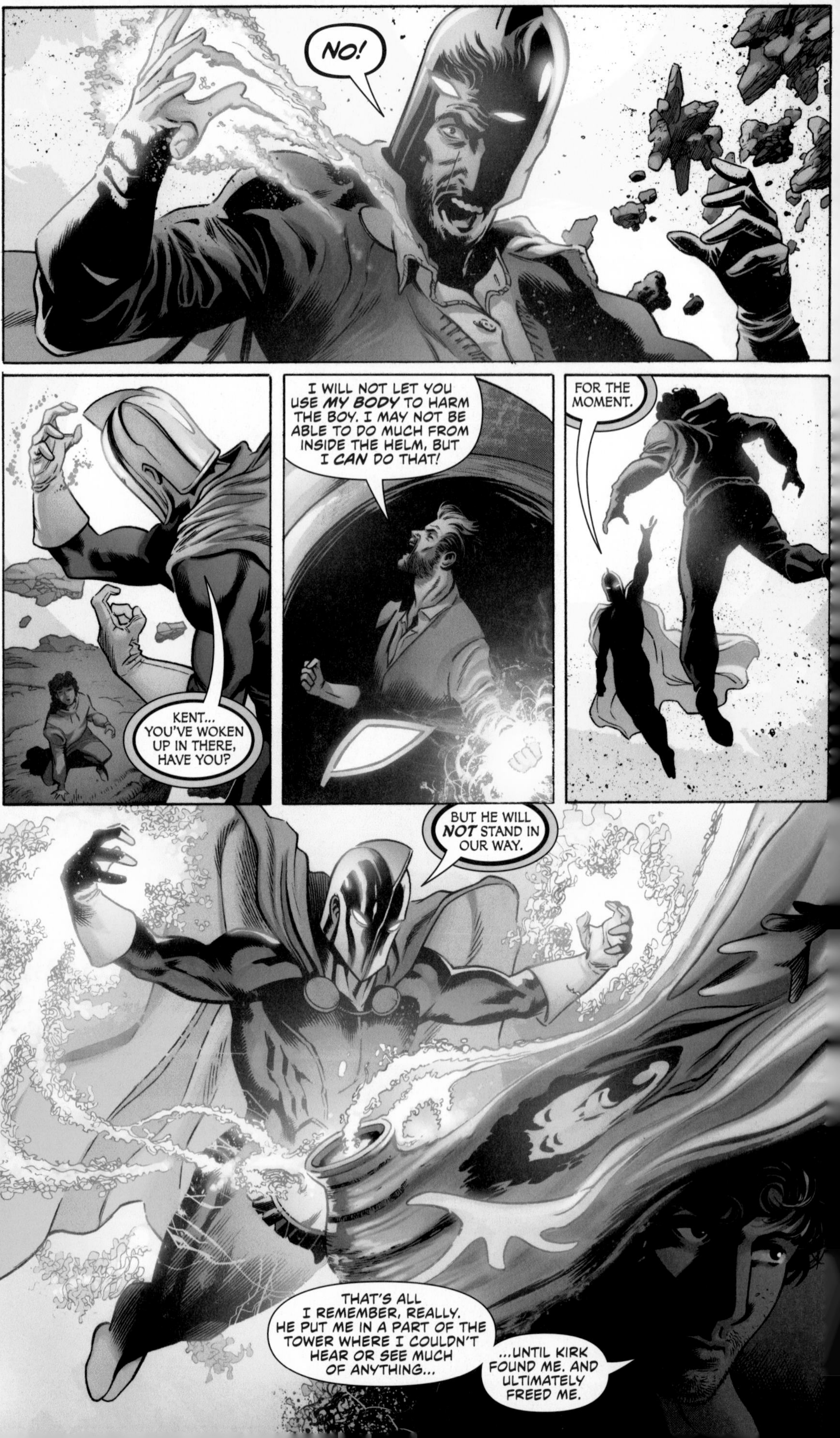
NO!
KENT... YOU'VE WOKEN UP IN THERE, HAVE YOU?
I WILL NOT LET YOU USE MY BODY TO HARM THE BOY. I MAY NOT BE ABLE TO DO MUCH FROM INSIDE THE HELM, BUT I CAN DO THAT!
FOR THE MOMENT.
BUT HE WILL NOT STAND IN OUR WAY.
THAT'S ALL I REMEMBER, REALLY. HE PUT ME IN A PART OF THE TOWER WHERE I COULDN'T HEAR OR SEE MUCH OF ANYTHING...
...UNTIL KIRK FOUND ME. AND ULTIMATELY FREED ME.

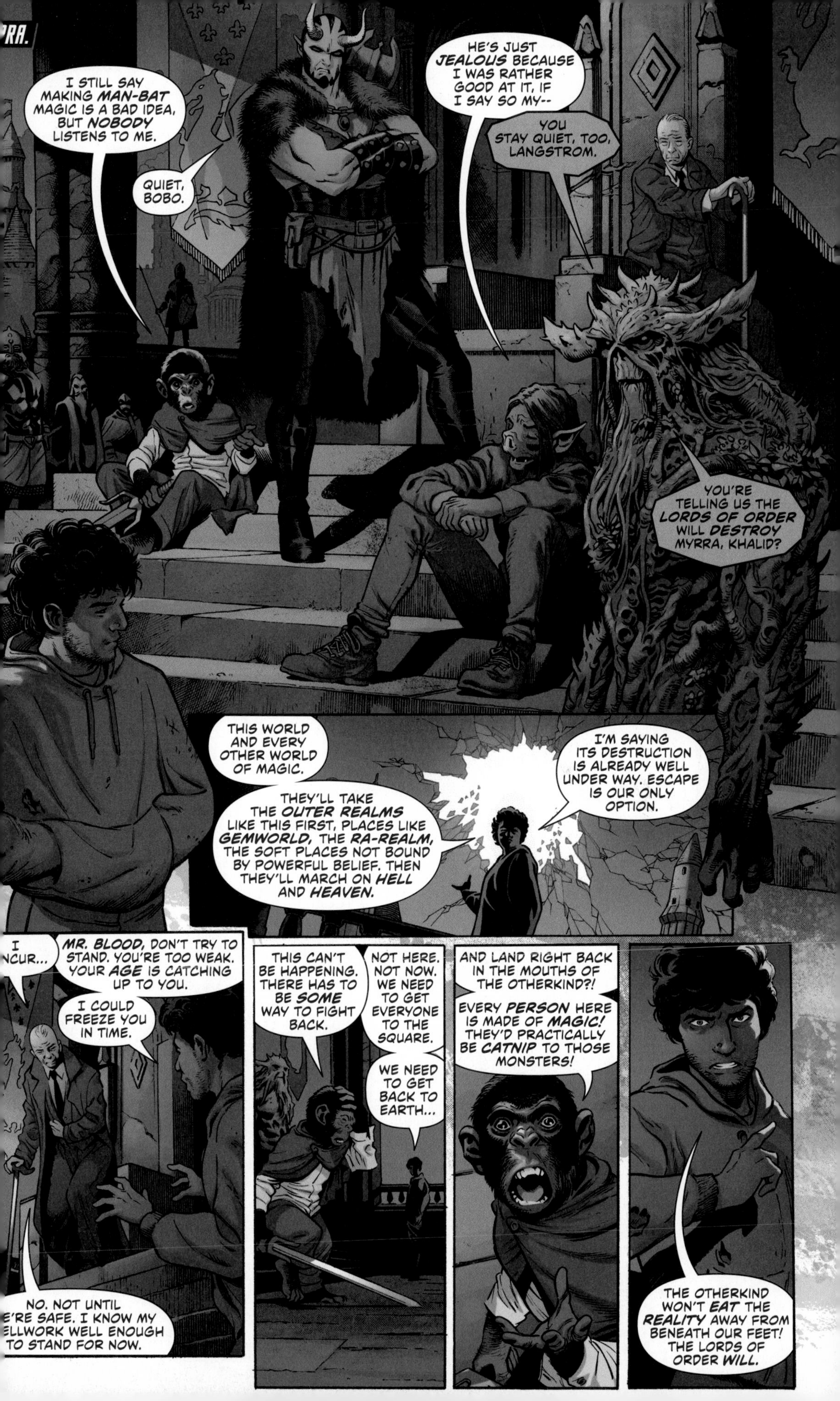

PRA.
I STILL SAY MAKING MAN-BAT MAGIC IS A BAD IDEA, BUT NOBODY LISTENS TO ME.
QUIET, BOBO.
HE'S JUST JEALOUS BECAUSE I WAS RATHER GOOD AT IT, IF I SAY SO MY--
YOU STAY QUIET, TOO, LANGSTROM.
YOU'RE TELLING US THE LORDS OF ORDER WILL DESTROY MYRRA, KHALID?
THIS WORLD AND EVERY OTHER WORLD OF MAGIC.
THEY'LL TAKE THE OUTER REALMS LIKE THIS FIRST, PLACES LIKE GEMWORLD, THE RA-REALM, THE SOFT PLACES NOT BOUND BY POWERFUL BELIEF. THEN THEY'LL MARCH ON HELL AND HEAVEN.
I'M SAYING ITS DESTRUCTION IS ALREADY WELL UNDER WAY. ESCAPE IS OUR ONLY OPTION.
I NCUR...
MR. BLOOD, DON'T TRY TO STAND. YOU'RE TOO WEAK. YOUR AGE IS CATCHING UP TO YOU.
I COULD FREEZE YOU IN TIME.
NO. NOT UNTIL E'RE SAFE. I KNOW MY ELLWORK WELL ENOUGH TO STAND FOR NOW.
THIS CAN'T BE HAPPENING. THERE HAS TO BE SOME WAY TO FIGHT BACK.
NOT HERE. NOT NOW. WE NEED TO GET EVERYONE TO THE SQUARE.
WE NEED TO GET BACK TO EARTH...
AND LAND RIGHT BACK IN THE MOUTHS OF THE OTHERKIND?!
EVERY PERSON HERE IS MADE OF MAGIC! THEY'D PRACTICALLY BE CATNIP TO THOSE MONSTERS!
THE OTHERKIND WON'T EAT THE REALITY AWAY FROM BENEATH OUR FEET! THE LORDS OF ORDER WILL.

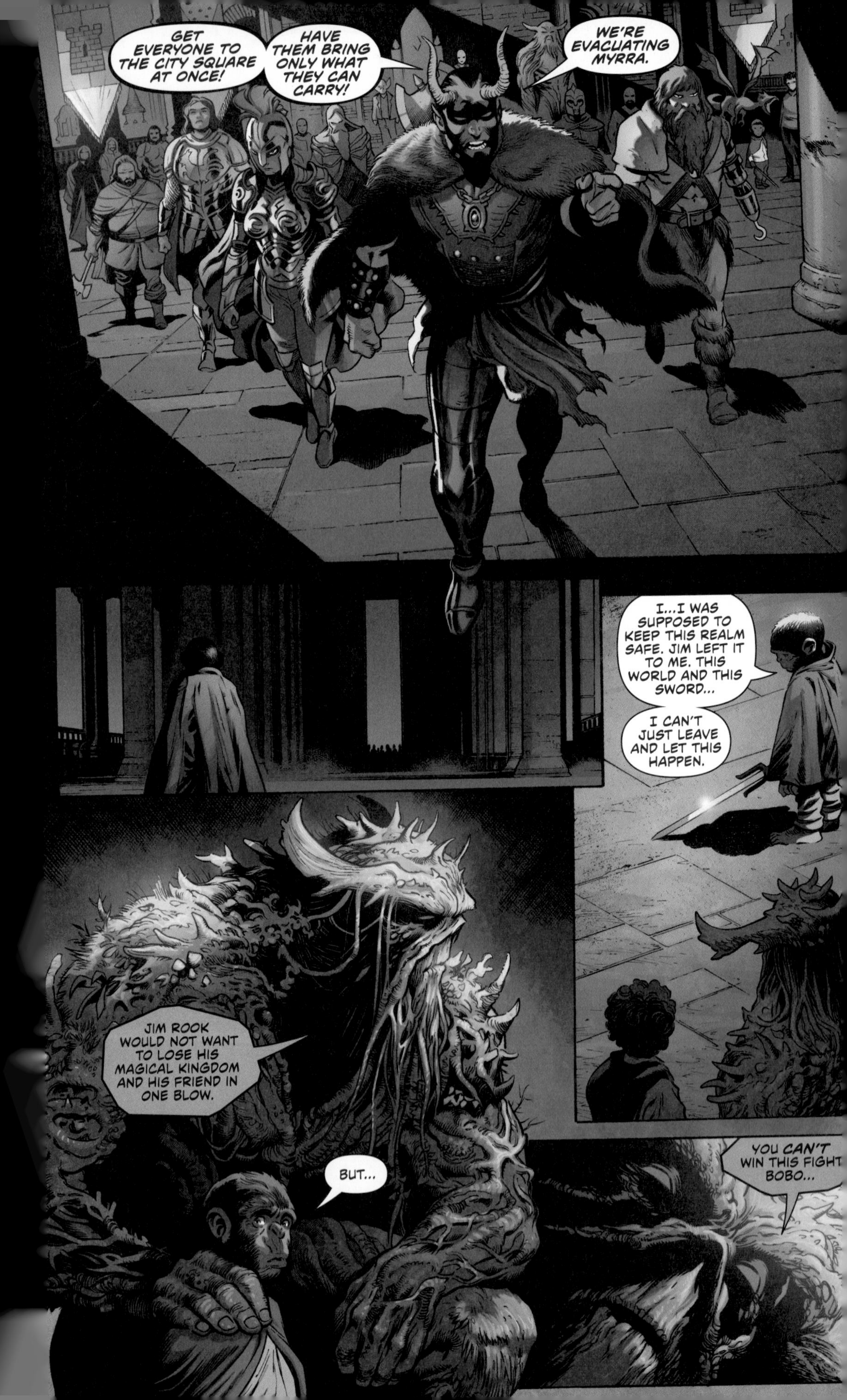
GET EVERYONE TO THE CITY SQUARE AT ONCE!
HAVE THEM BRING ONLY WHAT THEY CAN CARRY!
WE'RE EVACUATING MYRRA.
I...I WAS SUPPOSED TO KEEP THIS REALM SAFE. JIM LEFT IT TO ME. THIS WORLD AND THIS SWORD...
I CAN'T JUST LEAVE AND LET THIS HAPPEN.
JIM ROOK WOULD NOT WANT TO LOSE HIS MAGICAL KINGDOM AND HIS FRIEND IN ONE BLOW.
BUT...
YOU *CAN'T* WIN THIS FIGHT BOBO...

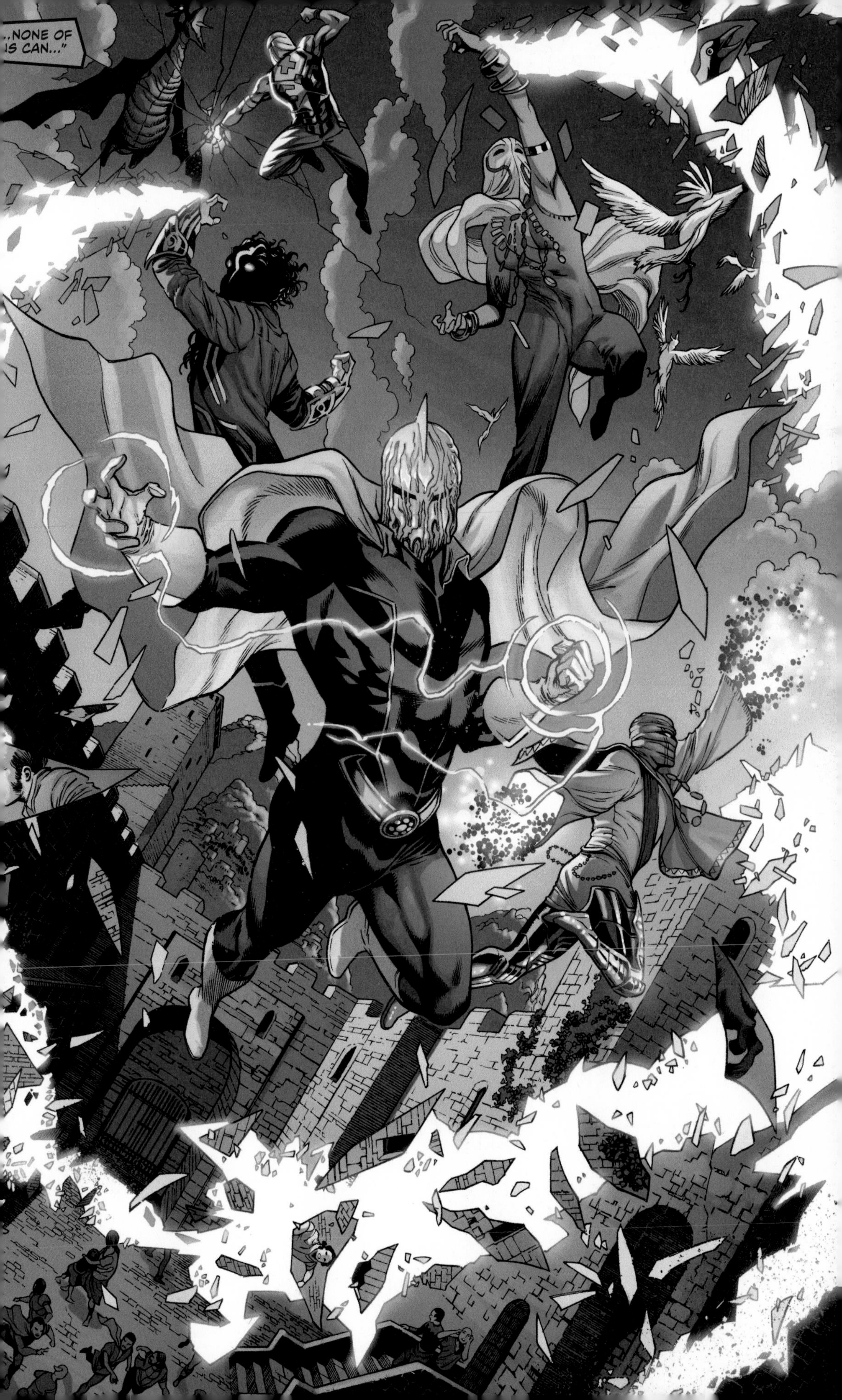

..NONE OF
IS CAN..."

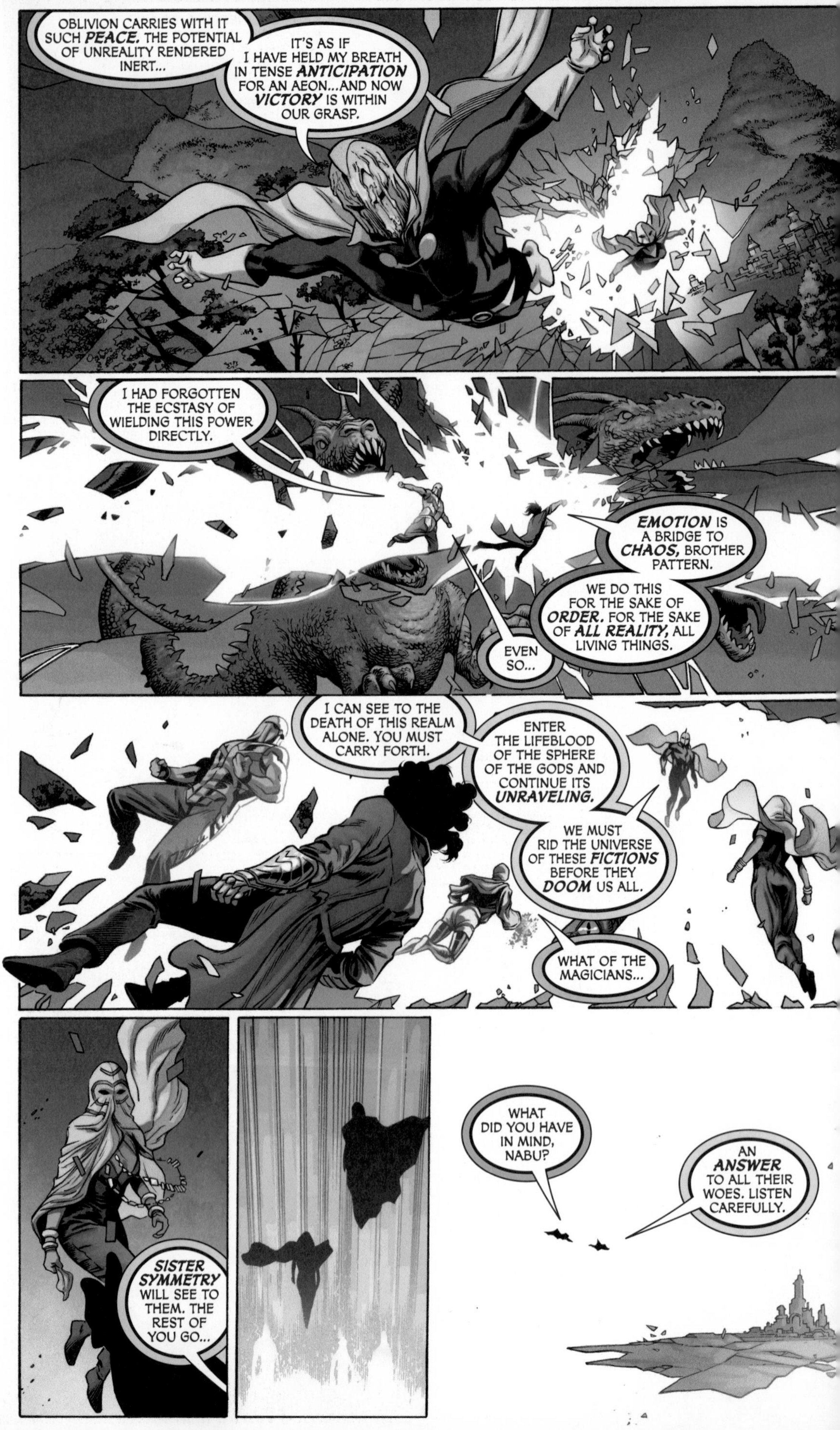
OBLIVION CARRIES WITH IT SUCH PEACE. THE POTENTIAL OF UNREALITY RENDERED INERT...
IT'S AS IF I HAVE HELD MY BREATH IN TENSE ANTICIPATION FOR AN AEON...AND NOW VICTORY IS WITHIN OUR GRASP.
I HAD FORGOTTEN THE ECSTASY OF WIELDING THIS POWER DIRECTLY.
EMOTION IS A BRIDGE TO CHAOS, BROTHER PATTERN.
WE DO THIS FOR THE SAKE OF ORDER. FOR THE SAKE OF ALL REALITY, ALL LIVING THINGS.
EVEN SO...
I CAN SEE TO THE DEATH OF THIS REALM ALONE. YOU MUST CARRY FORTH.
ENTER THE LIFEBLOOD OF THE SPHERE OF THE GODS AND CONTINUE ITS UNRAVELING.
WE MUST RID THE UNIVERSE OF THESE FICTIONS BEFORE THEY DOOM US ALL.
WHAT OF THE MAGICIANS...
SISTER SYMMETRY WILL SEE TO THEM. THE REST OF YOU GO...
WHAT DID YOU HAVE IN MIND, NABU?
AN ANSWER TO ALL THEIR WOES. LISTEN CAREFULLY.

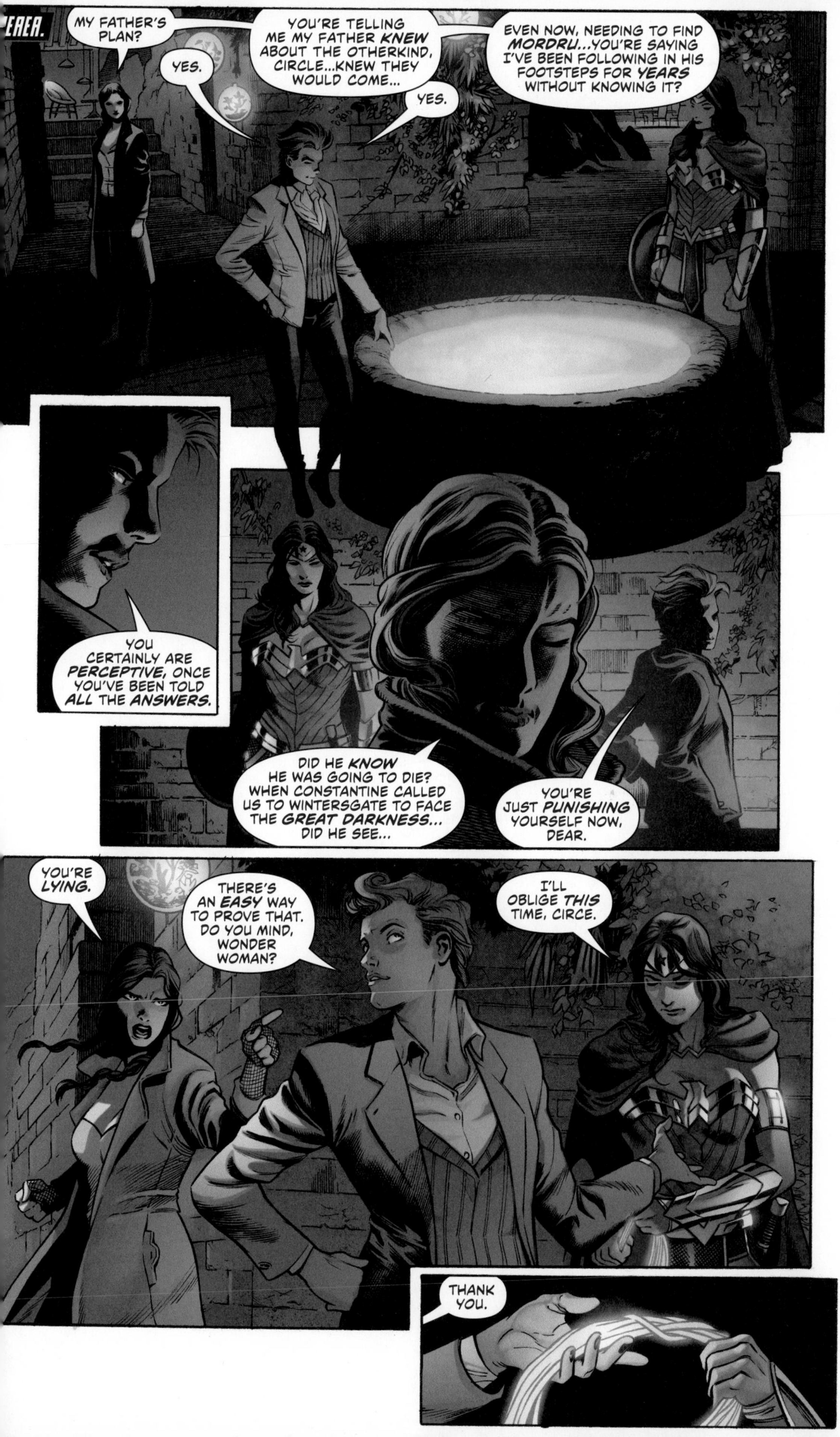
ERER.
MY FATHER'S PLAN?
YES.
YOU'RE TELLING ME MY FATHER KNEW ABOUT THE OTHERKIND, CIRCLE...KNEW THEY WOULD COME...
YES.
EVEN NOW, NEEDING TO FIND MORDRU...YOU'RE SAYING I'VE BEEN FOLLOWING IN HIS FOOTSTEPS FOR YEARS WITHOUT KNOWING IT?
YOU CERTAINLY ARE PERCEPTIVE, ONCE YOU'VE BEEN TOLD ALL THE ANSWERS.
DID HE KNOW HE WAS GOING TO DIE? WHEN CONSTANTINE CALLED US TO WINTERSGATE TO FACE THE GREAT DARKNESS... DID HE SEE...
YOU'RE JUST PUNISHING YOURSELF NOW, DEAR.
YOU'RE LYING.
THERE'S AN EASY WAY TO PROVE THAT. DO YOU MIND, WONDER WOMAN?
I'LL OBLIGE THIS TIME, CIRCE.
THANK YOU.

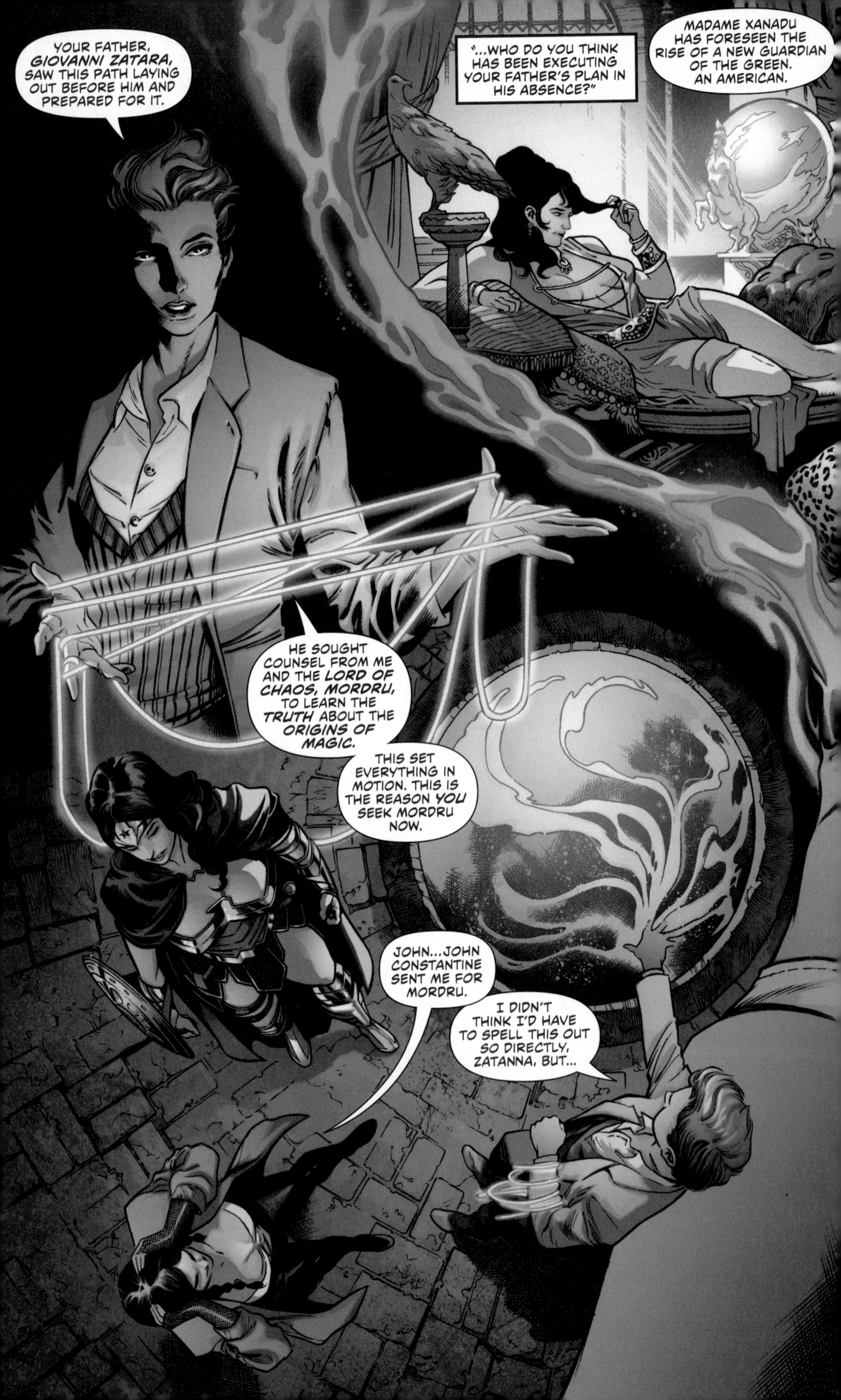
YOUR FATHER, GIOVANNI ZATARA, SAW THIS PATH LAYING OUT BEFORE HIM AND PREPARED FOR IT.
"...WHO DO YOU THINK HAS BEEN EXECUTING YOUR FATHER'S PLAN IN HIS ABSENCE?"
MADAME XANADU HAS FORESEEN THE RISE OF A NEW GUARDIAN OF THE GREEN. AN AMERICAN.
HE SOUGHT COUNSEL FROM ME AND THE LORD OF CHAOS, MORDRU, TO LEARN THE TRUTH ABOUT THE ORIGINS OF MAGIC.
THIS SET EVERYTHING IN MOTION. THIS IS THE REASON YOU SEEK MORDRU NOW.
JOHN...JOHN CONSTANTINE SENT ME FOR MORDRU.
I DIDN'T THINK I'D HAVE TO SPELL THIS OUT SO DIRECTLY, ZATANNA, BUT...

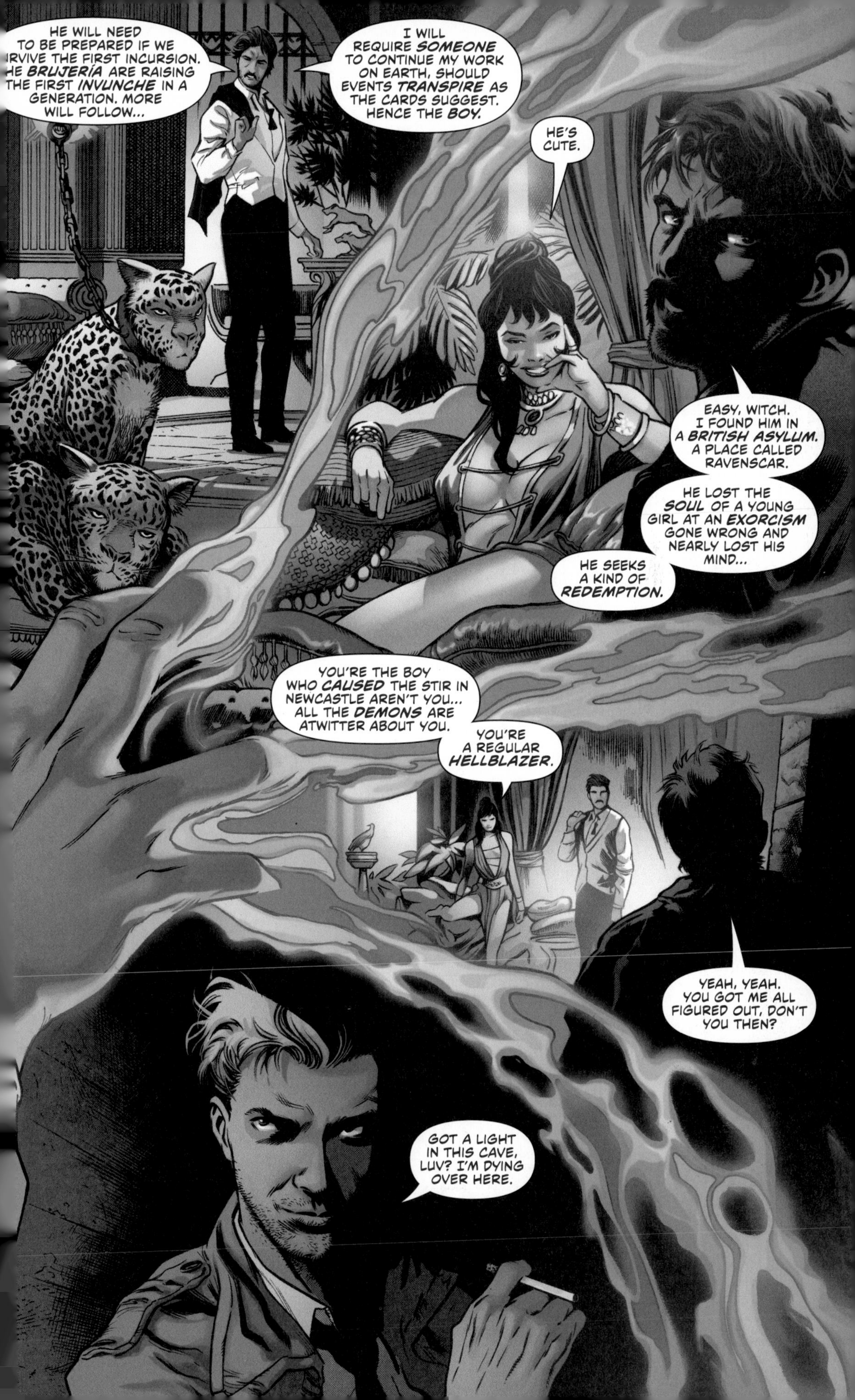
HE WILL NEED TO BE PREPARED IF WE IRVIVE THE FIRST INCURSION. HE BRUJERÍA ARE RAISING THE FIRST INVUNCHE IN A GENERATION. MORE WILL FOLLOW...
I WILL REQUIRE SOMEONE TO CONTINUE MY WORK ON EARTH, SHOULD EVENTS TRANSPIRE AS THE CARDS SUGGEST. HENCE THE BOY.
HE'S CUTE.
EASY, WITCH. I FOUND HIM IN A BRITISH ASYLUM. A PLACE CALLED RAVENSCAR.
HE LOST THE SOUL OF A YOUNG GIRL AT AN EXORCISM GONE WRONG AND NEARLY LOST HIS MIND...
HE SEEKS A KIND OF REDEMPTION.
YOU'RE THE BOY WHO CAUSED THE STIR IN NEWCASTLE AREN'T YOU... ALL THE DEMONS ARE ATWITTER ABOUT YOU.
YOU'RE A REGULAR HELLBLAZER.
YEAH, YEAH. YOU GOT ME ALL FIGURED OUT, DON'T YOU THEN?
GOT A LIGHT IN THIS CAVE, LUV? I'M DYING OVER HERE.

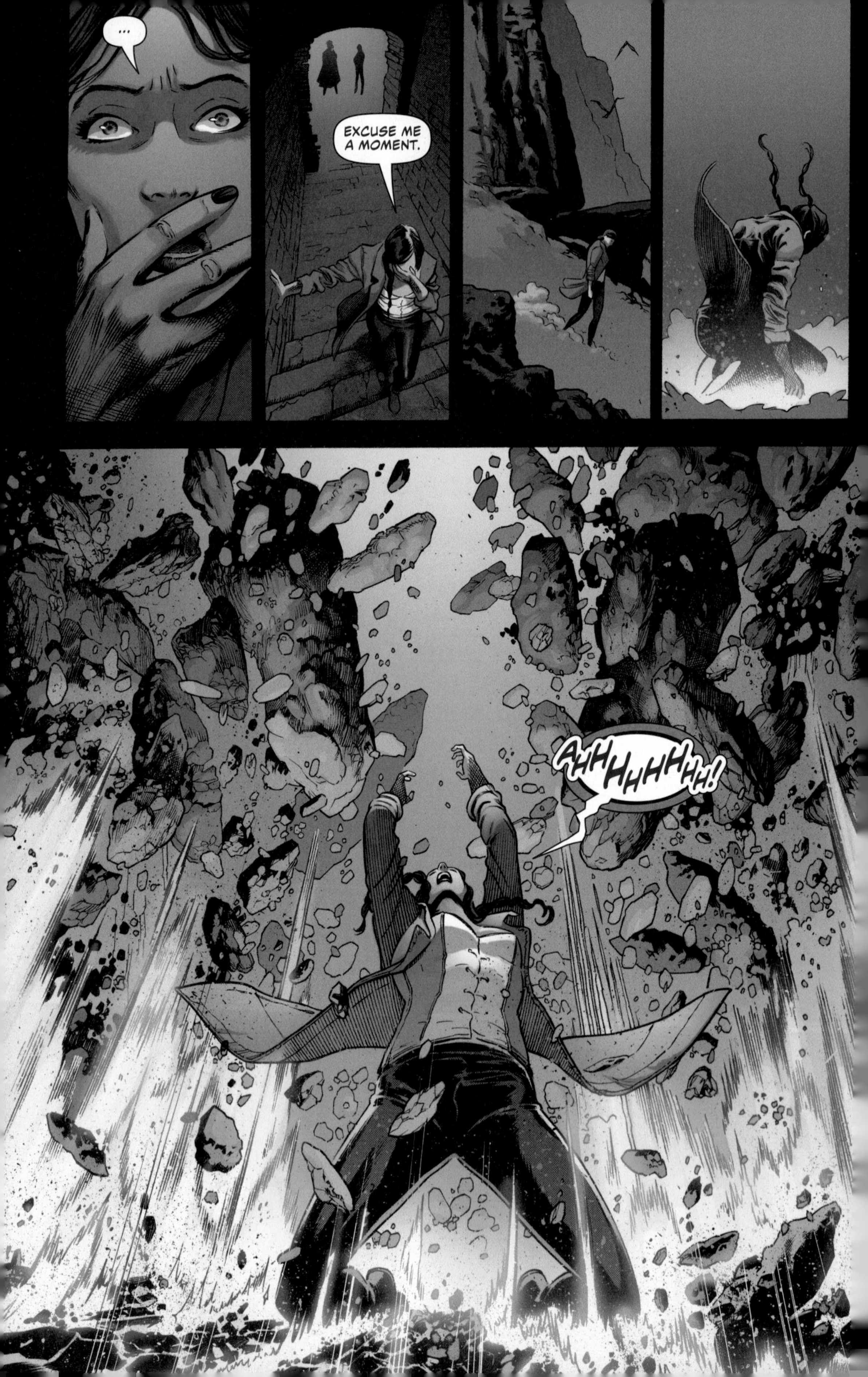
...
EXCUSE ME A MOMENT.
AHHHHHHHH!

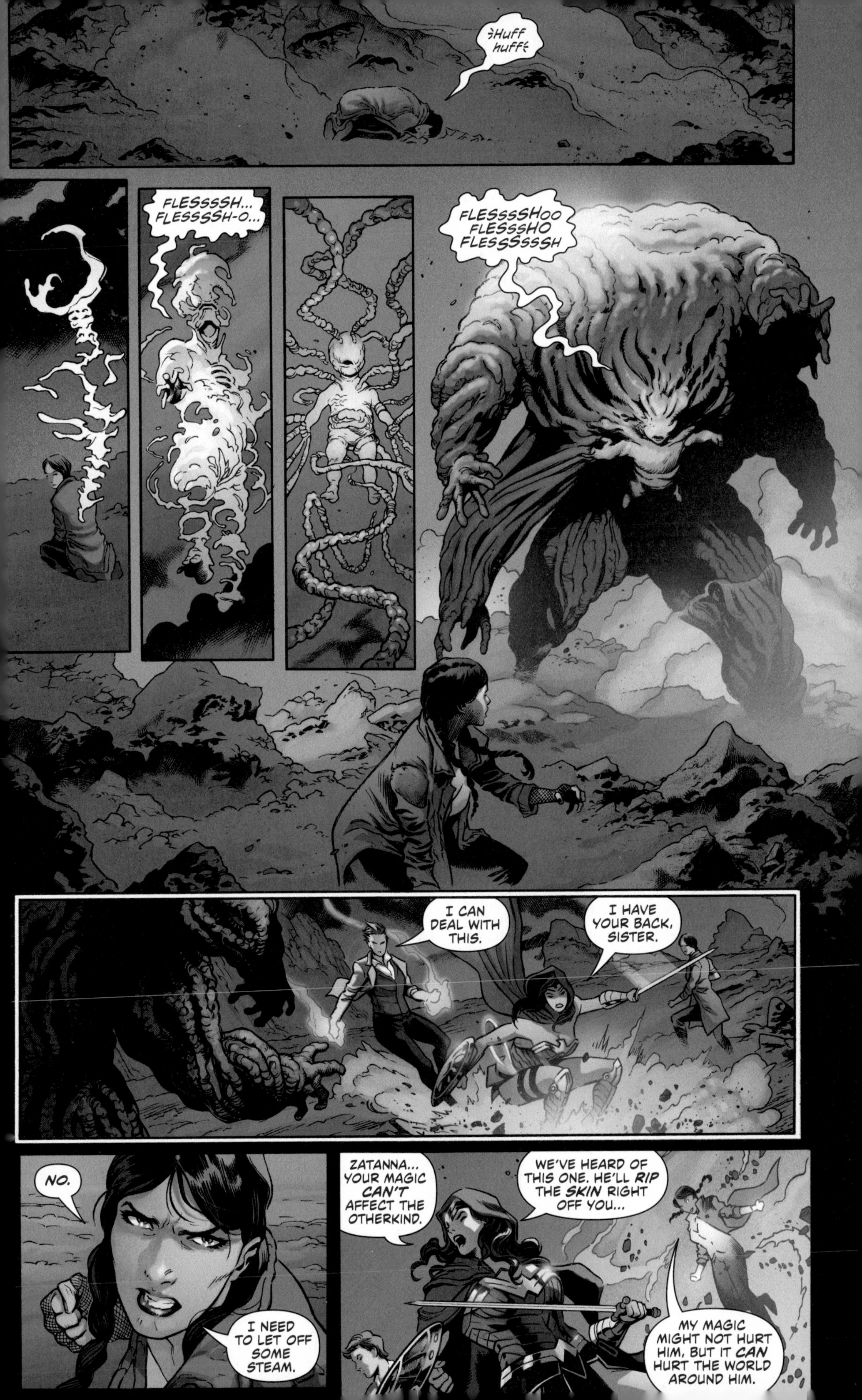
Huff huff
FLESSSSH... FLESSSSH-O...
FLESSSSHoo FLESSSHO FLESSSSSSH
I CAN DEAL WITH THIS.
I HAVE YOUR BACK, SISTER.
NO.
I NEED TO LET OFF SOME STEAM.
ZATANNA... YOUR MAGIC CAN'T AFFECT THE OTHERKIND.
WE'VE HEARD OF THIS ONE. HE'LL RIP THE SKIN RIGHT OFF YOU...
MY MAGIC MIGHT NOT HURT HIM, BUT IT CAN HURT THE WORLD AROUND HIM.

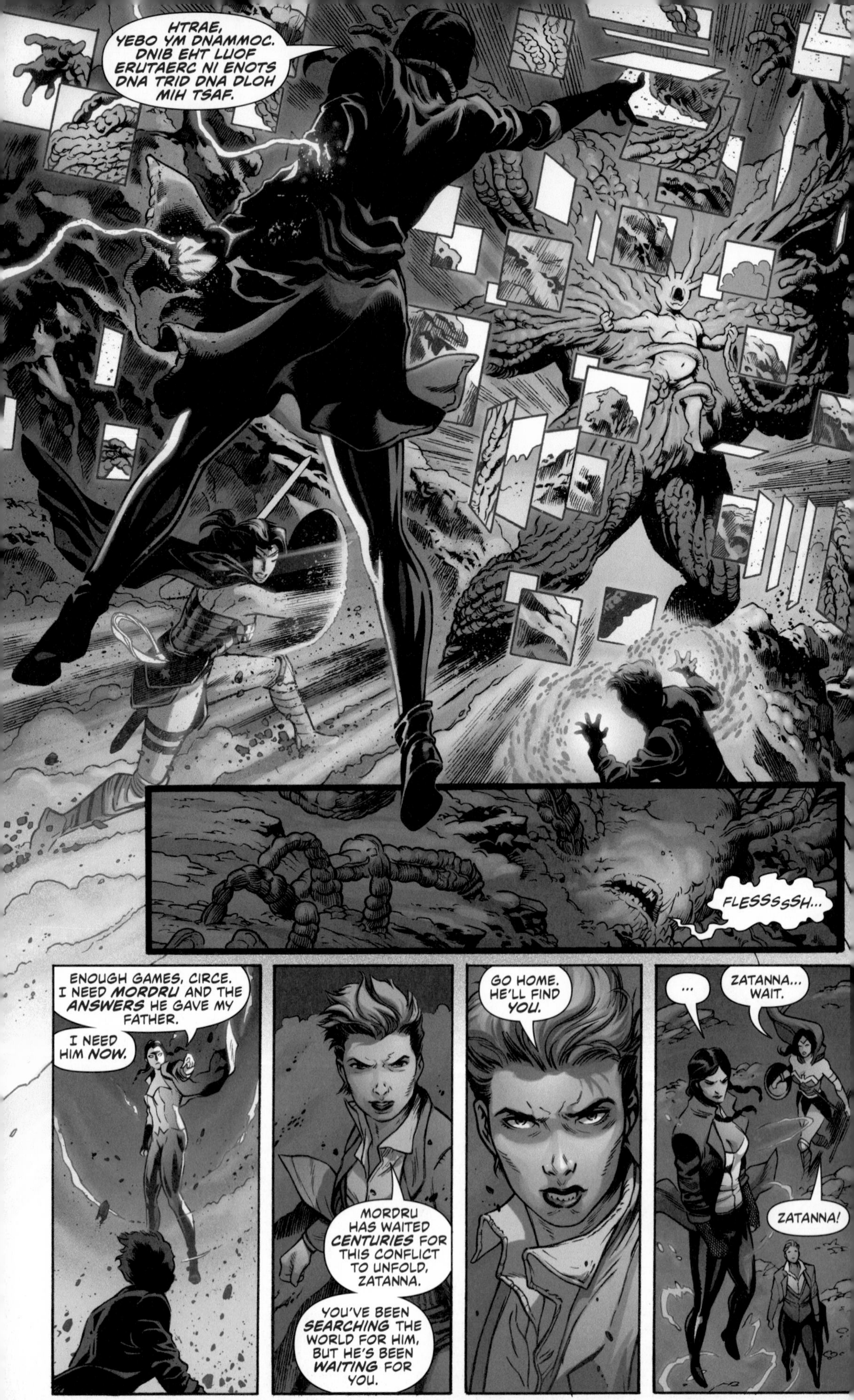
HTRAE, YEBO YM DNAMMOC. DNIB EHT LUOF ERUTAERC NI ENOTS DNA TRID DNA DLOH MIH TSAF.
FLESSSSSH...
ENOUGH GAMES, CIRCE. I NEED MORDRU AND THE ANSWERS HE GAVE MY FATHER.
I NEED HIM NOW.
MORDRU HAS WAITED CENTURIES FOR THIS CONFLICT TO UNFOLD, ZATANNA.
YOU'VE BEEN SEARCHING THE WORLD FOR HIM, BUT HE'S BEEN WAITING FOR YOU.
GO HOME. HE'LL FIND YOU.
...
ZATANNA... WAIT.
ZATANNA!

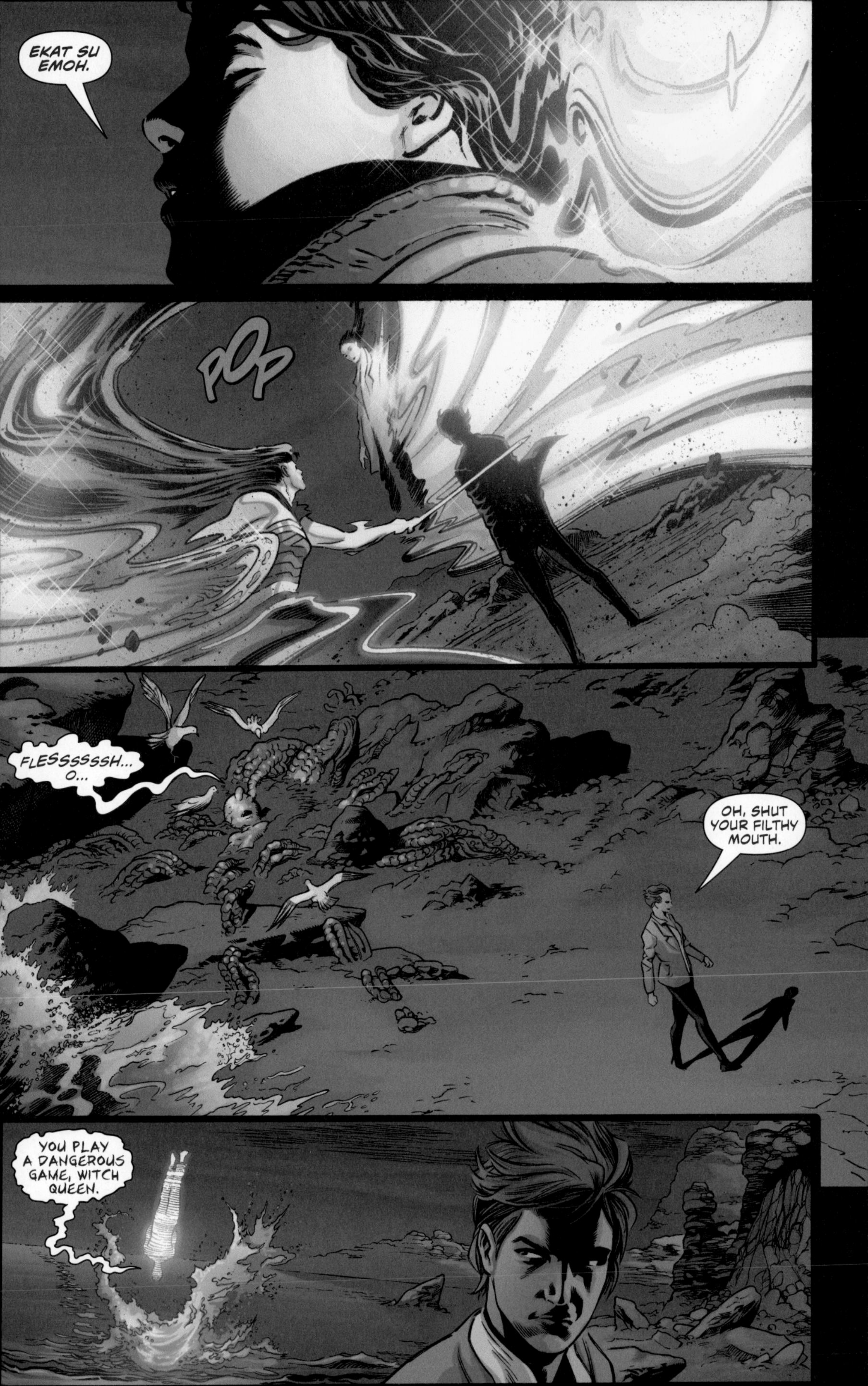
EKAT SU EMOH.
POP
FLESSSSSSH... O...
OH, SHUT YOUR FILTHY MOUTH.
YOU PLAY A DANGEROUS GAME, WITCH QUEEN.

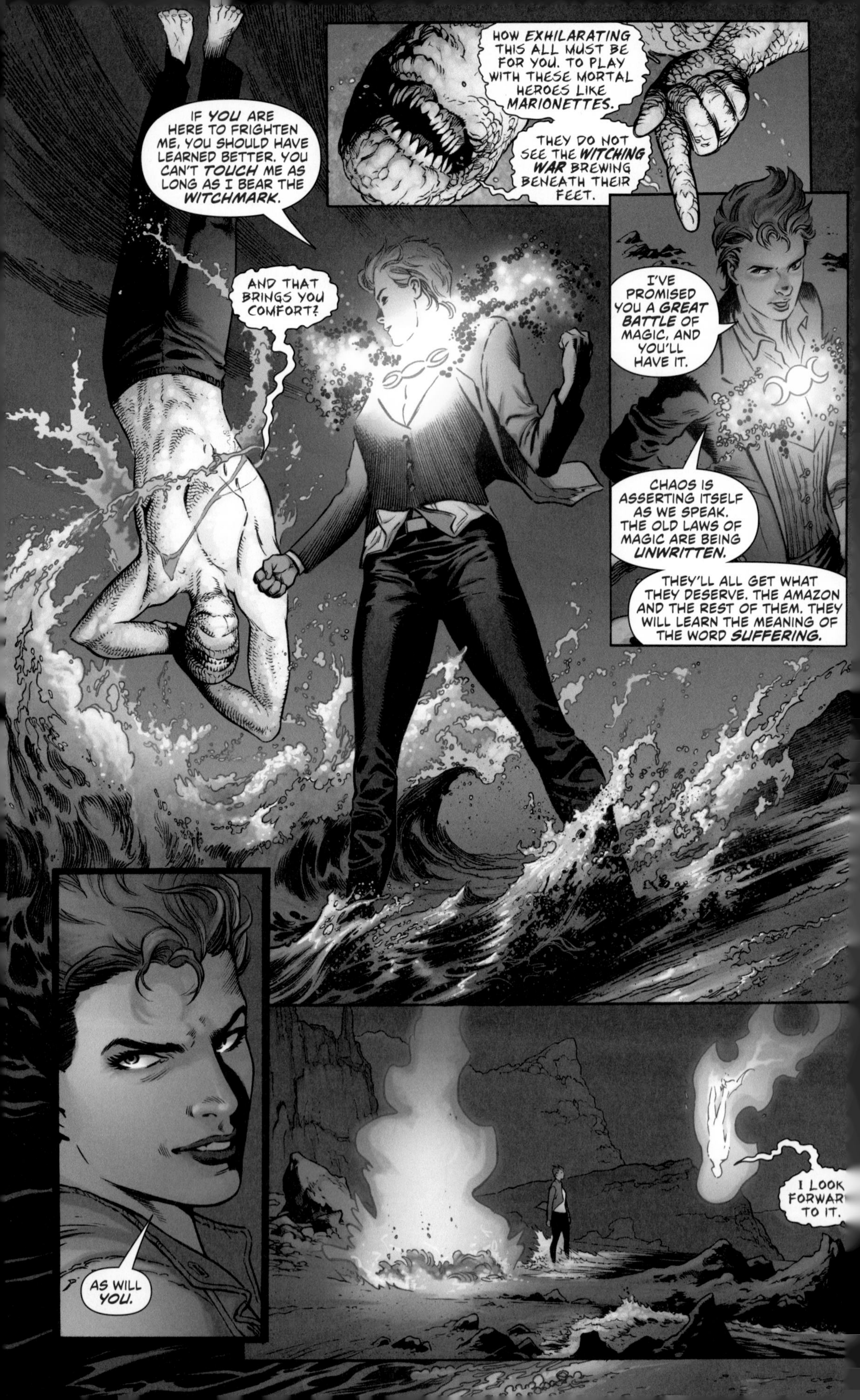
IF YOU ARE HERE TO FRIGHTEN ME, YOU SHOULD HAVE LEARNED BETTER. YOU CAN'T TOUCH ME AS LONG AS I BEAR THE WITCHMARK.
HOW EXHILARATING THIS ALL MUST BE FOR YOU. TO PLAY WITH THESE MORTAL HEROES LIKE MARIONETTES.
THEY DO NOT SEE THE WITCHING WAR BREWING BENEATH THEIR FEET.
AND THAT BRINGS YOU COMFORT?
I'VE PROMISED YOU A GREAT BATTLE OF MAGIC, AND YOU'LL HAVE IT.
CHAOS IS ASSERTING ITSELF AS WE SPEAK. THE OLD LAWS OF MAGIC ARE BEING UNWRITTEN.
THEY'LL ALL GET WHAT THEY DESERVE. THE AMAZON AND THE REST OF THEM. THEY WILL LEARN THE MEANING OF THE WORD SUFFERING.
I LOOK FORWAR TO IT.
AS WILL YOU.

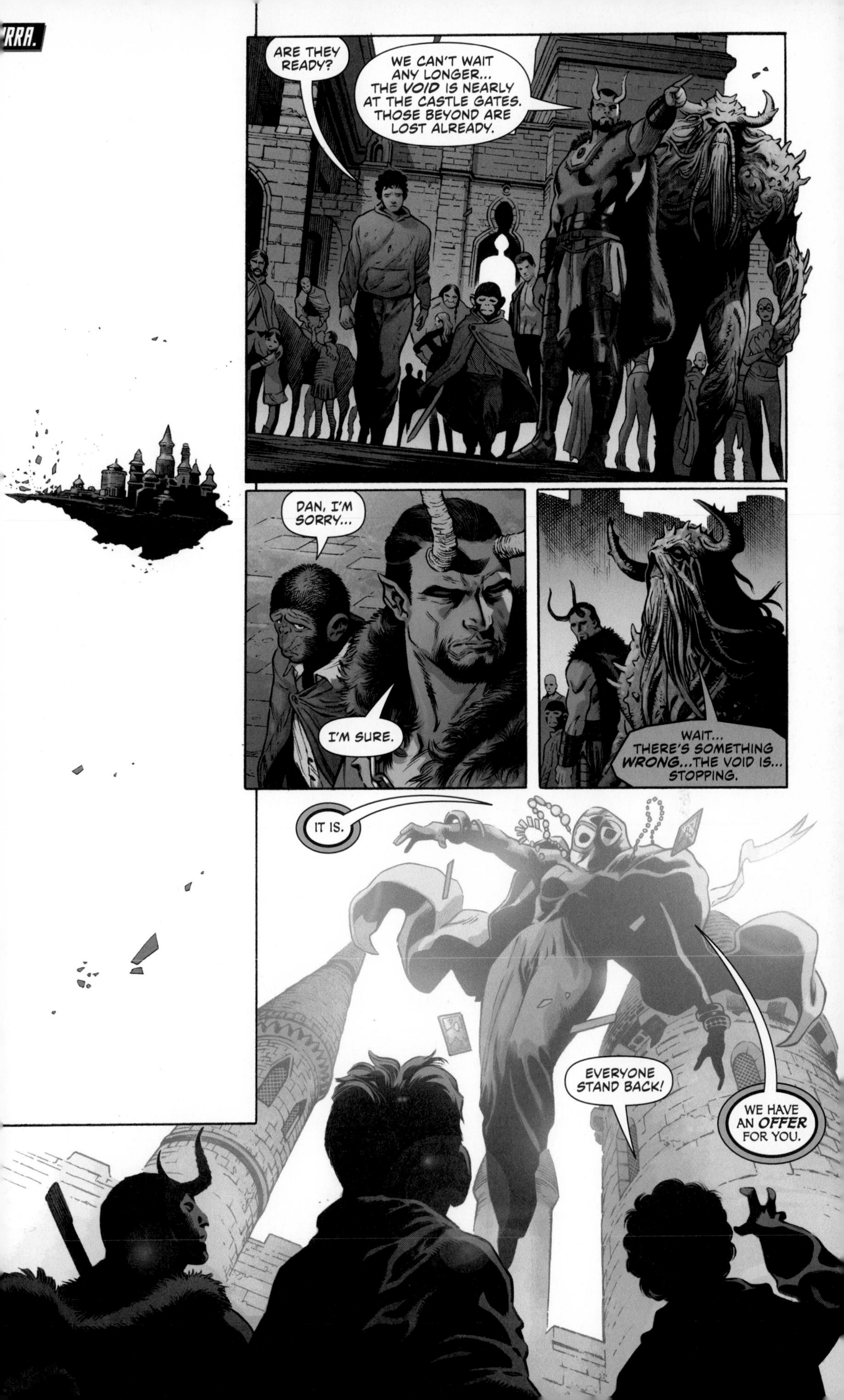
RRA.
ARE THEY READY?
WE CAN'T WAIT ANY LONGER... THE VOID IS NEARLY AT THE CASTLE GATES. THOSE BEYOND ARE LOST ALREADY.
DAN, I'M SORRY...
I'M SURE.
WAIT... THERE'S SOMETHING WRONG...THE VOID IS... STOPPING.
IT IS.
EVERYONE STAND BACK!
WE HAVE AN OFFER FOR YOU.

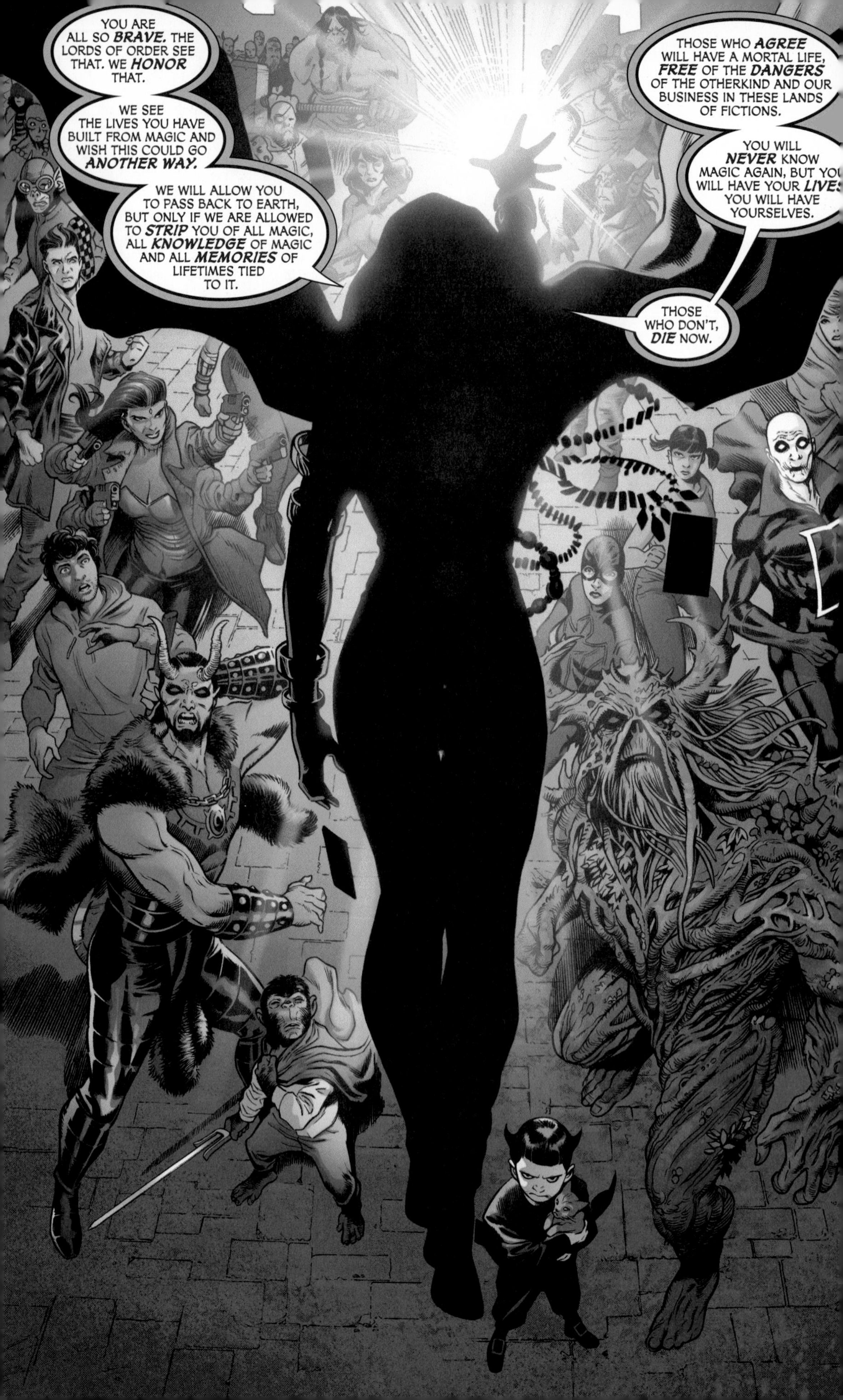
YOU ARE ALL SO BRAVE. THE LORDS OF ORDER SEE THAT. WE HONOR THAT.
WE SEE THE LIVES YOU HAVE BUILT FROM MAGIC AND WISH THIS COULD GO ANOTHER WAY.
WE WILL ALLOW YOU TO PASS BACK TO EARTH, BUT ONLY IF WE ARE ALLOWED TO STRIP YOU OF ALL MAGIC, ALL KNOWLEDGE OF MAGIC AND ALL MEMORIES OF LIFETIMES TIED TO IT.
THOSE WHO AGREE WILL HAVE A MORTAL LIFE, FREE OF THE DANGERS OF THE OTHERKIND AND OUR BUSINESS IN THESE LANDS OF FICTIONS.
YOU WILL NEVER KNOW MAGIC AGAIN, BUT YOU WILL HAVE YOUR LIVES. YOU WILL HAVE YOURSELVES.
THOSE WHO DON'T, DIE NOW.

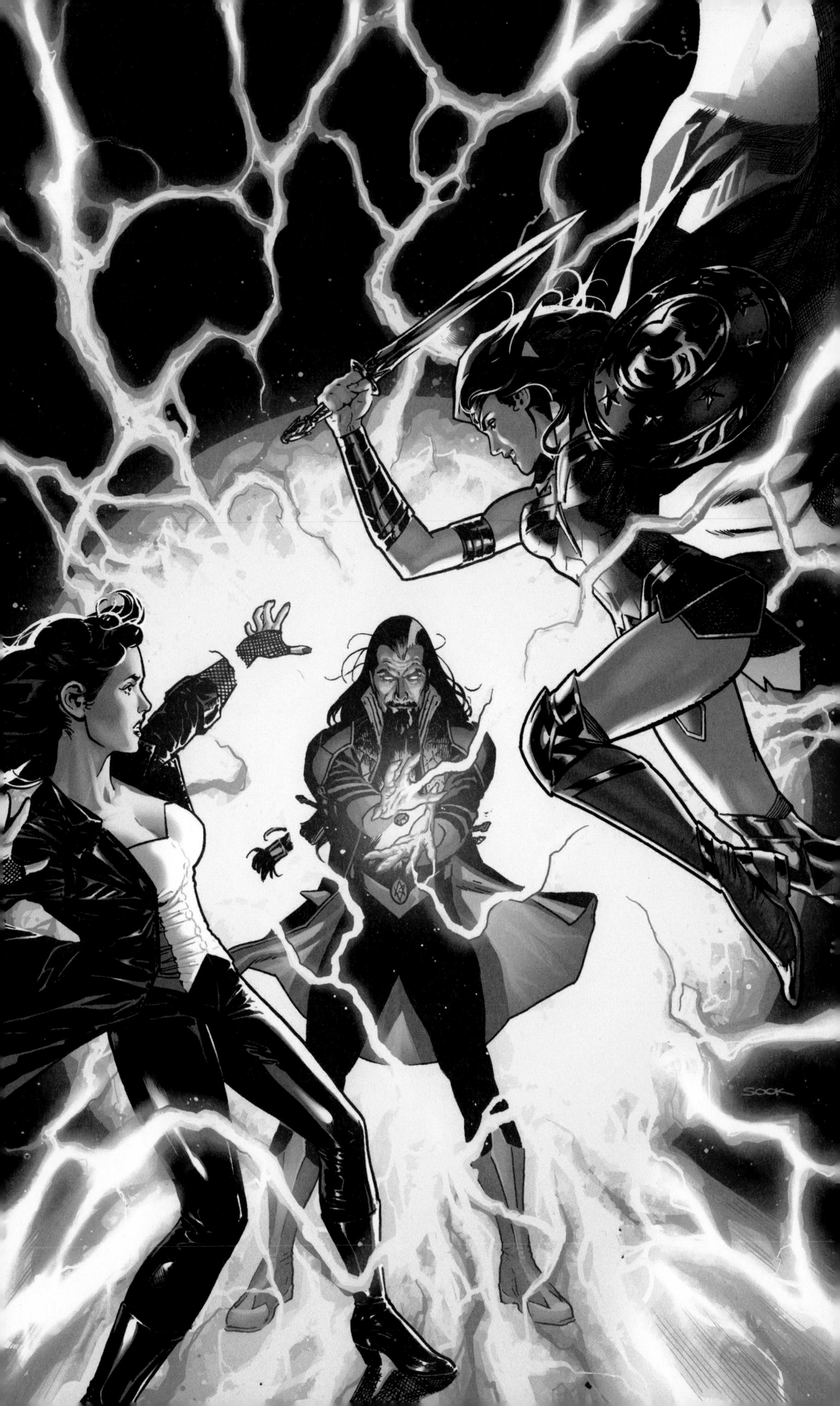
SOOK

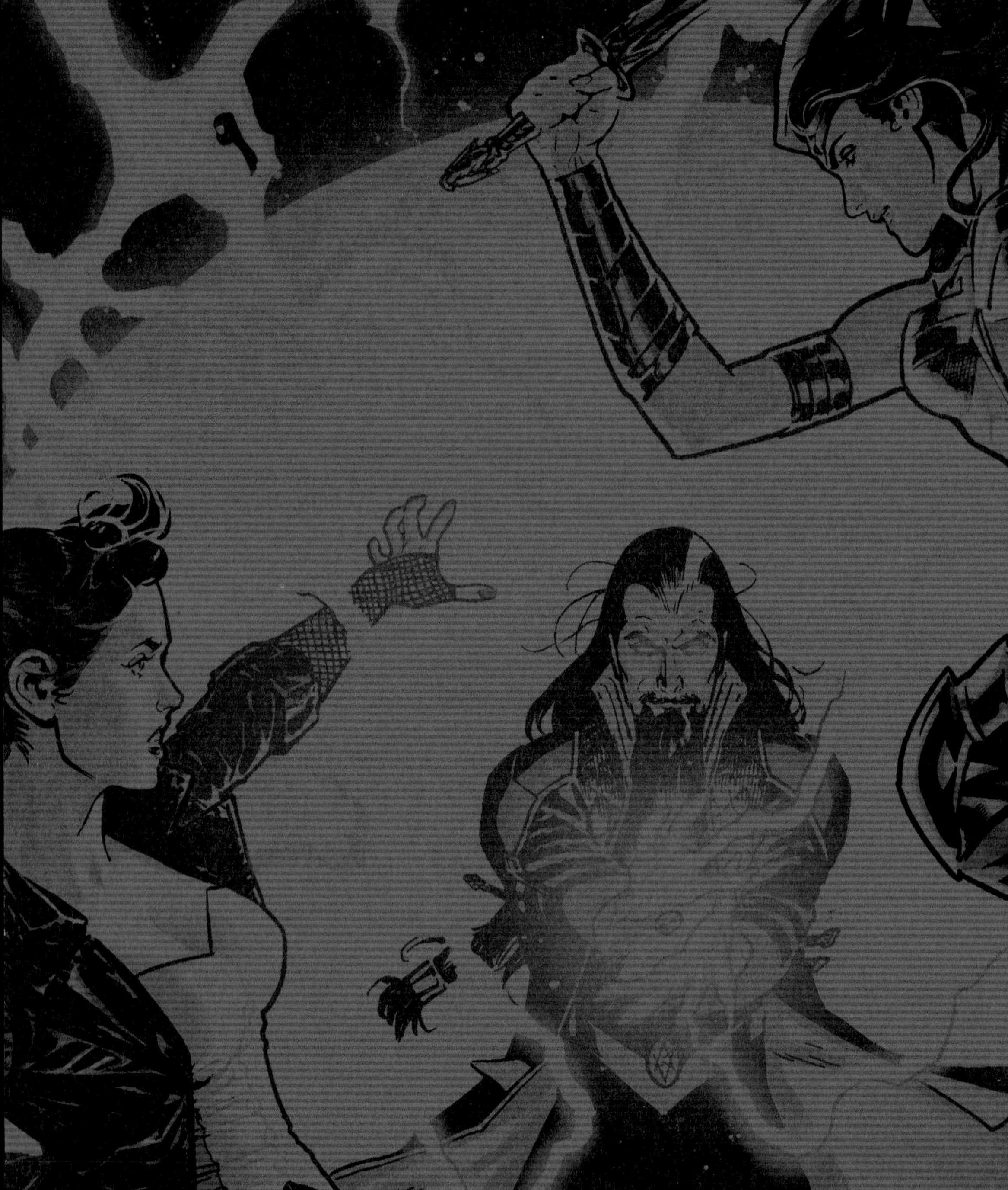

JUSTICE LEAGUE DARK
#11

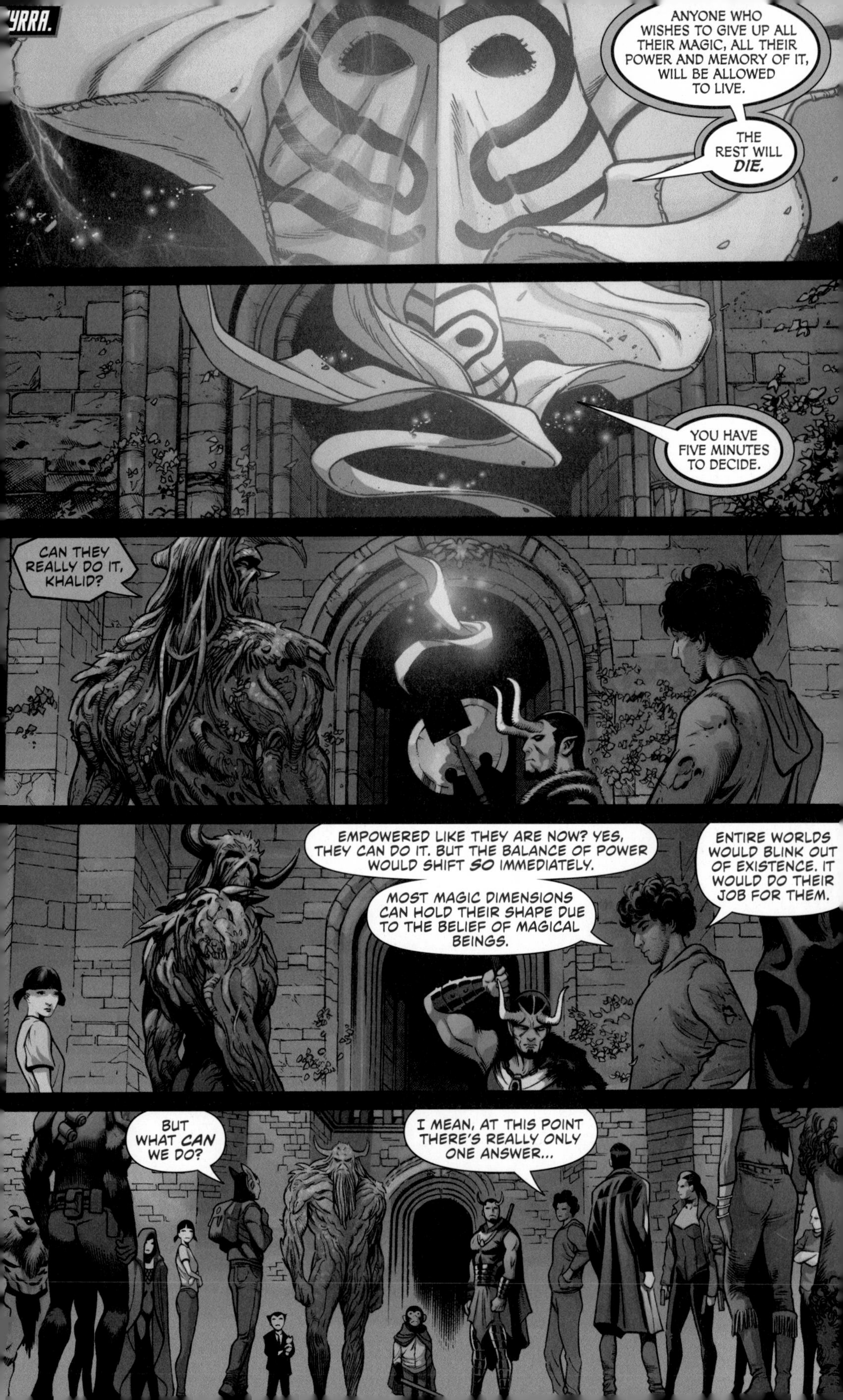
YRRA.
ANYONE WHO WISHES TO GIVE UP ALL THEIR MAGIC, ALL THEIR POWER AND MEMORY OF IT, WILL BE ALLOWED TO LIVE.
THE REST WILL *DIE.*
YOU HAVE FIVE MINUTES TO DECIDE.
CAN THEY REALLY DO IT, KHALID?
EMPOWERED LIKE THEY ARE NOW? YES, THEY CAN DO IT. BUT THE BALANCE OF POWER WOULD SHIFT *SO* IMMEDIATELY.
MOST MAGIC DIMENSIONS CAN HOLD THEIR SHAPE DUE TO THE BELIEF OF MAGICAL BEINGS.
ENTIRE WORLDS WOULD BLINK OUT OF EXISTENCE. IT WOULD DO THEIR JOB FOR THEM.
BUT WHAT *CAN* WE DO?
I MEAN, AT THIS POINT THERE'S REALLY ONLY ONE ANSWER...

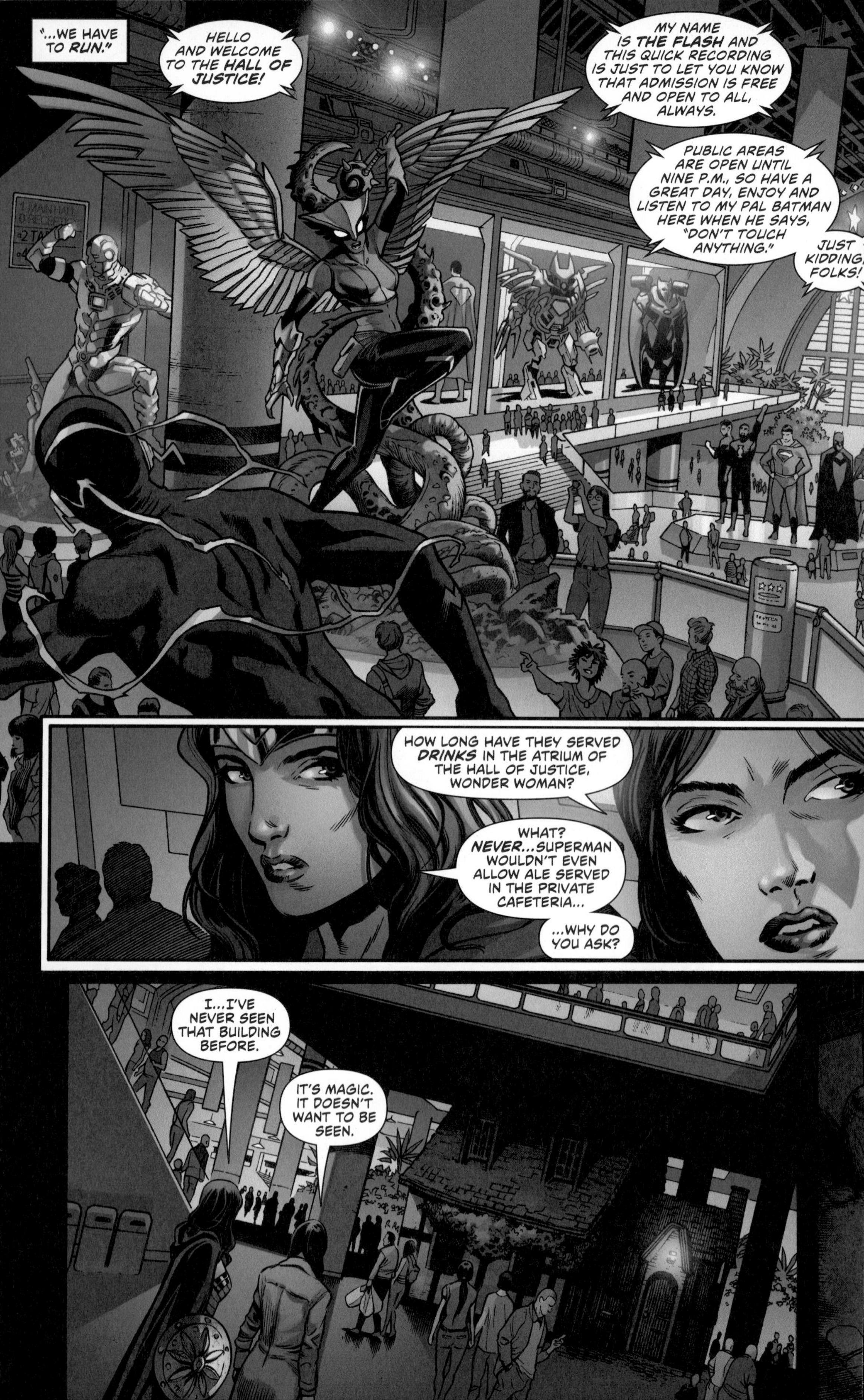
"...WE HAVE TO *RUN*."
HELLO AND WELCOME TO THE **HALL OF JUSTICE!**
MY NAME IS **THE FLASH** AND THIS QUICK RECORDING IS JUST TO LET YOU KNOW THAT ADMISSION IS FREE AND OPEN TO ALL, ALWAYS.
PUBLIC AREAS ARE OPEN UNTIL NINE P.M., SO HAVE A GREAT DAY, ENJOY AND LISTEN TO MY PAL BATMAN HERE WHEN HE SAYS, "DON'T TOUCH ANYTHING."
JUST KIDDING, FOLKS!
HOW LONG HAVE THEY SERVED ***DRINKS*** IN THE ATRIUM OF THE HALL OF JUSTICE, WONDER WOMAN?
WHAT? ***NEVER...*** SUPERMAN WOULDN'T EVEN ALLOW ALE SERVED IN THE PRIVATE CAFETERIA...
...WHY DO YOU ASK?
I...I'VE NEVER SEEN THAT BUILDING BEFORE.
IT'S MAGIC. IT DOESN'T WANT TO BE SEEN.

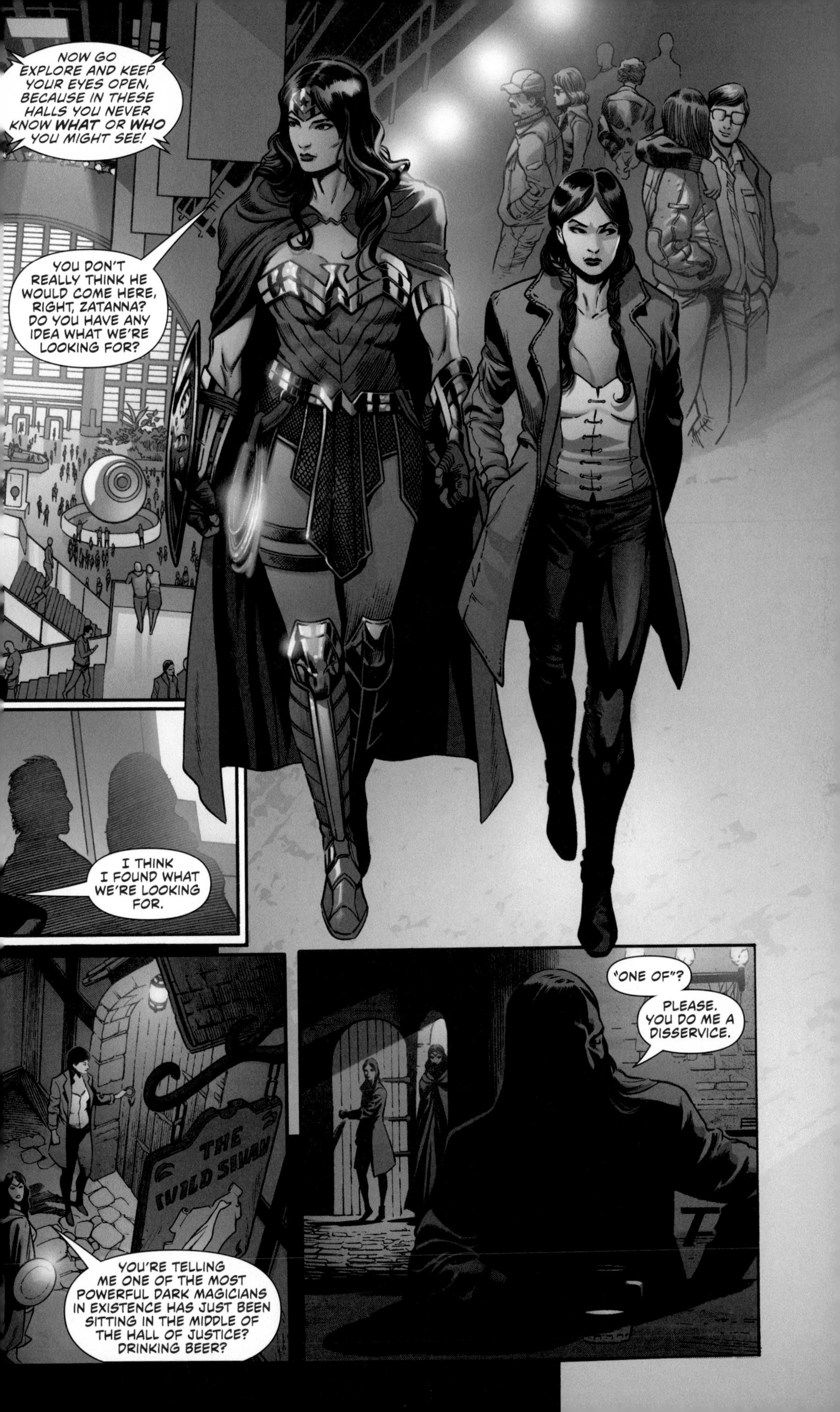
NOW GO EXPLORE AND KEEP YOUR EYES OPEN, BECAUSE IN THESE HALLS YOU NEVER KNOW WHAT OR WHO YOU MIGHT SEE!
YOU DON'T REALLY THINK HE WOULD COME HERE, RIGHT, ZATANNA? DO YOU HAVE ANY IDEA WHAT WE'RE LOOKING FOR?
I THINK I FOUND WHAT WE'RE LOOKING FOR.
THE WILD SWAN
YOU'RE TELLING ME ONE OF THE MOST POWERFUL DARK MAGICIANS IN EXISTENCE HAS JUST BEEN SITTING IN THE MIDDLE OF THE HALL OF JUSTICE? DRINKING BEER?
"ONE OF"?
PLEASE. YOU DO ME A DISSERVICE.

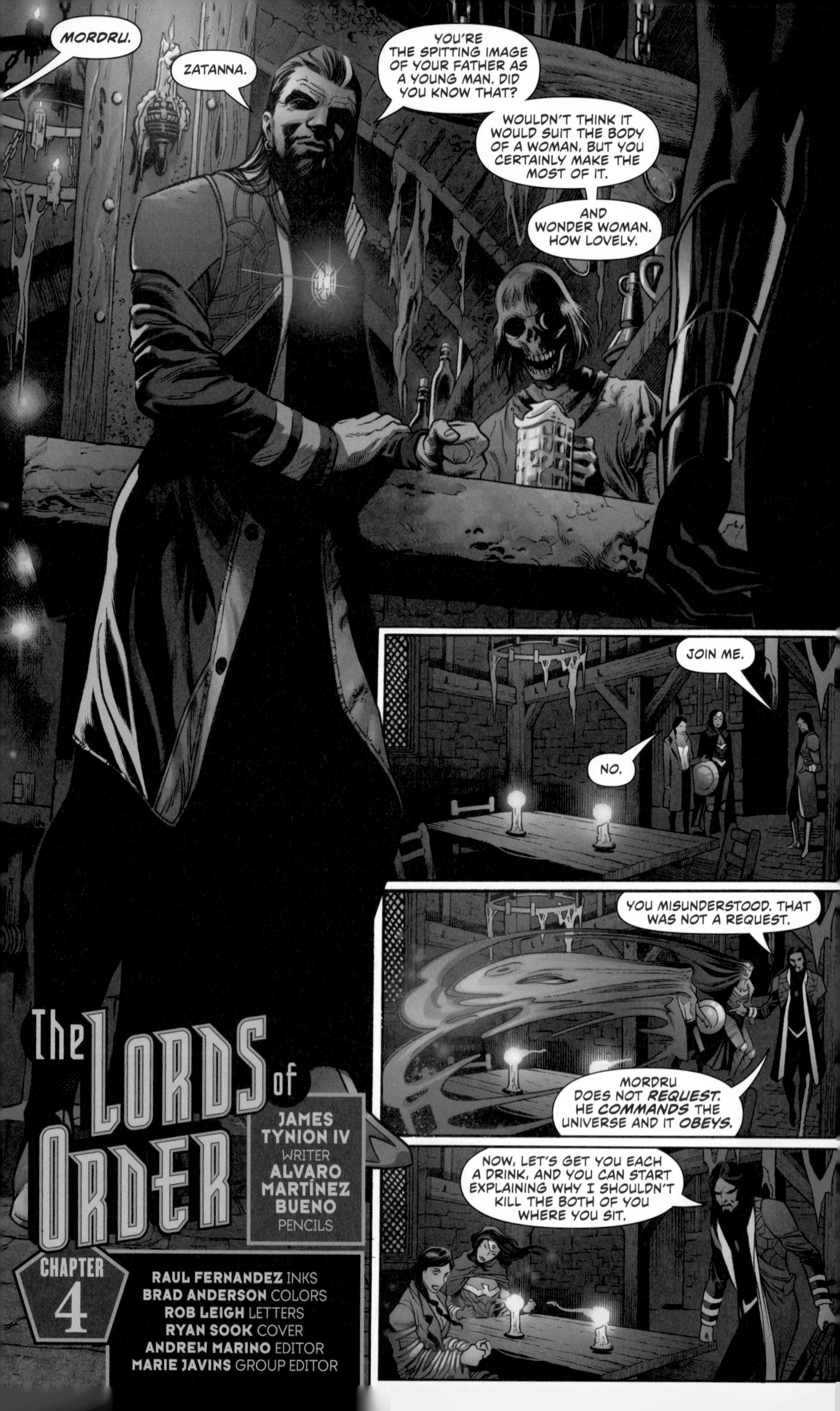
MORDRU.
ZATANNA.
YOU'RE THE SPITTING IMAGE OF YOUR FATHER AS A YOUNG MAN. DID YOU KNOW THAT?
WOULDN'T THINK IT WOULD SUIT THE BODY OF A WOMAN, BUT YOU CERTAINLY MAKE THE MOST OF IT.
AND WONDER WOMAN. HOW LOVELY.
The LORDS of ORDER
JAMES TYNION IV WRITER
ALVARO MARTÍNEZ BUENO PENCILS
CHAPTER 4
RAUL FERNANDEZ INKS
BRAD ANDERSON COLORS
ROB LEIGH LETTERS
RYAN SOOK COVER
ANDREW MARINO EDITOR
MARIE JAVINS GROUP EDITOR
JOIN ME.
NO.
YOU MISUNDERSTOOD. THAT WAS NOT A REQUEST.
MORDRU DOES NOT REQUEST. HE COMMANDS THE UNIVERSE AND IT OBEYS.
NOW, LET'S GET YOU EACH A DRINK, AND YOU CAN START EXPLAINING WHY I SHOULDN'T KILL THE BOTH OF YOU WHERE YOU SIT.

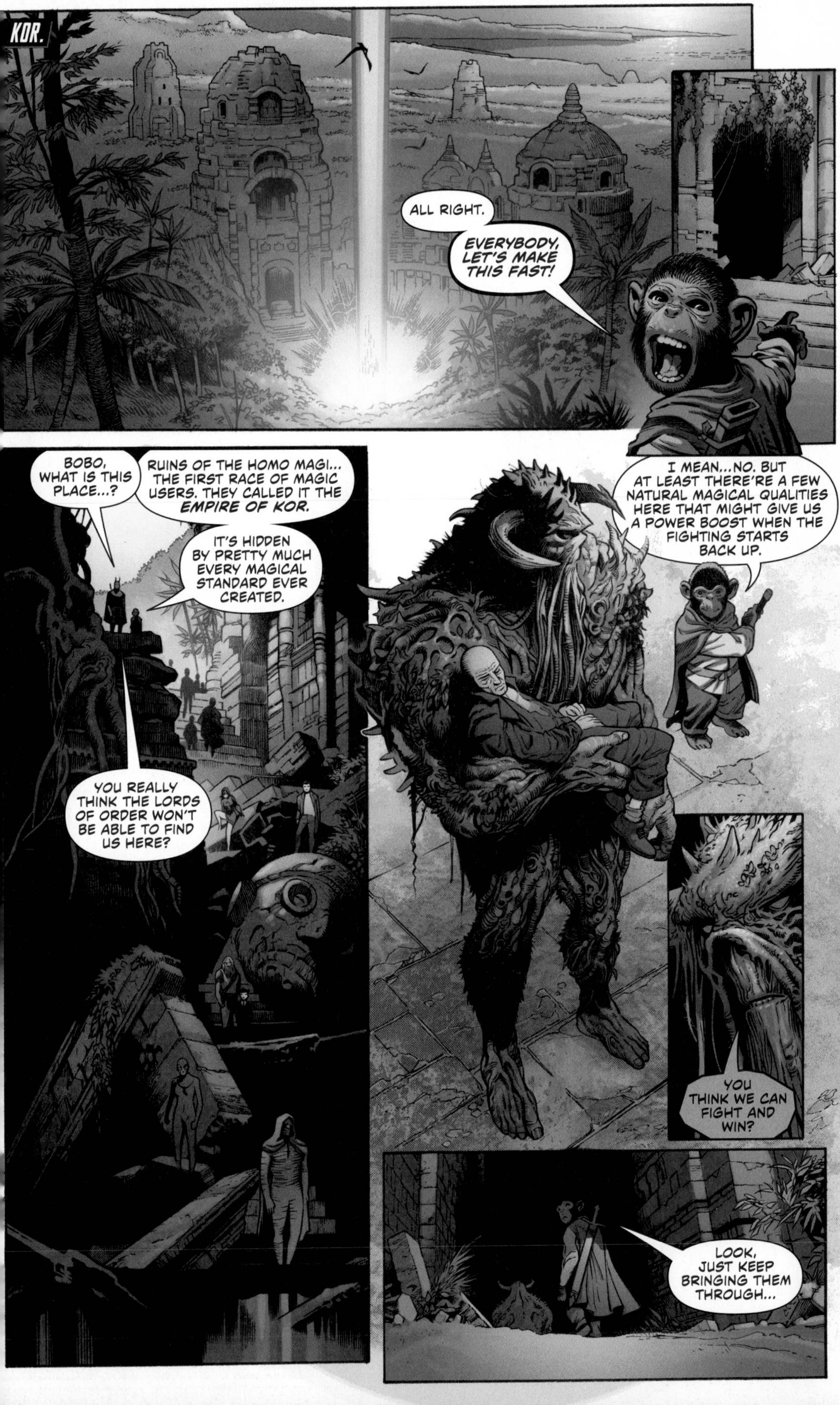
KOR.
ALL RIGHT.
EVERYBODY, LET'S MAKE THIS FAST!
BOBO, WHAT IS THIS PLACE...?
RUINS OF THE HOMO MAGI... THE FIRST RACE OF MAGIC USERS. THEY CALLED IT THE EMPIRE OF KOR.
IT'S HIDDEN BY PRETTY MUCH EVERY MAGICAL STANDARD EVER CREATED.
YOU REALLY THINK THE LORDS OF ORDER WON'T BE ABLE TO FIND US HERE?
I MEAN...NO. BUT AT LEAST THERE'RE A FEW NATURAL MAGICAL QUALITIES HERE THAT MIGHT GIVE US A POWER BOOST WHEN THE FIGHTING STARTS BACK UP.
YOU THINK WE CAN FIGHT AND WIN?
LOOK, JUST KEEP BRINGING THEM THROUGH...

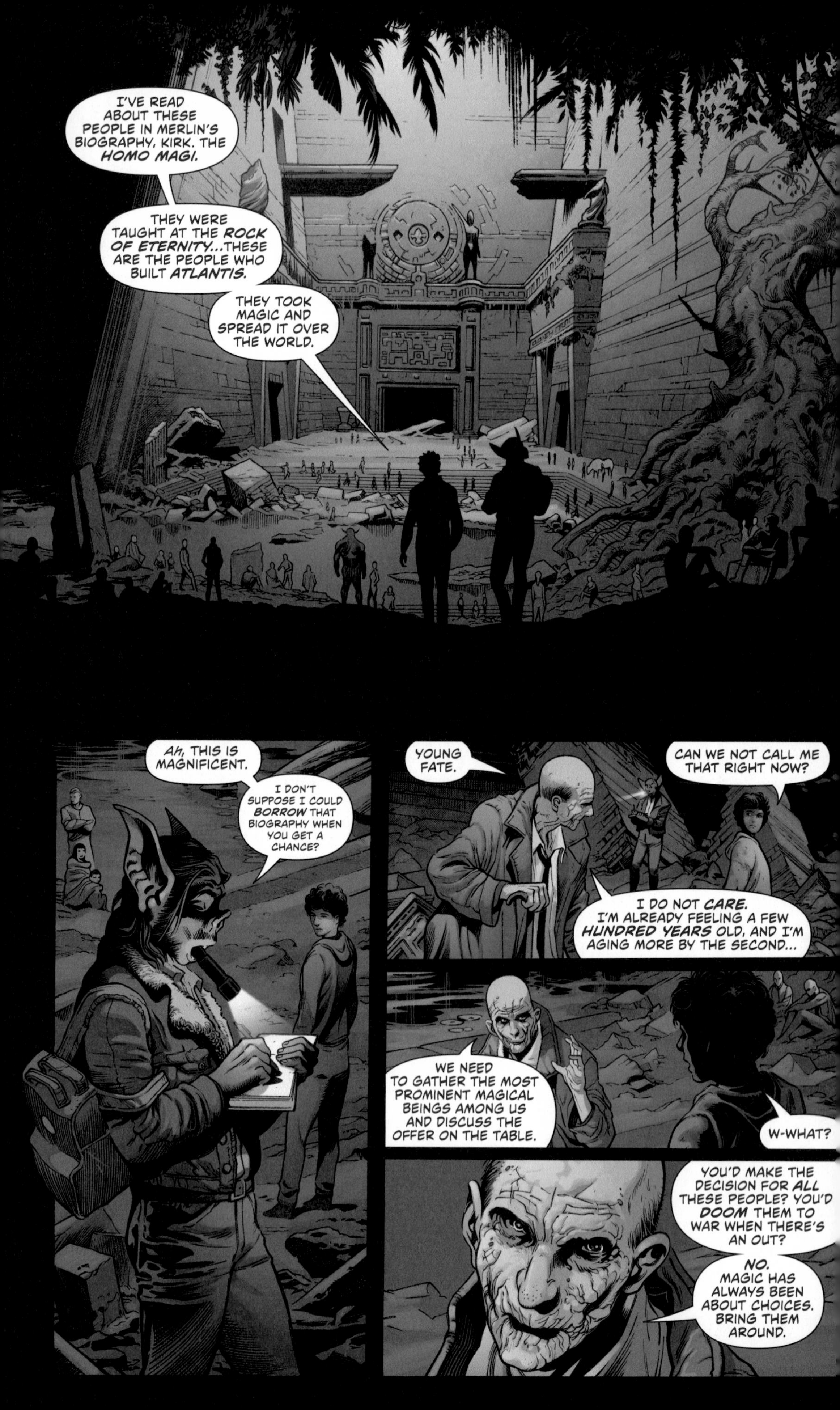
I'VE READ ABOUT THESE PEOPLE IN MERLIN'S BIOGRAPHY, KIRK. THE *HOMO MAGI.*
THEY WERE TAUGHT AT THE *ROCK OF ETERNITY*...THESE ARE THE PEOPLE WHO BUILT *ATLANTIS.*
THEY TOOK MAGIC AND SPREAD IT OVER THE WORLD.
Ah, THIS IS MAGNIFICENT.
I DON'T SUPPOSE I COULD *BORROW* THAT BIOGRAPHY WHEN YOU GET A CHANCE?
YOUNG FATE.
CAN WE NOT CALL ME THAT RIGHT NOW?
I DO NOT *CARE.* I'M ALREADY FEELING A FEW *HUNDRED YEARS* OLD, AND I'M AGING MORE BY THE SECOND...
WE NEED TO GATHER THE MOST PROMINENT MAGICAL BEINGS AMONG US AND DISCUSS THE OFFER ON THE TABLE.
W-WHAT?
YOU'D MAKE THE DECISION FOR *ALL* THESE PEOPLE? YOU'D *DOOM* THEM TO WAR WHEN THERE'S AN OUT?
NO. MAGIC HAS ALWAYS BEEN ABOUT CHOICES. BRING THEM AROUND.

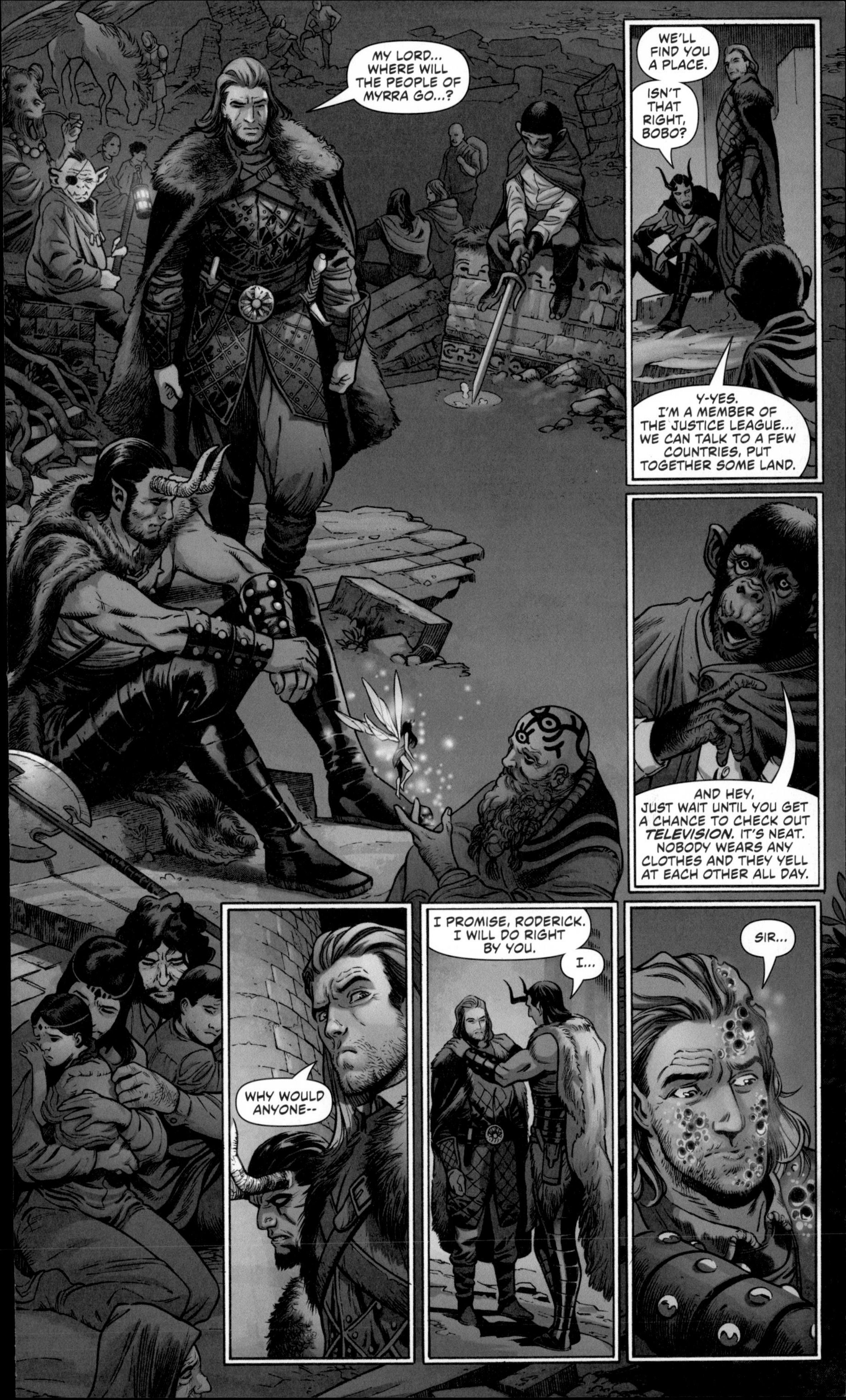
MY LORD... WHERE WILL THE PEOPLE OF MYRRA GO...?
WE'LL FIND YOU A PLACE.
ISN'T THAT RIGHT, BOBO?
Y-YES. I'M A MEMBER OF THE JUSTICE LEAGUE... WE CAN TALK TO A FEW COUNTRIES, PUT TOGETHER SOME LAND.
AND HEY, JUST WAIT UNTIL YOU GET A CHANCE TO CHECK OUT TELEVISION. IT'S NEAT. NOBODY WEARS ANY CLOTHES AND THEY YELL AT EACH OTHER ALL DAY.
WHY WOULD ANYONE--
I PROMISE, RODERICK. I WILL DO RIGHT BY YOU.
I...
SIR...

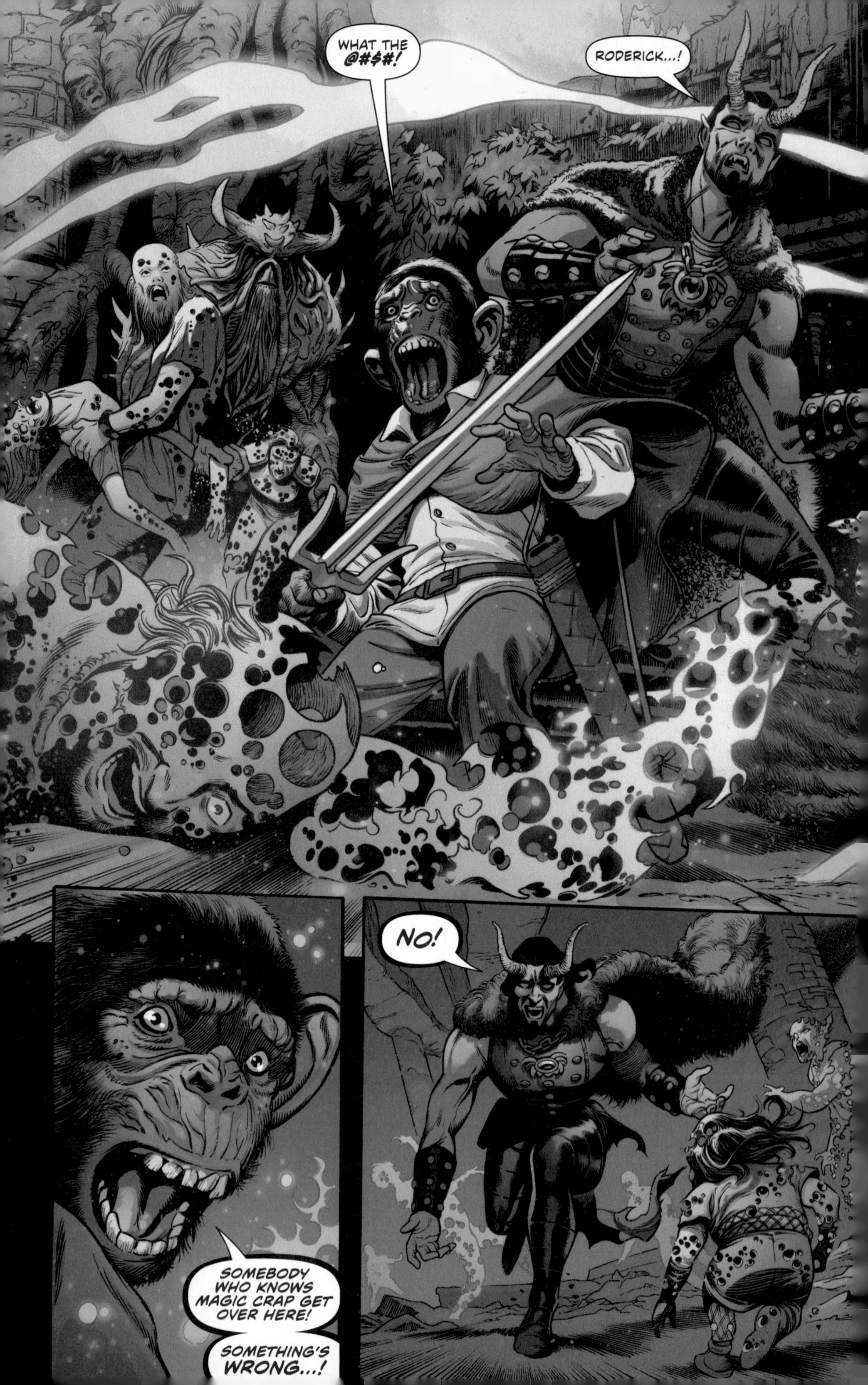
WHAT THE @#$#!
RODERICK...!
SOMEBODY WHO KNOWS MAGIC CRAP GET OVER HERE!
SOMETHING'S WRONG...!
NO!

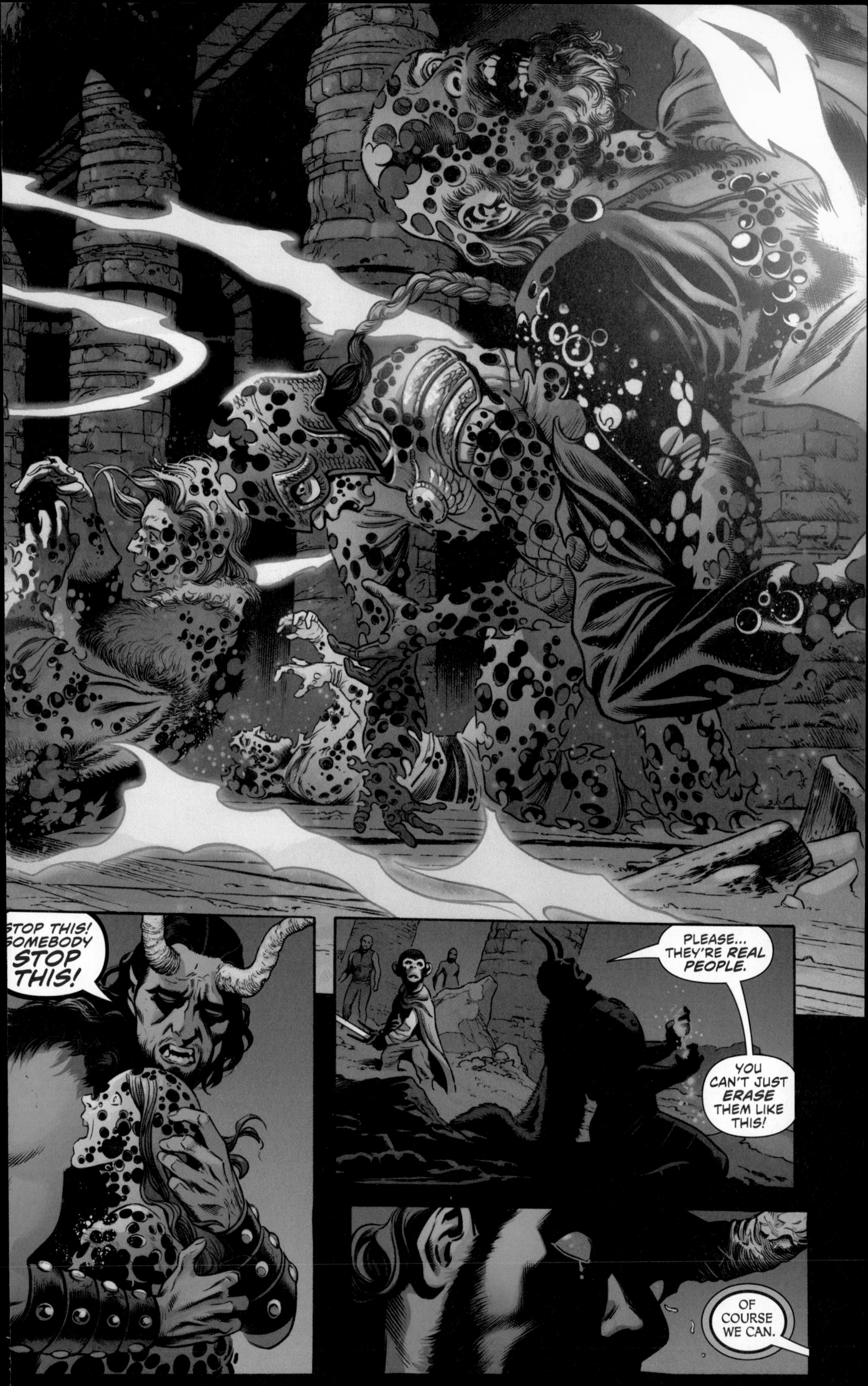
STOP THIS! SOMEBODY STOP THIS!
PLEASE... THEY'RE REAL PEOPLE.
YOU CAN'T JUST ERASE THEM LIKE THIS!
OF COURSE WE CAN.

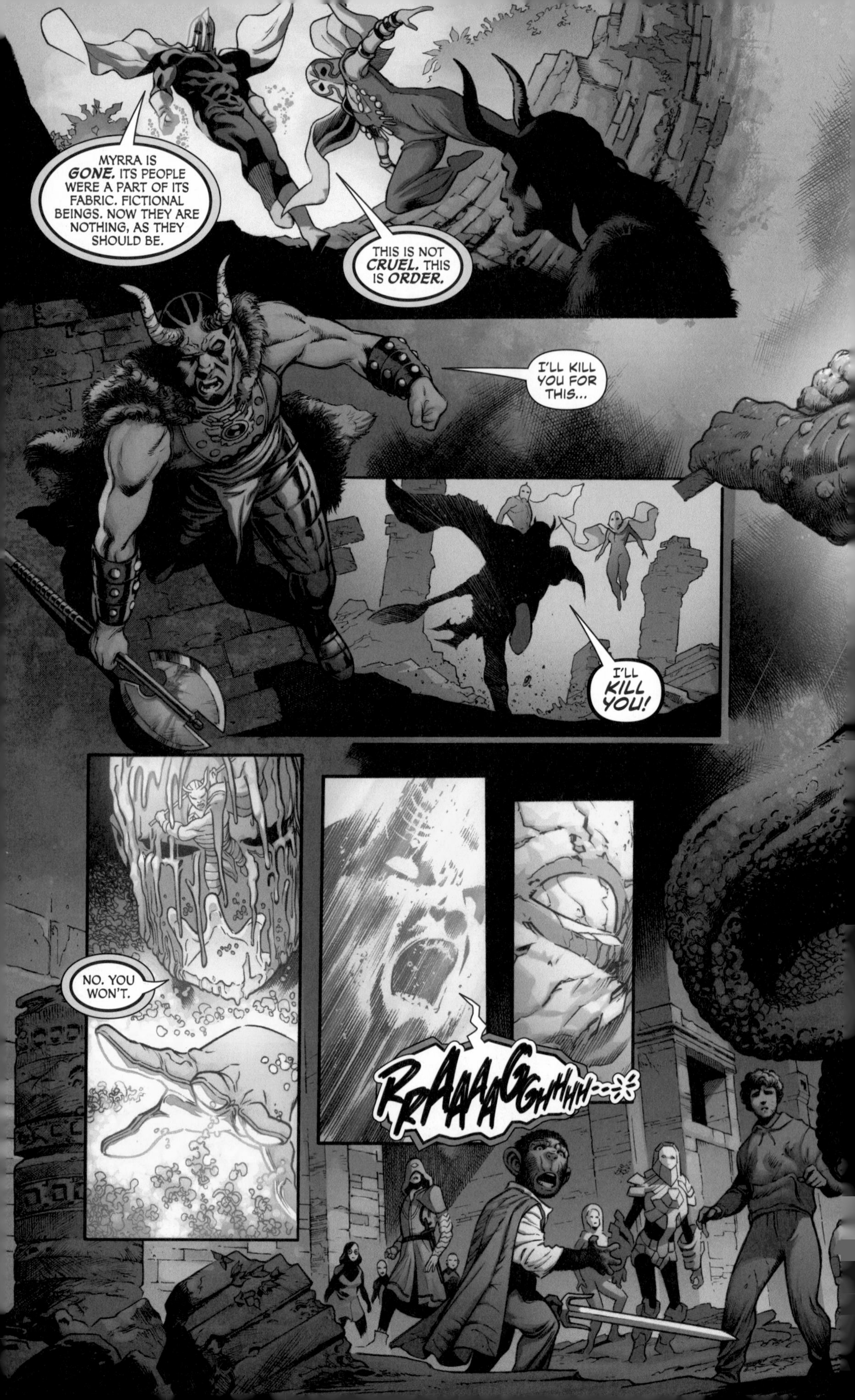
MYRRA IS GONE. ITS PEOPLE WERE A PART OF ITS FABRIC. FICTIONAL BEINGS. NOW THEY ARE NOTHING, AS THEY SHOULD BE.
THIS IS NOT CRUEL. THIS IS ORDER.
I'LL KILL YOU FOR THIS...
I'LL KILL YOU!
NO. YOU WON'T.
RRAAAAGGHHHH--!!

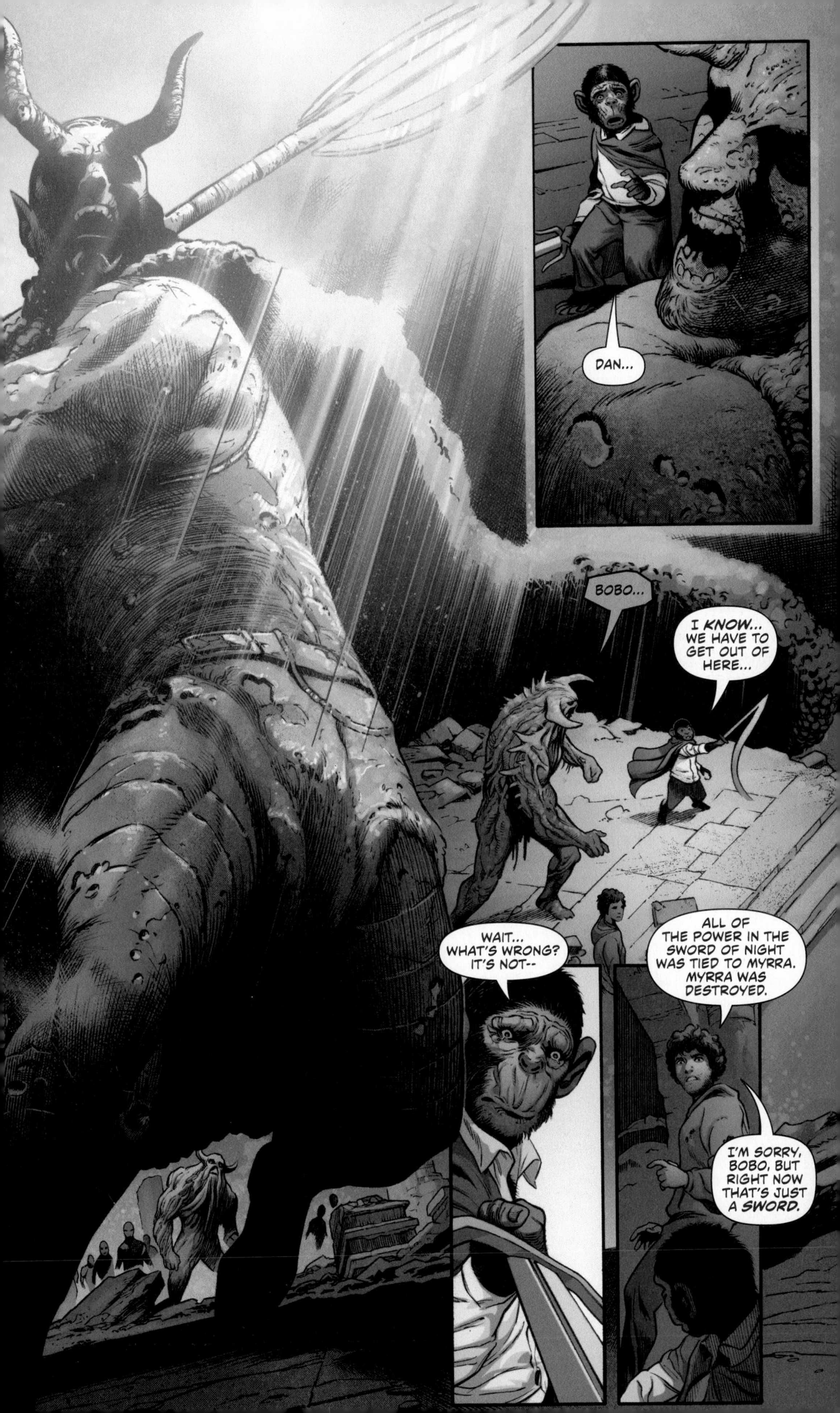
DAN...
BOBO...
I KNOW... WE HAVE TO GET OUT OF HERE...
WAIT... WHAT'S WRONG? IT'S NOT--
ALL OF THE POWER IN THE SWORD OF NIGHT WAS TIED TO MYRRA. MYRRA WAS DESTROYED.
I'M SORRY, BOBO, BUT RIGHT NOW THAT'S JUST A *SWORD*.

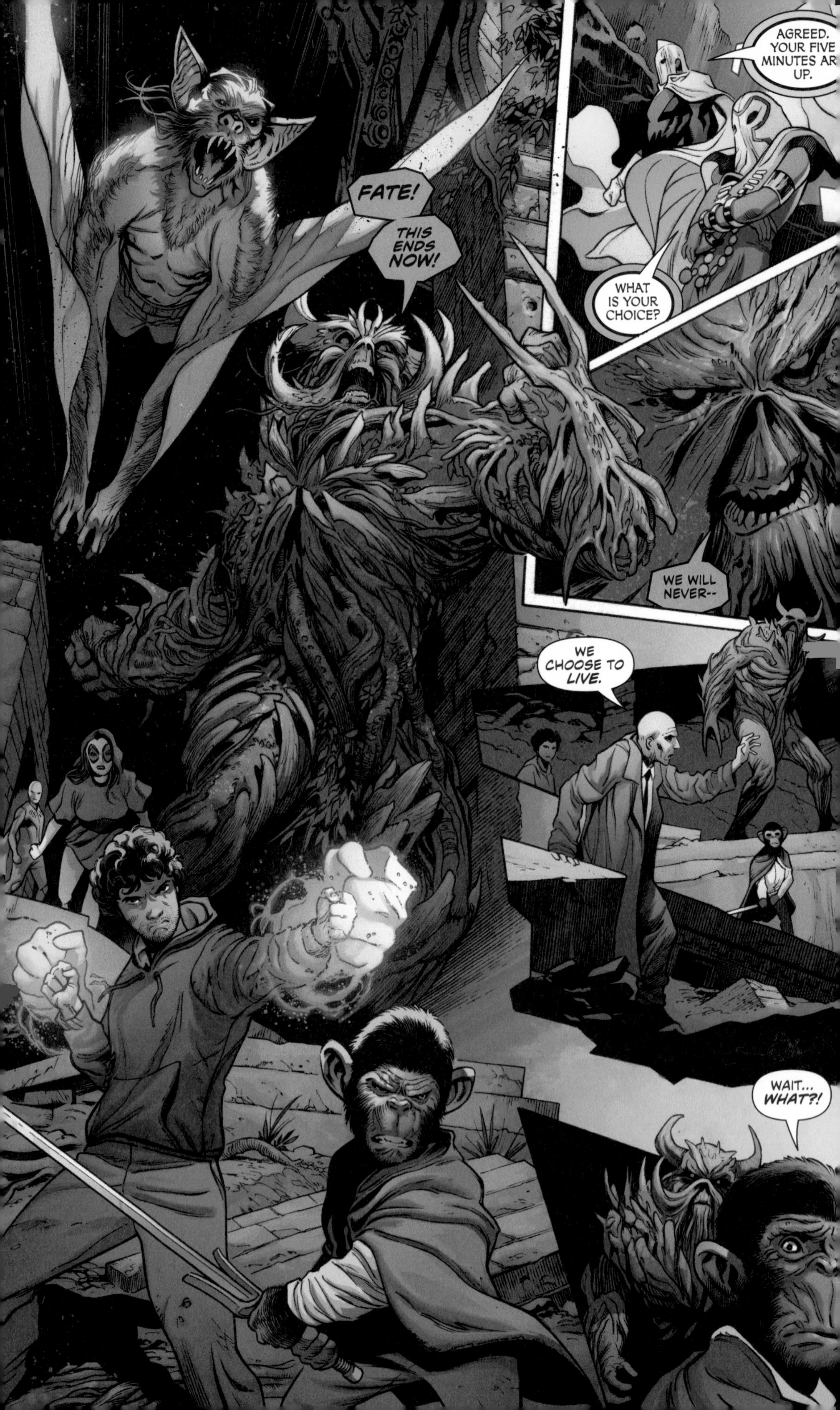
FATE!
THIS ENDS NOW!
AGREED. YOUR FIVE MINUTES AR UP.
WHAT IS YOUR CHOICE?
WE WILL NEVER--
WE CHOOSE TO LIVE.
WAIT... WHAT?!

THE *RUBY OF LIFE.*

WHAT A CURIOUS THING FOR YOUR FATHER TO SEND TO YOU FROM THE *GREAT DARKNESS.*

YOU KNOW, IT WAS MINED BY *NOMMO* IN *KOR* AT THE DAWN OF HUMANKIND. THIS MAY, IN FACT, BE THE *FIRST* MAGICAL ARTIFACT.

I REMEMBER HOW *ANGRY* THEY WERE WHEN IT WAS MADE. MY BROTHERS, SISTERS... WE HAD BROUGHT MAGIC INTO THIS WORLD THE *HARD* WAY.

WE THOUGHT WE WOULD BE THE *ONLY* ONES TO *WIELD* IT.

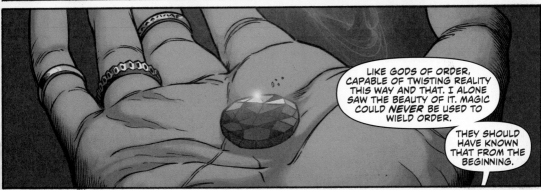

LIKE GODS OF ORDER, CAPABLE OF TWISTING REALITY THIS WAY AND THAT. I ALONE SAW THE BEAUTY OF IT. MAGIC COULD *NEVER* BE USED TO WIELD ORDER.

THEY SHOULD HAVE KNOWN THAT FROM THE BEGINNING.

MORDRU...

I DON'T...

YOU'VE SEEN PART OF THIS STORY. I CAN TASTE IT IN YOUR MIND.

YOU SAW THE LIFE OF *HECATE* BEFORE YOU SET THE OTHERKIND ON HER TO DEVOUR HER. YOU SAW THE LORDS OF ORDER. YOU SAW ME...

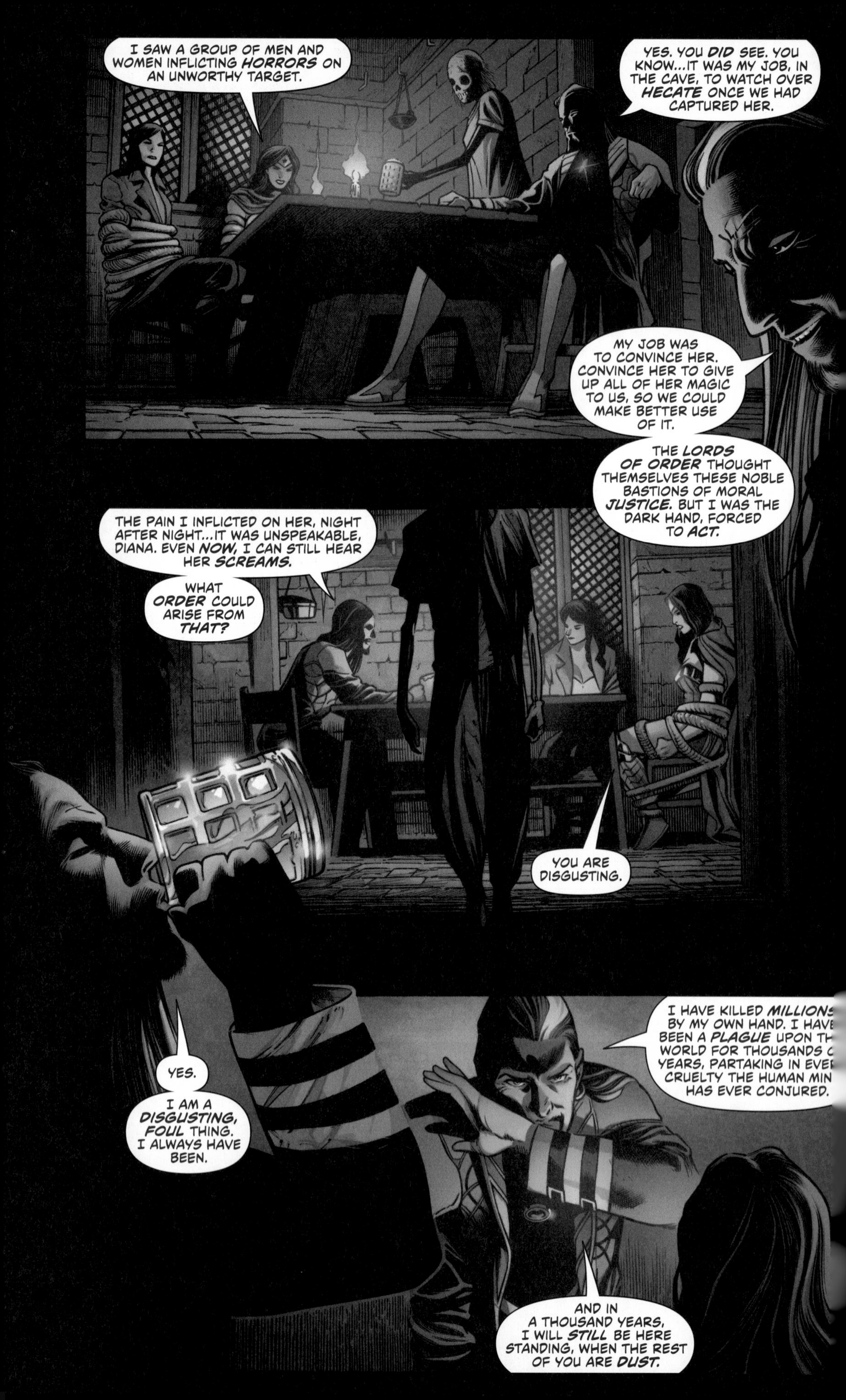

I SAW A GROUP OF MEN AND WOMEN INFLICTING HORRORS ON AN UNWORTHY TARGET.
YES. YOU DID SEE. YOU KNOW...IT WAS MY JOB, IN THE CAVE, TO WATCH OVER HECATE ONCE WE HAD CAPTURED HER.
MY JOB WAS TO CONVINCE HER. CONVINCE HER TO GIVE UP ALL OF HER MAGIC TO US, SO WE COULD MAKE BETTER USE OF IT.
THE LORDS OF ORDER THOUGHT THEMSELVES THESE NOBLE BASTIONS OF MORAL JUSTICE. BUT I WAS THE DARK HAND, FORCED TO ACT.
THE PAIN I INFLICTED ON HER, NIGHT AFTER NIGHT...IT WAS UNSPEAKABLE, DIANA. EVEN NOW, I CAN STILL HEAR HER SCREAMS.
WHAT ORDER COULD ARISE FROM THAT?
YOU ARE DISGUSTING.
YES.
I AM A DISGUSTING, FOUL THING. I ALWAYS HAVE BEEN.
I HAVE KILLED MILLIONS BY MY OWN HAND. I HAVE BEEN A PLAGUE UPON TH WORLD FOR THOUSANDS O YEARS, PARTAKING IN EVER CRUELTY THE HUMAN MIN HAS EVER CONJURED.
AND IN A THOUSAND YEARS, I WILL STILL BE HERE STANDING, WHEN THE REST OF YOU ARE DUST.

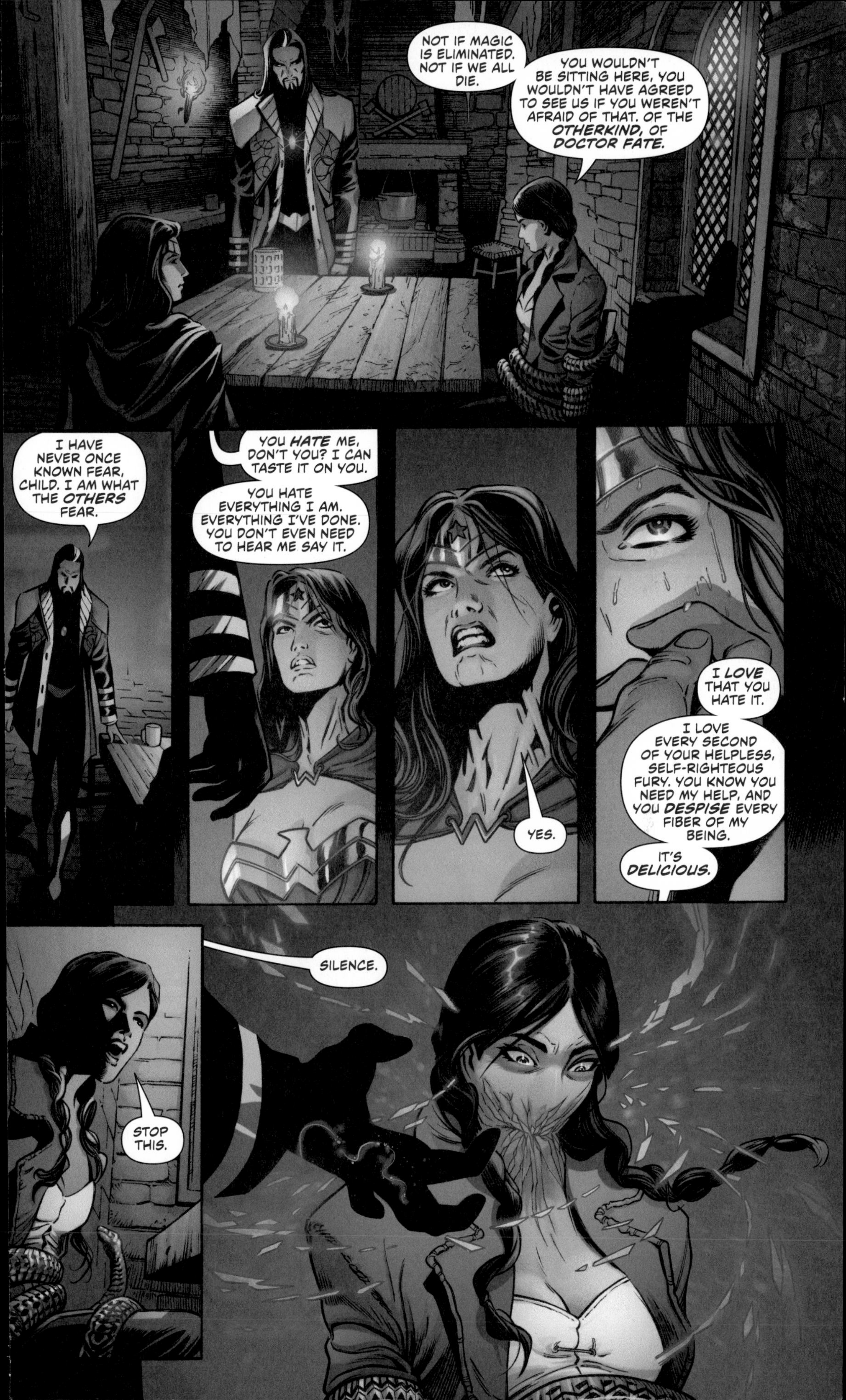
NOT IF MAGIC IS ELIMINATED. NOT IF WE ALL DIE.
YOU WOULDN'T BE SITTING HERE, YOU WOULDN'T HAVE AGREED TO SEE US IF YOU WEREN'T AFRAID OF THAT. OF THE OTHERKIND, OF DOCTOR FATE.
I HAVE NEVER ONCE KNOWN FEAR, CHILD. I AM WHAT THE OTHERS FEAR.
YOU HATE ME, DON'T YOU? I CAN TASTE IT ON YOU.
YOU HATE EVERYTHING I AM. EVERYTHING I'VE DONE. YOU DON'T EVEN NEED TO HEAR ME SAY IT.
YES.
I LOVE THAT YOU HATE IT.
I LOVE EVERY SECOND OF YOUR HELPLESS, SELF-RIGHTEOUS FURY. YOU KNOW YOU NEED MY HELP, AND YOU DESPISE EVERY FIBER OF MY BEING.
IT'S DELICIOUS.
SILENCE.
STOP THIS.

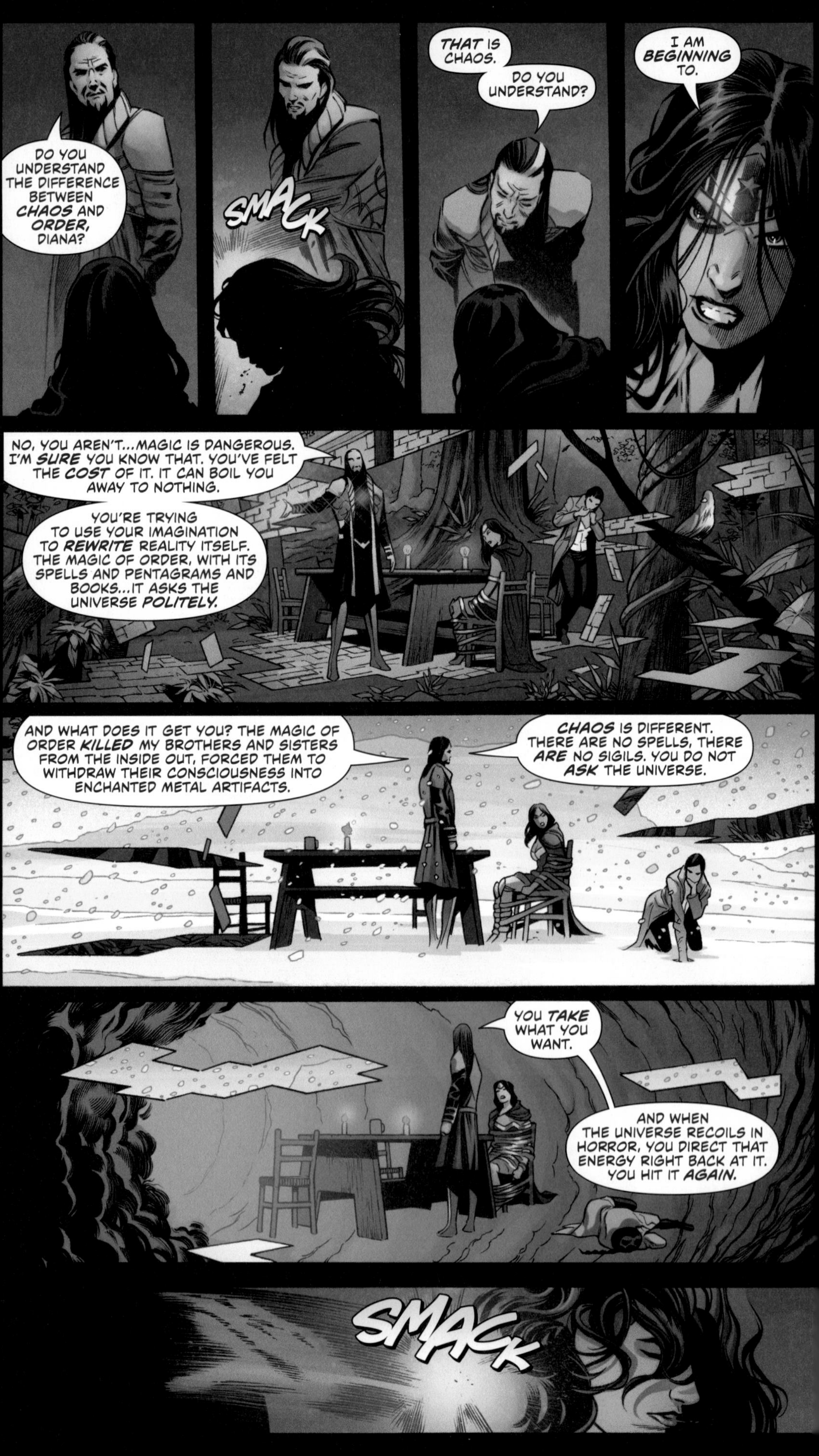
DO YOU UNDERSTAND THE DIFFERENCE BETWEEN CHAOS AND ORDER, DIANA?
SMACK
THAT IS CHAOS.
DO YOU UNDERSTAND?
I AM BEGINNING TO.
NO, YOU AREN'T...MAGIC IS DANGEROUS. I'M SURE YOU KNOW THAT. YOU'VE FELT THE COST OF IT. IT CAN BOIL YOU AWAY TO NOTHING.
YOU'RE TRYING TO USE YOUR IMAGINATION TO REWRITE REALITY ITSELF. THE MAGIC OF ORDER, WITH ITS SPELLS AND PENTAGRAMS AND BOOKS...IT ASKS THE UNIVERSE POLITELY.
AND WHAT DOES IT GET YOU? THE MAGIC OF ORDER KILLED MY BROTHERS AND SISTERS FROM THE INSIDE OUT, FORCED THEM TO WITHDRAW THEIR CONSCIOUSNESS INTO ENCHANTED METAL ARTIFACTS.
CHAOS IS DIFFERENT. THERE ARE NO SPELLS, THERE ARE NO SIGILS. YOU DO NOT ASK THE UNIVERSE.
YOU TAKE WHAT YOU WANT.
AND WHEN THE UNIVERSE RECOILS IN HORROR, YOU DIRECT THAT ENERGY RIGHT BACK AT IT. YOU HIT IT AGAIN.
SMACK

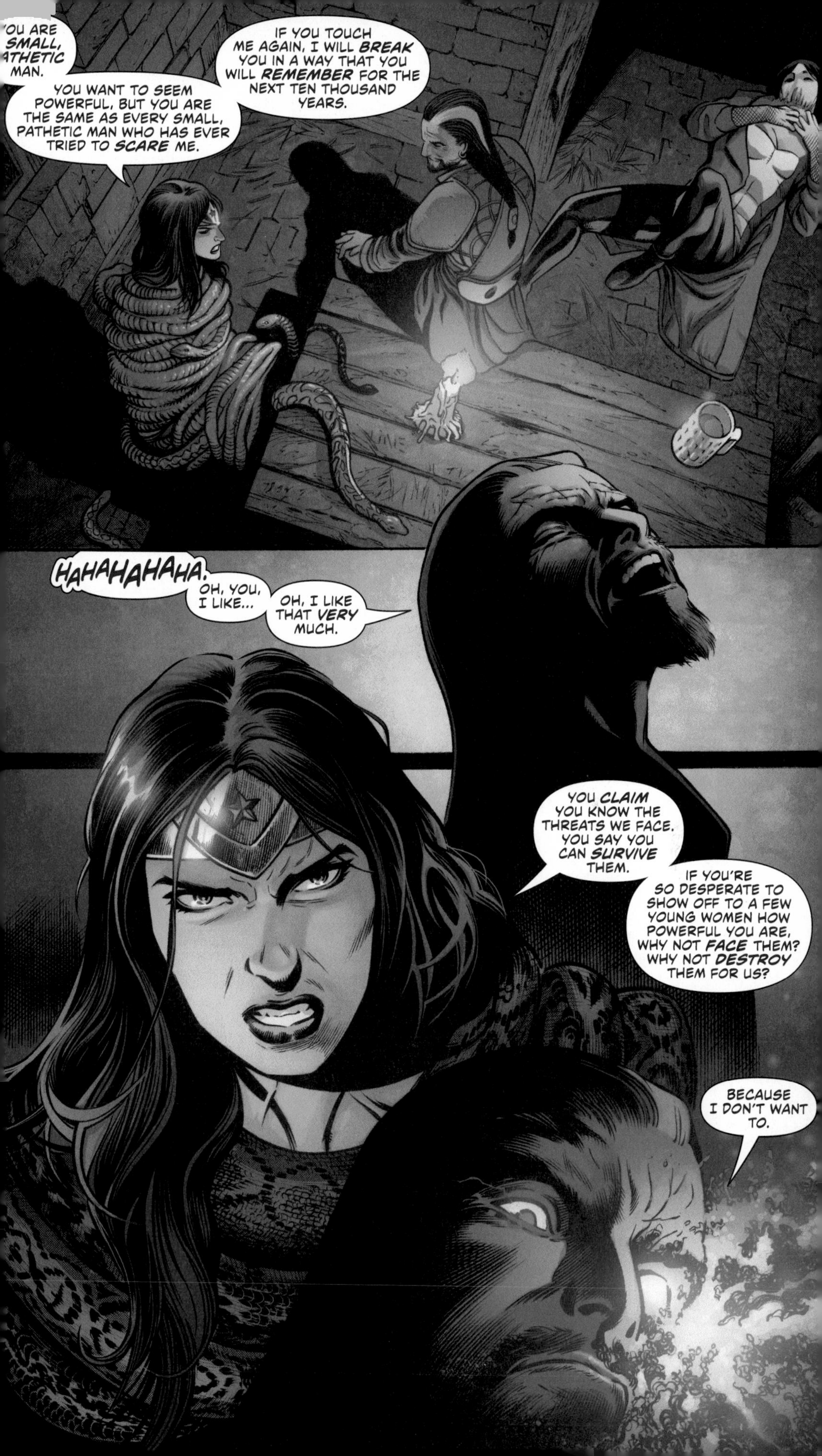
OU ARE SMALL, ATHETIC MAN.
YOU WANT TO SEEM POWERFUL, BUT YOU ARE THE SAME AS EVERY SMALL, PATHETIC MAN WHO HAS EVER TRIED TO SCARE ME.
IF YOU TOUCH ME AGAIN, I WILL BREAK YOU IN A WAY THAT YOU WILL REMEMBER FOR THE NEXT TEN THOUSAND YEARS.
HAHAHAHAHAHA.
OH, YOU, I LIKE...
OH, I LIKE THAT VERY MUCH.
YOU CLAIM YOU KNOW THE THREATS WE FACE. YOU SAY YOU CAN SURVIVE THEM.
IF YOU'RE SO DESPERATE TO SHOW OFF TO A FEW YOUNG WOMEN HOW POWERFUL YOU ARE, WHY NOT FACE THEM? WHY NOT DESTROY THEM FOR US?
BECAUSE I DON'T WANT TO.

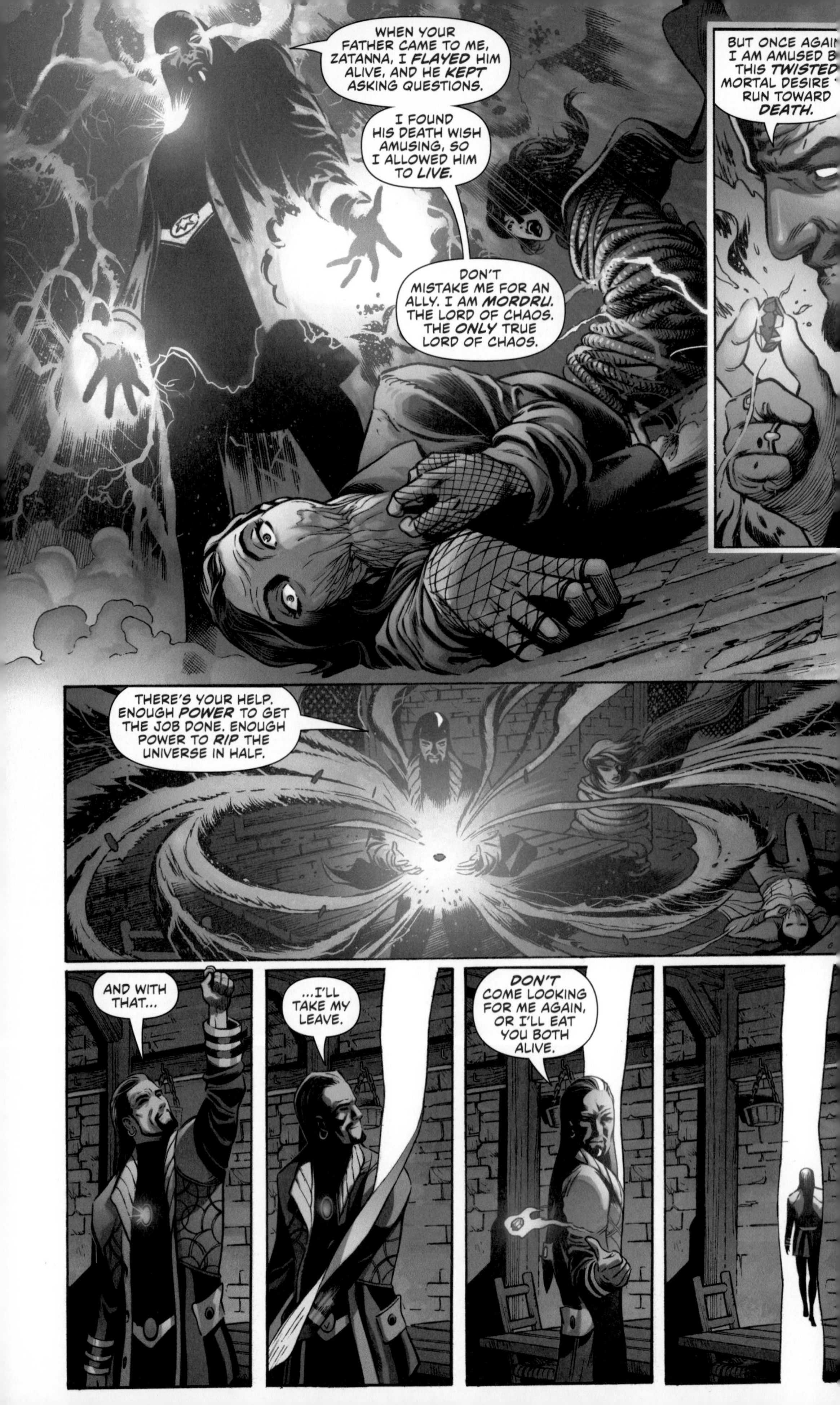
WHEN YOUR FATHER CAME TO ME, ZATANNA, I FLAYED HIM ALIVE, AND HE KEPT ASKING QUESTIONS.
I FOUND HIS DEATH WISH AMUSING, SO I ALLOWED HIM TO LIVE.
DON'T MISTAKE ME FOR AN ALLY. I AM MORDRU. THE LORD OF CHAOS. THE ONLY TRUE LORD OF CHAOS.
BUT ONCE AGAIN I AM AMUSED B THIS TWISTED MORTAL DESIRE RUN TOWARD DEATH.
THERE'S YOUR HELP. ENOUGH POWER TO GET THE JOB DONE. ENOUGH POWER TO RIP THE UNIVERSE IN HALF.
AND WITH THAT...
...I'LL TAKE MY LEAVE.
DON'T COME LOOKING FOR ME AGAIN, OR I'LL EAT YOU BOTH ALIVE.

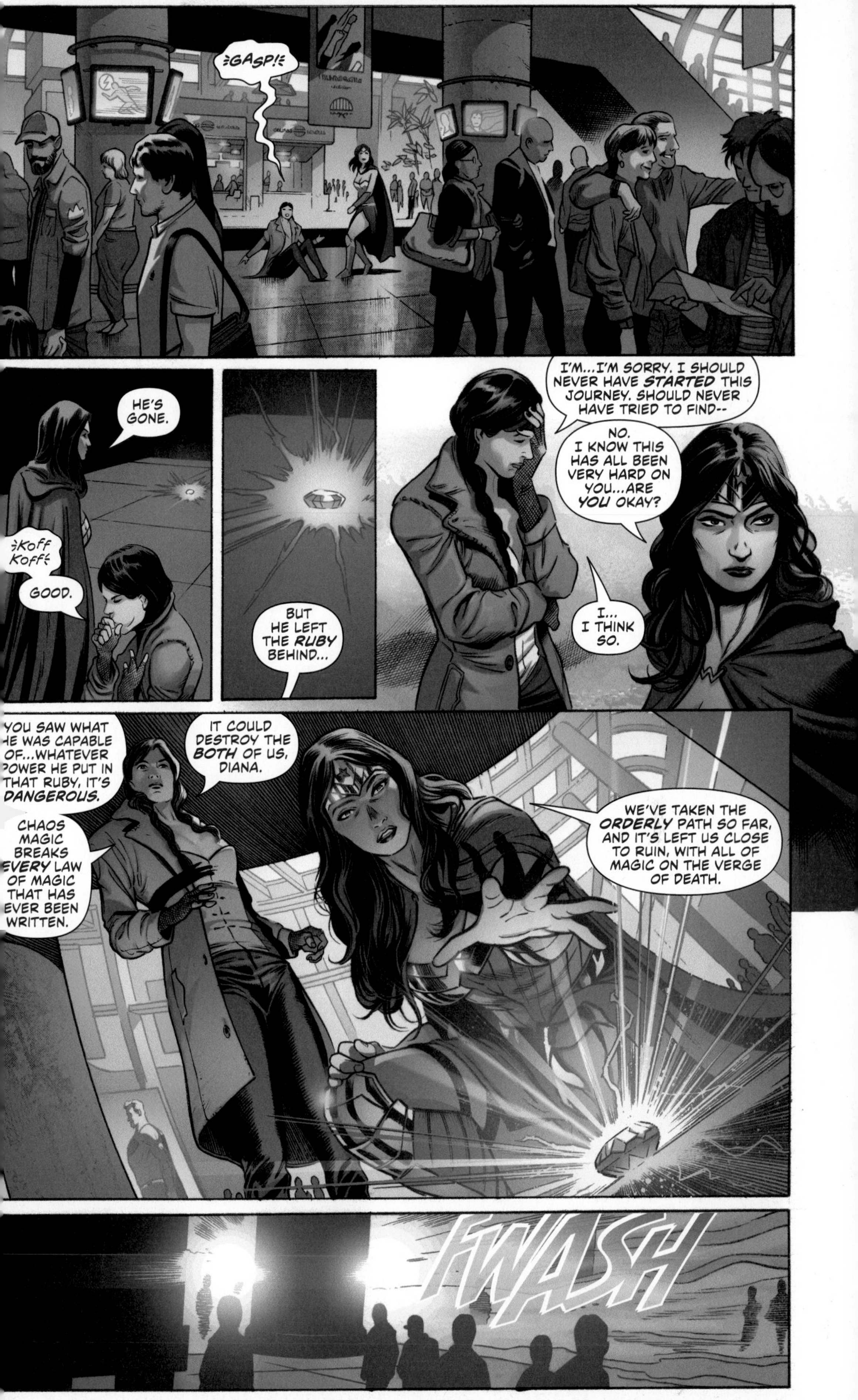
GASP!
HE'S GONE.
KOFF KOFF
GOOD.
BUT HE LEFT THE RUBY BEHIND...
I'M...I'M SORRY. I SHOULD NEVER HAVE STARTED THIS JOURNEY. SHOULD NEVER HAVE TRIED TO FIND--
NO. I KNOW THIS HAS ALL BEEN VERY HARD ON YOU...ARE YOU OKAY?
I... I THINK SO.
YOU SAW WHAT HE WAS CAPABLE OF...WHATEVER POWER HE PUT IN THAT RUBY, IT'S DANGEROUS.
IT COULD DESTROY THE BOTH OF US, DIANA.
CHAOS MAGIC BREAKS EVERY LAW OF MAGIC THAT HAS EVER BEEN WRITTEN.
WE'VE TAKEN THE ORDERLY PATH SO FAR, AND IT'S LEFT US CLOSE TO RUIN, WITH ALL OF MAGIC ON THE VERGE OF DEATH.
FWASH

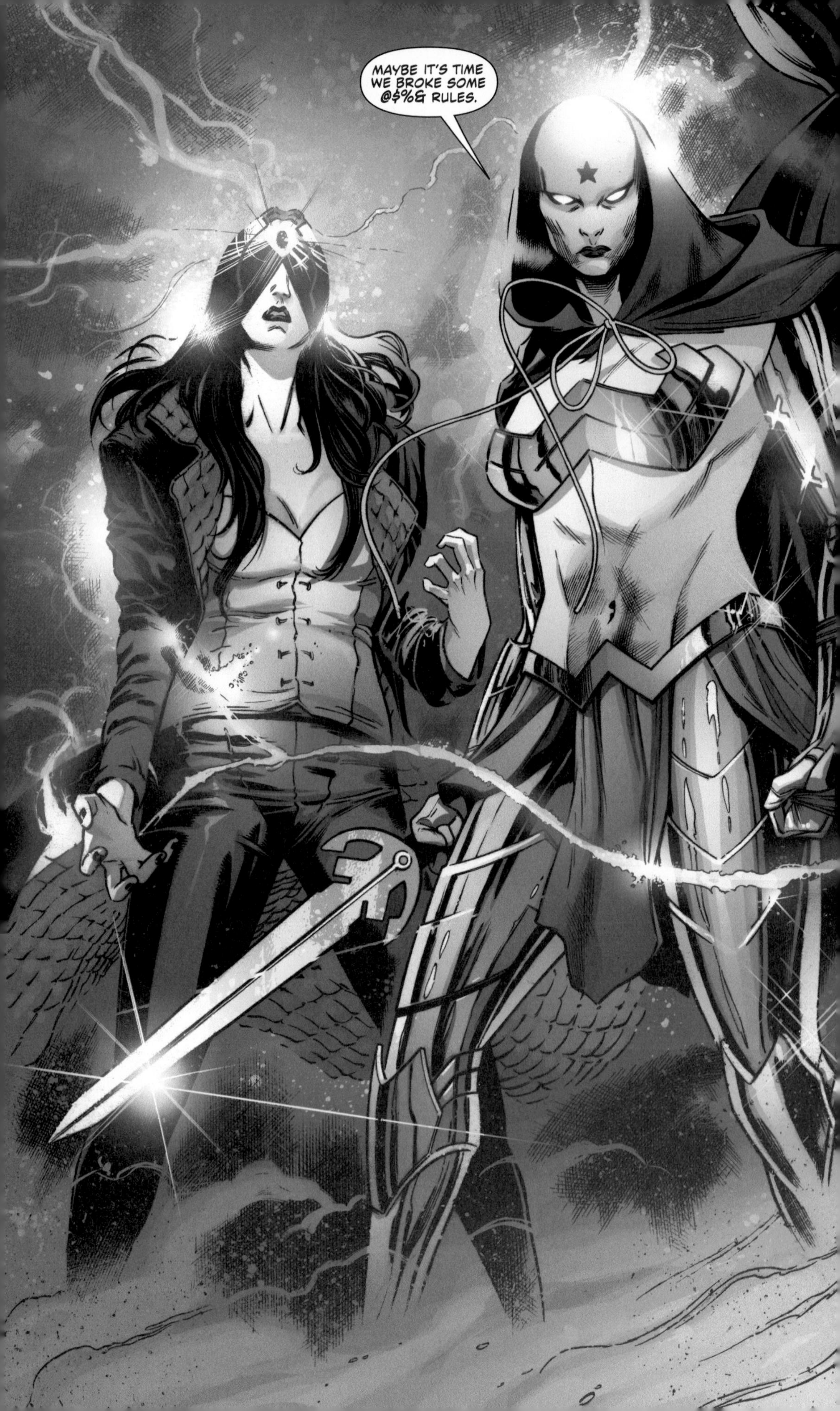
MAYBE IT'S TIME WE BROKE SOME @$%& RULES.

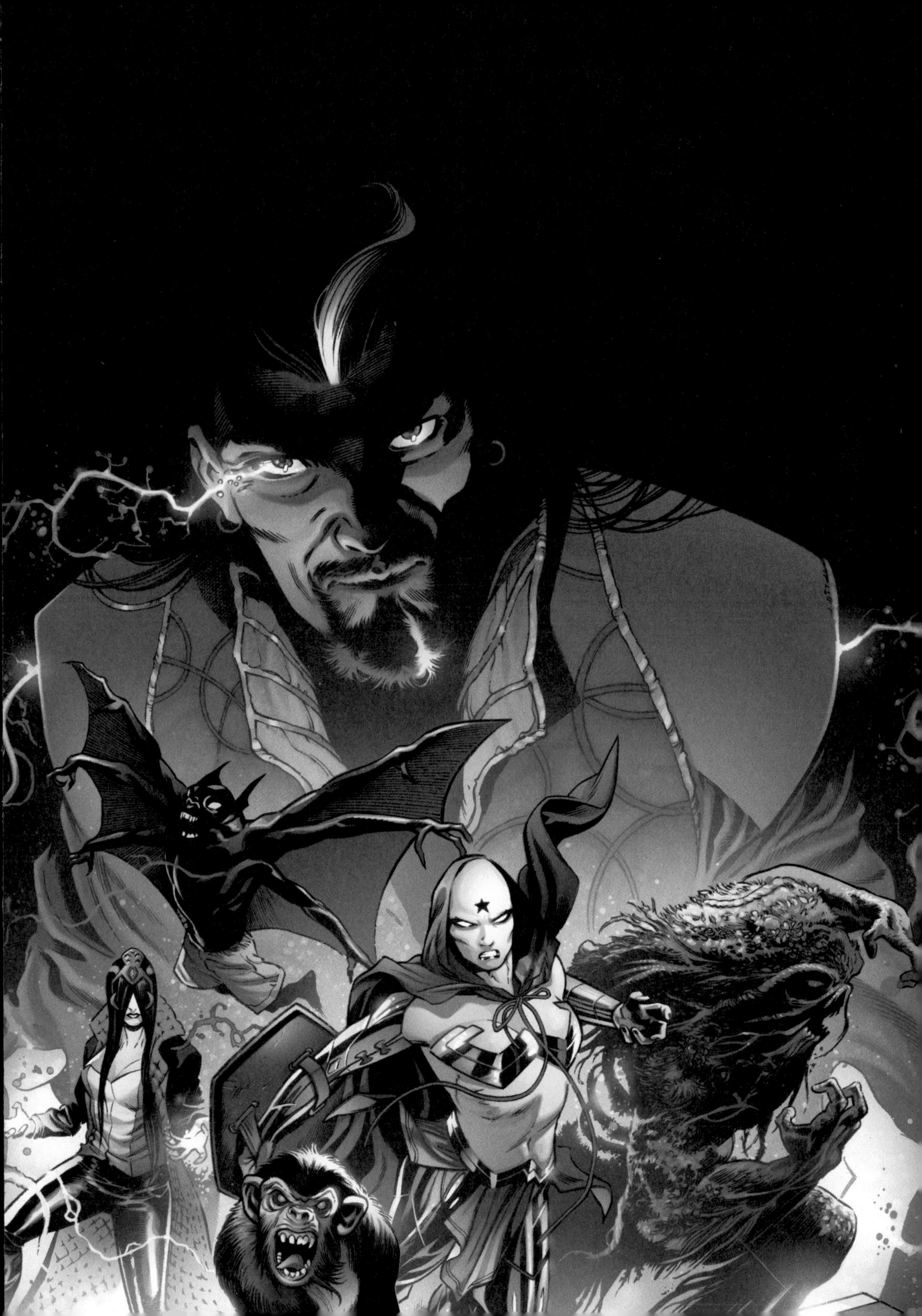

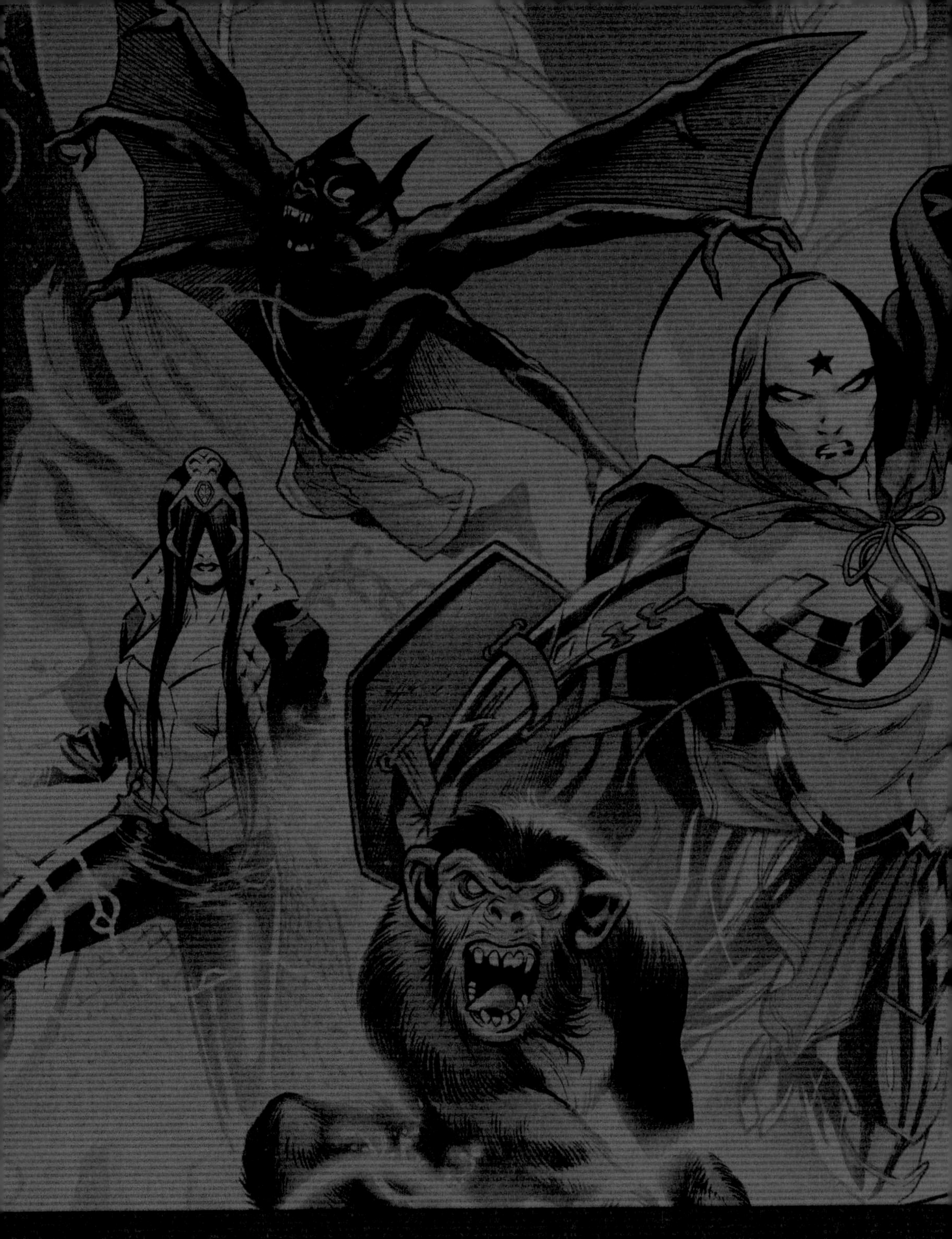

JUSTICE LEAGUE DARK

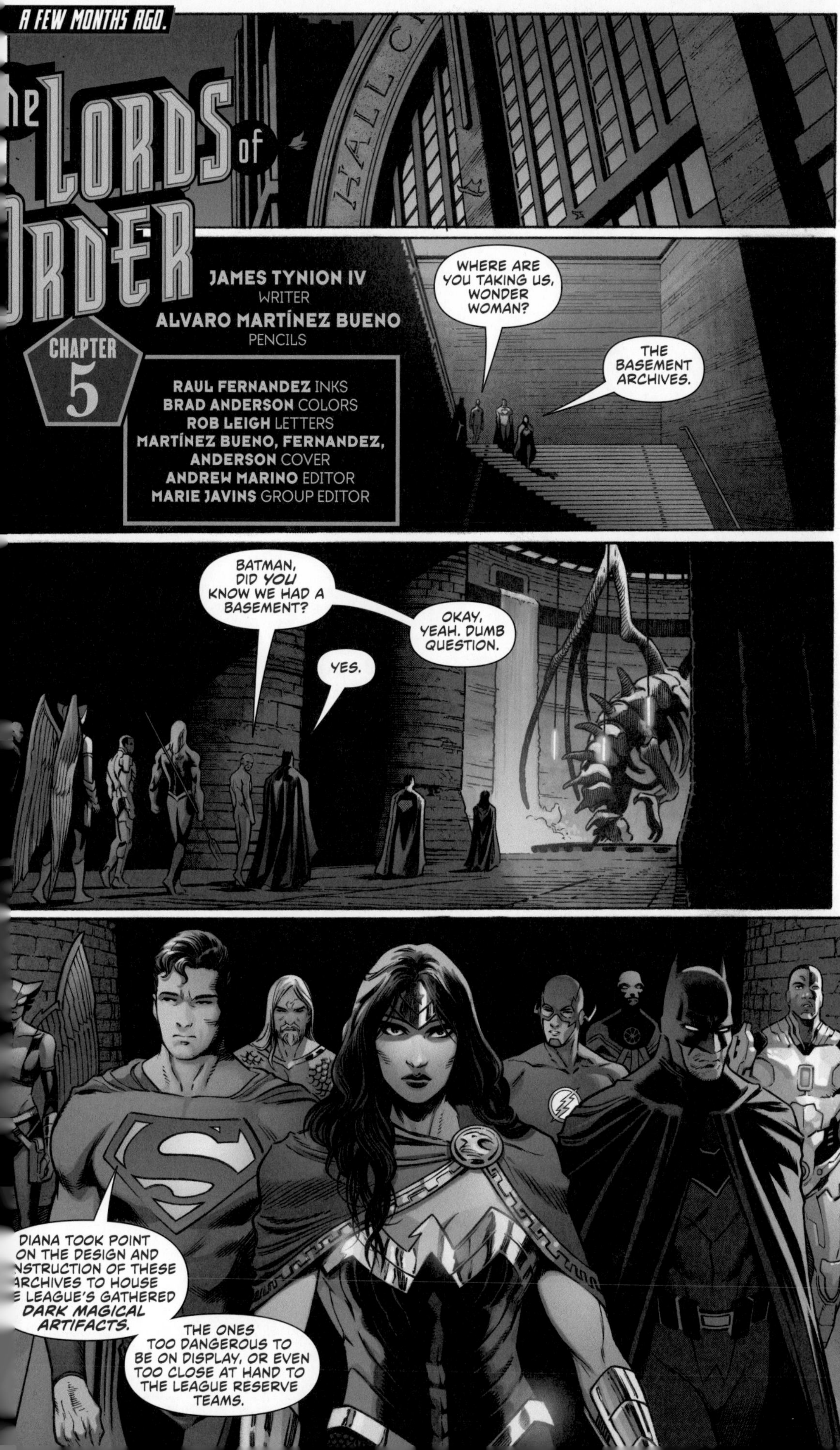

A FEW MONTHS AGO.
LORDS of ORDER
JAMES TYNION IV
WRITER
ALVARO MARTÍNEZ BUENO
PENCILS
CHAPTER 5
RAUL FERNANDEZ INKS
BRAD ANDERSON COLORS
ROB LEIGH LETTERS
MARTÍNEZ BUENO, FERNANDEZ, ANDERSON COVER
ANDREW MARINO EDITOR
MARIE JAVINS GROUP EDITOR
WHERE ARE YOU TAKING US, WONDER WOMAN?
THE BASEMENT ARCHIVES.
BATMAN, DID *YOU* KNOW WE HAD A BASEMENT?
YES.
OKAY, YEAH. DUMB QUESTION.
DIANA TOOK POINT ON THE DESIGN AND NSTRUCTION OF THESE ARCHIVES TO HOUSE E LEAGUE'S GATHERED ***DARK MAGICAL ARTIFACTS.***
THE ONES TOO DANGEROUS TO BE ON DISPLAY, OR EVEN TOO CLOSE AT HAND TO THE LEAGUE RESERVE TEAMS.

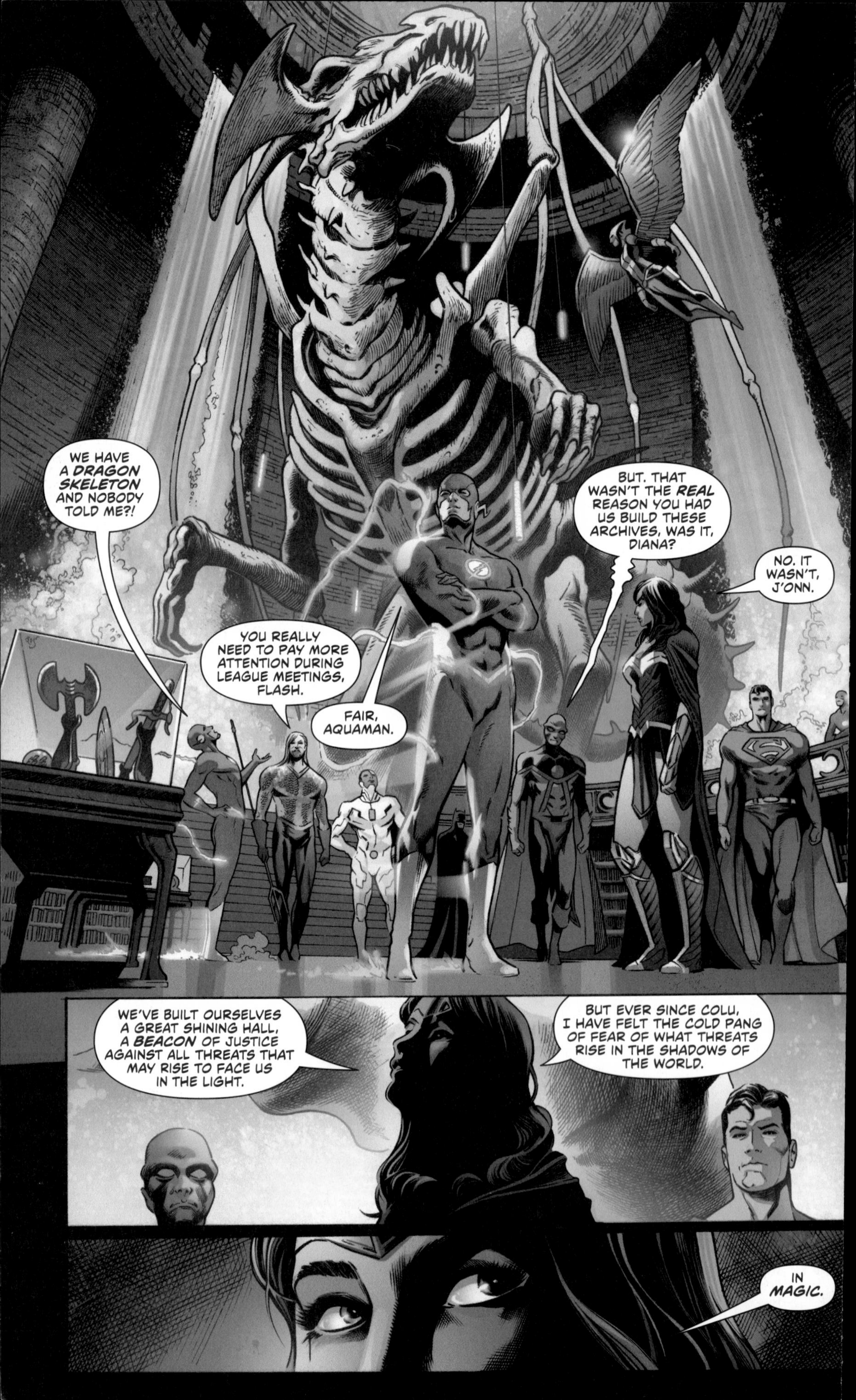

WE HAVE A *DRAGON SKELETON* AND NOBODY TOLD ME?!
YOU REALLY NEED TO PAY MORE ATTENTION DURING LEAGUE MEETINGS, FLASH.
FAIR, AQUAMAN.
BUT. THAT WASN'T THE *REAL* REASON YOU HAD US BUILD THESE ARCHIVES, WAS IT, DIANA?
NO. IT WASN'T, J'ONN.
WE'VE BUILT OURSELVES A GREAT SHINING HALL, A *BEACON* OF JUSTICE AGAINST ALL THREATS THAT MAY RISE TO FACE US IN THE LIGHT.
BUT EVER SINCE COLU, I HAVE FELT THE COLD PANG OF FEAR OF WHAT THREATS RISE IN THE SHADOWS OF THE WORLD.
IN *MAGIC*.

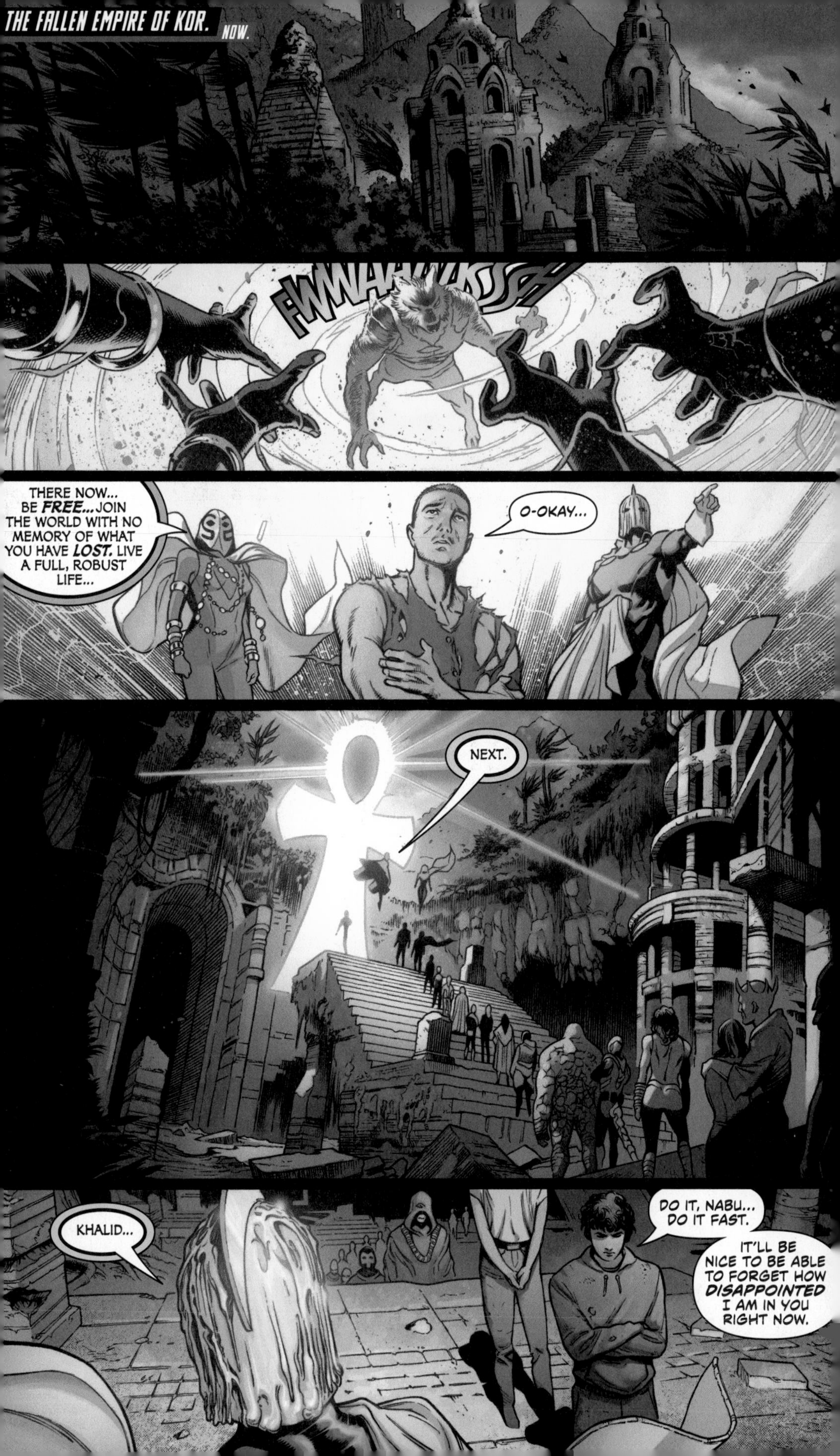
THE FALLEN EMPIRE OF KOR.
NOW.
FWWAHHKSSH
THERE NOW... BE FREE...JOIN THE WORLD WITH NO MEMORY OF WHAT YOU HAVE LOST. LIVE A FULL, ROBUST LIFE...
O-OKAY...
NEXT.
KHALID...
DO IT, NABU... DO IT FAST.
IT'LL BE NICE TO BE ABLE TO FORGET HOW DISAPPOINTED I AM IN YOU RIGHT NOW.

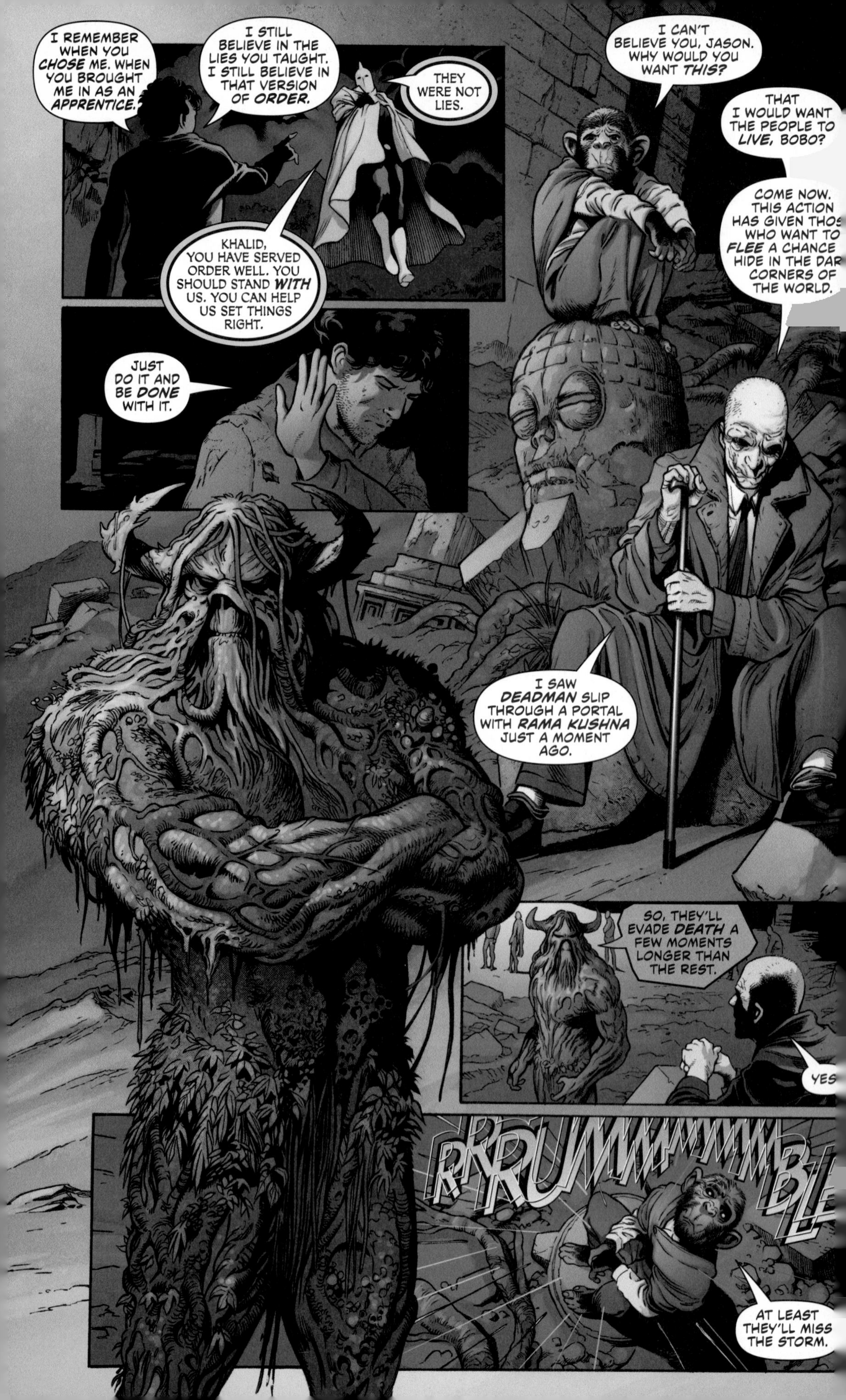
I REMEMBER WHEN YOU CHOSE ME. WHEN YOU BROUGHT ME IN AS AN APPRENTICE.
I STILL BELIEVE IN THE LIES YOU TAUGHT. I STILL BELIEVE IN THAT VERSION OF ORDER.
THEY WERE NOT LIES.
KHALID, YOU HAVE SERVED ORDER WELL. YOU SHOULD STAND WITH US. YOU CAN HELP US SET THINGS RIGHT.
JUST DO IT AND BE DONE WITH IT.
I CAN'T BELIEVE YOU, JASON. WHY WOULD YOU WANT THIS?
THAT I WOULD WANT THE PEOPLE TO LIVE, BOBO?
COME NOW. THIS ACTION HAS GIVEN THOS WHO WANT TO FLEE A CHANCE HIDE IN THE DAR CORNERS OF THE WORLD.
I SAW DEADMAN SLIP THROUGH A PORTAL WITH RAMA KUSHNA JUST A MOMENT AGO.
SO, THEY'LL EVADE DEATH A FEW MOMENTS LONGER THAN THE REST.
YES
RRRUMMMMMMBLE
AT LEAST THEY'LL MISS THE STORM.

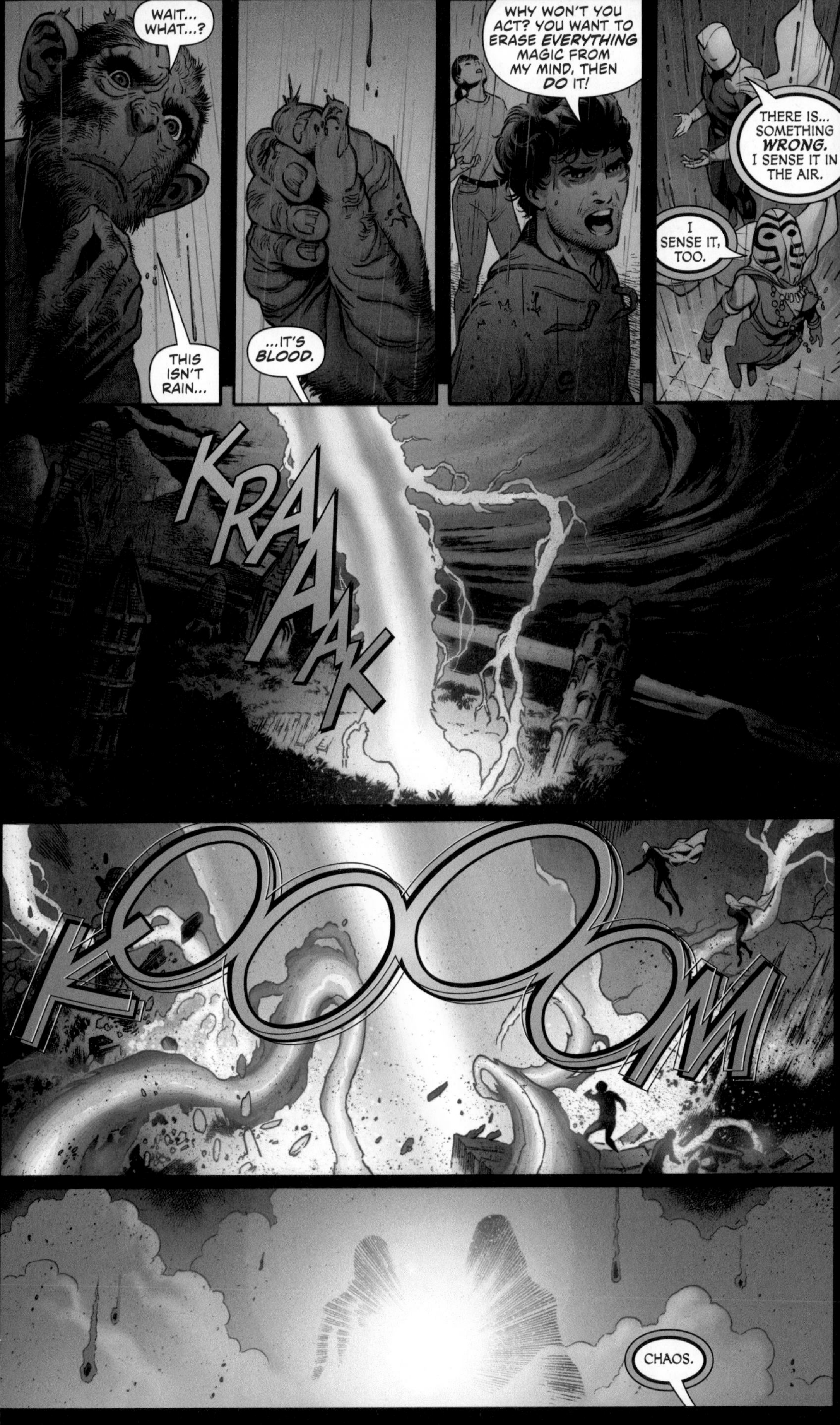
WAIT... WHAT...?
THIS ISN'T RAIN...
...IT'S BLOOD.
WHY WON'T YOU ACT? YOU WANT TO ERASE EVERYTHING MAGIC FROM MY MIND, THEN DO IT!
THERE IS... SOMETHING WRONG. I SENSE IT IN THE AIR.
I SENSE IT, TOO.
KRAAAK
KOOOOM
CHAOS.

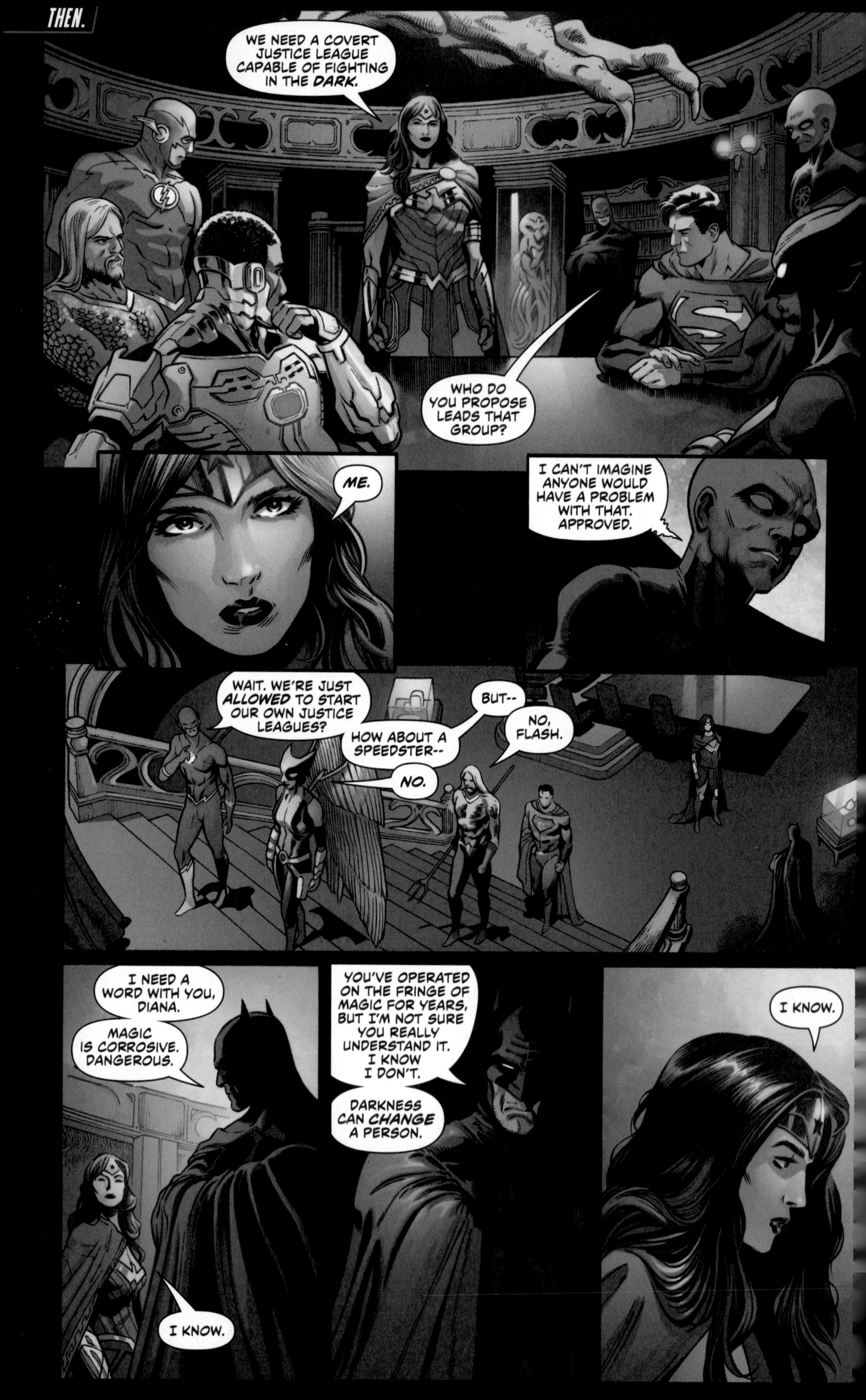
THEN.
WE NEED A COVERT JUSTICE LEAGUE CAPABLE OF FIGHTING IN THE DARK.
WHO DO YOU PROPOSE LEADS THAT GROUP?
ME.
I CAN'T IMAGINE ANYONE WOULD HAVE A PROBLEM WITH THAT. APPROVED.
WAIT. WE'RE JUST ALLOWED TO START OUR OWN JUSTICE LEAGUES?
BUT--
HOW ABOUT A SPEEDSTER--
NO, FLASH.
NO.
I NEED A WORD WITH YOU, DIANA.
MAGIC IS CORROSIVE. DANGEROUS.
I KNOW.
YOU'VE OPERATED ON THE FRINGE OF MAGIC FOR YEARS, BUT I'M NOT SURE YOU REALLY UNDERSTAND IT. I KNOW I DON'T.
DARKNESS CAN CHANGE A PERSON.
I KNOW.

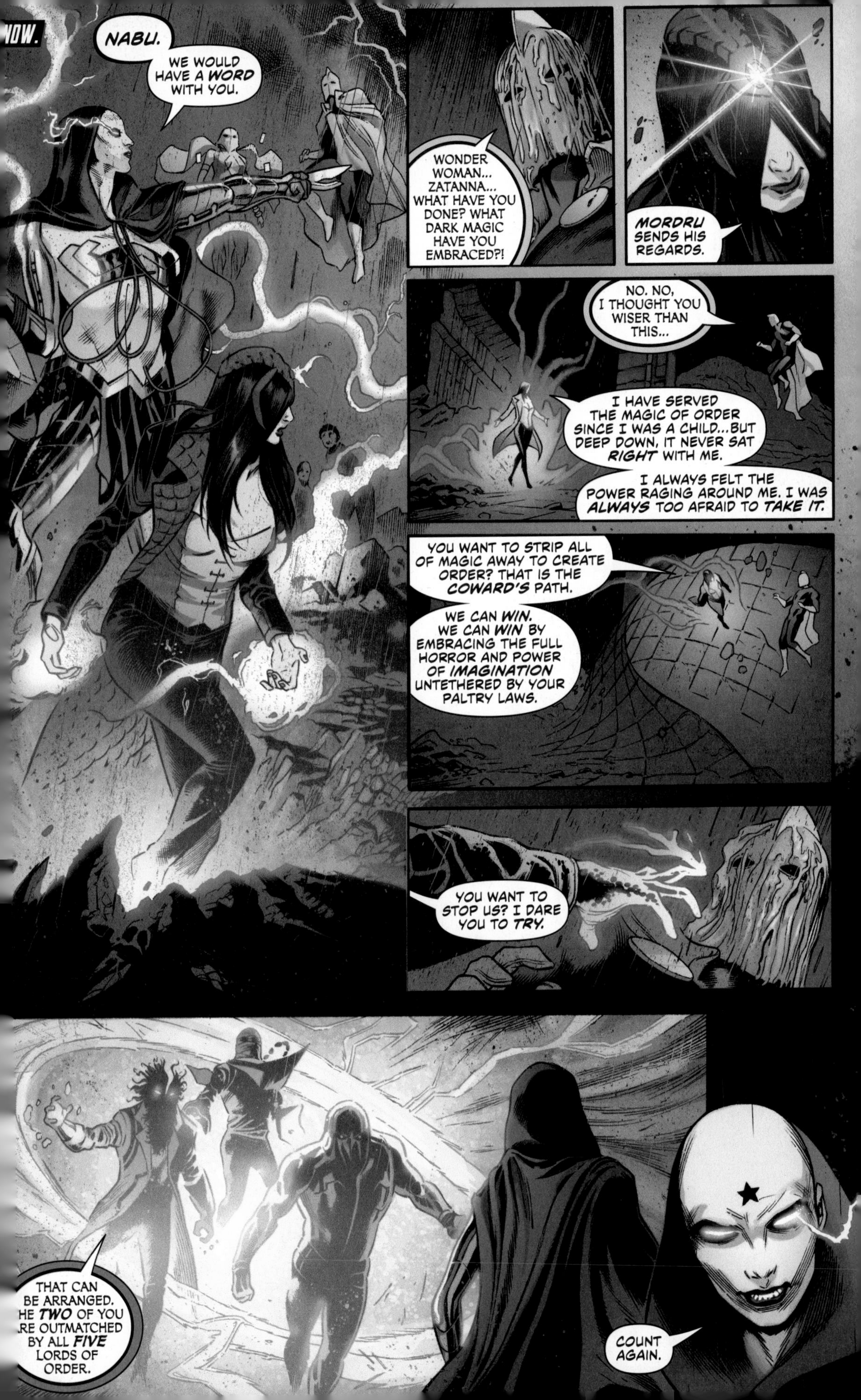
NOW.
NABU.
WE WOULD HAVE A WORD WITH YOU.
WONDER WOMAN... ZATANNA... WHAT HAVE YOU DONE? WHAT DARK MAGIC HAVE YOU EMBRACED?!
MORDRU SENDS HIS REGARDS.
NO. NO, I THOUGHT YOU WISER THAN THIS...
I HAVE SERVED THE MAGIC OF ORDER SINCE I WAS A CHILD...BUT DEEP DOWN, IT NEVER SAT RIGHT WITH ME.
I ALWAYS FELT THE POWER RAGING AROUND ME. I WAS ALWAYS TOO AFRAID TO TAKE IT.
YOU WANT TO STRIP ALL OF MAGIC AWAY TO CREATE ORDER? THAT IS THE COWARD'S PATH.
WE CAN WIN. WE CAN WIN BY EMBRACING THE FULL HORROR AND POWER OF IMAGINATION UNTETHERED BY YOUR PALTRY LAWS.
YOU WANT TO STOP US? I DARE YOU TO TRY.
THAT CAN BE ARRANGED. HE TWO OF YOU RE OUTMATCHED BY ALL FIVE LORDS OF ORDER.
COUNT AGAIN.

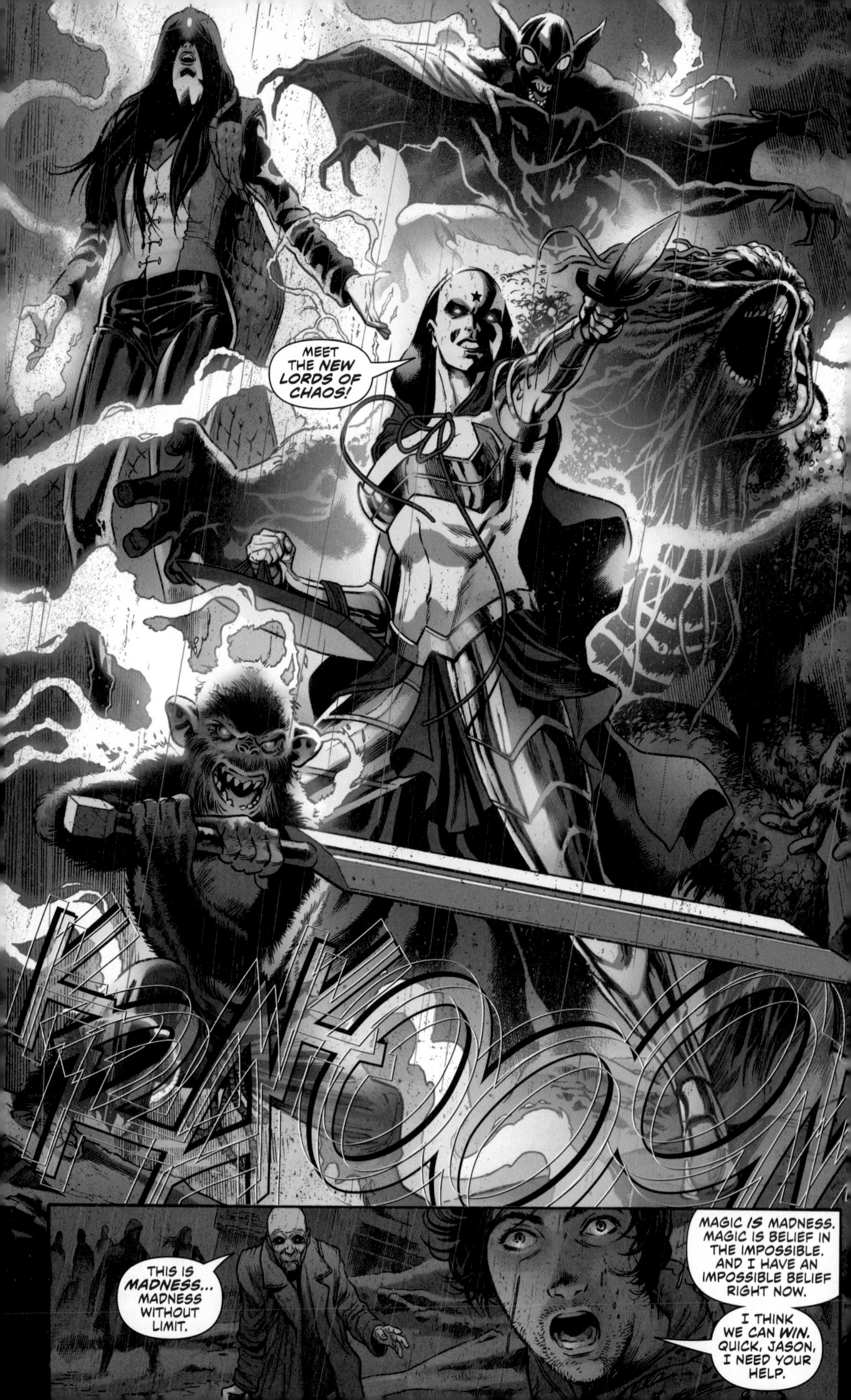

MEET THE NEW LORDS OF CHAOS!
THIS IS MADNESS... MADNESS WITHOUT LIMIT.
MAGIC IS MADNESS. MAGIC IS BELIEF IN THE IMPOSSIBLE. AND I HAVE AN IMPOSSIBLE BELIEF RIGHT NOW.
I THINK WE CAN WIN. QUICK, JASON, I NEED YOUR HELP.

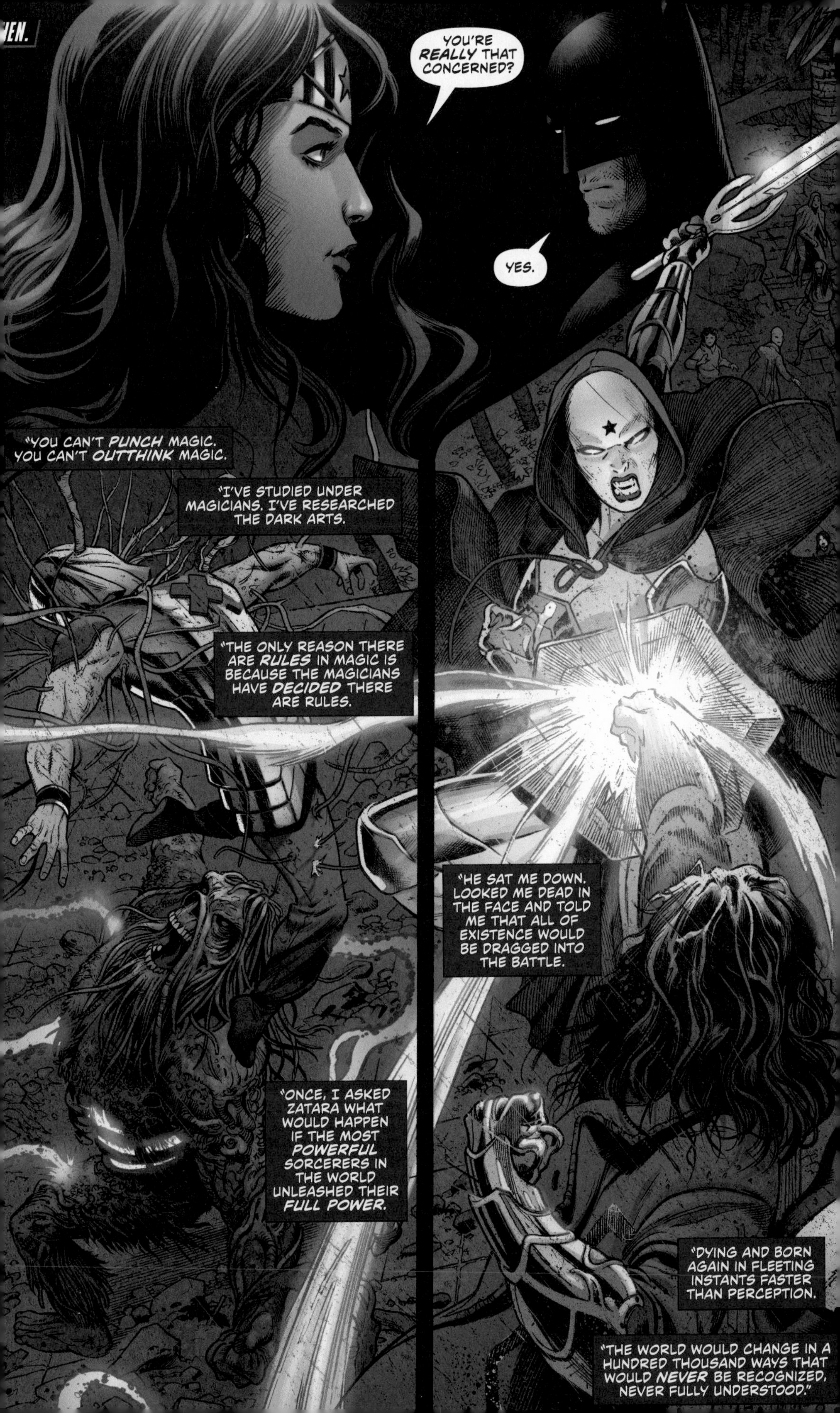

EN.
YOU'RE REALLY THAT CONCERNED?
YES.
"YOU CAN'T PUNCH MAGIC. YOU CAN'T OUTTHINK MAGIC.
"I'VE STUDIED UNDER MAGICIANS. I'VE RESEARCHED THE DARK ARTS.
"THE ONLY REASON THERE ARE RULES IN MAGIC IS BECAUSE THE MAGICIANS HAVE DECIDED THERE ARE RULES.
"ONCE, I ASKED ZATARA WHAT WOULD HAPPEN IF THE MOST POWERFUL SORCERERS IN THE WORLD UNLEASHED THEIR FULL POWER.
"HE SAT ME DOWN. LOOKED ME DEAD IN THE FACE AND TOLD ME THAT ALL OF EXISTENCE WOULD BE DRAGGED INTO THE BATTLE.
"DYING AND BORN AGAIN IN FLEETING INSTANTS FASTER THAN PERCEPTION.
"THE WORLD WOULD CHANGE IN A HUNDRED THOUSAND WAYS THAT WOULD NEVER BE RECOGNIZED, NEVER FULLY UNDERSTOOD."

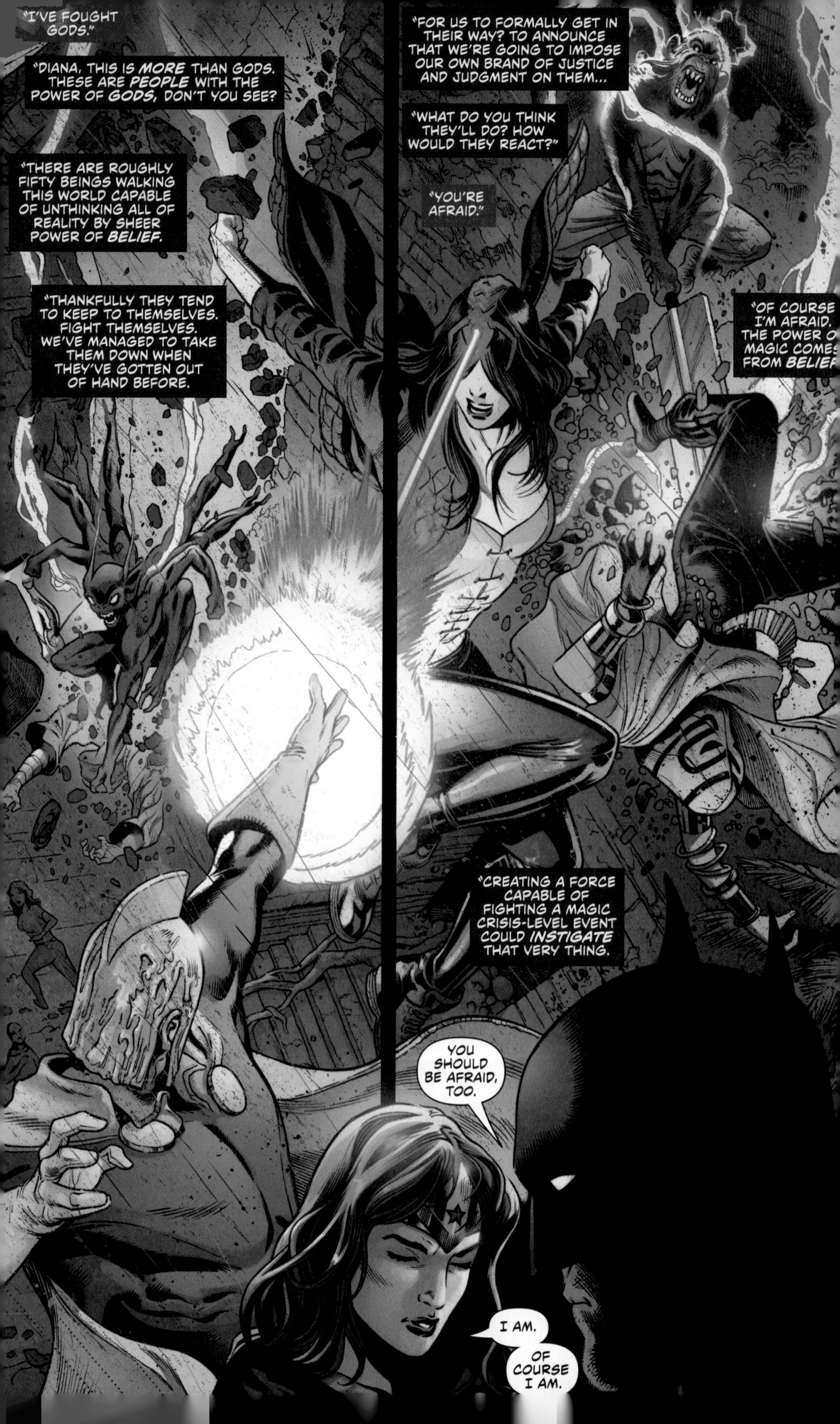
"I'VE FOUGHT GODS."
"DIANA, THIS IS MORE THAN GODS. THESE ARE PEOPLE WITH THE POWER OF GODS, DON'T YOU SEE?
"THERE ARE ROUGHLY FIFTY BEINGS WALKING THIS WORLD CAPABLE OF UNTHINKING ALL OF REALITY BY SHEER POWER OF BELIEF.
"THANKFULLY THEY TEND TO KEEP TO THEMSELVES. FIGHT THEMSELVES. WE'VE MANAGED TO TAKE THEM DOWN WHEN THEY'VE GOTTEN OUT OF HAND BEFORE.
"FOR US TO FORMALLY GET IN THEIR WAY? TO ANNOUNCE THAT WE'RE GOING TO IMPOSE OUR OWN BRAND OF JUSTICE AND JUDGMENT ON THEM...
"WHAT DO YOU THINK THEY'LL DO? HOW WOULD THEY REACT?"
"YOU'RE AFRAID."
"CREATING A FORCE CAPABLE OF FIGHTING A MAGIC CRISIS-LEVEL EVENT COULD INSTIGATE THAT VERY THING.
YOU SHOULD BE AFRAID, TOO.
I AM.
OF COURSE I AM.

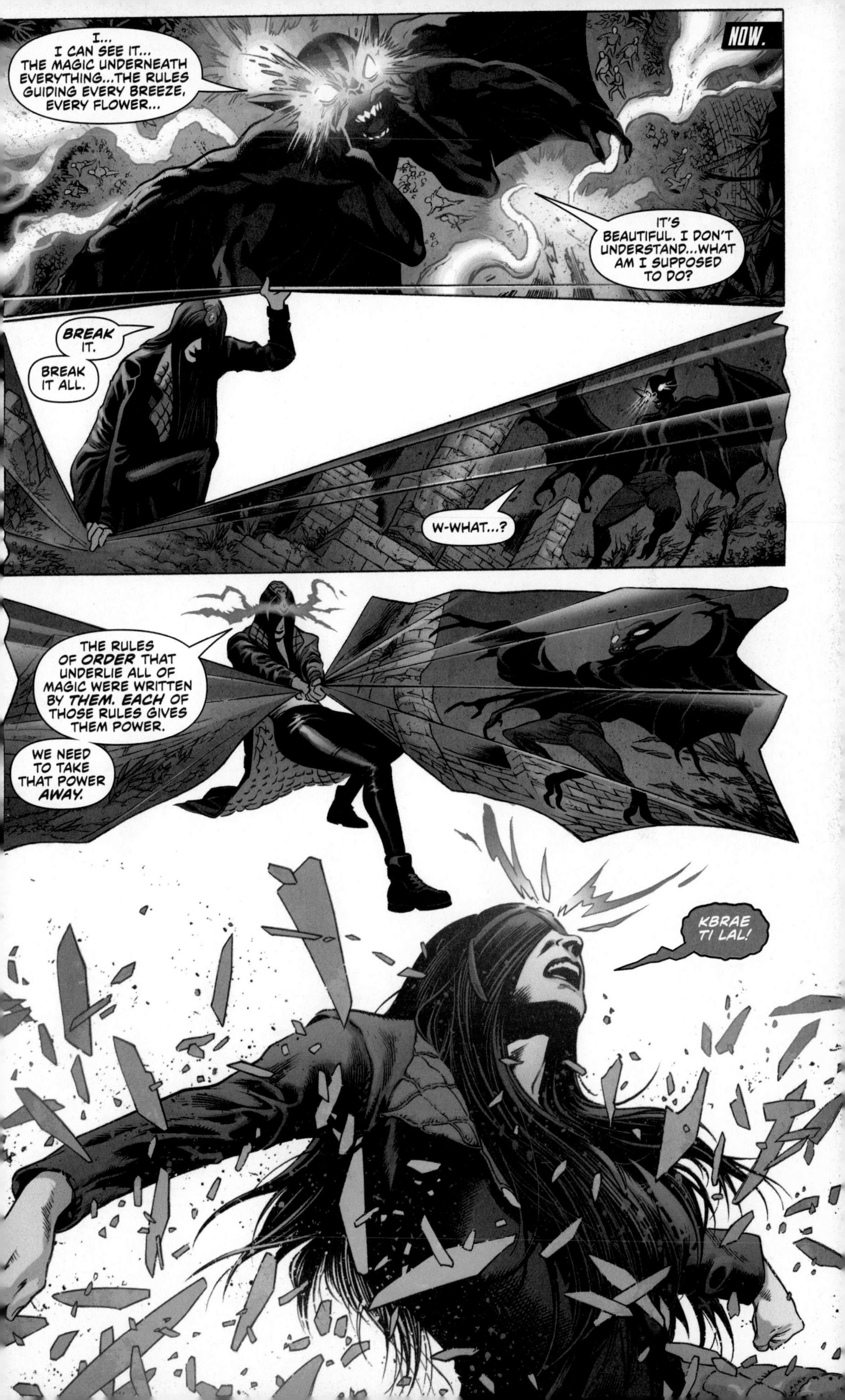
NOW.
I... I CAN SEE IT... THE MAGIC UNDERNEATH EVERYTHING...THE RULES GUIDING EVERY BREEZE, EVERY FLOWER...
IT'S BEAUTIFUL. I DON'T UNDERSTAND...WHAT AM I SUPPOSED TO DO?
BREAK IT.
BREAK IT ALL.
W-WHAT...?
THE RULES OF ORDER THAT UNDERLIE ALL OF MAGIC WERE WRITTEN BY THEM. EACH OF THOSE RULES GIVES THEM POWER.
WE NEED TO TAKE THAT POWER AWAY.
KBRAE TI LAL!

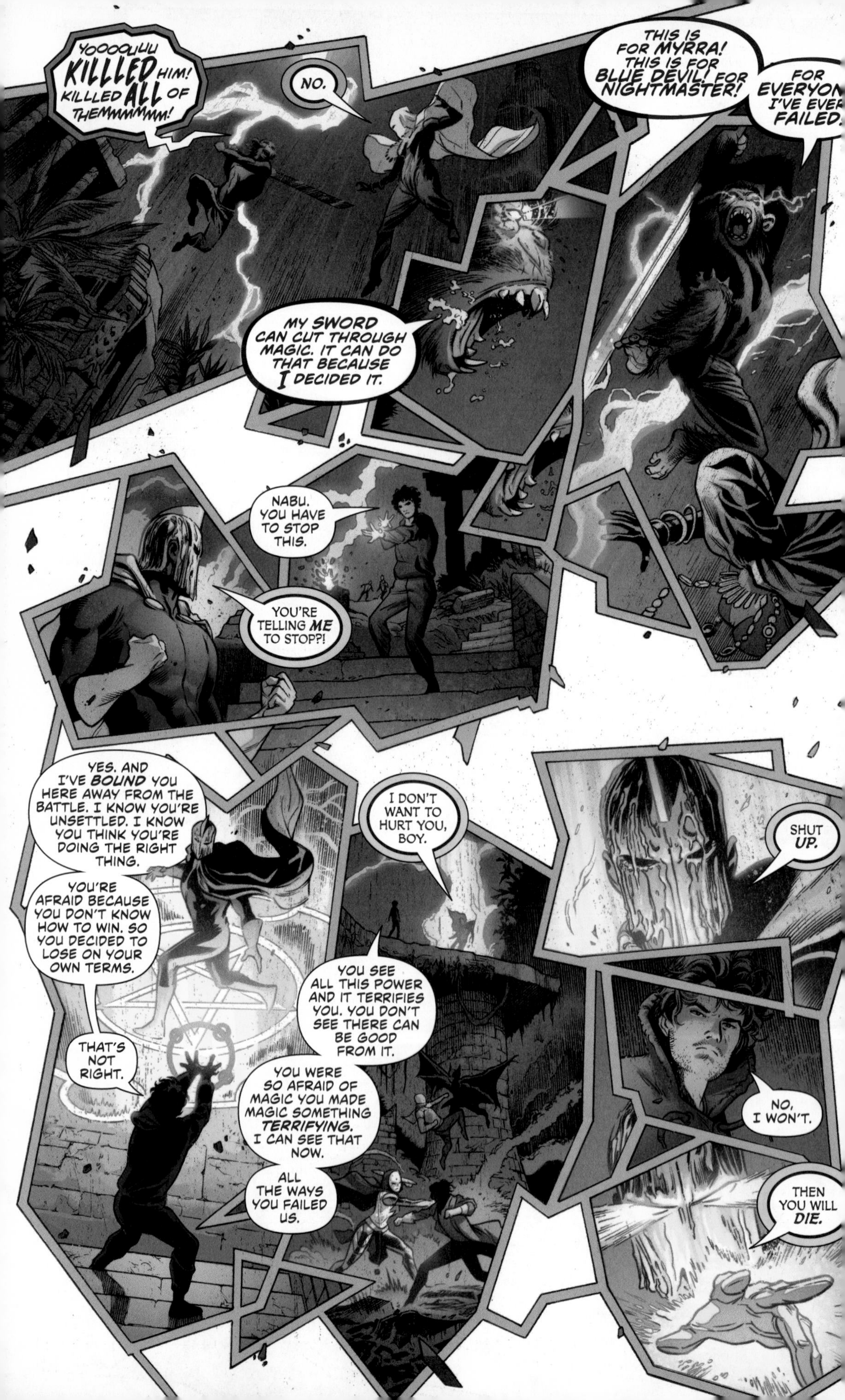
YOOOOUUU KILLED HIM! KILLED ALL OF THEMMMMMM!
NO.
THIS IS FOR MYRRA! THIS IS FOR BLUE DEVIL! FOR NIGHTMASTER!
FOR EVERYON I'VE EVER FAILED!
MY SWORD CAN CUT THROUGH MAGIC. IT CAN DO THAT BECAUSE I DECIDED IT.
NABU. YOU HAVE TO STOP THIS.
YOU'RE TELLING ME TO STOP?!
YES. AND I'VE BOUND YOU HERE AWAY FROM THE BATTLE. I KNOW YOU'RE UNSETTLED. I KNOW YOU THINK YOU'RE DOING THE RIGHT THING.
YOU'RE AFRAID BECAUSE YOU DON'T KNOW HOW TO WIN. SO YOU DECIDED TO LOSE ON YOUR OWN TERMS.
THAT'S NOT RIGHT.
I DON'T WANT TO HURT YOU, BOY.
YOU SEE ALL THIS POWER AND IT TERRIFIES YOU. YOU DON'T SEE THERE CAN BE GOOD FROM IT.
YOU WERE SO AFRAID OF MAGIC YOU MADE MAGIC SOMETHING TERRIFYING. I CAN SEE THAT NOW.
ALL THE WAYS YOU FAILED US.
SHUT UP.
NO, I WON'T.
THEN YOU WILL DIE.

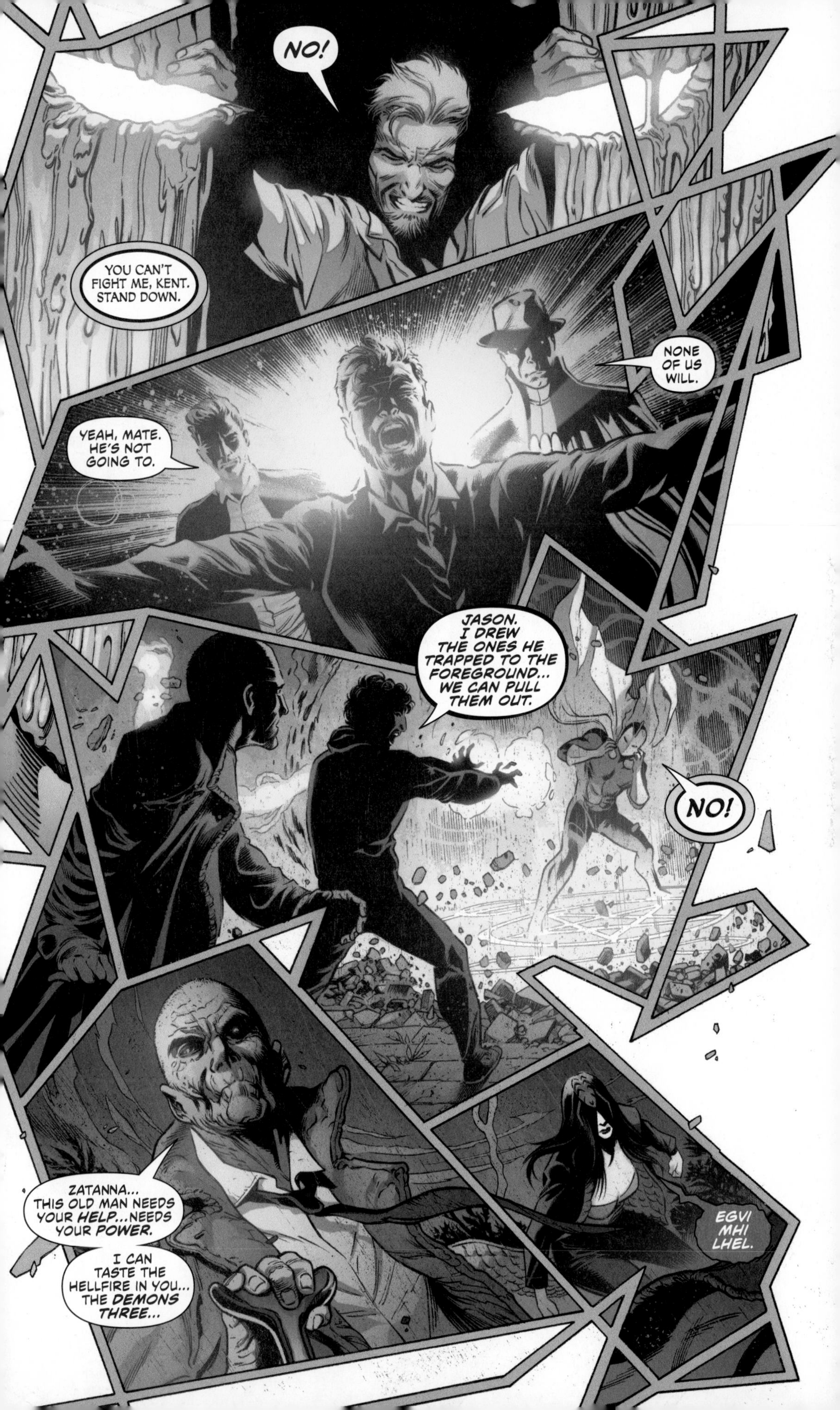
NO!
YOU CAN'T FIGHT ME, KENT. STAND DOWN.
NONE OF US WILL.
YEAH, MATE. HE'S NOT GOING TO.
JASON. I DREW THE ONES HE TRAPPED TO THE FOREGROUND... WE CAN PULL THEM OUT.
NO!
ZATANNA... THIS OLD MAN NEEDS YOUR HELP...NEEDS YOUR POWER.
I CAN TASTE THE HELLFIRE IN YOU... THE DEMONS THREE...
EGVI MHI LHEL.

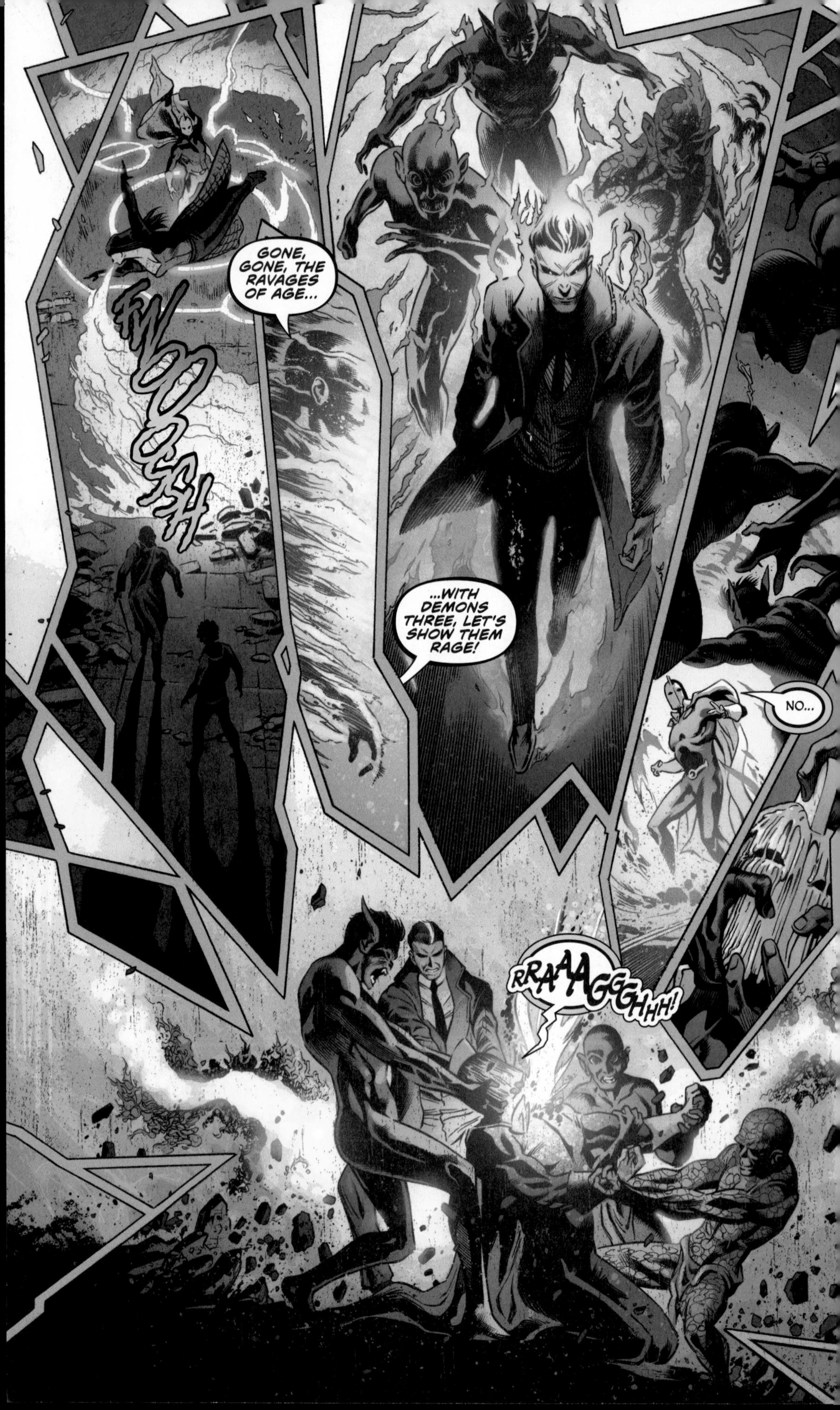
GONE, GONE, THE RAVAGES OF AGE...
FWOOOSH
...WITH DEMONS THREE, LET'S SHOW THEM RAGE!
NO...
RRAAAAGGGHHH!

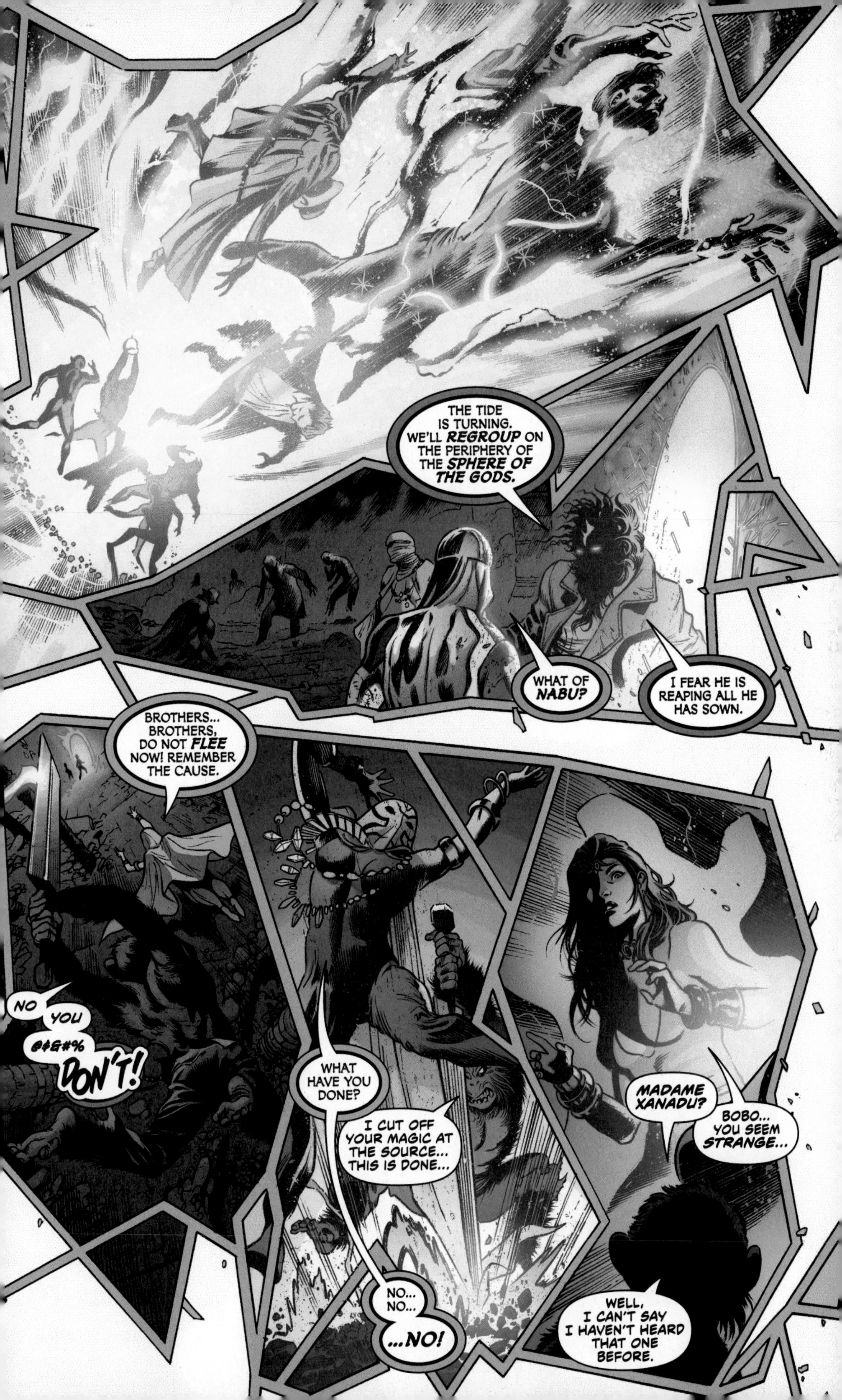
THE TIDE IS TURNING. WE'LL REGROUP ON THE PERIPHERY OF THE SPHERE OF THE GODS.
WHAT OF NABU?
I FEAR HE IS REAPING ALL HE HAS SOWN.
BROTHERS... BROTHERS, DO NOT FLEE NOW! REMEMBER THE CAUSE.
NO YOU @$&#% DON'T!
WHAT HAVE YOU DONE?
I CUT OFF YOUR MAGIC AT THE SOURCE... THIS IS DONE...
NO... NO...
...NO!
MADAME XANADU?
BOBO... YOU SEEM STRANGE...
WELL, I CAN'T SAY I HAVEN'T HEARD THAT ONE BEFORE.

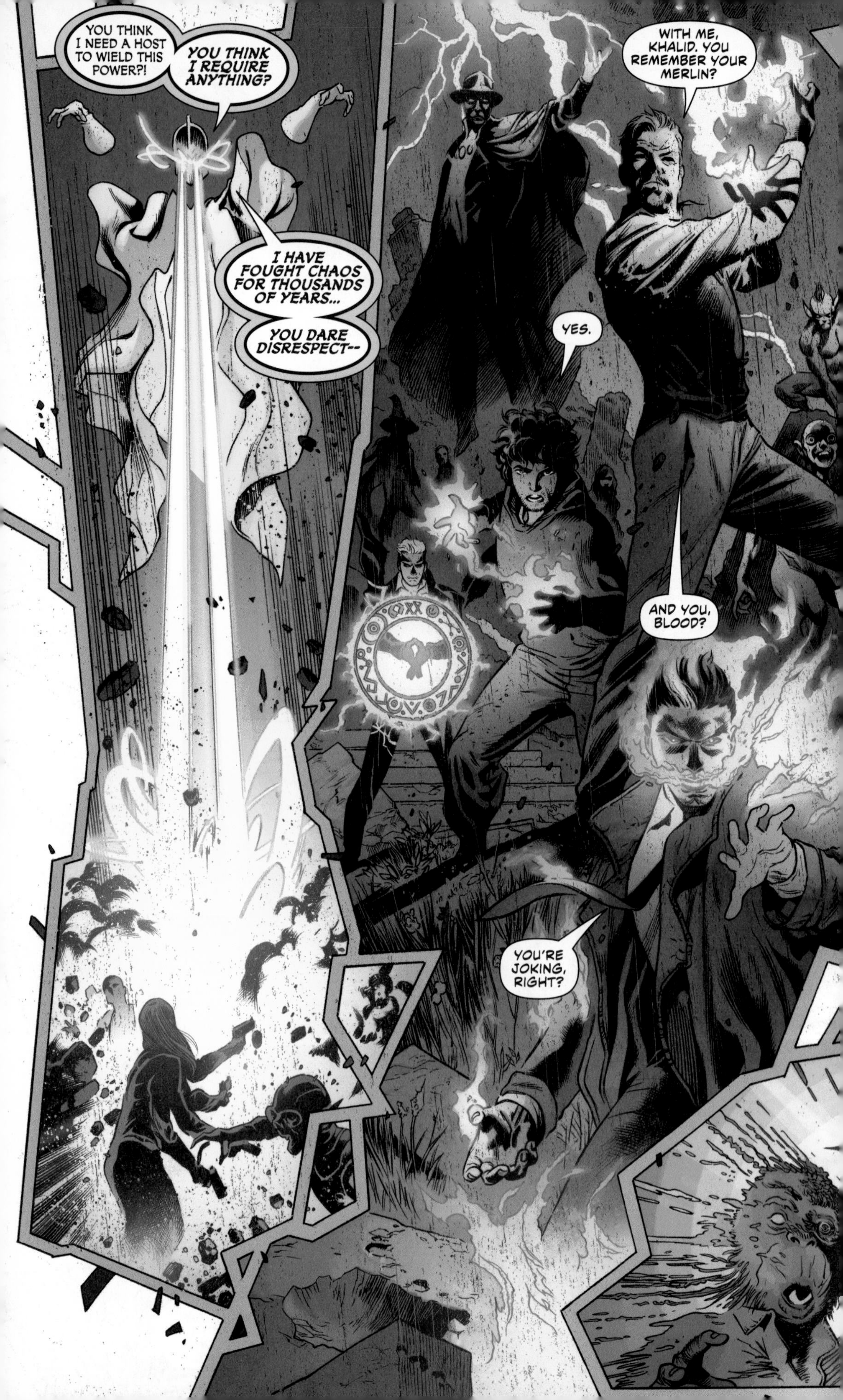

YOU THINK I NEED A HOST TO WIELD THIS POWER?!
YOU THINK I REQUIRE ANYTHING?
I HAVE FOUGHT CHAOS FOR THOUSANDS OF YEARS...
YOU DARE DISRESPECT--
WITH ME, KHALID. YOU REMEMBER YOUR MERLIN?
YES.
AND YOU, BLOOD?
YOU'RE JOKING, RIGHT?

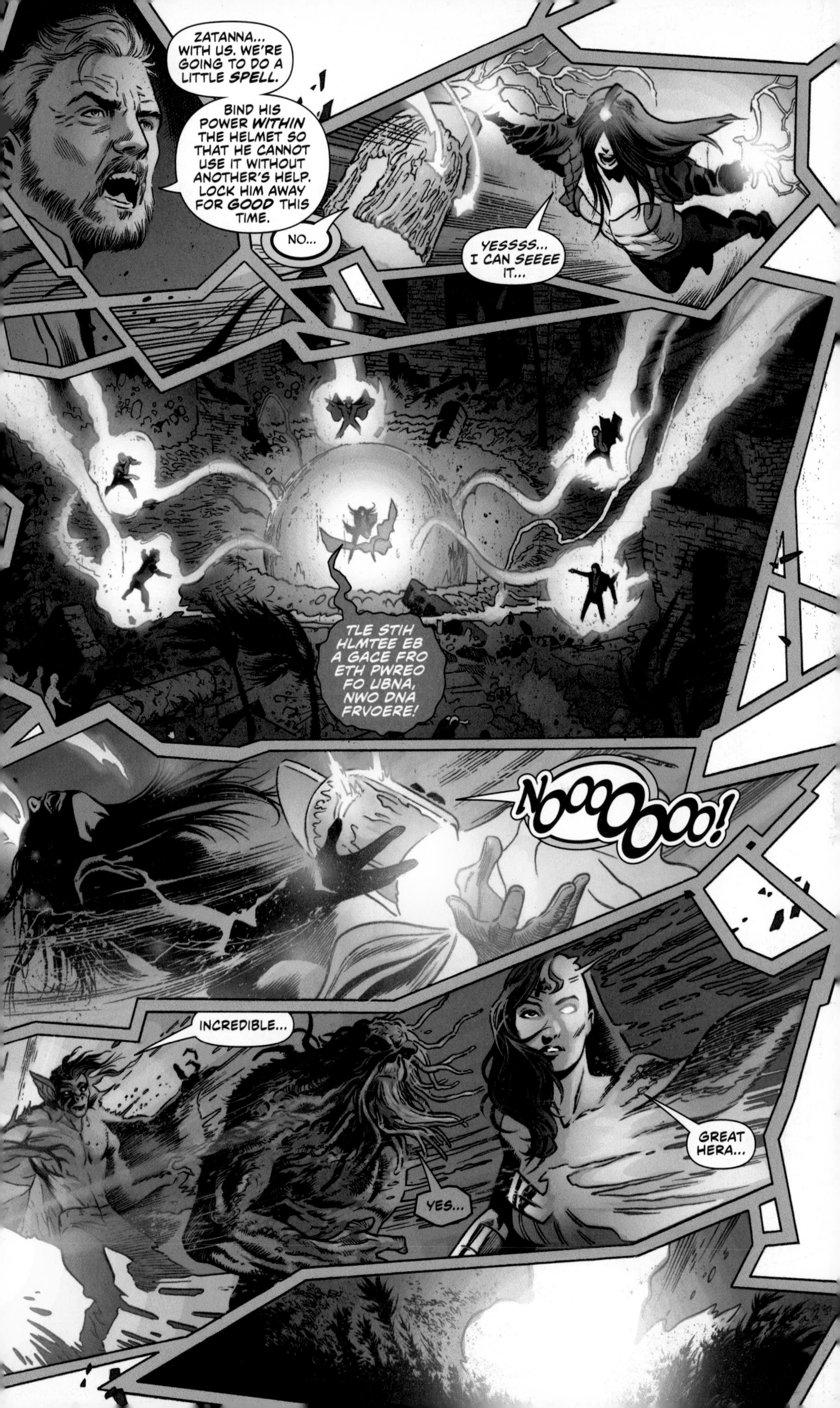

ZATANNA... WITH US. WE'RE GOING TO DO A LITTLE SPELL.
BIND HIS POWER WITHIN THE HELMET SO THAT HE CANNOT USE IT WITHOUT ANOTHER'S HELP. LOCK HIM AWAY FOR GOOD THIS TIME.
NO...
YESSSS... I CAN SEEEE IT...
TLE STIH HLMTEE EB A GACE FRO ETH PWREO FO UBNA, NWO DNA FRVOERE!
NOOOOOOO!
INCREDIBLE...
GREAT HERA...
YES...

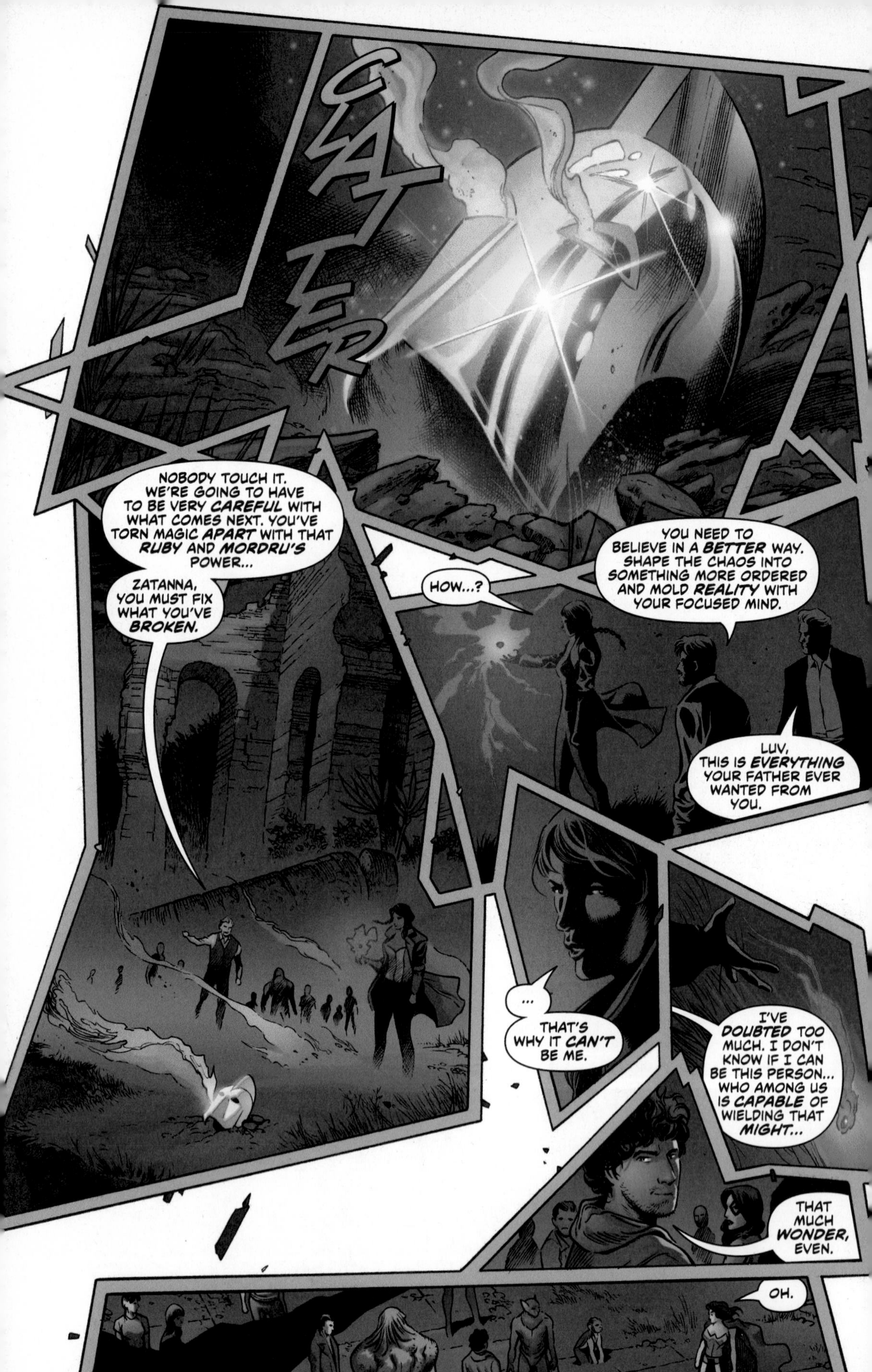
CLATTER
NOBODY TOUCH IT. WE'RE GOING TO HAVE TO BE VERY CAREFUL WITH WHAT COMES NEXT. YOU'VE TORN MAGIC APART WITH THAT RUBY AND MORDRU'S POWER...
ZATANNA, YOU MUST FIX WHAT YOU'VE BROKEN.
HOW...?
YOU NEED TO BELIEVE IN A BETTER WAY. SHAPE THE CHAOS INTO SOMETHING MORE ORDERED AND MOLD REALITY WITH YOUR FOCUSED MIND.
LUV, THIS IS EVERYTHING YOUR FATHER EVER WANTED FROM YOU.
... THAT'S WHY IT CAN'T BE ME.
I'VE DOUBTED TOO MUCH. I DON'T KNOW IF I CAN BE THIS PERSON... WHO AMONG US IS CAPABLE OF WIELDING THAT MIGHT...
THAT MUCH WONDER, EVEN.
OH.

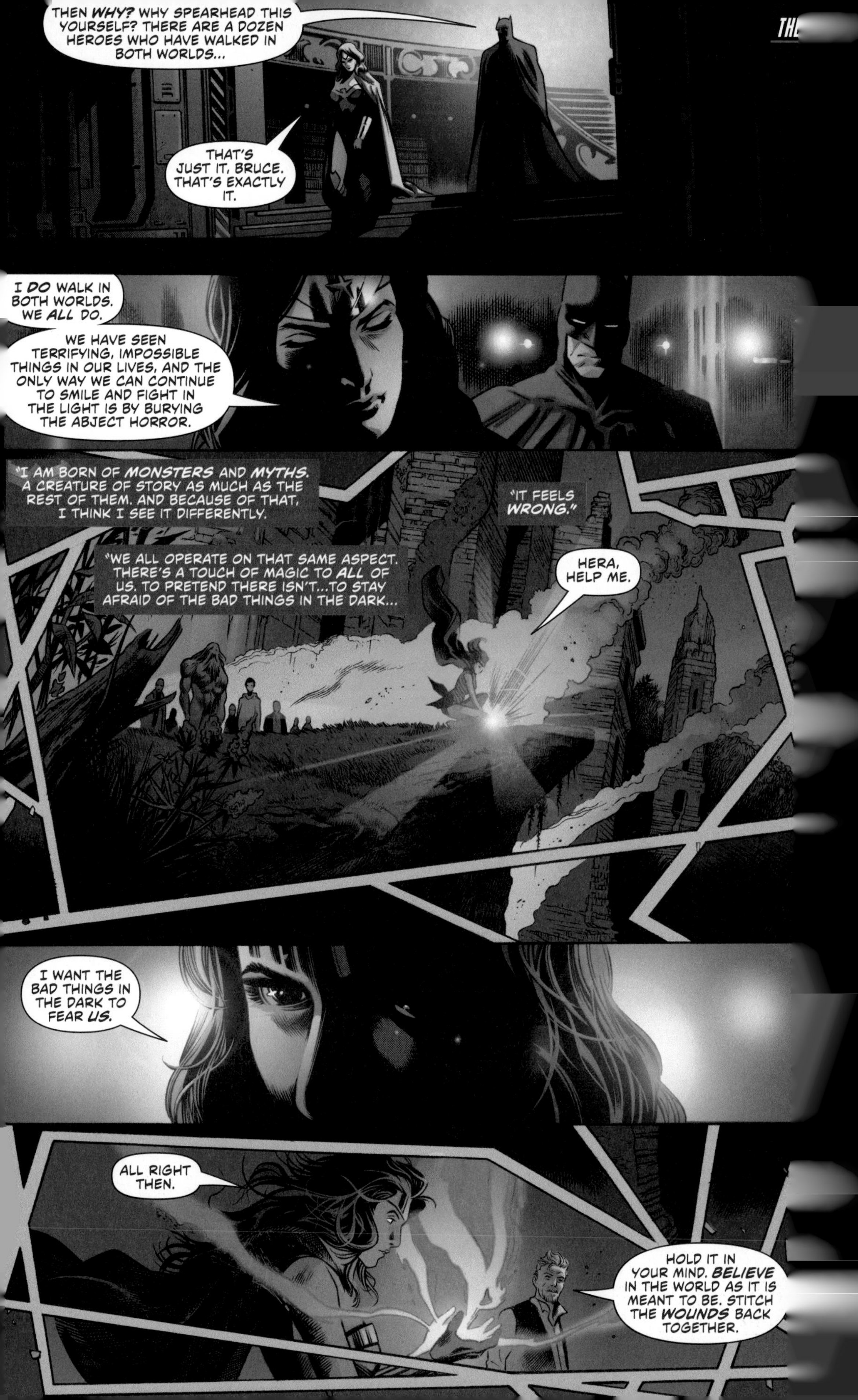
THEN WHY? WHY SPEARHEAD THIS YOURSELF? THERE ARE A DOZEN HEROES WHO HAVE WALKED IN BOTH WORLDS...
THAT'S JUST IT, BRUCE. THAT'S EXACTLY IT.
I DO WALK IN BOTH WORLDS. WE ALL DO.
WE HAVE SEEN TERRIFYING, IMPOSSIBLE THINGS IN OUR LIVES, AND THE ONLY WAY WE CAN CONTINUE TO SMILE AND FIGHT IN THE LIGHT IS BY BURYING THE ABJECT HORROR.
"I AM BORN OF MONSTERS AND MYTHS. A CREATURE OF STORY AS MUCH AS THE REST OF THEM. AND BECAUSE OF THAT, I THINK I SEE IT DIFFERENTLY.
"IT FEELS WRONG."
"WE ALL OPERATE ON THAT SAME ASPECT. THERE'S A TOUCH OF MAGIC TO ALL OF US. TO PRETEND THERE ISN'T...TO STAY AFRAID OF THE BAD THINGS IN THE DARK...
HERA, HELP ME.
I WANT THE BAD THINGS IN THE DARK TO FEAR US.
ALL RIGHT THEN.
HOLD IT IN YOUR MIND. BELIEVE IN THE WORLD AS IT IS MEANT TO BE. STITCH THE WOUNDS BACK TOGETHER.

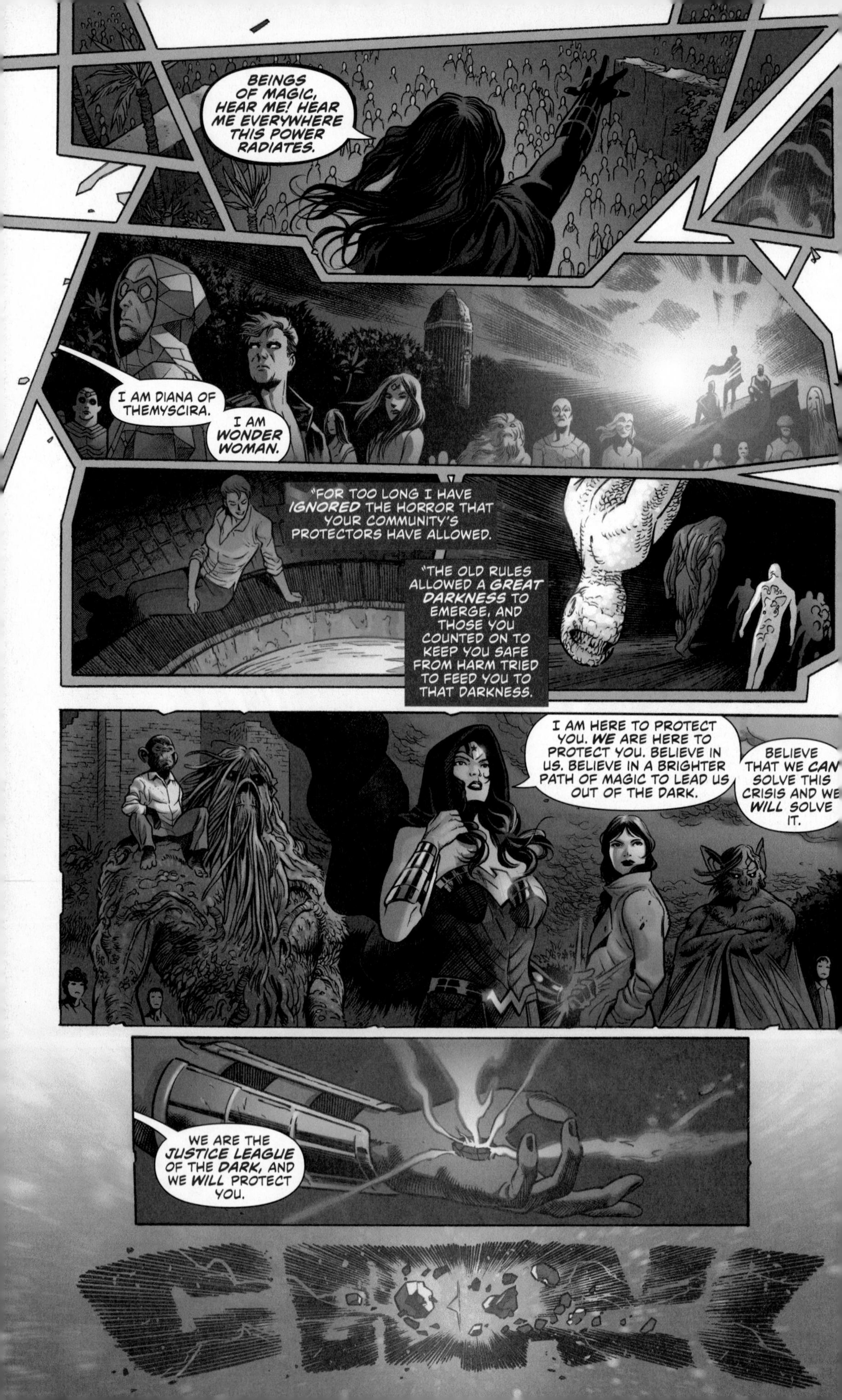

BEINGS OF MAGIC, HEAR ME! HEAR ME EVERYWHERE THIS POWER RADIATES.
I AM DIANA OF THEMYSCIRA.
I AM WONDER WOMAN.
"FOR TOO LONG I HAVE IGNORED THE HORROR THAT YOUR COMMUNITY'S PROTECTORS HAVE ALLOWED.
"THE OLD RULES ALLOWED A GREAT DARKNESS TO EMERGE, AND THOSE YOU COUNTED ON TO KEEP YOU SAFE FROM HARM TRIED TO FEED YOU TO THAT DARKNESS.
I AM HERE TO PROTECT YOU. WE ARE HERE TO PROTECT YOU. BELIEVE IN US. BELIEVE IN A BRIGHTER PATH OF MAGIC TO LEAD US OUT OF THE DARK.
BELIEVE THAT WE CAN SOLVE THIS CRISIS AND WE WILL SOLVE IT.
WE ARE THE JUSTICE LEAGUE OF THE DARK, AND WE WILL PROTECT YOU.

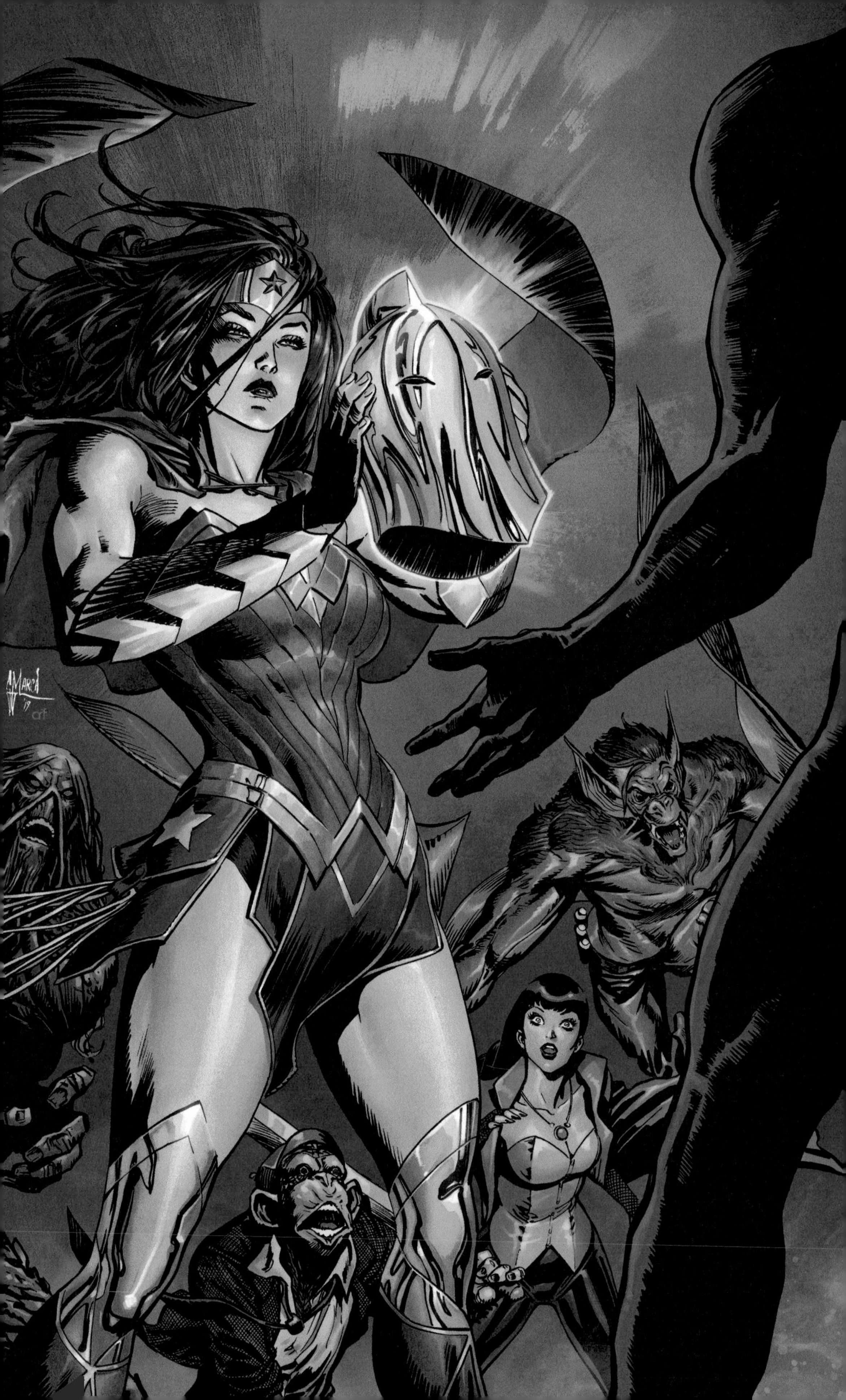

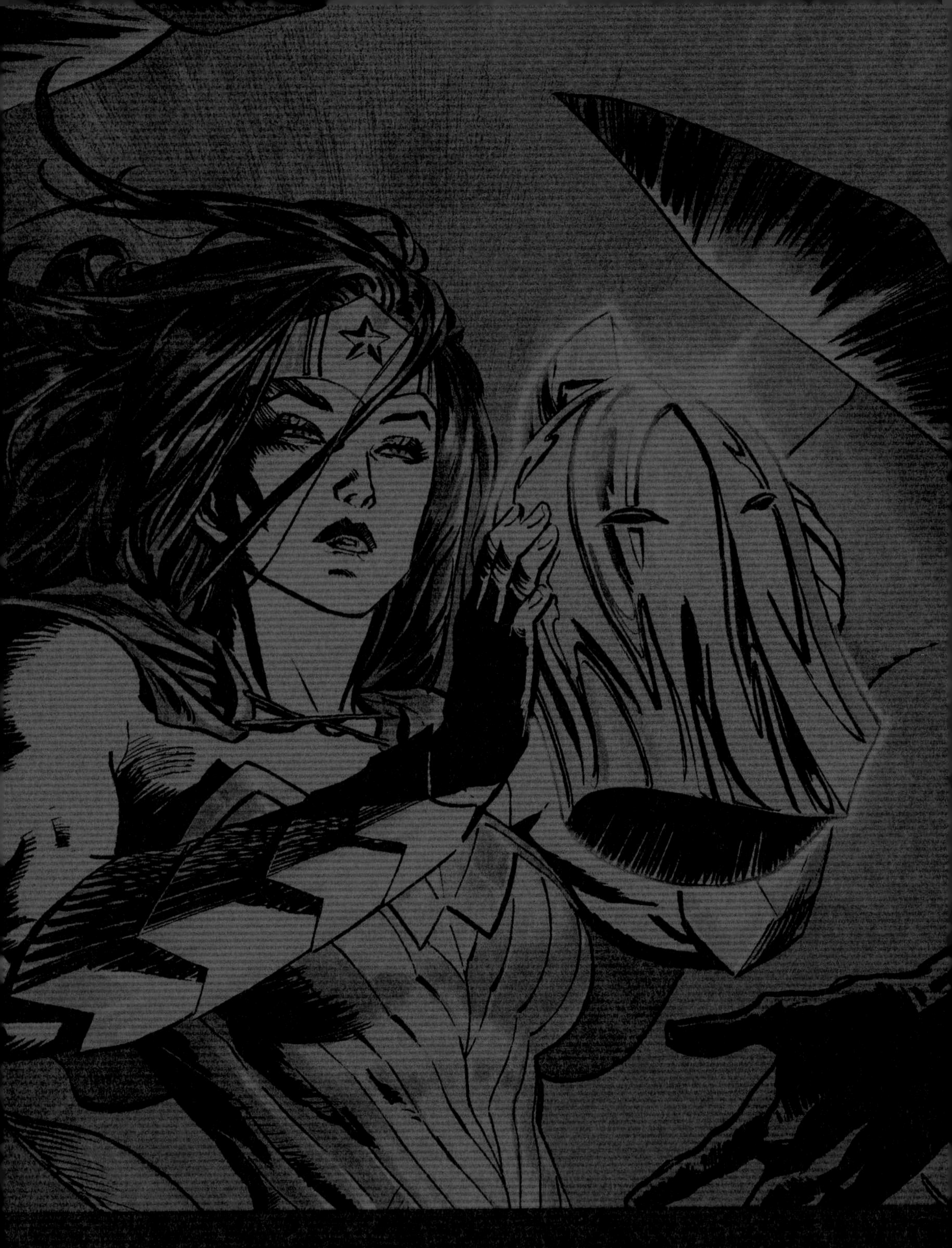

JUSTICE LEAGUE DARK

#13

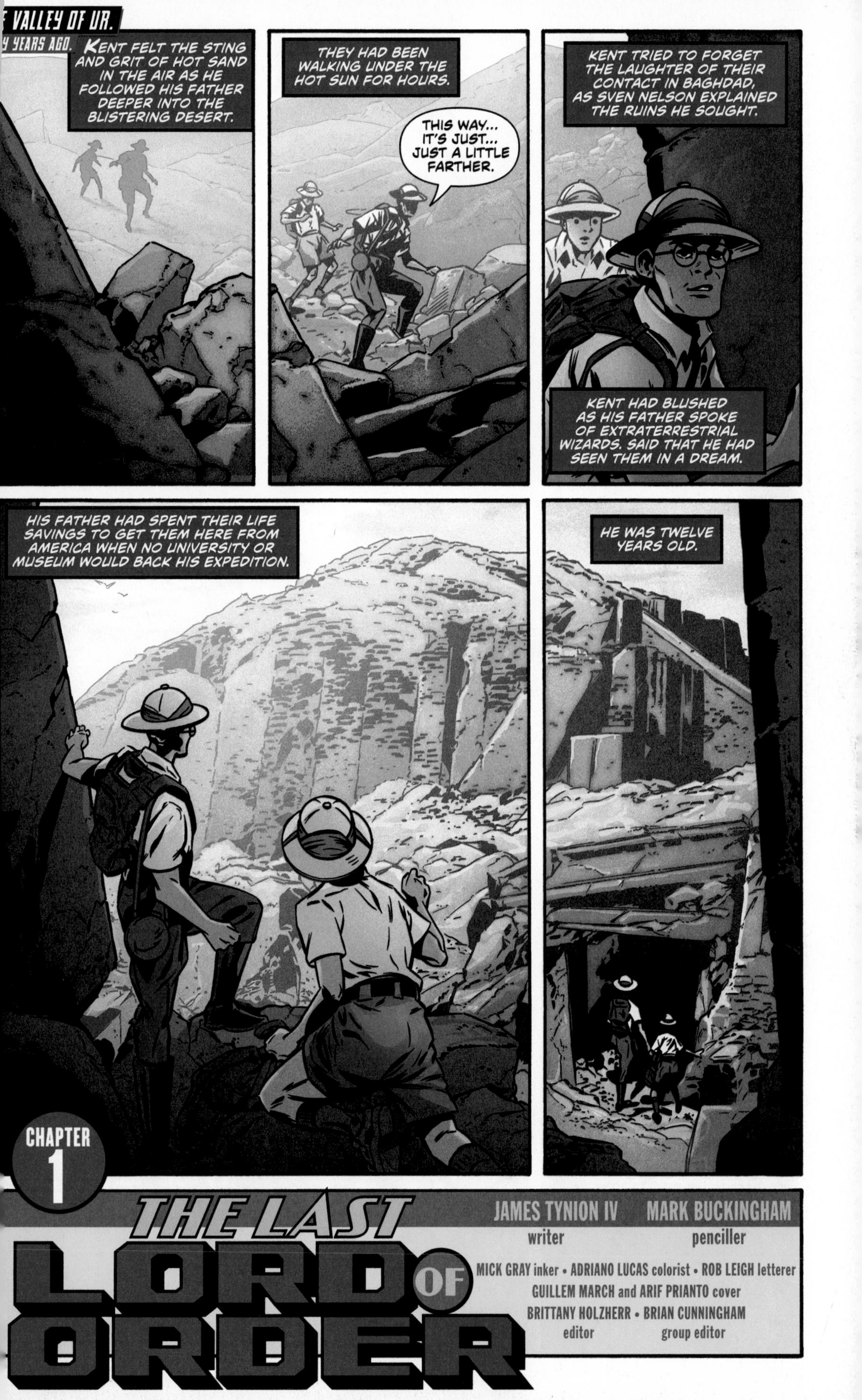

VALLEY OF UR.
YEARS AGO.
KENT FELT THE STING AND GRIT OF HOT SAND IN THE AIR AS HE FOLLOWED HIS FATHER DEEPER INTO THE BLISTERING DESERT.
THEY HAD BEEN WALKING UNDER THE HOT SUN FOR HOURS.
THIS WAY... IT'S JUST... JUST A LITTLE FARTHER.
KENT TRIED TO FORGET THE LAUGHTER OF THEIR CONTACT IN BAGHDAD, AS SVEN NELSON EXPLAINED THE RUINS HE SOUGHT.
KENT HAD BLUSHED AS HIS FATHER SPOKE OF EXTRATERRESTRIAL WIZARDS. SAID THAT HE HAD SEEN THEM IN A DREAM.
HIS FATHER HAD SPENT THEIR LIFE SAVINGS TO GET THEM HERE FROM AMERICA WHEN NO UNIVERSITY OR MUSEUM WOULD BACK HIS EXPEDITION.
HE WAS TWELVE YEARS OLD.
CHAPTER 1
THE LAST LORD OF ORDER
JAMES TYNION IV writer
MARK BUCKINGHAM penciller
MICK GRAY inker • ADRIANO LUCAS colorist • ROB LEIGH letterer
GUILLEM MARCH and ARIF PRIANTO cover
BRITTANY HOLZHERR • BRIAN CUNNINGHAM
editor group editor

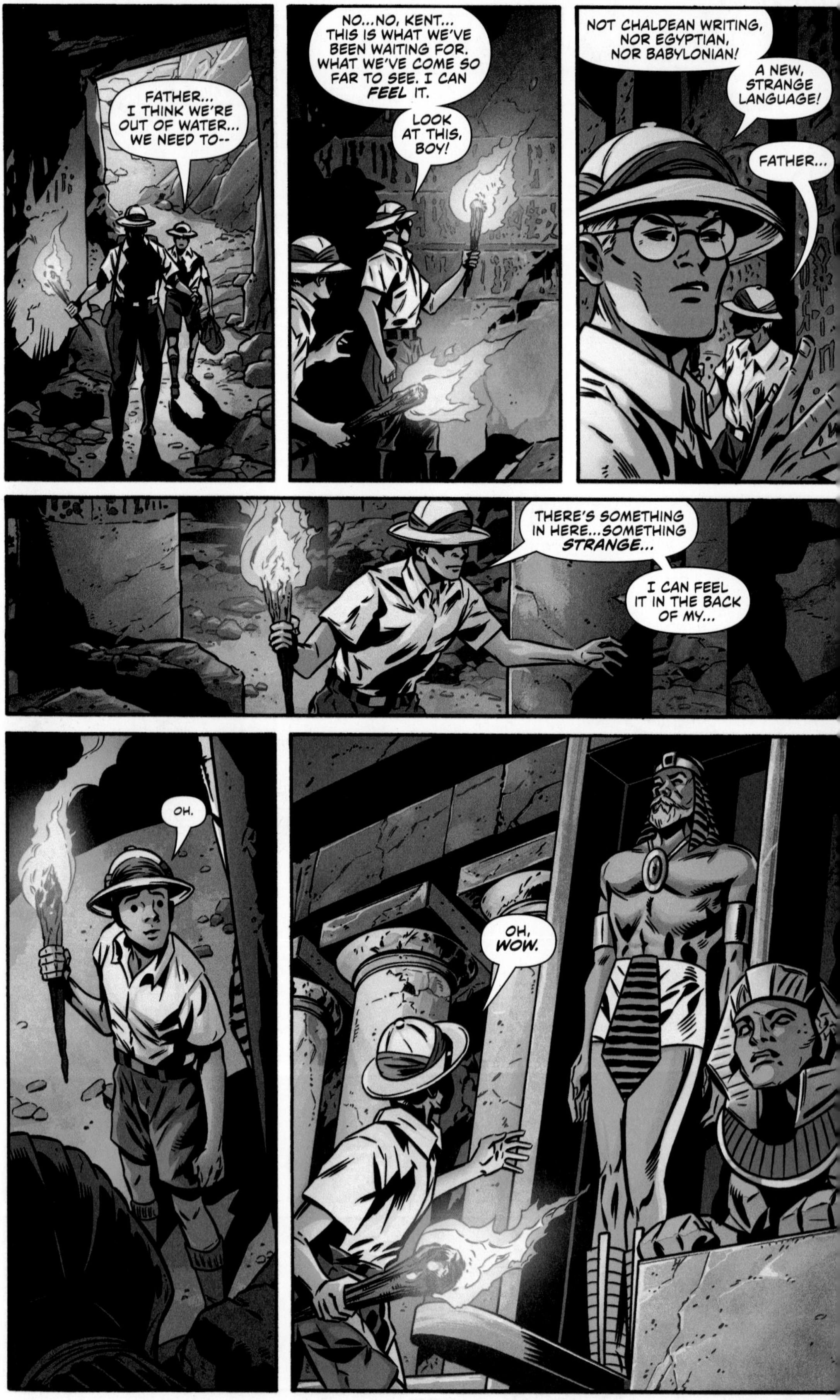

FATHER... I THINK WE'RE OUT OF WATER... WE NEED TO--
NO...NO, KENT... THIS IS WHAT WE'VE BEEN WAITING FOR. WHAT WE'VE COME SO FAR TO SEE. I CAN FEEL IT.
LOOK AT THIS, BOY!
NOT CHALDEAN WRITING, NOR EGYPTIAN, NOR BABYLONIAN!
A NEW, STRANGE LANGUAGE!
FATHER...
THERE'S SOMETHING IN HERE...SOMETHING STRANGE...
I CAN FEEL IT IN THE BACK OF MY...
OH.
OH, WOW.

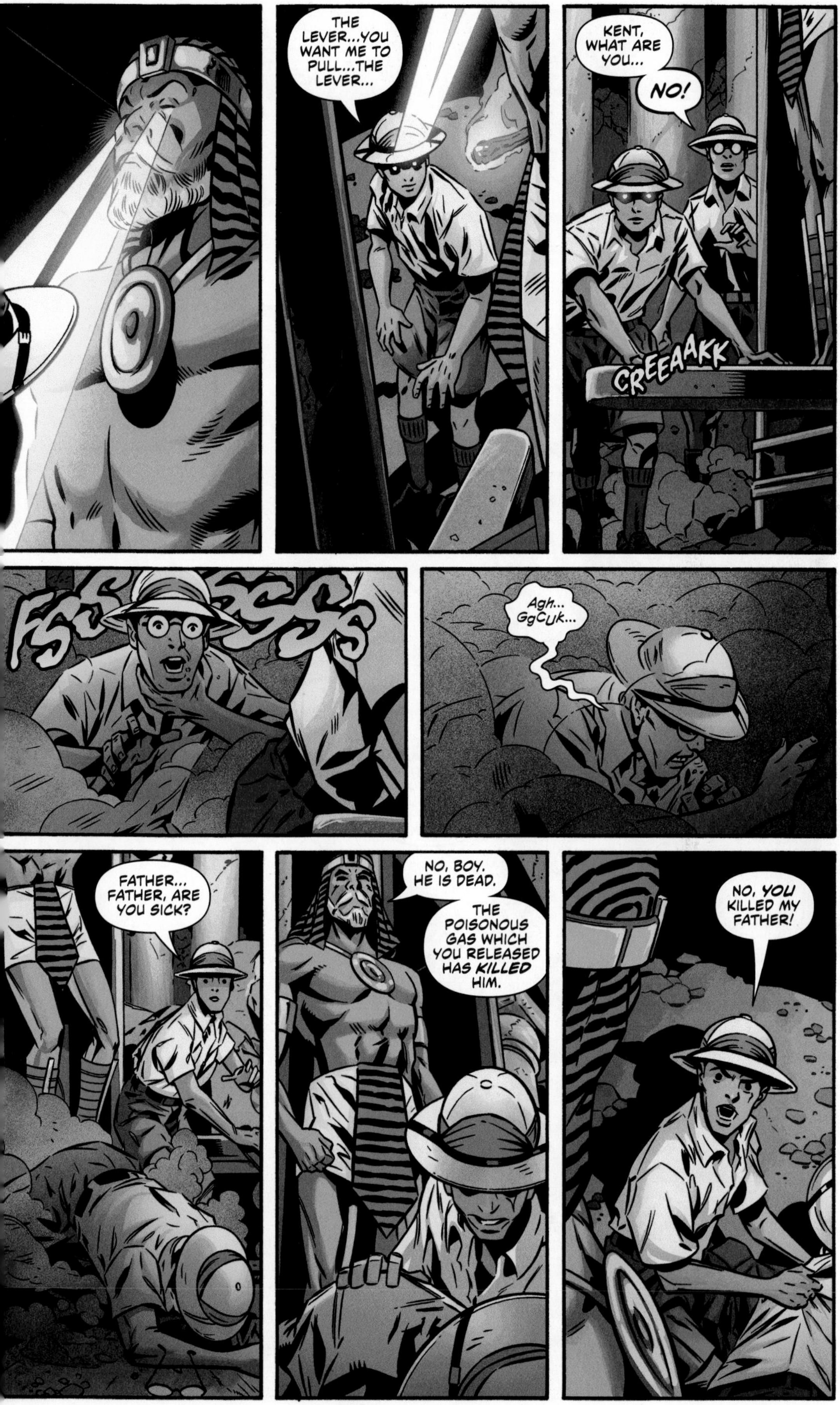
THE LEVER...YOU WANT ME TO PULL...THE LEVER...
KENT, WHAT ARE YOU...
NO!
CREEAAKK
Agh... GgCUK...
FATHER... FATHER, ARE YOU SICK?
NO, BOY. HE IS DEAD.
THE POISONOUS GAS WHICH YOU RELEASED HAS KILLED HIM.
NO, YOU KILLED MY FATHER!

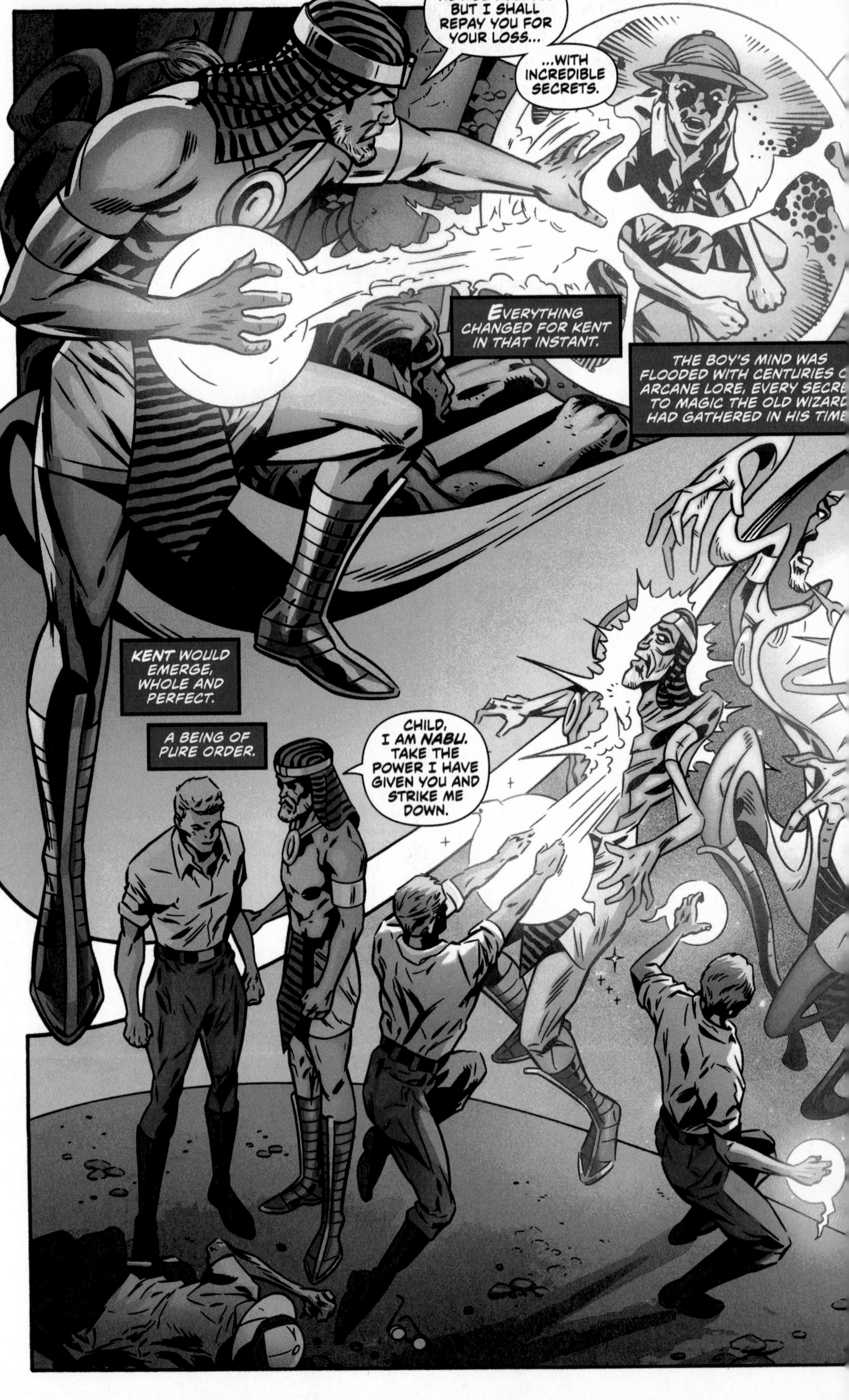
IT COULD NOT BE HELPED, BUT I SHALL REPAY YOU FOR YOUR LOSS...
...WITH INCREDIBLE SECRETS.
EVERYTHING CHANGED FOR KENT IN THAT INSTANT.
THE BOY'S MIND WAS FLOODED WITH CENTURIES OF ARCANE LORE, EVERY SECRET TO MAGIC THE OLD WIZARD HAD GATHERED IN HIS TIME.
KENT WOULD EMERGE, WHOLE AND PERFECT.
A BEING OF PURE ORDER.
CHILD, I AM NABU. TAKE THE POWER I HAVE GIVEN YOU AND STRIKE ME DOWN.

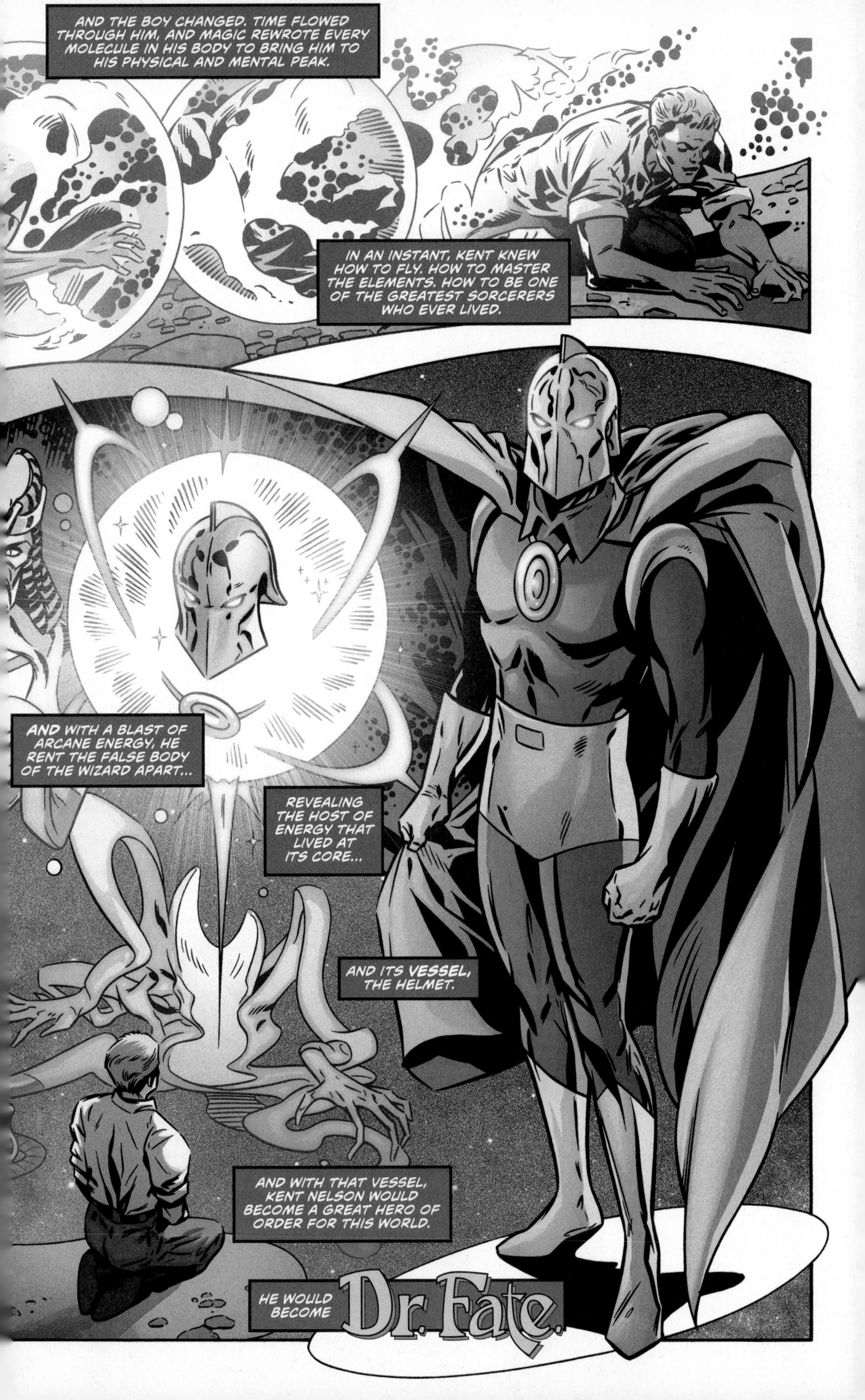
AND THE BOY CHANGED. TIME FLOWED THROUGH HIM, AND MAGIC REWROTE EVERY MOLECULE IN HIS BODY TO BRING HIM TO HIS PHYSICAL AND MENTAL PEAK.
IN AN INSTANT, KENT KNEW HOW TO FLY. HOW TO MASTER THE ELEMENTS. HOW TO BE ONE OF THE GREATEST SORCERERS WHO EVER LIVED.
AND WITH A BLAST OF ARCANE ENERGY, HE RENT THE FALSE BODY OF THE WIZARD APART...
REVEALING THE HOST OF ENERGY THAT LIVED AT ITS CORE...
AND ITS VESSEL, THE HELMET.
AND WITH THAT VESSEL, KENT NELSON WOULD BECOME A GREAT HERO OF ORDER FOR THIS WORLD.
HE WOULD BECOME
Dr. Fate.

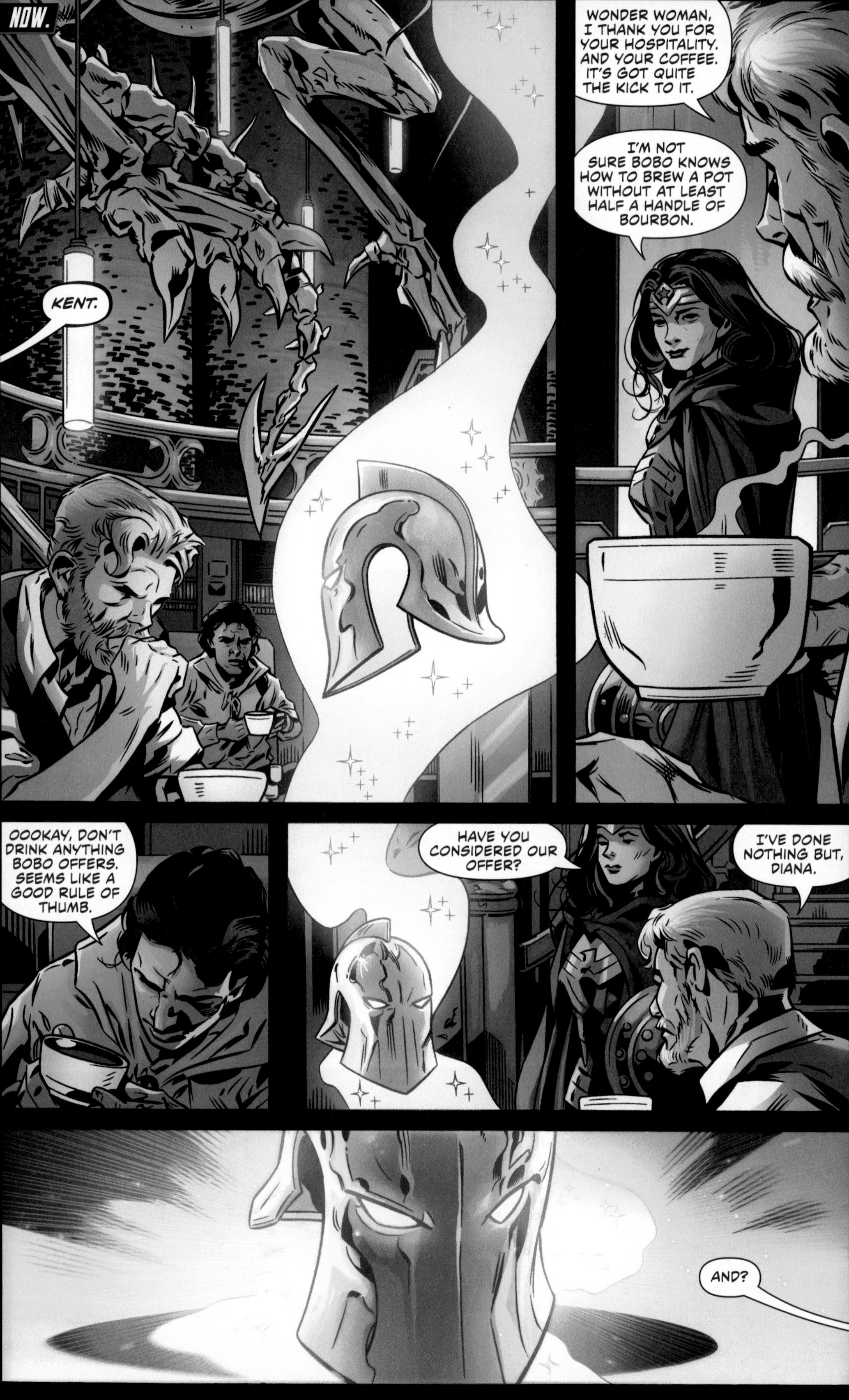
NOW.
KENT.
WONDER WOMAN, I THANK YOU FOR YOUR HOSPITALITY. AND YOUR COFFEE. IT'S GOT QUITE THE KICK TO IT.
I'M NOT SURE BOBO KNOWS HOW TO BREW A POT WITHOUT AT LEAST HALF A HANDLE OF BOURBON.
OOOKAY, DON'T DRINK ANYTHING BOBO OFFERS. SEEMS LIKE A GOOD RULE OF THUMB.
HAVE YOU CONSIDERED OUR OFFER?
I'VE DONE NOTHING BUT, DIANA.
AND?

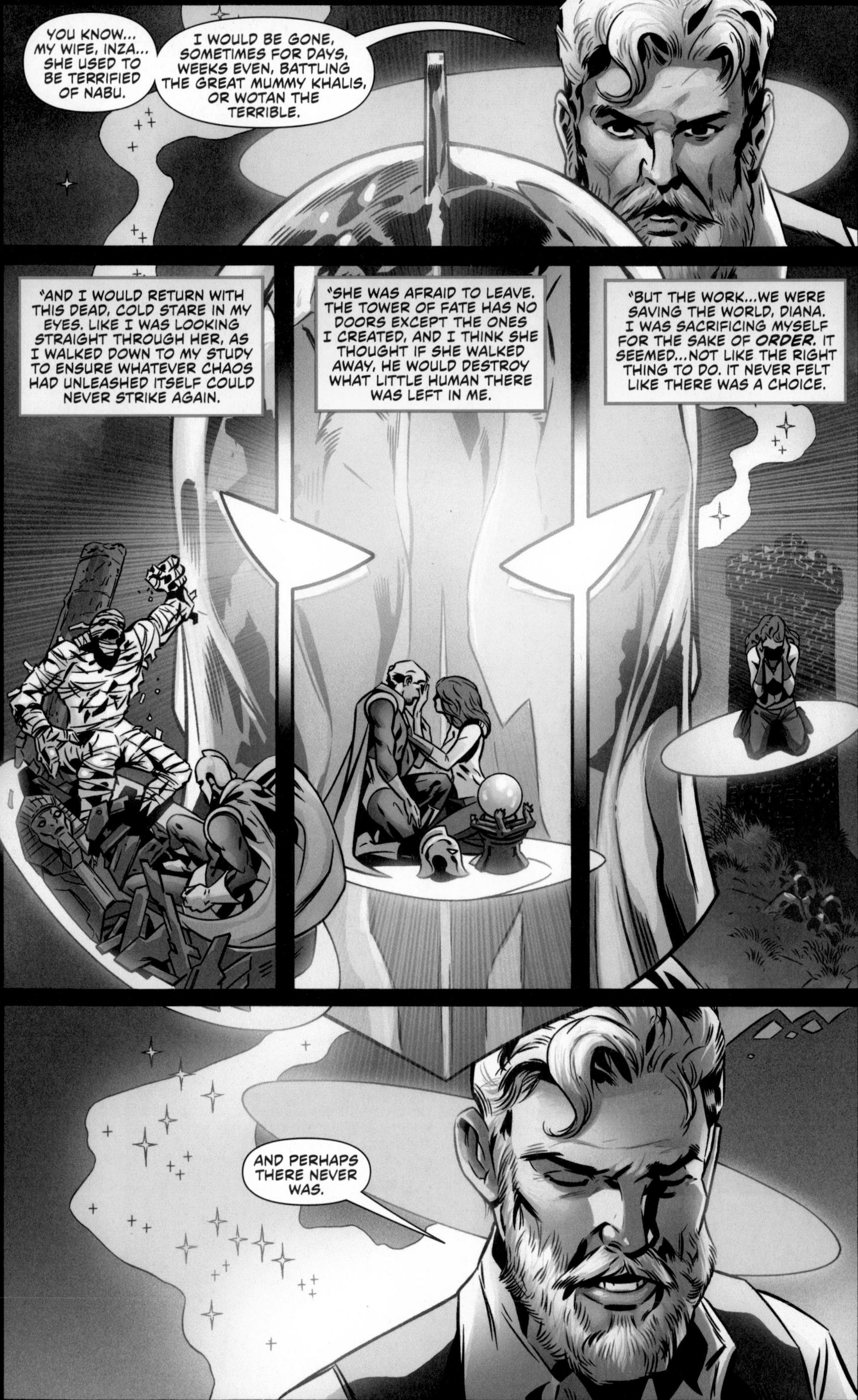
YOU KNOW... MY WIFE, INZA... SHE USED TO BE TERRIFIED OF NABU.
I WOULD BE GONE, SOMETIMES FOR DAYS, WEEKS EVEN, BATTLING THE GREAT MUMMY KHALIS, OR WOTAN THE TERRIBLE.
"AND I WOULD RETURN WITH THIS DEAD, COLD STARE IN MY EYES. LIKE I WAS LOOKING STRAIGHT THROUGH HER, AS I WALKED DOWN TO MY STUDY TO ENSURE WHATEVER CHAOS HAD UNLEASHED ITSELF COULD NEVER STRIKE AGAIN.
"SHE WAS AFRAID TO LEAVE. THE TOWER OF FATE HAS NO DOORS EXCEPT THE ONES I CREATED, AND I THINK SHE THOUGHT IF SHE WALKED AWAY, HE WOULD DESTROY WHAT LITTLE HUMAN THERE WAS LEFT IN ME.
"BUT THE WORK...WE WERE SAVING THE WORLD, DIANA. I WAS SACRIFICING MYSELF FOR THE SAKE OF *ORDER*. IT SEEMED...NOT LIKE THE RIGHT THING TO DO. IT NEVER FELT LIKE THERE WAS A CHOICE.
AND PERHAPS THERE NEVER WAS.

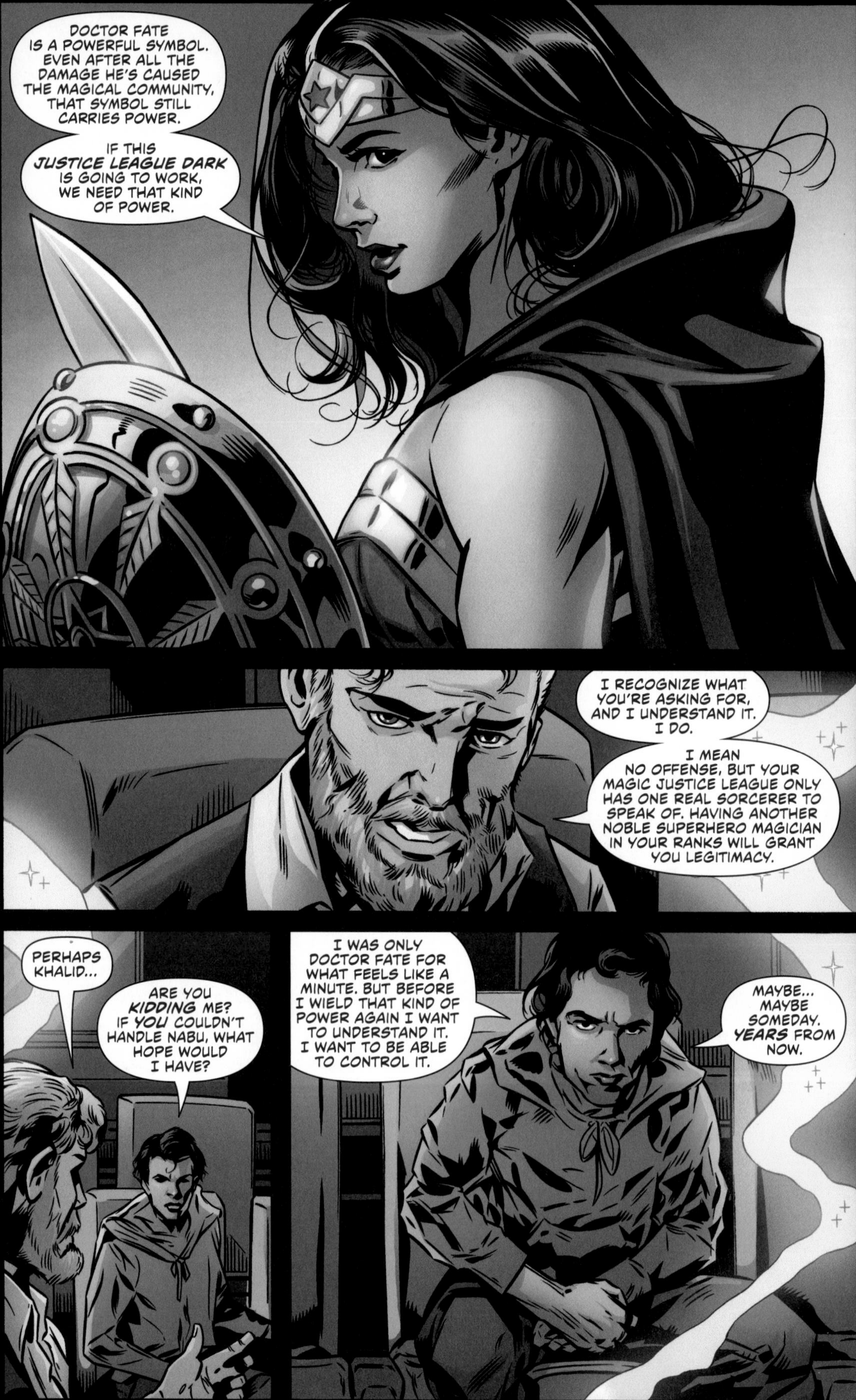
DOCTOR FATE IS A POWERFUL SYMBOL. EVEN AFTER ALL THE DAMAGE HE'S CAUSED THE MAGICAL COMMUNITY, THAT SYMBOL STILL CARRIES POWER.
IF THIS *JUSTICE LEAGUE DARK* IS GOING TO WORK, WE NEED THAT KIND OF POWER.
I RECOGNIZE WHAT YOU'RE ASKING FOR, AND I UNDERSTAND IT. I DO.
I MEAN NO OFFENSE, BUT YOUR MAGIC JUSTICE LEAGUE ONLY HAS ONE REAL SORCERER TO SPEAK OF. HAVING ANOTHER NOBLE SUPERHERO MAGICIAN IN YOUR RANKS WILL GRANT YOU LEGITIMACY.
PERHAPS KHALID...
ARE YOU ***KIDDING*** ME? IF ***YOU*** COULDN'T HANDLE NABU, WHAT HOPE WOULD I HAVE?
I WAS ONLY DOCTOR FATE FOR WHAT FEELS LIKE A MINUTE. BUT BEFORE I WIELD THAT KIND OF POWER AGAIN I WANT TO UNDERSTAND IT. I WANT TO BE ABLE TO CONTROL IT.
MAYBE... MAYBE SOMEDAY. ***YEARS*** FROM NOW.

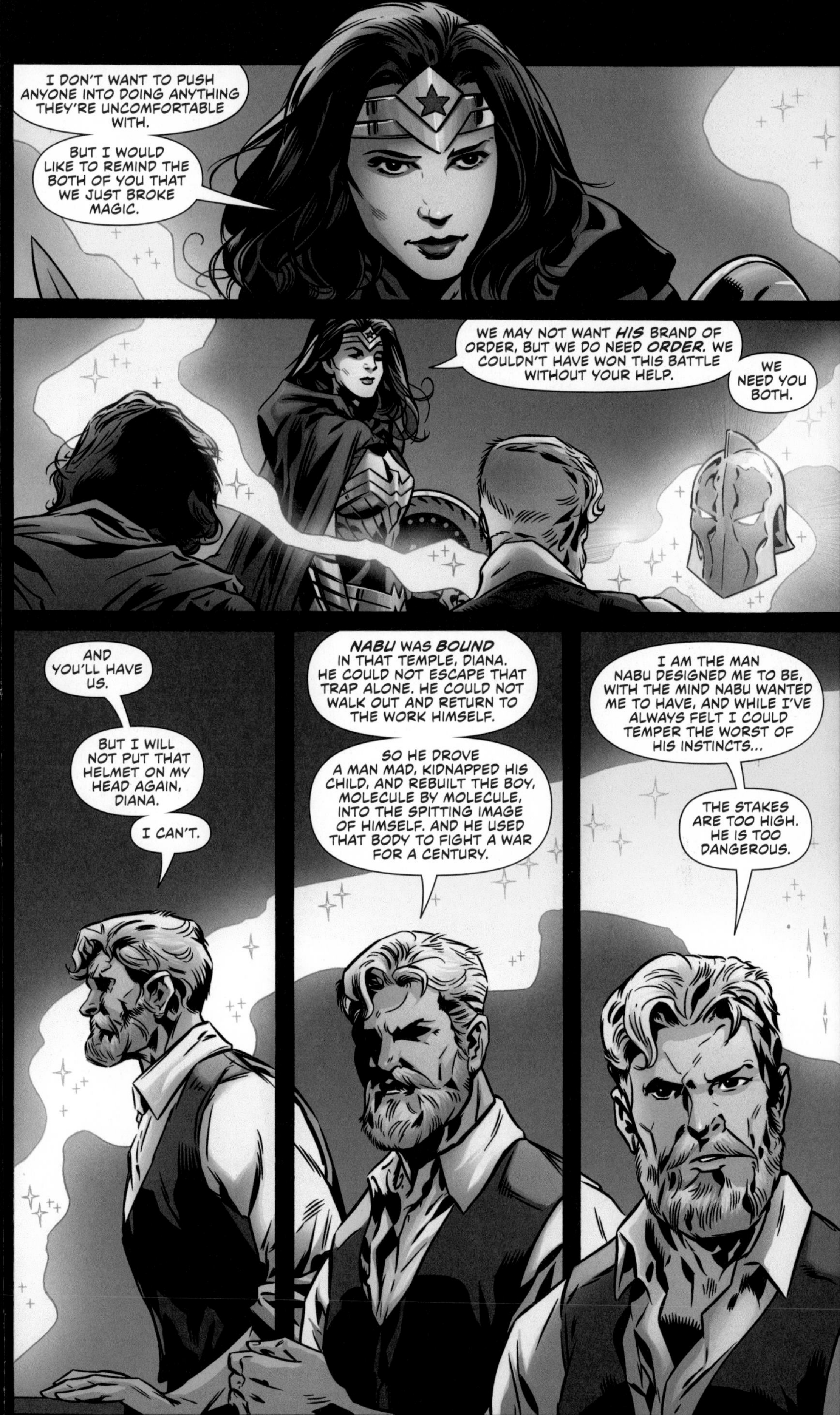
I DON'T WANT TO PUSH ANYONE INTO DOING ANYTHING THEY'RE UNCOMFORTABLE WITH.
BUT I WOULD LIKE TO REMIND THE BOTH OF YOU THAT WE JUST BROKE MAGIC.
WE MAY NOT WANT *HIS* BRAND OF ORDER, BUT WE DO NEED *ORDER*. WE COULDN'T HAVE WON THIS BATTLE WITHOUT YOUR HELP.
WE NEED YOU BOTH.
AND YOU'LL HAVE US.
BUT I WILL NOT PUT THAT HELMET ON MY HEAD AGAIN, DIANA.
I CAN'T.
NABU WAS *BOUND* IN THAT TEMPLE, DIANA. HE COULD NOT ESCAPE THAT TRAP ALONE. HE COULD NOT WALK OUT AND RETURN TO THE WORK HIMSELF.
SO HE DROVE A MAN MAD, KIDNAPPED HIS CHILD, AND REBUILT THE BOY, MOLECULE BY MOLECULE, INTO THE SPITTING IMAGE OF HIMSELF. AND HE USED THAT BODY TO FIGHT A WAR FOR A CENTURY.
I AM THE MAN NABU DESIGNED ME TO BE, WITH THE MIND NABU WANTED ME TO HAVE, AND WHILE I'VE ALWAYS FELT I COULD TEMPER THE WORST OF HIS INSTINCTS...
THE STAKES ARE TOO HIGH. HE IS TOO DANGEROUS.

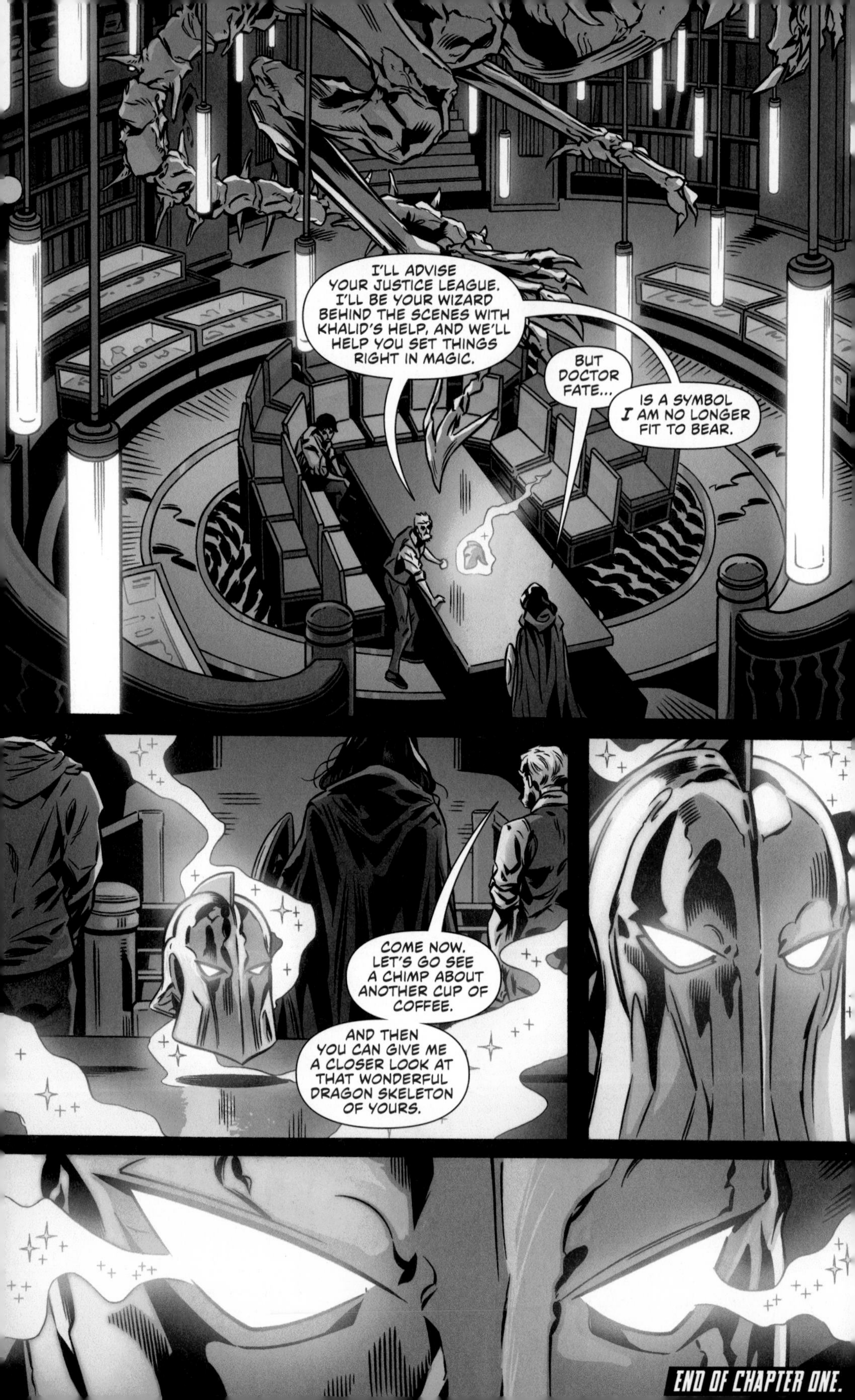
I'LL ADVISE YOUR JUSTICE LEAGUE. I'LL BE YOUR WIZARD BEHIND THE SCENES WITH KHALID'S HELP, AND WE'LL HELP YOU SET THINGS RIGHT IN MAGIC.
BUT DOCTOR FATE...
IS A SYMBOL I AM NO LONGER FIT TO BEAR.
COME NOW. LET'S GO SEE A CHIMP ABOUT ANOTHER CUP OF COFFEE.
AND THEN YOU CAN GIVE ME A CLOSER LOOK AT THAT WONDERFUL DRAGON SKELETON OF YOURS.
END OF CHAPTER ONE.

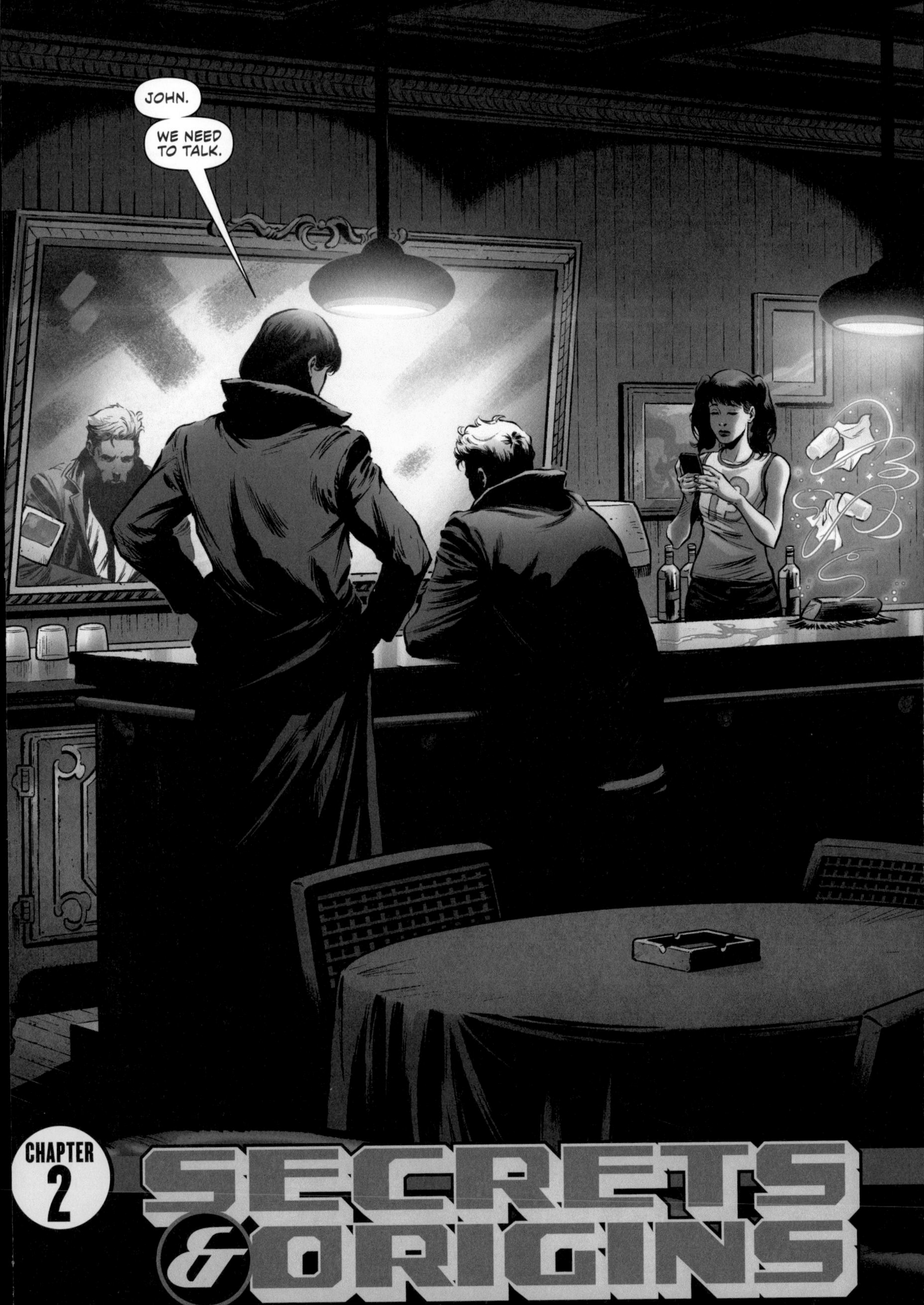
JOHN.
WE NEED TO TALK.

CHAPTER 2 SECRETS & ORIGINS

JAMES TYNION IV writer • DANIEL SAMPERE penciller • JUAN ALBARRAN inker • ADRIANO LUCAS colorist • ROB LEIGH letterer

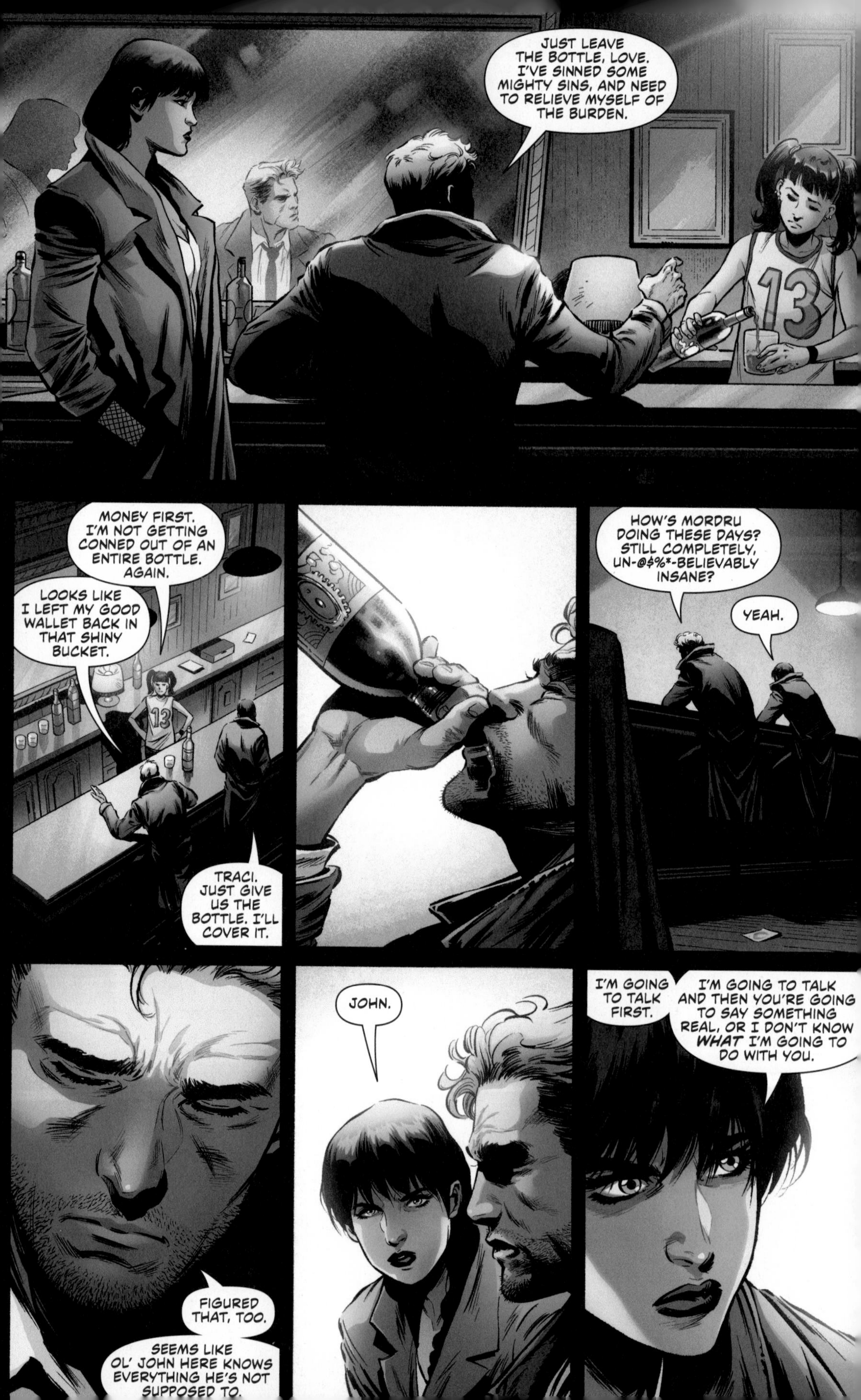
JUST LEAVE THE BOTTLE, LOVE. I'VE SINNED SOME MIGHTY SINS, AND NEED TO RELIEVE MYSELF OF THE BURDEN.
13
MONEY FIRST. I'M NOT GETTING CONNED OUT OF AN ENTIRE BOTTLE. AGAIN.
LOOKS LIKE I LEFT MY GOOD WALLET BACK IN THAT SHINY BUCKET.
TRACI. JUST GIVE US THE BOTTLE. I'LL COVER IT.
HOW'S MORDRU DOING THESE DAYS? STILL COMPLETELY, UN-@$%*-BELIEVABLY INSANE?
YEAH.
FIGURED THAT, TOO.
SEEMS LIKE OL' JOHN HERE KNOWS EVERYTHING HE'S NOT SUPPOSED TO.
JOHN.
I'M GOING TO TALK FIRST.
I'M GOING TO TALK AND THEN YOU'RE GOING TO SAY SOMETHING REAL, OR I DON'T KNOW *WHAT* I'M GOING TO DO WITH YOU.

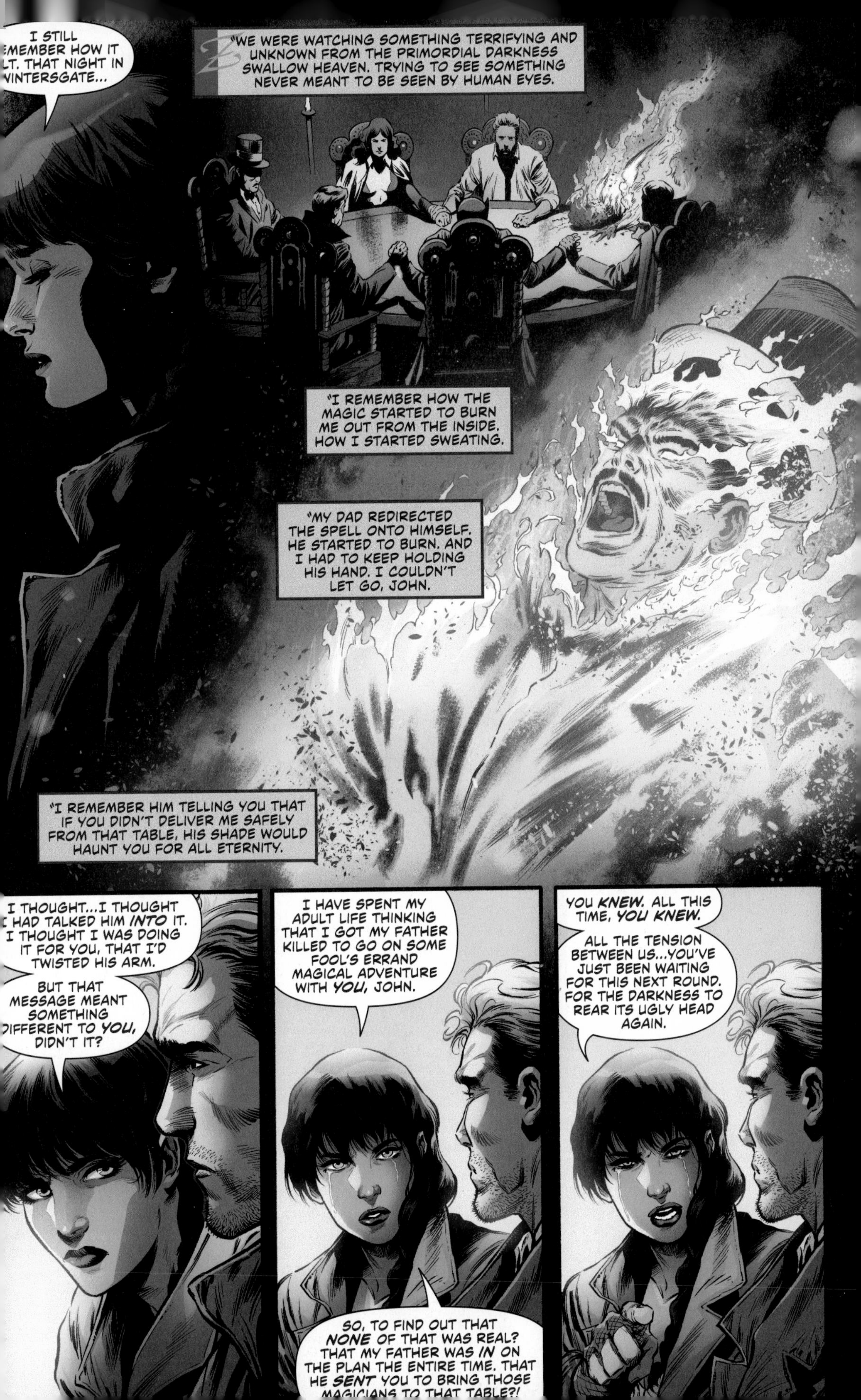
I STILL REMEMBER HOW IT FELT. THAT NIGHT IN WINTERSGATE...
"WE WERE WATCHING SOMETHING TERRIFYING AND UNKNOWN FROM THE PRIMORDIAL DARKNESS SWALLOW HEAVEN. TRYING TO SEE SOMETHING NEVER MEANT TO BE SEEN BY HUMAN EYES.
"I REMEMBER HOW THE MAGIC STARTED TO BURN ME OUT FROM THE INSIDE. HOW I STARTED SWEATING.
"MY DAD REDIRECTED THE SPELL ONTO HIMSELF. HE STARTED TO BURN. AND I HAD TO KEEP HOLDING HIS HAND. I COULDN'T LET GO, JOHN.
"I REMEMBER HIM TELLING YOU THAT IF YOU DIDN'T DELIVER ME SAFELY FROM THAT TABLE, HIS SHADE WOULD HAUNT YOU FOR ALL ETERNITY.
I THOUGHT...I THOUGHT I HAD TALKED HIM *INTO* IT. I THOUGHT I WAS DOING IT FOR YOU, THAT I'D TWISTED HIS ARM.
BUT THAT MESSAGE MEANT SOMETHING DIFFERENT TO *YOU*, DIDN'T IT?
I HAVE SPENT MY ADULT LIFE THINKING THAT I GOT MY FATHER KILLED TO GO ON SOME FOOL'S ERRAND MAGICAL ADVENTURE WITH *YOU*, JOHN.
SO, TO FIND OUT THAT *NONE* OF THAT WAS REAL? THAT MY FATHER WAS *IN* ON THE PLAN THE ENTIRE TIME. THAT HE *SENT* YOU TO BRING THOSE MAGICIANS TO THAT TABLE?!
YOU *KNEW*. ALL THIS TIME, *YOU KNEW*.
ALL THE TENSION BETWEEN US...YOU'VE JUST BEEN WAITING FOR THIS NEXT ROUND. FOR THE DARKNESS TO REAR ITS UGLY HEAD AGAIN.

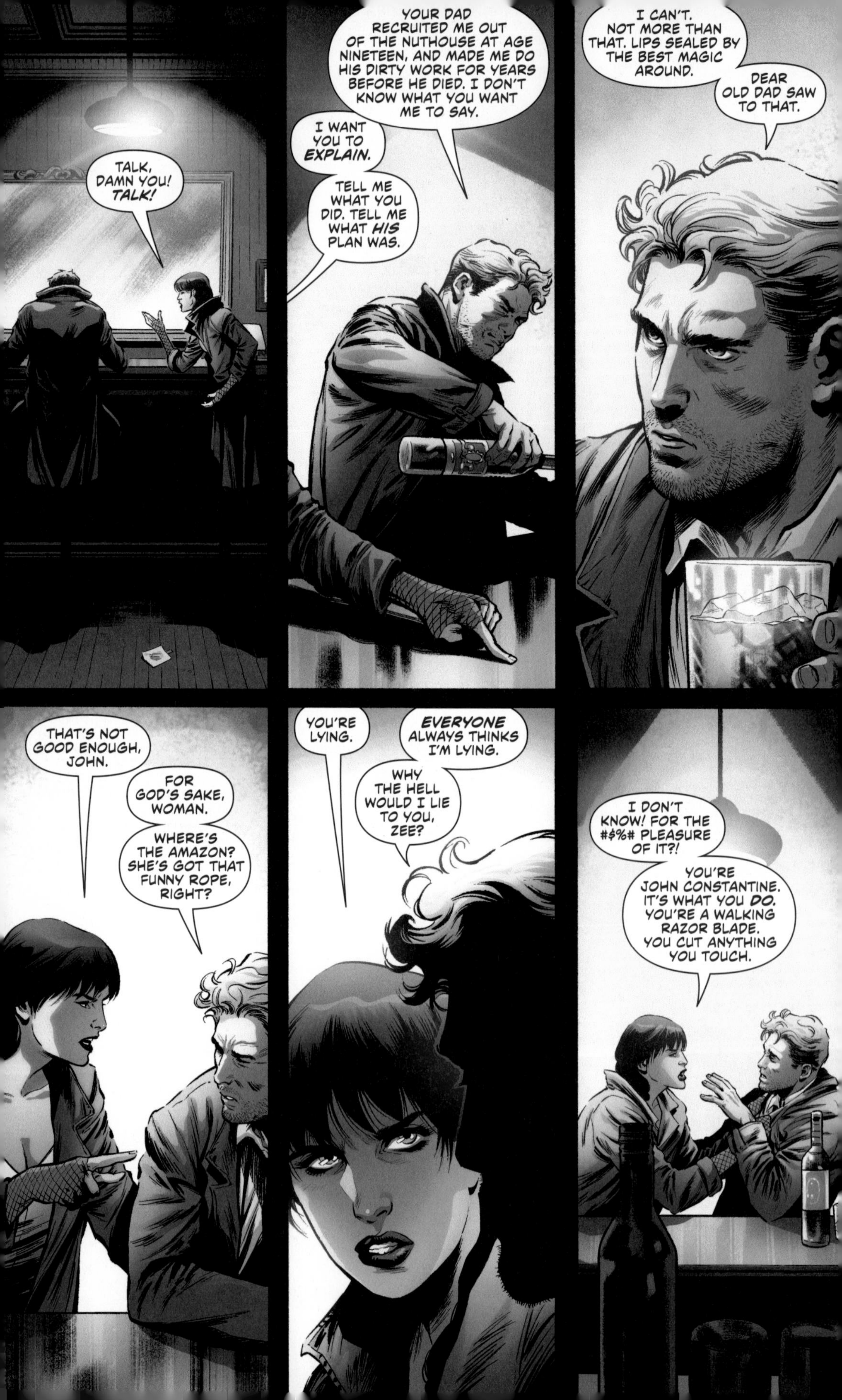
TALK, DAMN YOU! TALK!
YOUR DAD RECRUITED ME OUT OF THE NUTHOUSE AT AGE NINETEEN, AND MADE ME DO HIS DIRTY WORK FOR YEARS BEFORE HE DIED. I DON'T KNOW WHAT YOU WANT ME TO SAY.
I WANT YOU TO EXPLAIN.
TELL ME WHAT YOU DID. TELL ME WHAT HIS PLAN WAS.
I CAN'T. NOT MORE THAN THAT. LIPS SEALED BY THE BEST MAGIC AROUND.
DEAR OLD DAD SAW TO THAT.
THAT'S NOT GOOD ENOUGH, JOHN.
FOR GOD'S SAKE, WOMAN.
WHERE'S THE AMAZON? SHE'S GOT THAT FUNNY ROPE, RIGHT?
YOU'RE LYING.
EVERYONE ALWAYS THINKS I'M LYING.
WHY THE HELL WOULD I LIE TO YOU, ZEE?
I DON'T KNOW! FOR THE #$%# PLEASURE OF IT?!
YOU'RE JOHN CONSTANTINE. IT'S WHAT YOU DO. YOU'RE A WALKING RAZOR BLADE. YOU CUT ANYTHING YOU TOUCH.

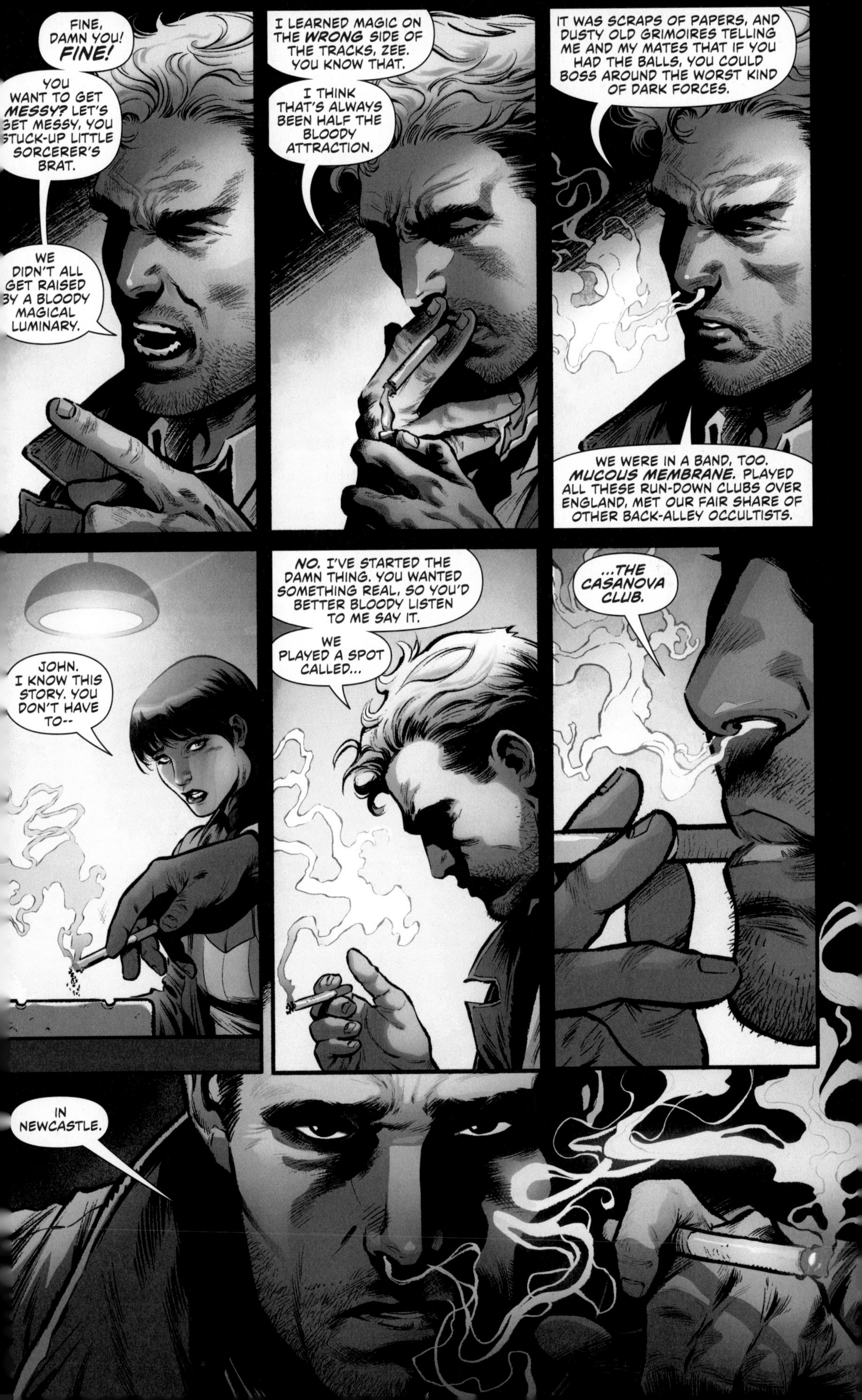
FINE, DAMN YOU! FINE!
YOU WANT TO GET MESSY? LET'S GET MESSY, YOU STUCK-UP LITTLE SORCERER'S BRAT.
WE DIDN'T ALL GET RAISED BY A BLOODY MAGICAL LUMINARY.
I LEARNED MAGIC ON THE WRONG SIDE OF THE TRACKS, ZEE. YOU KNOW THAT.
I THINK THAT'S ALWAYS BEEN HALF THE BLOODY ATTRACTION.
IT WAS SCRAPS OF PAPERS, AND DUSTY OLD GRIMOIRES TELLING ME AND MY MATES THAT IF YOU HAD THE BALLS, YOU COULD BOSS AROUND THE WORST KIND OF DARK FORCES.
WE WERE IN A BAND, TOO. MUCOUS MEMBRANE. PLAYED ALL THESE RUN-DOWN CLUBS OVER ENGLAND, MET OUR FAIR SHARE OF OTHER BACK-ALLEY OCCULTISTS.
JOHN. I KNOW THIS STORY. YOU DON'T HAVE TO--
NO. I'VE STARTED THE DAMN THING. YOU WANTED SOMETHING REAL, SO YOU'D BETTER BLOODY LISTEN TO ME SAY IT.
WE PLAYED A SPOT CALLED...
...THE CASANOVA CLUB.
IN NEWCASTLE.

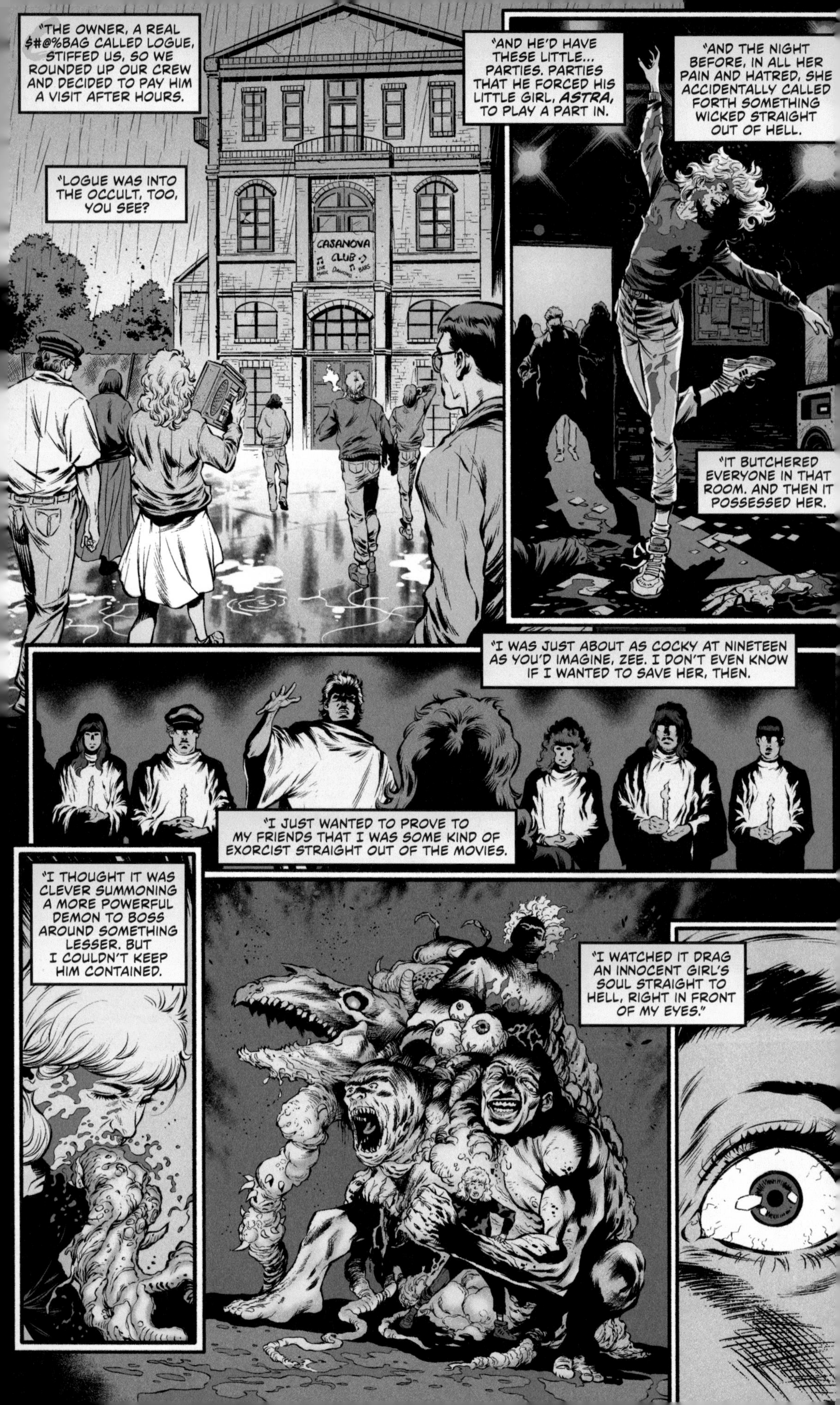

"THE OWNER, A REAL $#@%BAG CALLED LOGUE, STIFFED US, SO WE ROUNDED UP OUR CREW AND DECIDED TO PAY HIM A VISIT AFTER HOURS.
"LOGUE WAS INTO THE OCCULT, TOO, YOU SEE?
CASANOVA CLUB
LIVE MUSIC DANCING BARS
"AND HE'D HAVE THESE LITTLE... PARTIES. PARTIES THAT HE FORCED HIS LITTLE GIRL, ASTRA, TO PLAY A PART IN.
"AND THE NIGHT BEFORE, IN ALL HER PAIN AND HATRED, SHE ACCIDENTALLY CALLED FORTH SOMETHING WICKED STRAIGHT OUT OF HELL.
"IT BUTCHERED EVERYONE IN THAT ROOM. AND THEN IT POSSESSED HER.
"I WAS JUST ABOUT AS COCKY AT NINETEEN AS YOU'D IMAGINE, ZEE. I DON'T EVEN KNOW IF I WANTED TO SAVE HER, THEN.
"I JUST WANTED TO PROVE TO MY FRIENDS THAT I WAS SOME KIND OF EXORCIST STRAIGHT OUT OF THE MOVIES.
"I THOUGHT IT WAS CLEVER SUMMONING A MORE POWERFUL DEMON TO BOSS AROUND SOMETHING LESSER. BUT I COULDN'T KEEP HIM CONTAINED.
"I WATCHED IT DRAG AN INNOCENT GIRL'S SOUL STRAIGHT TO HELL, RIGHT IN FRONT OF MY EYES."

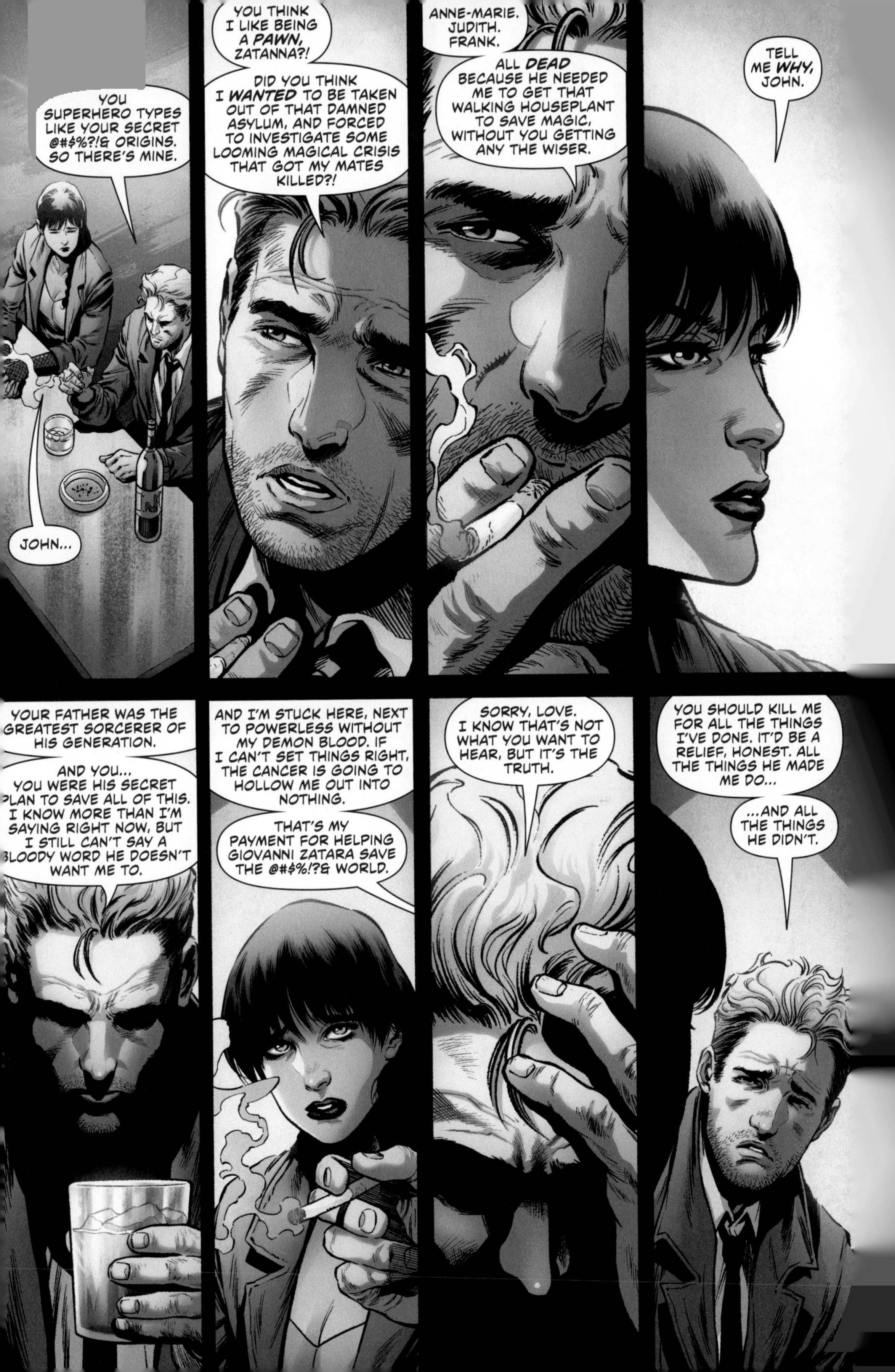
YOU SUPERHERO TYPES LIKE YOUR SECRET @#$%?!& ORIGINS. SO THERE'S MINE.
JOHN...
YOU THINK I LIKE BEING A PAWN, ZATANNA?!
DID YOU THINK I WANTED TO BE TAKEN OUT OF THAT DAMNED ASYLUM, AND FORCED TO INVESTIGATE SOME LOOMING MAGICAL CRISIS THAT GOT MY MATES KILLED?!
ANNE-MARIE. JUDITH. FRANK.
ALL DEAD BECAUSE HE NEEDED ME TO GET THAT WALKING HOUSEPLANT TO SAVE MAGIC, WITHOUT YOU GETTING ANY THE WISER.
TELL ME WHY, JOHN.
YOUR FATHER WAS THE GREATEST SORCERER OF HIS GENERATION.
AND YOU... YOU WERE HIS SECRET PLAN TO SAVE ALL OF THIS. I KNOW MORE THAN I'M SAYING RIGHT NOW, BUT I STILL CAN'T SAY A BLOODY WORD HE DOESN'T WANT ME TO.
AND I'M STUCK HERE, NEXT TO POWERLESS WITHOUT MY DEMON BLOOD. IF I CAN'T SET THINGS RIGHT, THE CANCER IS GOING TO HOLLOW ME OUT INTO NOTHING.
THAT'S MY PAYMENT FOR HELPING GIOVANNI ZATARA SAVE THE @#$%!?& WORLD.
SORRY, LOVE. I KNOW THAT'S NOT WHAT YOU WANT TO HEAR, BUT IT'S THE TRUTH.
YOU SHOULD KILL ME FOR ALL THE THINGS I'VE DONE. IT'D BE A RELIEF, HONEST. ALL THE THINGS HE MADE ME DO...
...AND ALL THE THINGS HE DIDN'T.

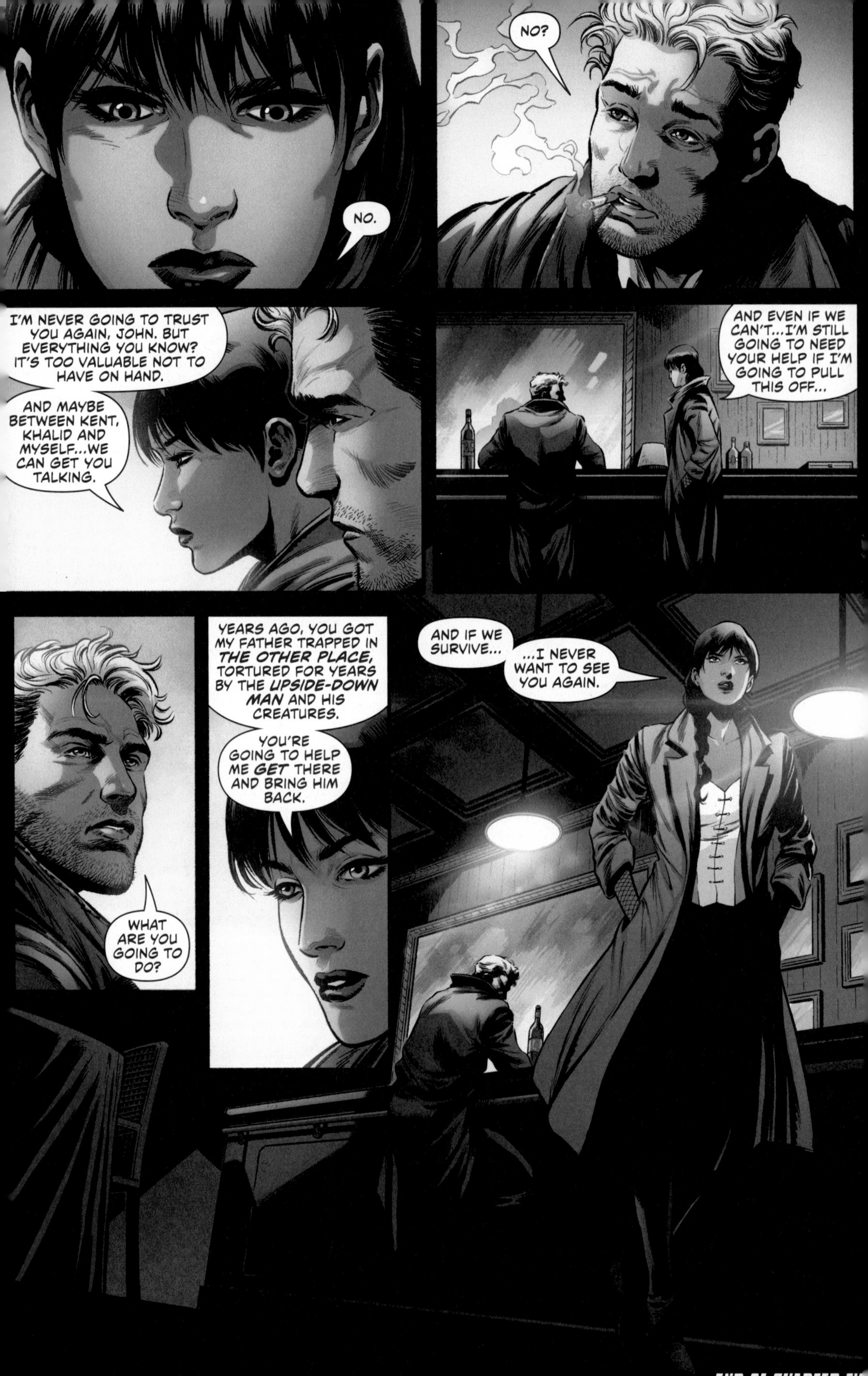
NO.
NO?
I'M NEVER GOING TO TRUST YOU AGAIN, JOHN. BUT EVERYTHING YOU KNOW? IT'S TOO VALUABLE NOT TO HAVE ON HAND.
AND MAYBE BETWEEN KENT, KHALID AND MYSELF...WE CAN GET YOU TALKING.
AND EVEN IF WE CAN'T...I'M STILL GOING TO NEED YOUR HELP IF I'M GOING TO PULL THIS OFF...
WHAT ARE YOU GOING TO DO?
YEARS AGO, YOU GOT MY FATHER TRAPPED IN THE OTHER PLACE, TORTURED FOR YEARS BY THE UPSIDE-DOWN MAN AND HIS CREATURES.
YOU'RE GOING TO HELP ME GET THERE AND BRING HIM BACK.
AND IF WE SURVIVE...
...I NEVER WANT TO SEE YOU AGAIN.

END OF CHAPTER TW

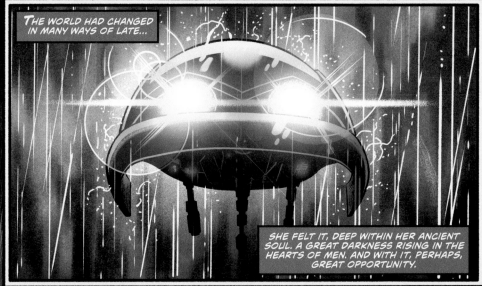

THE WORLD HAD CHANGED IN MANY WAYS OF LATE...

SHE FELT IT, DEEP WITHIN HER ANCIENT SOUL. A GREAT DARKNESS RISING IN THE HEARTS OF MEN. AND WITH IT, PERHAPS, GREAT OPPORTUNITY.

DOOM WAS COMING, AND THE MORTALS HAD BEGUN TO CHEER ITS ARRIVAL.

AFTER ALL, THAT'S WHAT THE MAN ON THE TELEVISION HAD SAID, WASN'T IT? THIS WAS TO BE A *YEAR OF THE VILLAIN*, AND THEY WOULD *ALL* BE VILLAINS TOGETHER. IN DOOM THEY MAY FIND GREAT POWER.

CHAPTER **3**

THE WITCHING WAY

JAMES TYNION IV writer • DANIEL SAMPERE penciller • JUAN ALBARRAN inker • ADRIANO LUCAS colorist • ROB LEIGH letterer

SHE CERTAINLY WOULD. HER MACHINATIONS WERE ALREADY SPRINGING TO LIFE, READY TO DRAG THE MAGICAL WORLD TOWARD WAR.

THIS MOMENT COULD BE OF USE TO HER...PERHAPS, IN MORE WAYS THAN SHE EXPECTED.

HELLO, YOU STRANGE MACHINE...

...I SENSE YOU HAVE SOMETHING TO TELL ME, DO YOU NOT?

CIRCE, THIS IS LUTHOR.

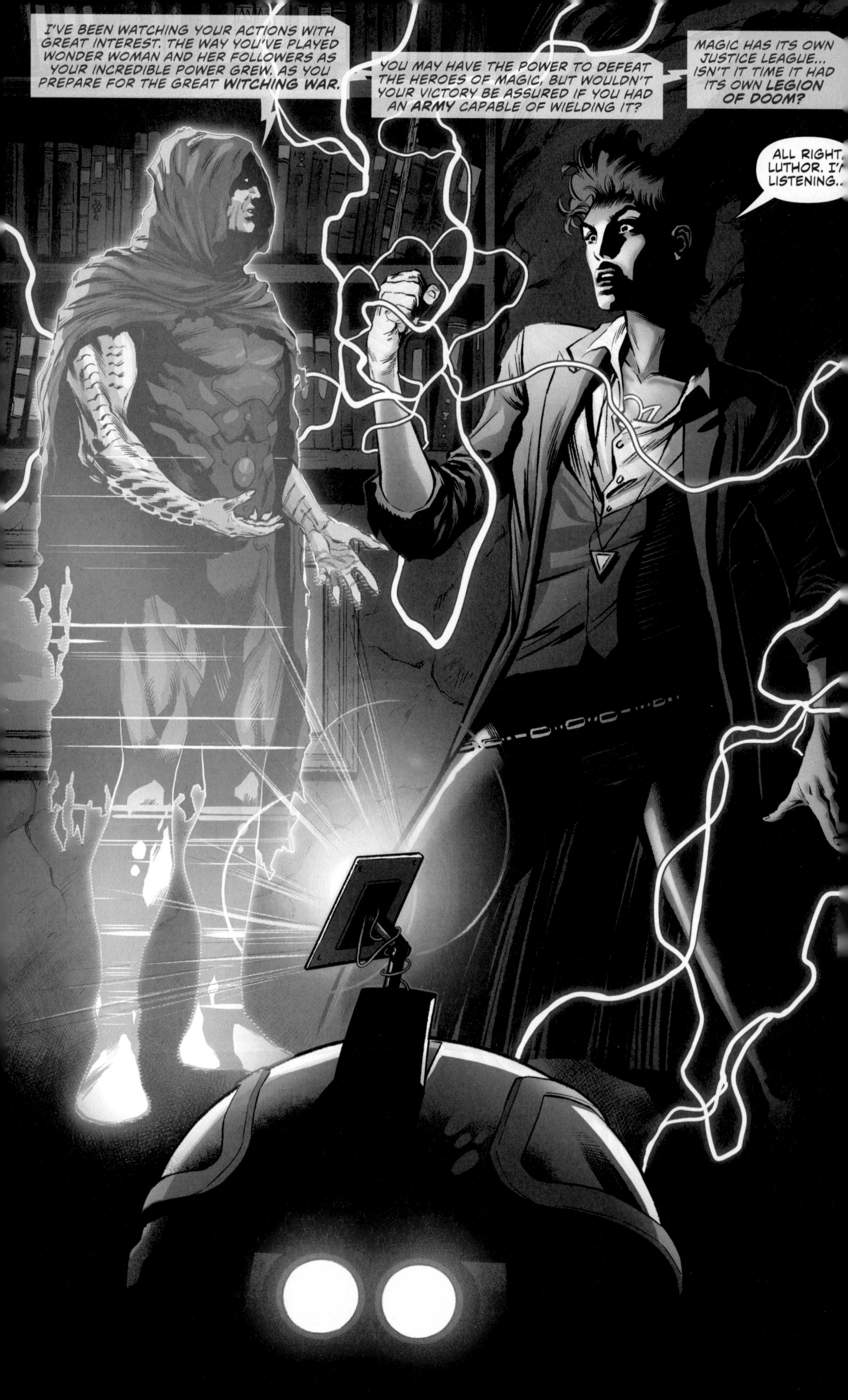

I'VE BEEN WATCHING YOUR ACTIONS WITH GREAT INTEREST. THE WAY YOU'VE PLAYED WONDER WOMAN AND HER FOLLOWERS AS YOUR INCREDIBLE POWER GREW. AS YOU PREPARE FOR THE GREAT WITCHING WAR.
YOU MAY HAVE THE POWER TO DEFEAT THE HEROES OF MAGIC, BUT WOULDN'T YOUR VICTORY BE ASSURED IF YOU HAD AN ARMY CAPABLE OF WIELDING IT?
MAGIC HAS ITS OWN JUSTICE LEAGUE... ISN'T IT TIME IT HAD ITS OWN LEGION OF DOOM?
ALL RIGHT, LUTHOR. I'M LISTENING...

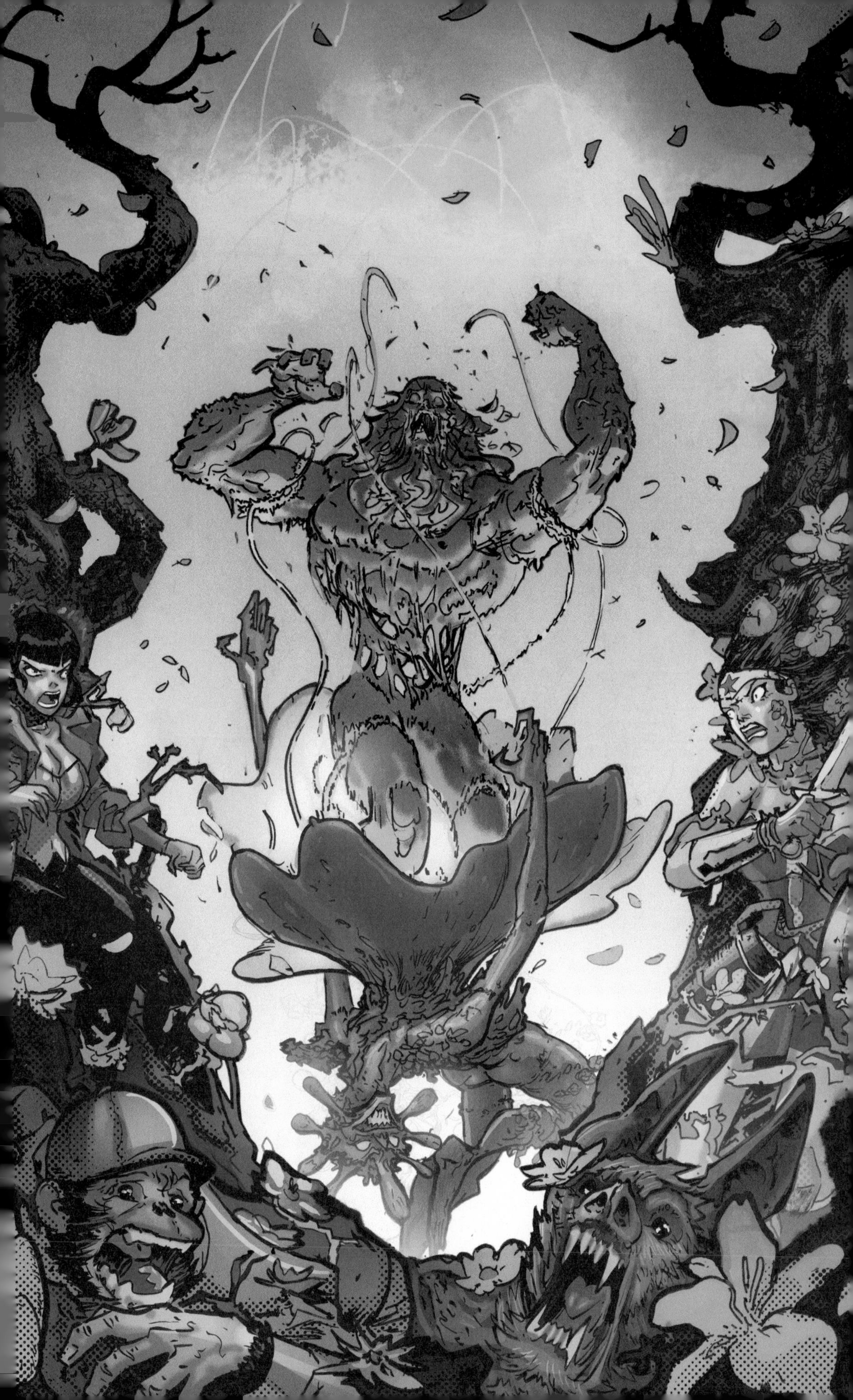

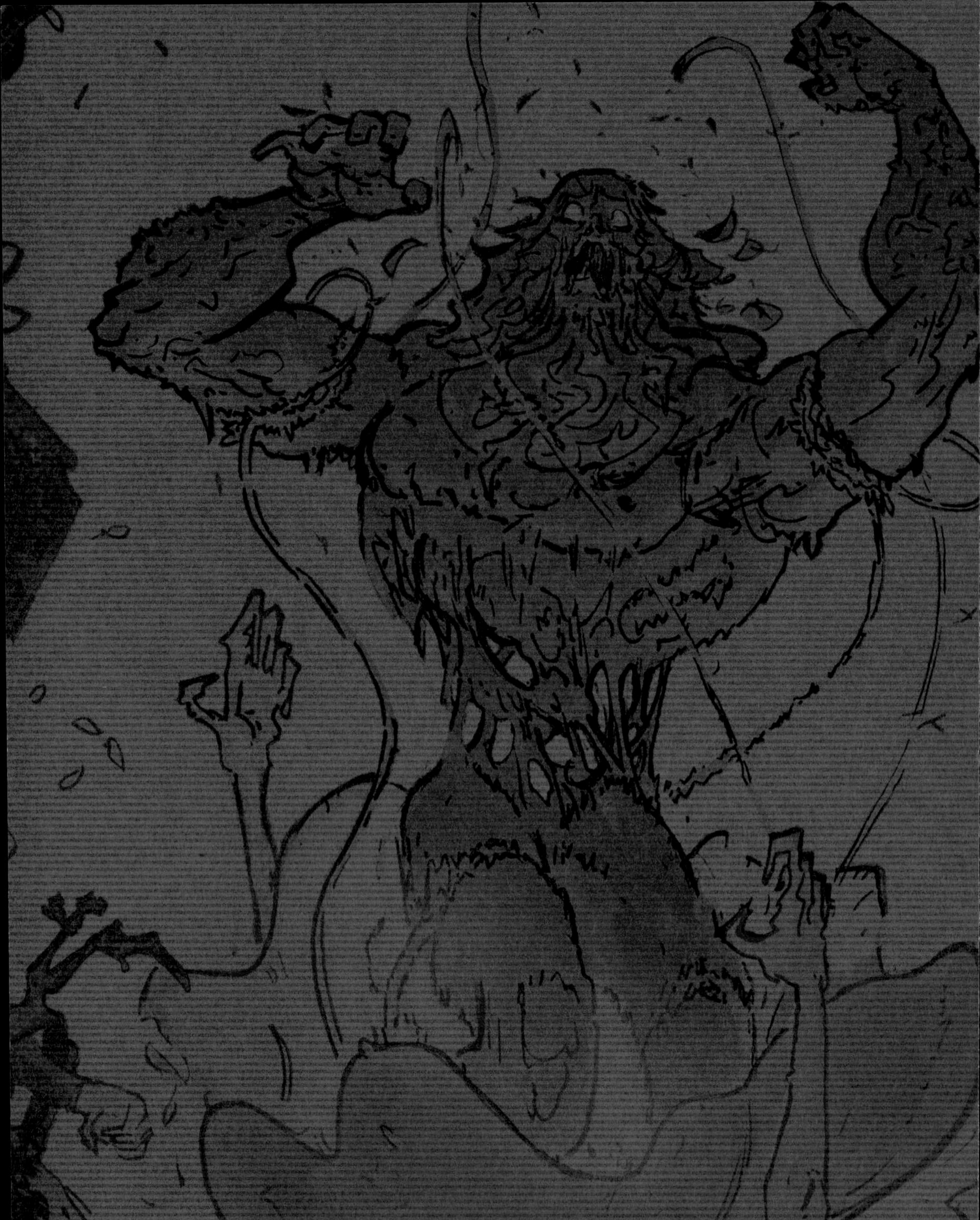

JUSTICE LEAGUE DARK
ANNUAL #1

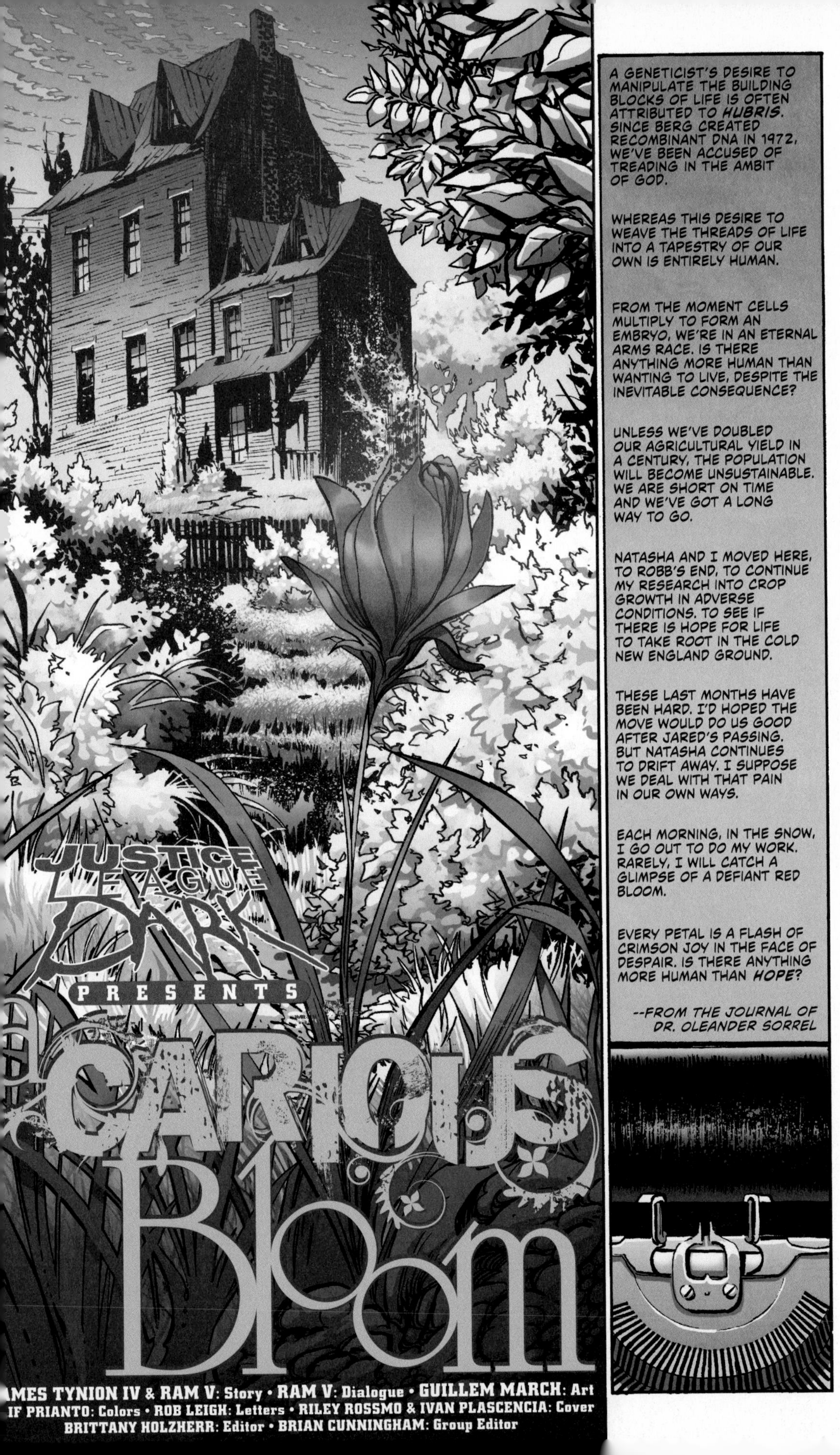

A GENETICIST'S DESIRE TO MANIPULATE THE BUILDING BLOCKS OF LIFE IS OFTEN ATTRIBUTED TO *HUBRIS*. SINCE BERG CREATED RECOMBINANT DNA IN 1972, WE'VE BEEN ACCUSED OF TREADING IN THE AMBIT OF GOD.
WHEREAS THIS DESIRE TO WEAVE THE THREADS OF LIFE INTO A TAPESTRY OF OUR OWN IS ENTIRELY HUMAN.
FROM THE MOMENT CELLS MULTIPLY TO FORM AN EMBRYO, WE'RE IN AN ETERNAL ARMS RACE. IS THERE ANYTHING MORE HUMAN THAN WANTING TO LIVE, DESPITE THE INEVITABLE CONSEQUENCE?
UNLESS WE'VE DOUBLED OUR AGRICULTURAL YIELD IN A CENTURY, THE POPULATION WILL BECOME UNSUSTAINABLE. WE ARE SHORT ON TIME AND WE'VE GOT A LONG WAY TO GO.
NATASHA AND I MOVED HERE, TO ROBB'S END, TO CONTINUE MY RESEARCH INTO CROP GROWTH IN ADVERSE CONDITIONS. TO SEE IF THERE IS HOPE FOR LIFE TO TAKE ROOT IN THE COLD NEW ENGLAND GROUND.
THESE LAST MONTHS HAVE BEEN HARD. I'D HOPED THE MOVE WOULD DO US GOOD AFTER JARED'S PASSING. BUT NATASHA CONTINUES TO DRIFT AWAY. I SUPPOSE WE DEAL WITH THAT PAIN IN OUR OWN WAYS.
EACH MORNING, IN THE SNOW, I GO OUT TO DO MY WORK. RARELY, I WILL CATCH A GLIMPSE OF A DEFIANT RED BLOOM.
EVERY PETAL IS A FLASH OF CRIMSON JOY IN THE FACE OF DESPAIR. IS THERE ANYTHING MORE HUMAN THAN *HOPE*?
--FROM THE JOURNAL OF DR. OLEANDER SORREL
JUSTICE LEAGUE DARK
PRESENTS
CARIOUS
Bloom
AMES TYNION IV & RAM V: Story • RAM V: Dialogue • GUILLEM MARCH: Art
IF PRIANTO: Colors • ROB LEIGH: Letters • RILEY ROSSMO & IVAN PLASCENCIA: Cover
BRITTANY HOLZHERR: Editor • BRIAN CUNNINGHAM: Group Editor

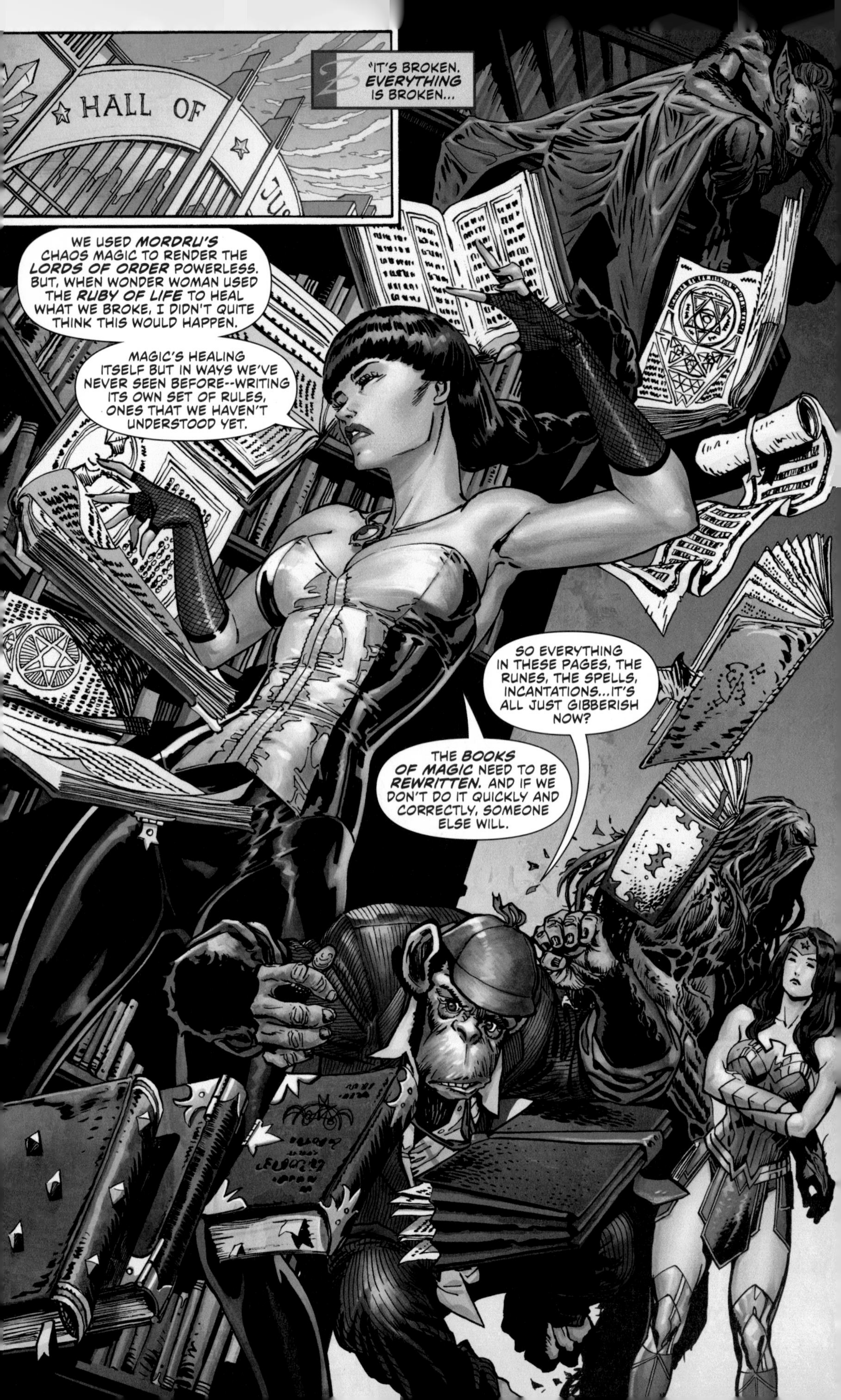

HALL OF
JUS
"IT'S BROKEN. EVERYTHING IS BROKEN...
WE USED MORDRU'S CHAOS MAGIC TO RENDER THE LORDS OF ORDER POWERLESS. BUT, WHEN WONDER WOMAN USED THE RUBY OF LIFE TO HEAL WHAT WE BROKE, I DIDN'T QUITE THINK THIS WOULD HAPPEN.
MAGIC'S HEALING ITSELF BUT IN WAYS WE'VE NEVER SEEN BEFORE--WRITING ITS OWN SET OF RULES, ONES THAT WE HAVEN'T UNDERSTOOD YET.
SO EVERYTHING IN THESE PAGES, THE RUNES, THE SPELLS, INCANTATIONS...IT'S ALL JUST GIBBERISH NOW?
THE BOOKS OF MAGIC NEED TO BE REWRITTEN. AND IF WE DON'T DO IT QUICKLY AND CORRECTLY, SOMEONE ELSE WILL.

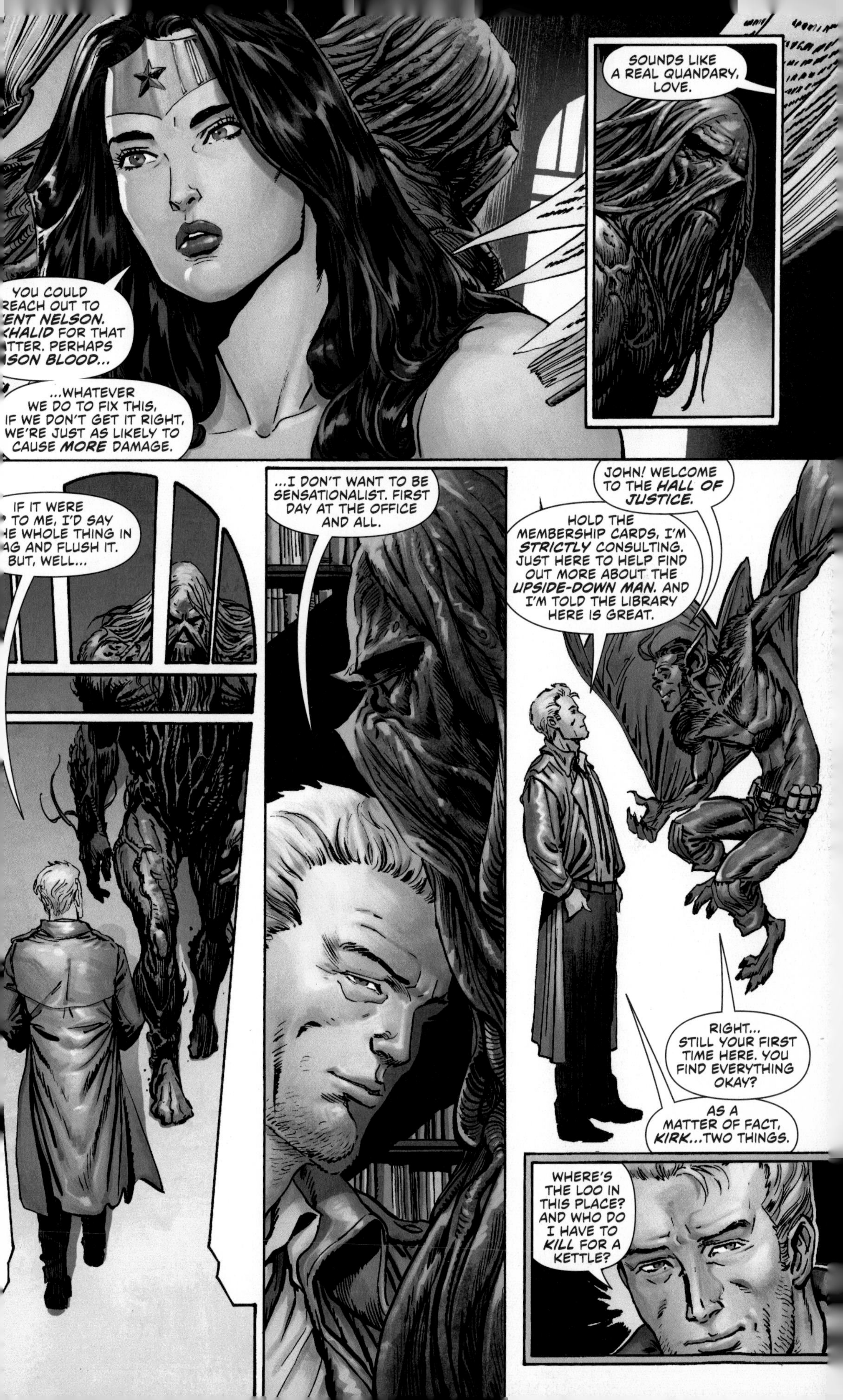

YOU COULD REACH OUT TO ENT NELSON. KHALID FOR THAT ATTER. PERHAPS SON BLOOD...
...WHATEVER WE DO TO FIX THIS, IF WE DON'T GET IT RIGHT, WE'RE JUST AS LIKELY TO CAUSE *MORE* DAMAGE.
SOUNDS LIKE A REAL QUANDARY, LOVE.
IF IT WERE TO ME, I'D SAY HE WHOLE THING IN AG AND FLUSH IT. BUT, WELL...
...I DON'T WANT TO BE SENSATIONALIST. FIRST DAY AT THE OFFICE AND ALL.
JOHN! WELCOME TO THE *HALL OF JUSTICE.*
HOLD THE MEMBERSHIP CARDS, I'M *STRICTLY* CONSULTING. JUST HERE TO HELP FIND OUT MORE ABOUT THE *UPSIDE-DOWN MAN.* AND I'M TOLD THE LIBRARY HERE IS GREAT.
RIGHT... STILL YOUR FIRST TIME HERE. YOU FIND EVERYTHING OKAY?
AS A MATTER OF FACT, *KIRK*...TWO THINGS.
WHERE'S THE LOO IN THIS PLACE? AND WHO DO I HAVE TO *KILL* FOR A KETTLE?

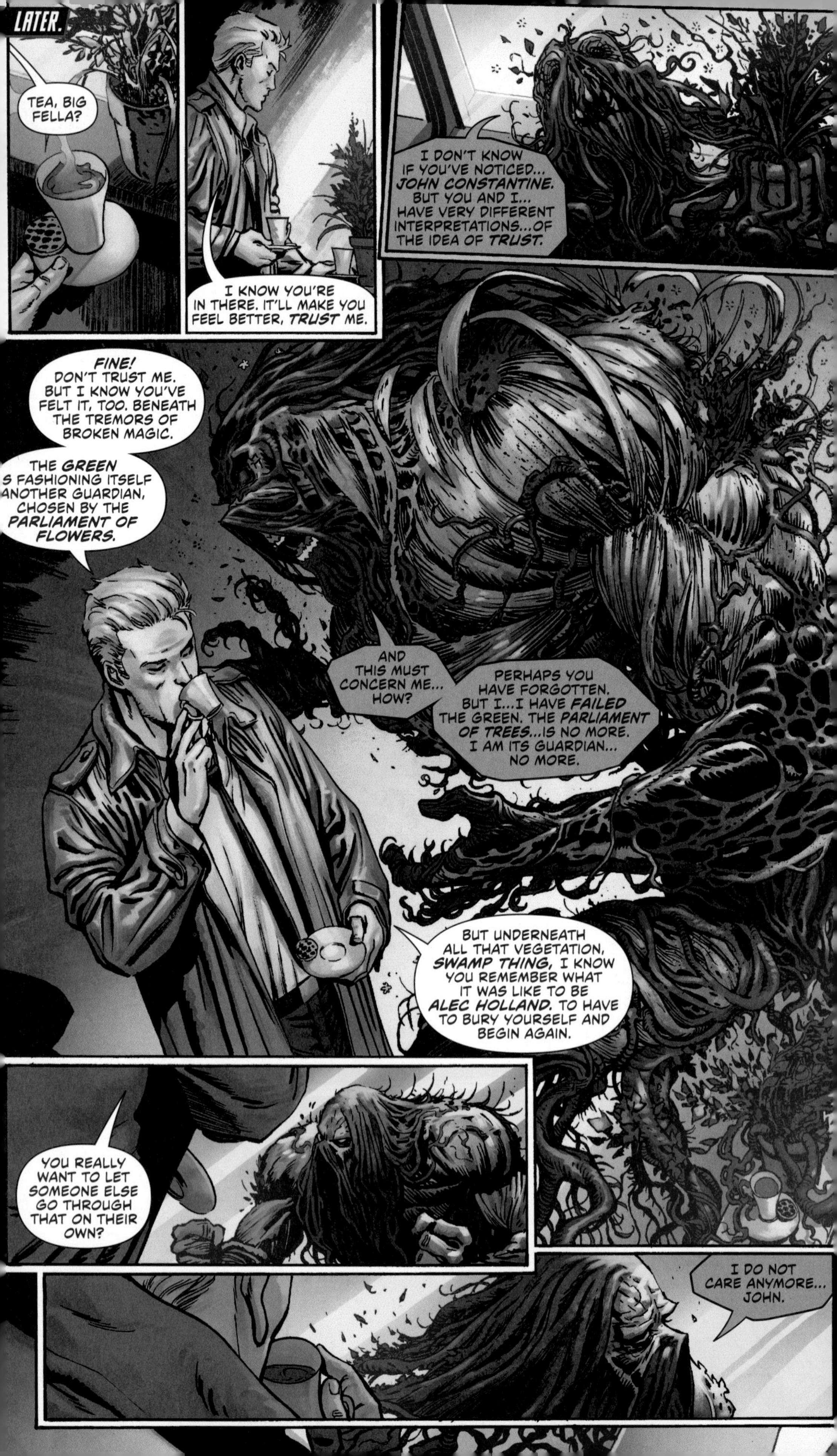
LATER.
TEA, BIG FELLA?
I KNOW YOU'RE IN THERE. IT'LL MAKE YOU FEEL BETTER, TRUST ME.
I DON'T KNOW IF YOU'VE NOTICED... JOHN CONSTANTINE. BUT YOU AND I... HAVE VERY DIFFERENT INTERPRETATIONS...OF THE IDEA OF TRUST.
FINE! DON'T TRUST ME. BUT I KNOW YOU'VE FELT IT, TOO. BENEATH THE TREMORS OF BROKEN MAGIC.
THE GREEN S FASHIONING ITSELF ANOTHER GUARDIAN, CHOSEN BY THE PARLIAMENT OF FLOWERS.
AND THIS MUST CONCERN ME... HOW?
PERHAPS YOU HAVE FORGOTTEN. BUT I...I HAVE FAILED THE GREEN. THE PARLIAMENT OF TREES...IS NO MORE. I AM ITS GUARDIAN... NO MORE.
BUT UNDERNEATH ALL THAT VEGETATION, SWAMP THING, I KNOW YOU REMEMBER WHAT IT WAS LIKE TO BE ALEC HOLLAND. TO HAVE TO BURY YOURSELF AND BEGIN AGAIN.
YOU REALLY WANT TO LET SOMEONE ELSE GO THROUGH THAT ON THEIR OWN?
I DO NOT CARE ANYMORE... JOHN.

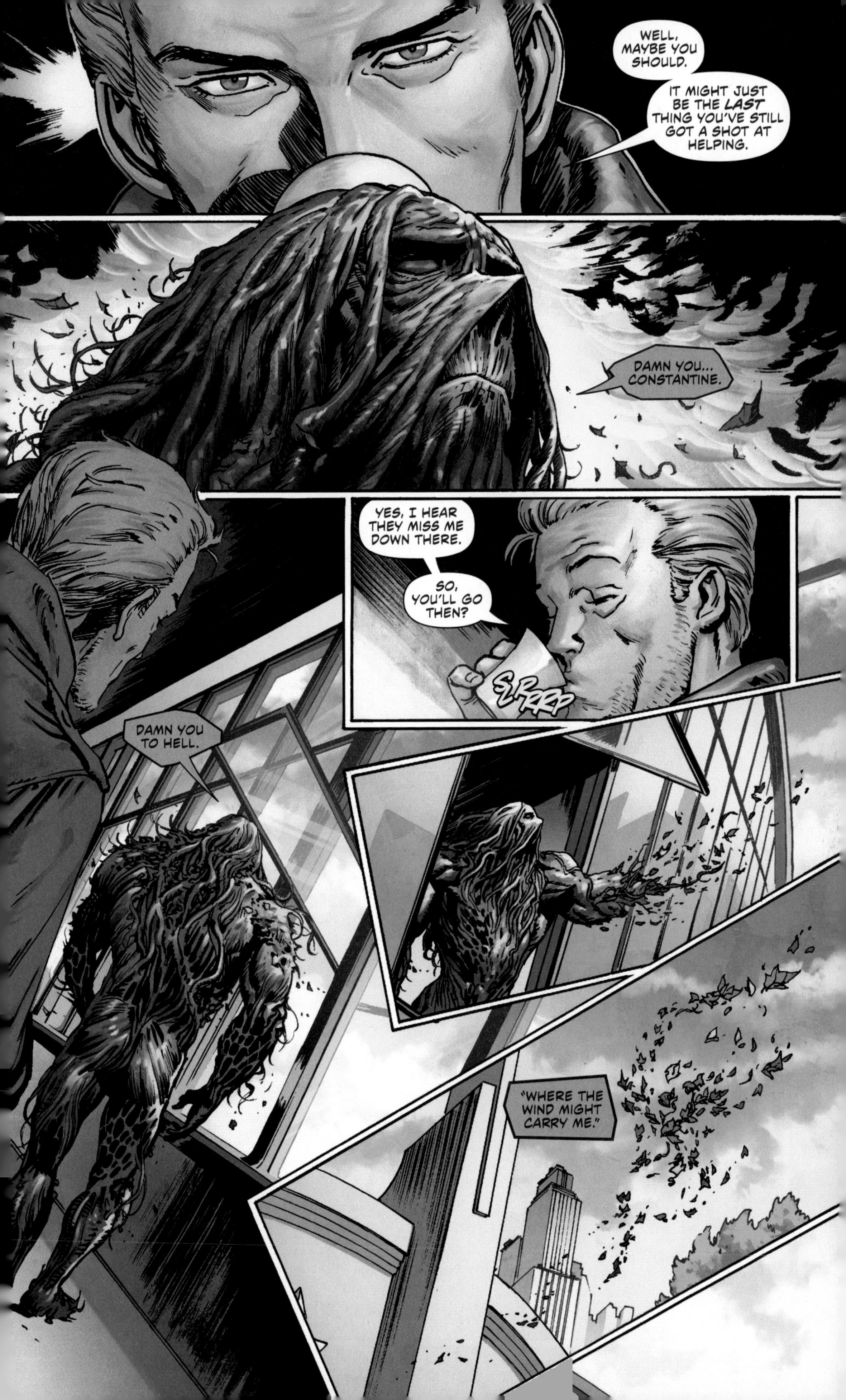
WELL, MAYBE YOU SHOULD.
IT MIGHT JUST BE THE *LAST* THING YOU'VE STILL GOT A SHOT AT HELPING.
DAMN YOU... CONSTANTINE.
YES, I HEAR THEY MISS ME DOWN THERE.
SO, YOU'LL GO THEN?
SLRRRP
DAMN YOU TO HELL.
"WHERE THE WIND MIGHT CARRY ME."

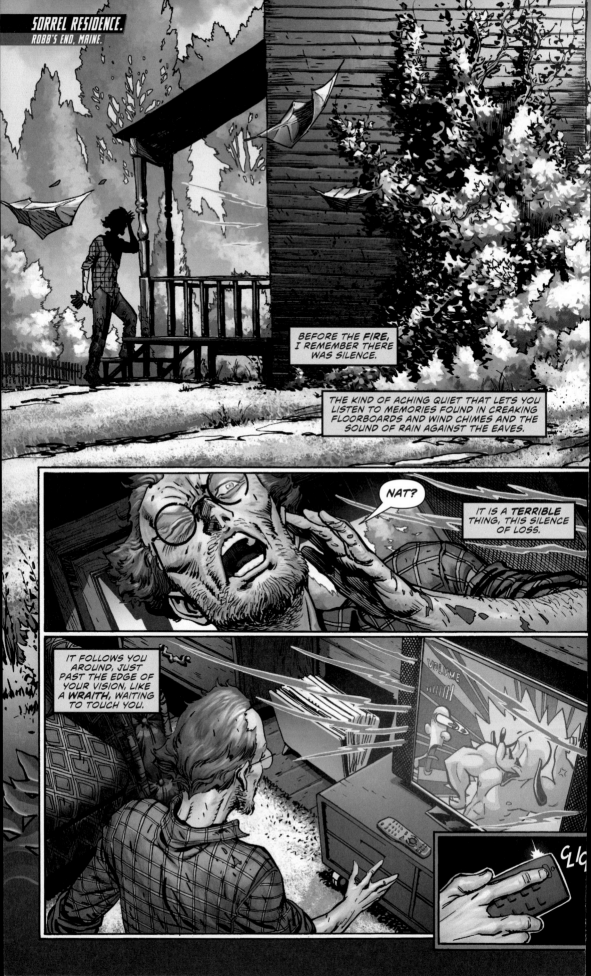

SORREL RESIDENCE.
ROBB'S END, MAINE.

BEFORE THE FIRE,
I REMEMBER THERE
WAS SILENCE.

THE KIND OF ACHING QUIET THAT LETS YOU
LISTEN TO MEMORIES FOUND IN CREAKING
FLOORBOARDS AND WIND CHIMES AND THE
SOUND OF RAIN AGAINST THE EAVES.

NAT?

IT IS A TERRIBLE
THING, THIS SILENCE
OF LOSS.

IT FOLLOWS YOU
AROUND, JUST
PAST THE EDGE OF
YOUR VISION, LIKE
A WRAITH, WAITING
TO TOUCH YOU.

VOLUME

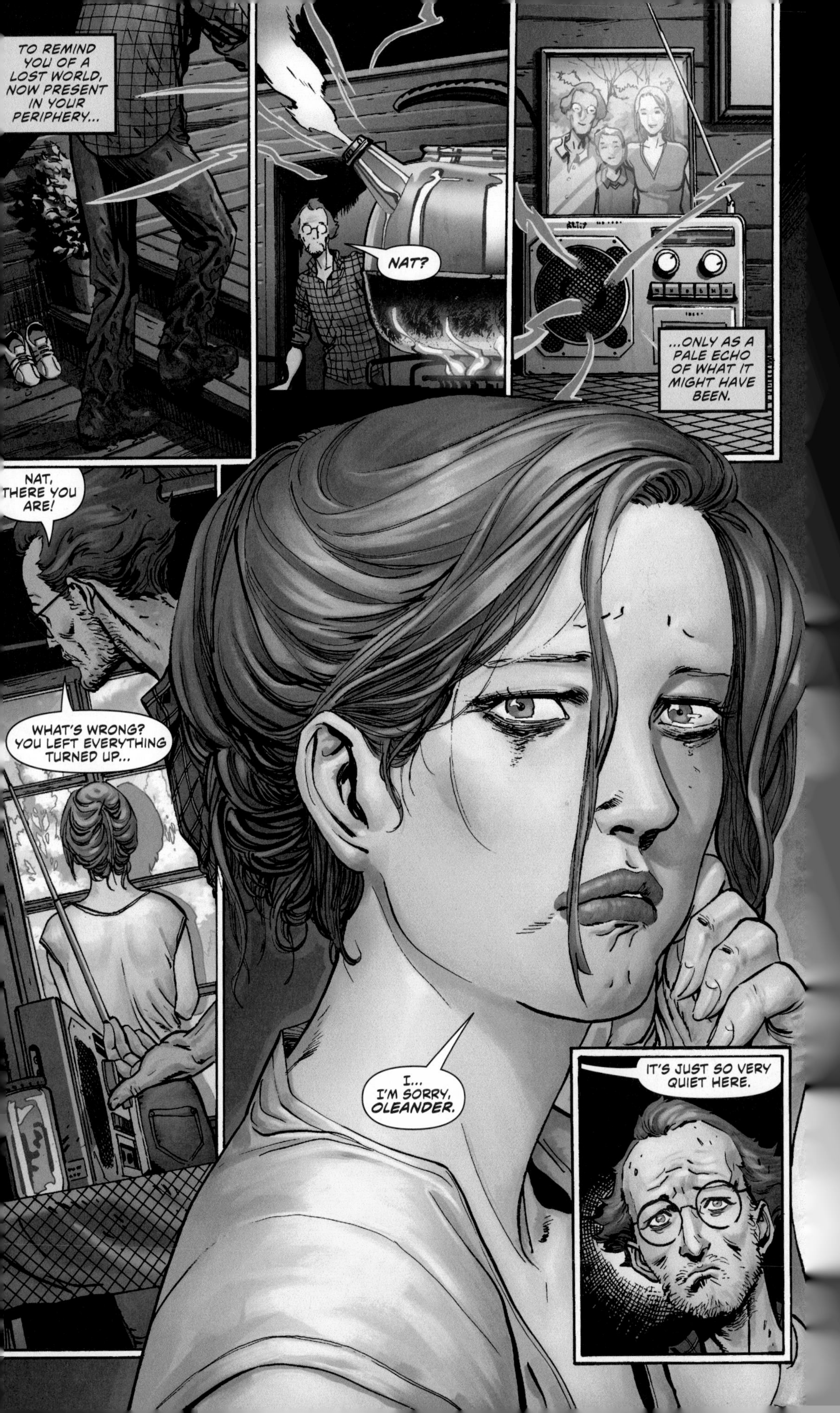
TO REMIND YOU OF A LOST WORLD, NOW PRESENT IN YOUR PERIPHERY...
NAT?
...ONLY AS A PALE ECHO OF WHAT IT MIGHT HAVE BEEN.
NAT, THERE YOU ARE!
WHAT'S WRONG? YOU LEFT EVERYTHING TURNED UP...
I... I'M SORRY, OLEANDER.
IT'S JUST SO VERY QUIET HERE.

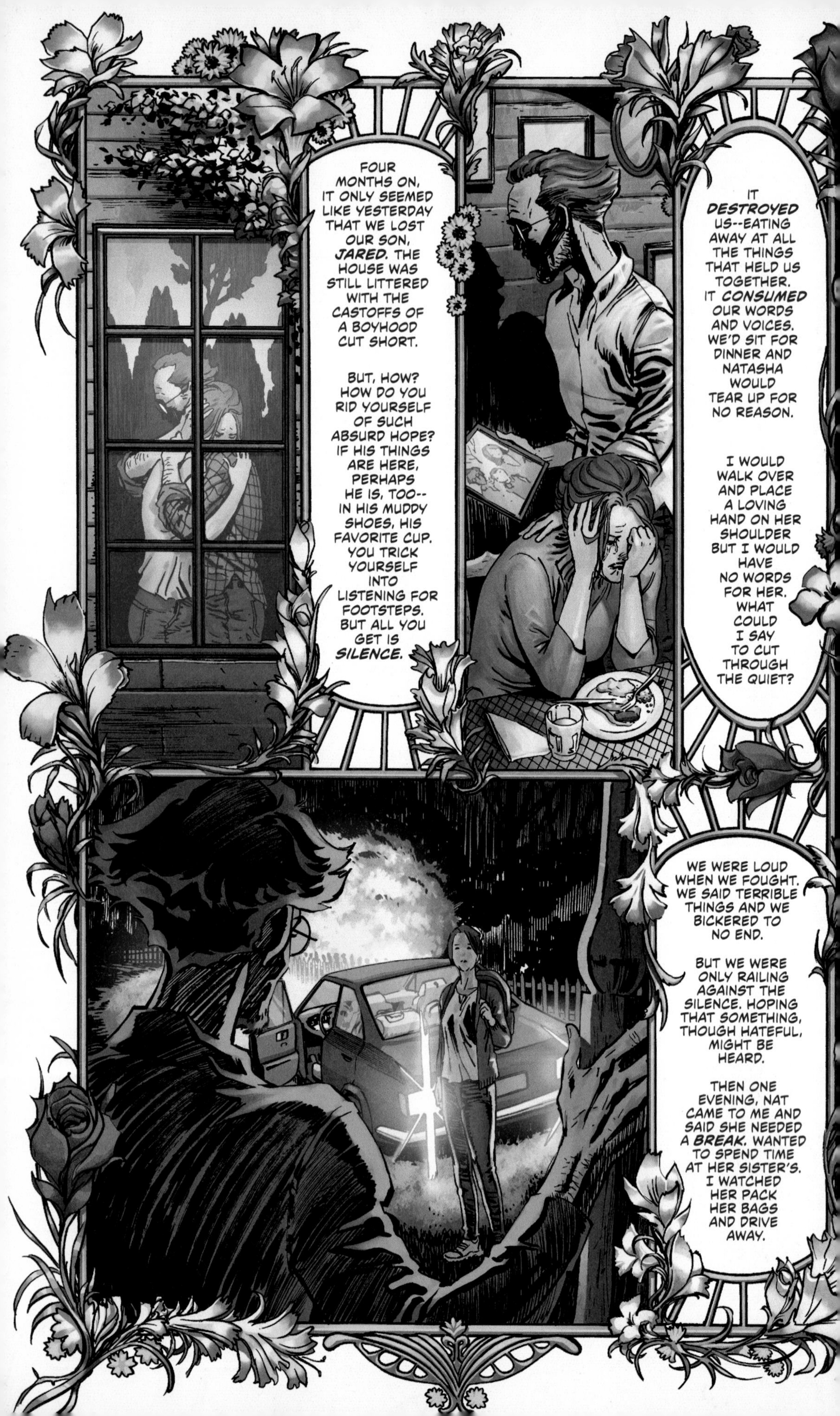
FOUR MONTHS ON, IT ONLY SEEMED LIKE YESTERDAY THAT WE LOST OUR SON, JARED. THE HOUSE WAS STILL LITTERED WITH THE CASTOFFS OF A BOYHOOD CUT SHORT.
BUT, HOW? HOW DO YOU RID YOURSELF OF SUCH ABSURD HOPE? IF HIS THINGS ARE HERE, PERHAPS HE IS, TOO-- IN HIS MUDDY SHOES, HIS FAVORITE CUP. YOU TRICK YOURSELF INTO LISTENING FOR FOOTSTEPS. BUT ALL YOU GET IS SILENCE.
IT DESTROYED US--EATING AWAY AT ALL THE THINGS THAT HELD US TOGETHER. IT CONSUMED OUR WORDS AND VOICES. WE'D SIT FOR DINNER AND NATASHA WOULD TEAR UP FOR NO REASON.
I WOULD WALK OVER AND PLACE A LOVING HAND ON HER SHOULDER BUT I WOULD HAVE NO WORDS FOR HER. WHAT COULD I SAY TO CUT THROUGH THE QUIET?
WE WERE LOUD WHEN WE FOUGHT. WE SAID TERRIBLE THINGS AND WE BICKERED TO NO END.
BUT WE WERE ONLY RAILING AGAINST THE SILENCE. HOPING THAT SOMETHING, THOUGH HATEFUL, MIGHT BE HEARD.
THEN ONE EVENING, NAT CAME TO ME AND SAID SHE NEEDED A BREAK. WANTED TO SPEND TIME AT HER SISTER'S. I WATCHED HER PACK HER BAGS AND DRIVE AWAY.

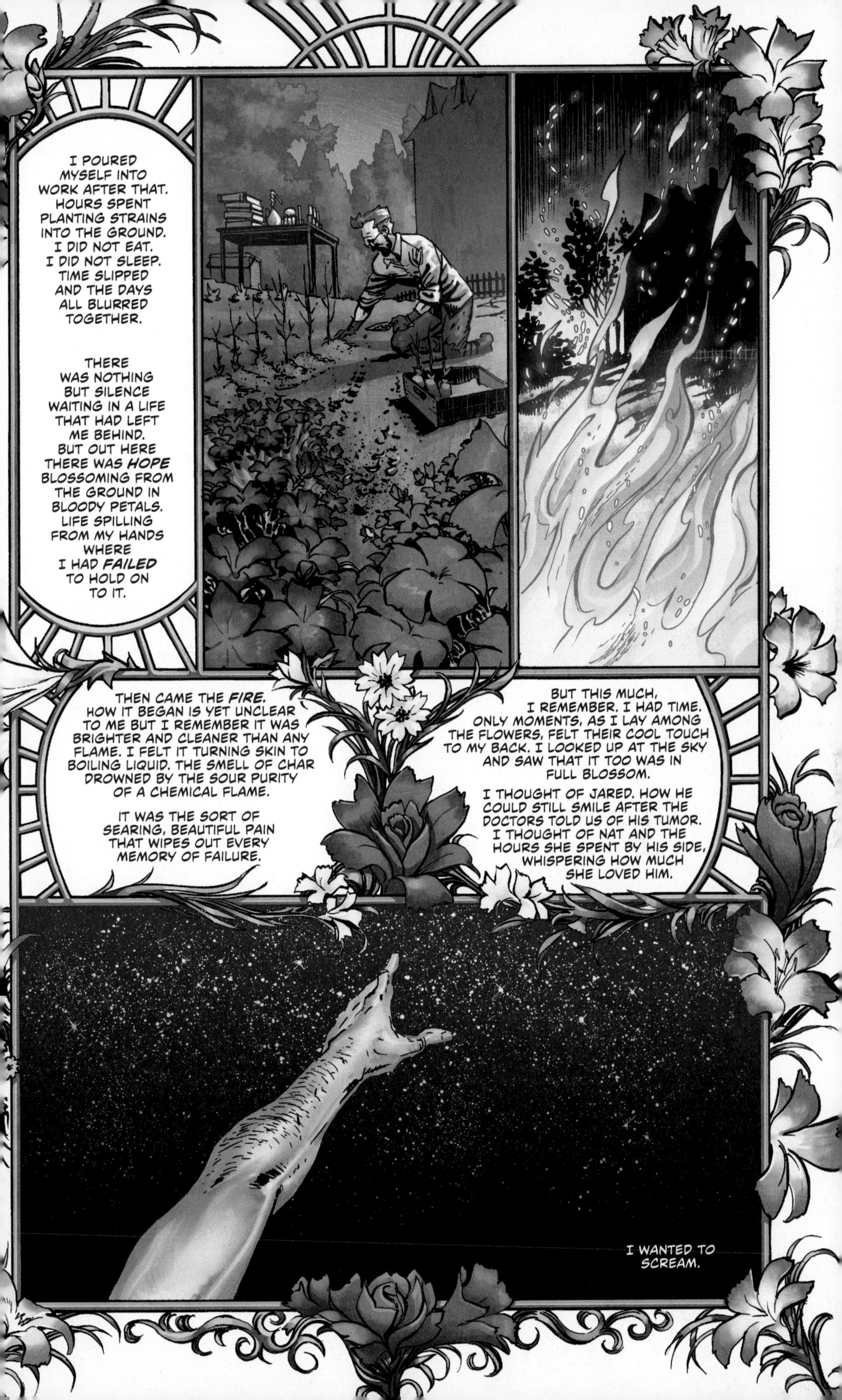
I POURED MYSELF INTO WORK AFTER THAT. HOURS SPENT PLANTING STRAINS INTO THE GROUND. I DID NOT EAT. I DID NOT SLEEP. TIME SLIPPED AND THE DAYS ALL BLURRED TOGETHER.
THERE WAS NOTHING BUT SILENCE WAITING IN A LIFE THAT HAD LEFT ME BEHIND. BUT OUT HERE THERE WAS *HOPE* BLOSSOMING FROM THE GROUND IN BLOODY PETALS. LIFE SPILLING FROM MY HANDS WHERE I HAD *FAILED* TO HOLD ON TO IT.
THEN CAME THE *FIRE.* HOW IT BEGAN IS YET UNCLEAR TO ME BUT I REMEMBER IT WAS BRIGHTER AND CLEANER THAN ANY FLAME. I FELT IT TURNING SKIN TO BOILING LIQUID. THE SMELL OF CHAR DROWNED BY THE SOUR PURITY OF A CHEMICAL FLAME.
IT WAS THE SORT OF SEARING, BEAUTIFUL PAIN THAT WIPES OUT EVERY MEMORY OF FAILURE.
BUT THIS MUCH, I REMEMBER. I HAD TIME. ONLY MOMENTS, AS I LAY AMONG THE FLOWERS, FELT THEIR COOL TOUCH TO MY BACK. I LOOKED UP AT THE SKY AND SAW THAT IT TOO WAS IN FULL BLOSSOM.
I THOUGHT OF JARED. HOW HE COULD STILL SMILE AFTER THE DOCTORS TOLD US OF HIS TUMOR. I THOUGHT OF NAT AND THE HOURS SHE SPENT BY HIS SIDE, WHISPERING HOW MUCH SHE LOVED HIM.
I WANTED TO SCREAM.

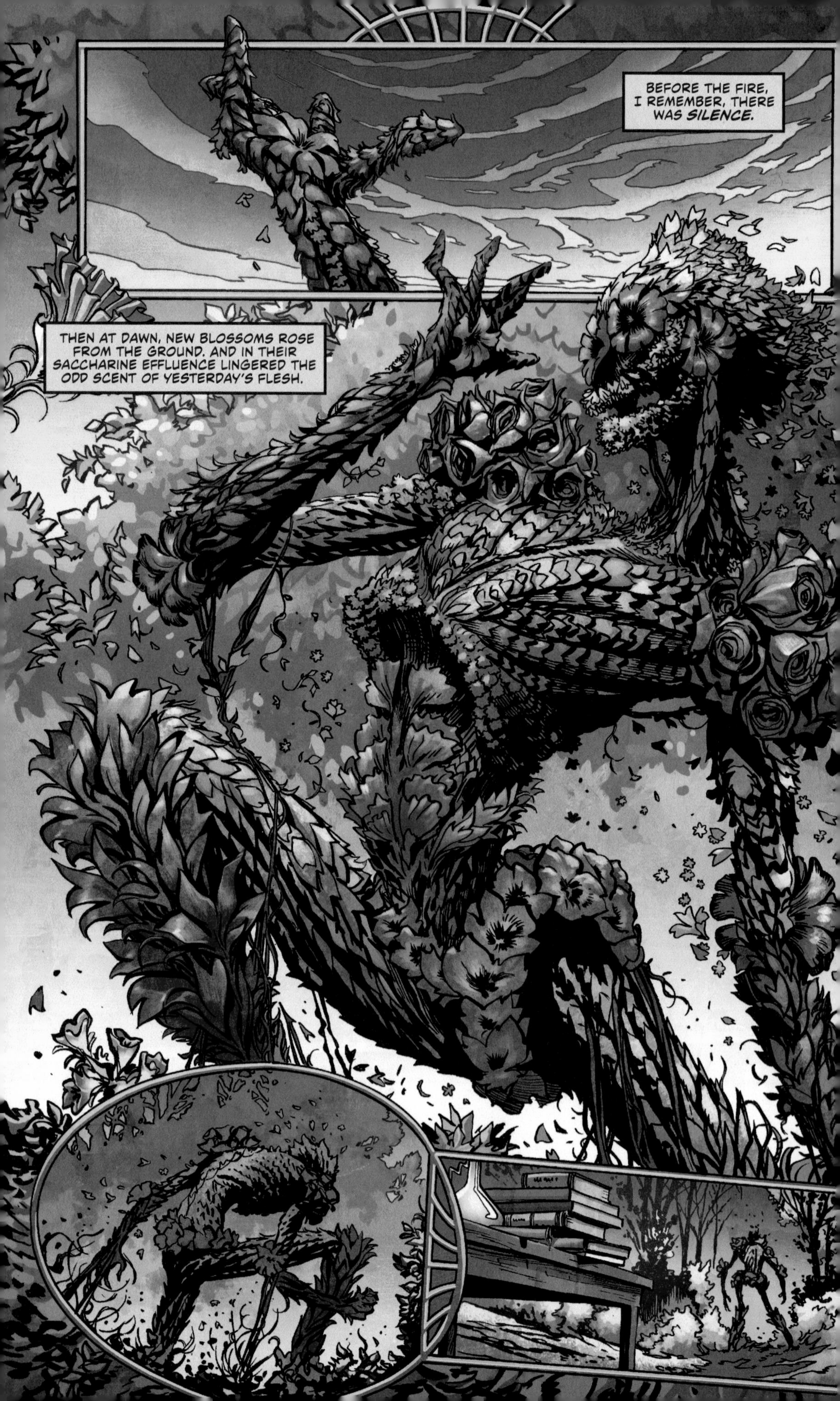
BEFORE THE FIRE, I REMEMBER, THERE WAS SILENCE.
THEN AT DAWN, NEW BLOSSOMS ROSE FROM THE GROUND. AND IN THEIR SACCHARINE EFFLUENCE LINGERED THE ODD SCENT OF YESTERDAY'S FLESH.

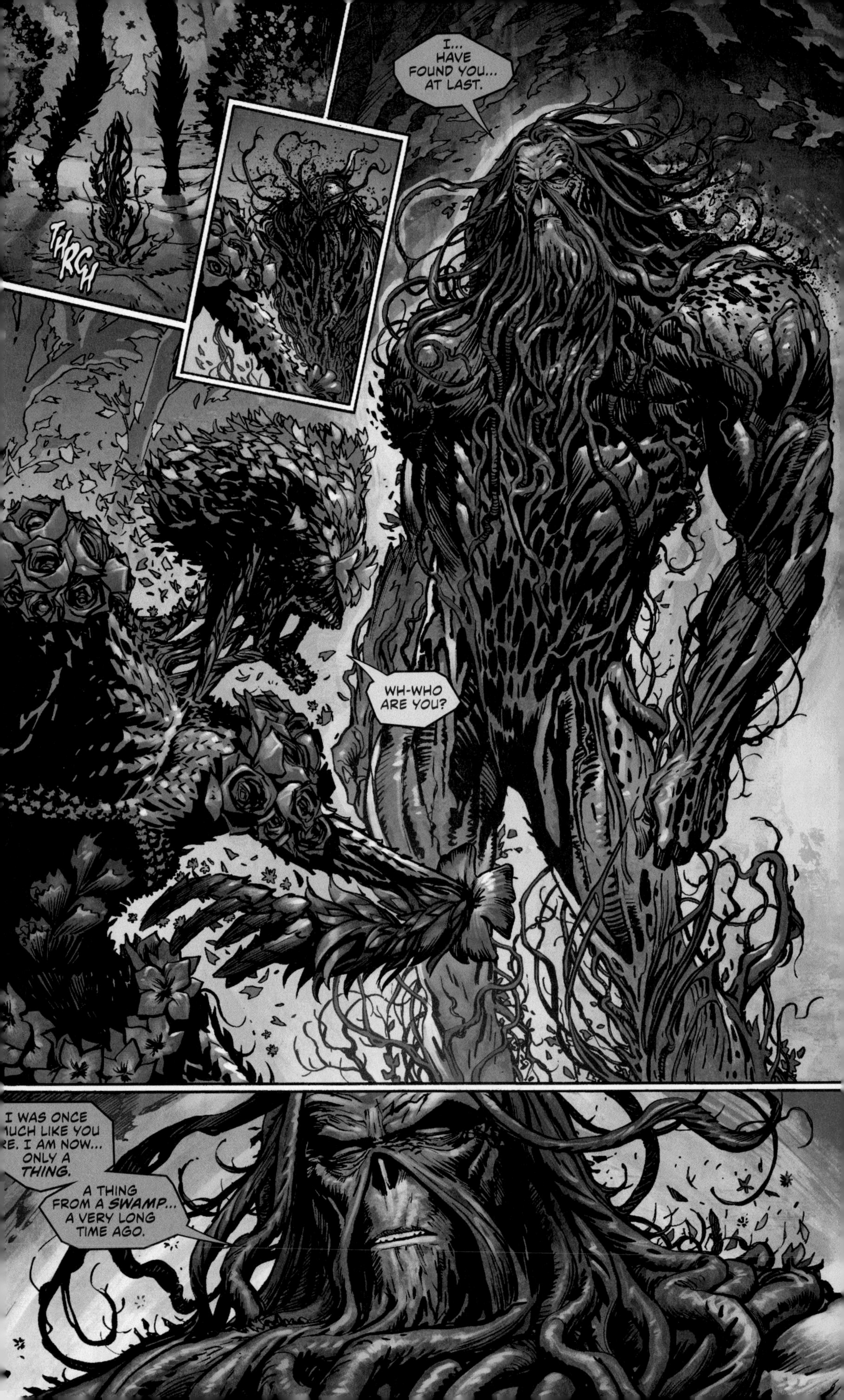
THRCH
I... HAVE FOUND YOU... AT LAST.
WH-WHO ARE YOU?
I WAS ONCE MUCH LIKE YOU ARE. I AM NOW... ONLY A THING.
A THING FROM A SWAMP... A VERY LONG TIME AGO.

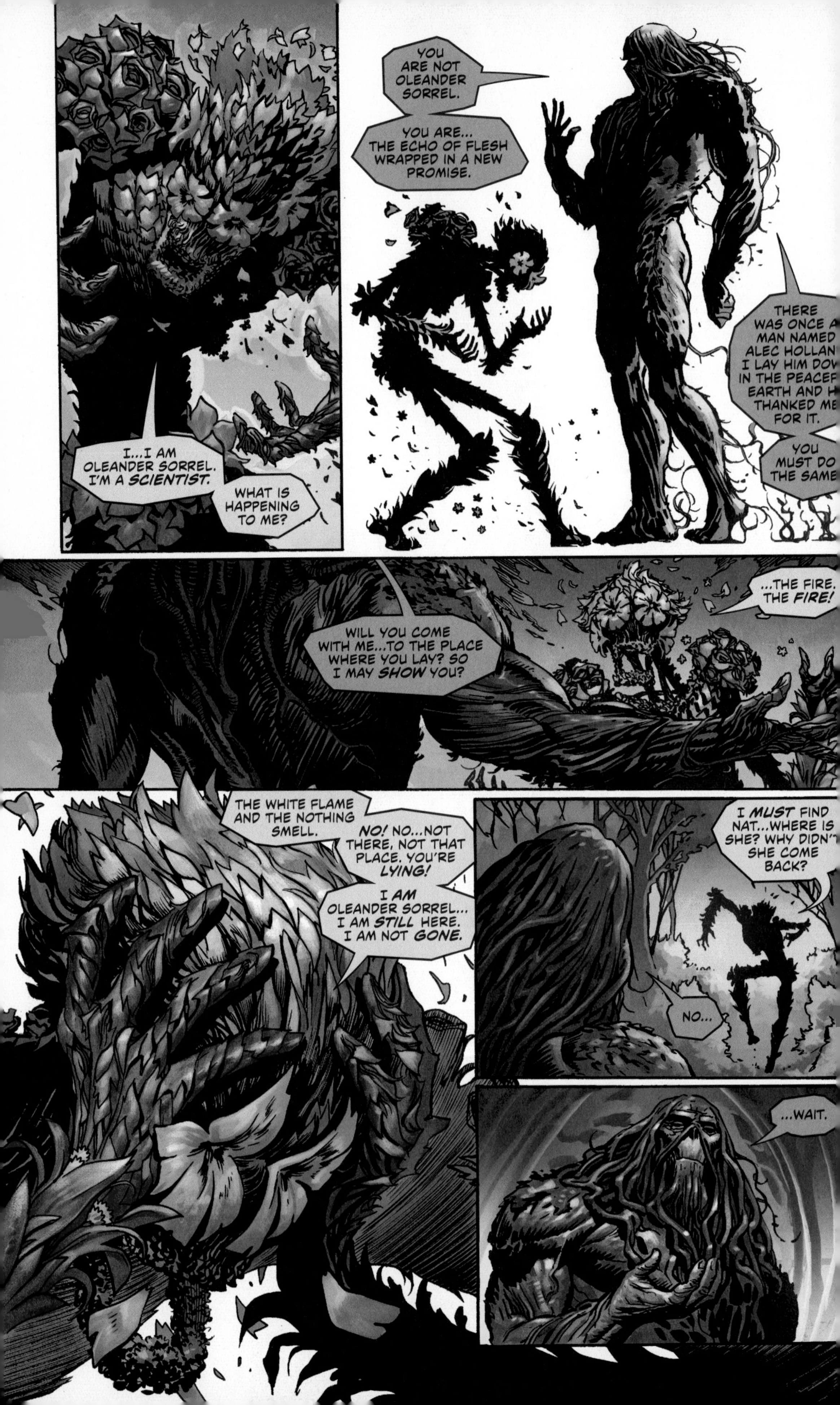

I...I AM OLEANDER SORREL. I'M A SCIENTIST.
WHAT IS HAPPENING TO ME?
YOU ARE NOT OLEANDER SORREL.
YOU ARE... THE ECHO OF FLESH WRAPPED IN A NEW PROMISE.
THERE WAS ONCE A MAN NAMED ALEC HOLLAN I LAY HIM DOV IN THE PEACEF EARTH AND H THANKED ME FOR IT.
YOU MUST DO THE SAME
WILL YOU COME WITH ME...TO THE PLACE WHERE YOU LAY? SO I MAY SHOW YOU?
...THE FIRE. THE FIRE!
THE WHITE FLAME AND THE NOTHING SMELL.
NO! NO...NOT THERE, NOT THAT PLACE. YOU'RE LYING!
I AM OLEANDER SORREL... I AM STILL HERE. I AM NOT GONE.
I MUST FIND NAT...WHERE IS SHE? WHY DIDN'T SHE COME BACK?
NO...
...WAIT.

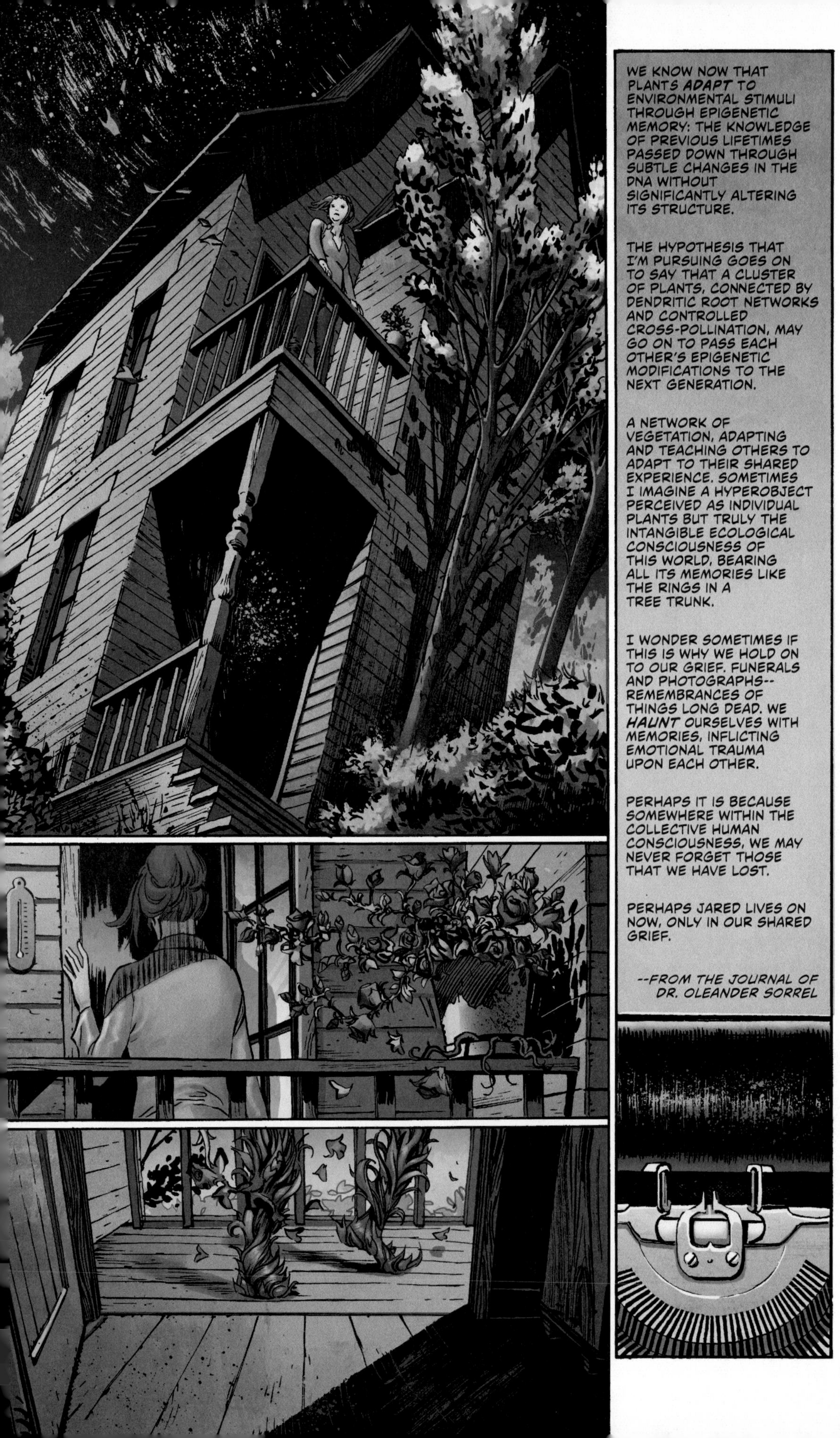
WE KNOW NOW THAT PLANTS *ADAPT* TO ENVIRONMENTAL STIMULI THROUGH EPIGENETIC MEMORY: THE KNOWLEDGE OF PREVIOUS LIFETIMES PASSED DOWN THROUGH SUBTLE CHANGES IN THE DNA WITHOUT SIGNIFICANTLY ALTERING ITS STRUCTURE.
THE HYPOTHESIS THAT I'M PURSUING GOES ON TO SAY THAT A CLUSTER OF PLANTS, CONNECTED BY DENDRITIC ROOT NETWORKS AND CONTROLLED CROSS-POLLINATION, MAY GO ON TO PASS EACH OTHER'S EPIGENETIC MODIFICATIONS TO THE NEXT GENERATION.
A NETWORK OF VEGETATION, ADAPTING AND TEACHING OTHERS TO ADAPT TO THEIR SHARED EXPERIENCE. SOMETIMES I IMAGINE A HYPEROBJECT PERCEIVED AS INDIVIDUAL PLANTS BUT TRULY THE INTANGIBLE ECOLOGICAL CONSCIOUSNESS OF THIS WORLD, BEARING ALL ITS MEMORIES LIKE THE RINGS IN A TREE TRUNK.
I WONDER SOMETIMES IF THIS IS WHY WE HOLD ON TO OUR GRIEF. FUNERALS AND PHOTOGRAPHS-- REMEMBRANCES OF THINGS LONG DEAD. WE *HAUNT* OURSELVES WITH MEMORIES, INFLICTING EMOTIONAL TRAUMA UPON EACH OTHER.
PERHAPS IT IS BECAUSE SOMEWHERE WITHIN THE COLLECTIVE HUMAN CONSCIOUSNESS, WE MAY NEVER FORGET THOSE THAT WE HAVE LOST.
PERHAPS JARED LIVES ON NOW, ONLY IN OUR SHARED GRIEF.
--FROM THE JOURNAL OF DR. OLEANDER SORREL

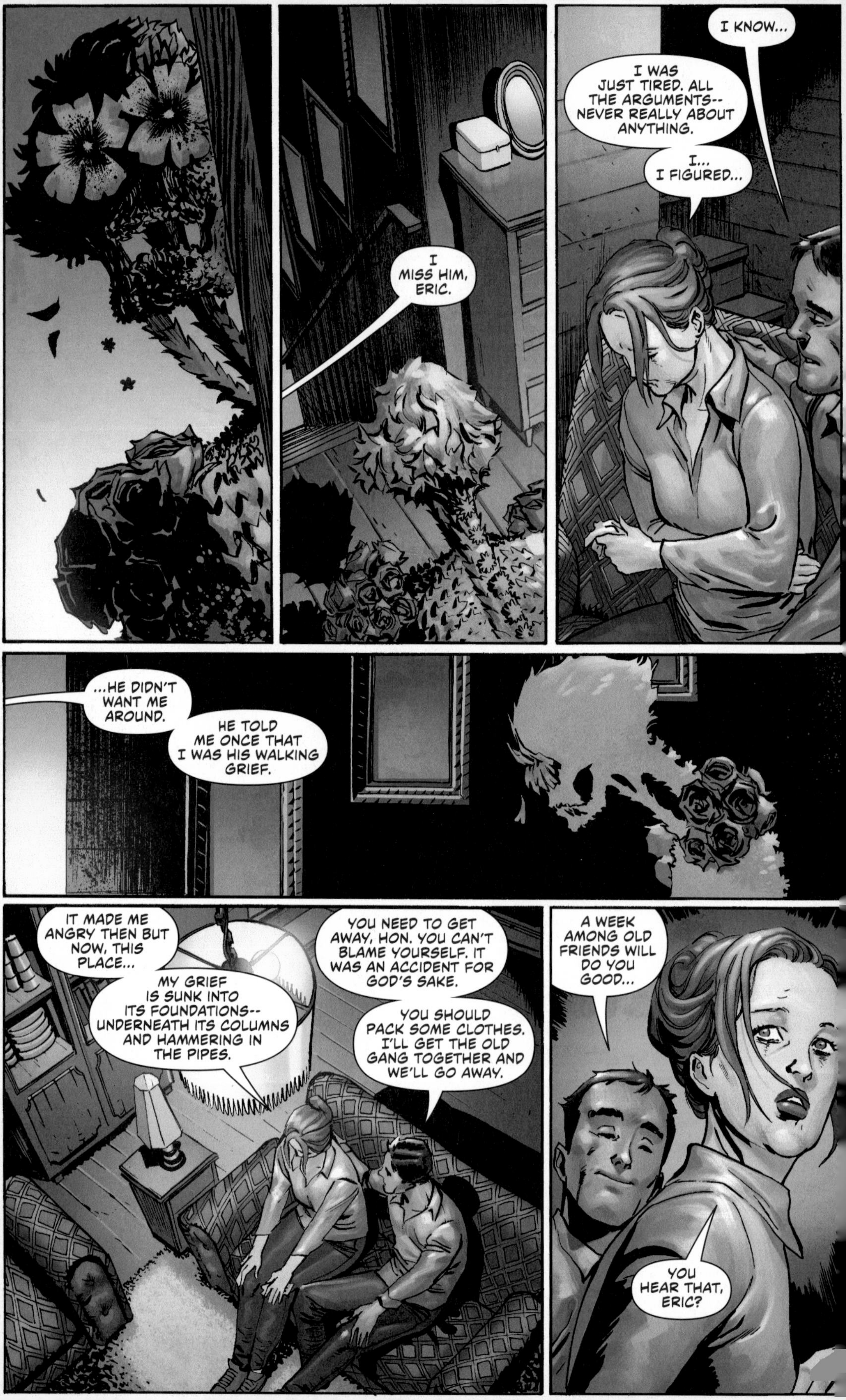
I MISS HIM, ERIC.
I KNOW...
I WAS JUST TIRED. ALL THE ARGUMENTS-- NEVER REALLY ABOUT ANYTHING.
I... I FIGURED...
...HE DIDN'T WANT ME AROUND.
HE TOLD ME ONCE THAT I WAS HIS WALKING GRIEF.
IT MADE ME ANGRY THEN BUT NOW, THIS PLACE...
MY GRIEF IS SUNK INTO ITS FOUNDATIONS-- UNDERNEATH ITS COLUMNS AND HAMMERING IN THE PIPES.
YOU NEED TO GET AWAY, HON. YOU CAN'T BLAME YOURSELF. IT WAS AN ACCIDENT FOR GOD'S SAKE.
YOU SHOULD PACK SOME CLOTHES. I'LL GET THE OLD GANG TOGETHER AND WE'LL GO AWAY.
A WEEK AMONG OLD FRIENDS WILL DO YOU GOOD...
YOU HEAR THAT, ERIC?

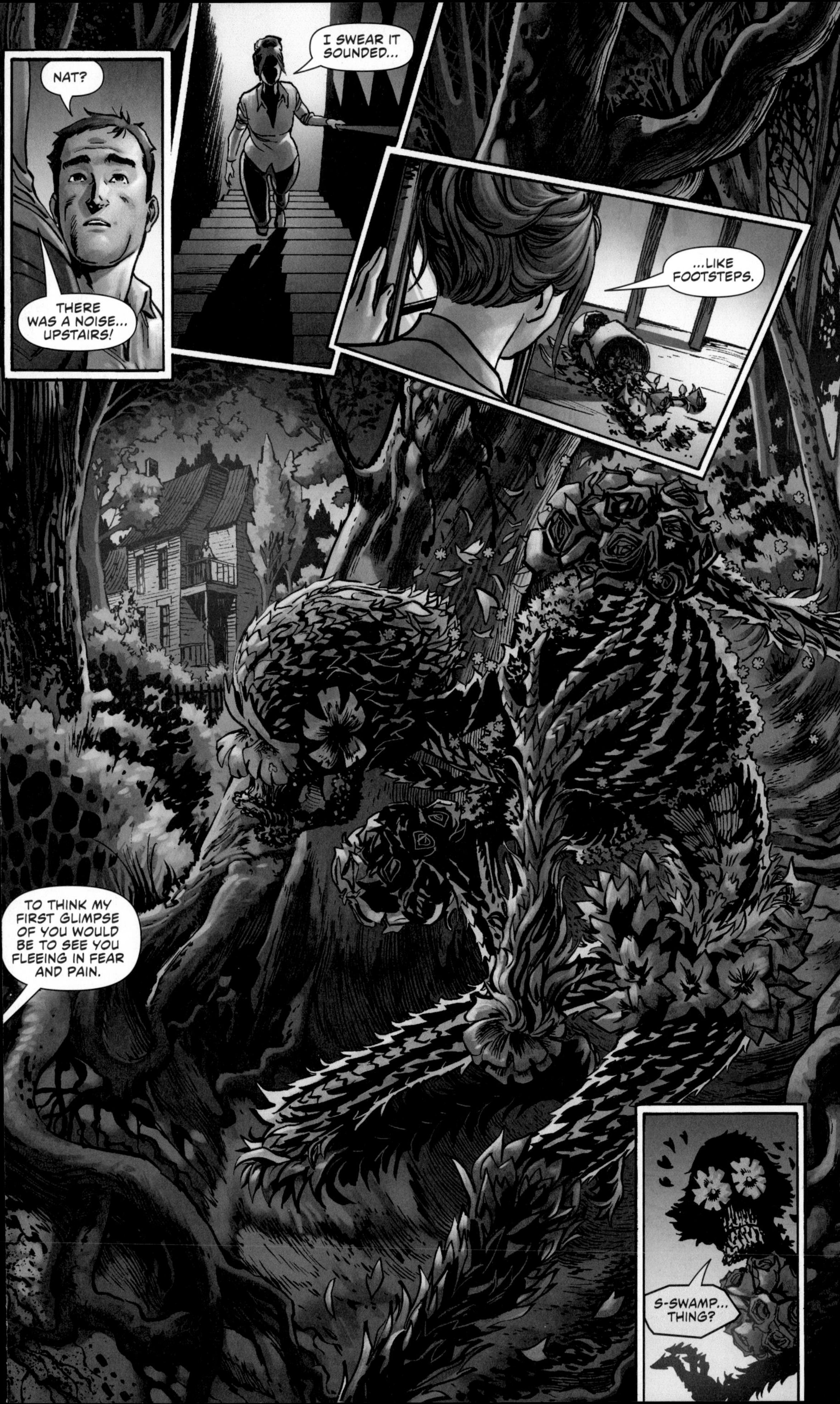
NAT?
THERE WAS A NOISE... UPSTAIRS!
I SWEAR IT SOUNDED...
...LIKE FOOTSTEPS.
TO THINK MY FIRST GLIMPSE OF YOU WOULD BE TO SEE YOU FLEEING IN FEAR AND PAIN.
S-SWAMP... THING?

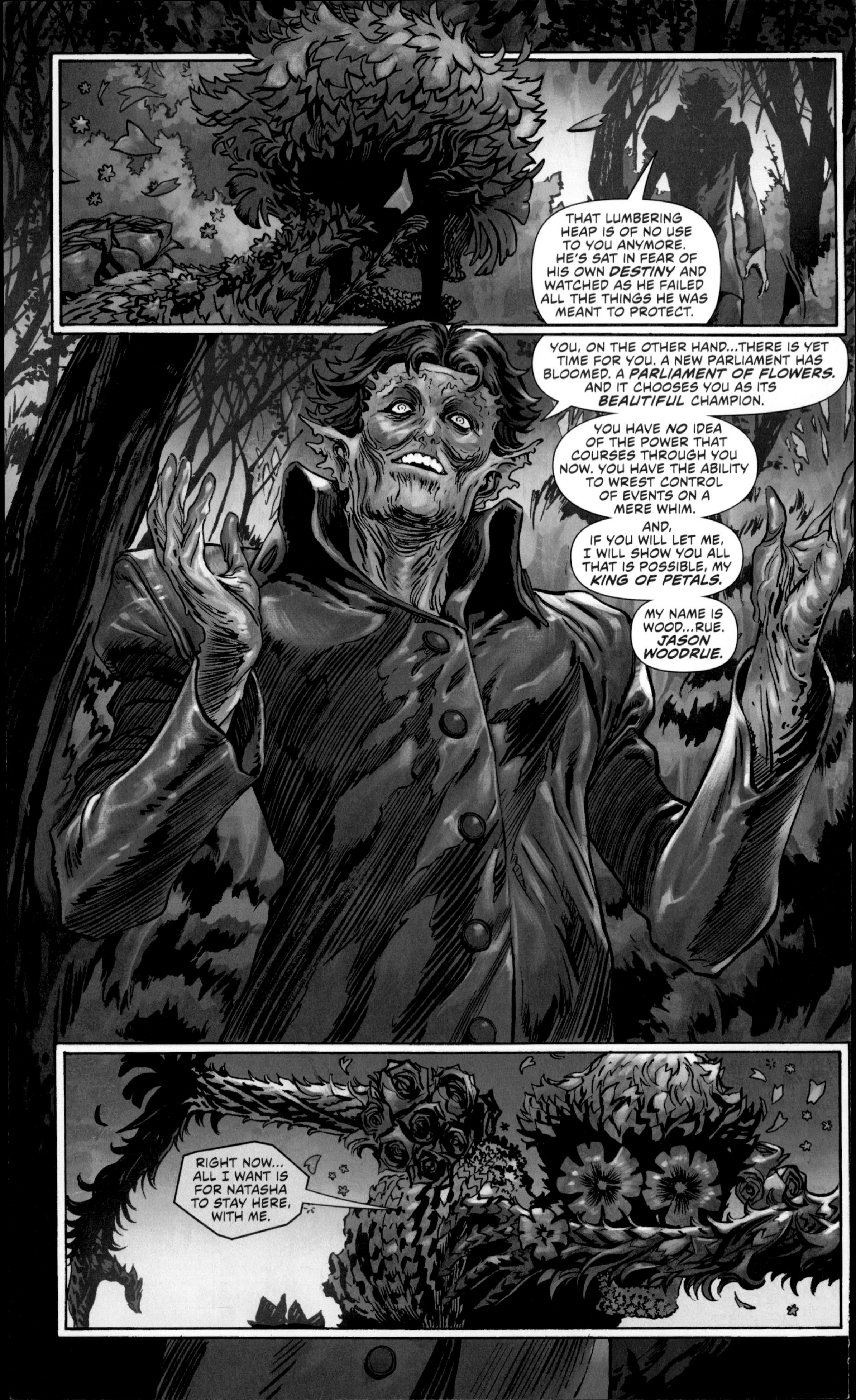
THAT LUMBERING HEAP IS OF NO USE TO YOU ANYMORE. HE'S SAT IN FEAR OF HIS OWN DESTINY AND WATCHED AS HE FAILED ALL THE THINGS HE WAS MEANT TO PROTECT.
YOU, ON THE OTHER HAND...THERE IS YET TIME FOR YOU. A NEW PARLIAMENT HAS BLOOMED. A PARLIAMENT OF FLOWERS. AND IT CHOOSES YOU AS ITS BEAUTIFUL CHAMPION.
YOU HAVE NO IDEA OF THE POWER THAT COURSES THROUGH YOU NOW. YOU HAVE THE ABILITY TO WREST CONTROL OF EVENTS ON A MERE WHIM.
AND, IF YOU WILL LET ME, I WILL SHOW YOU ALL THAT IS POSSIBLE, MY KING OF PETALS.
MY NAME IS WOOD...RUE. JASON WOODRUE.
RIGHT NOW... ALL I WANT IS FOR NATASHA TO STAY HERE, WITH ME.

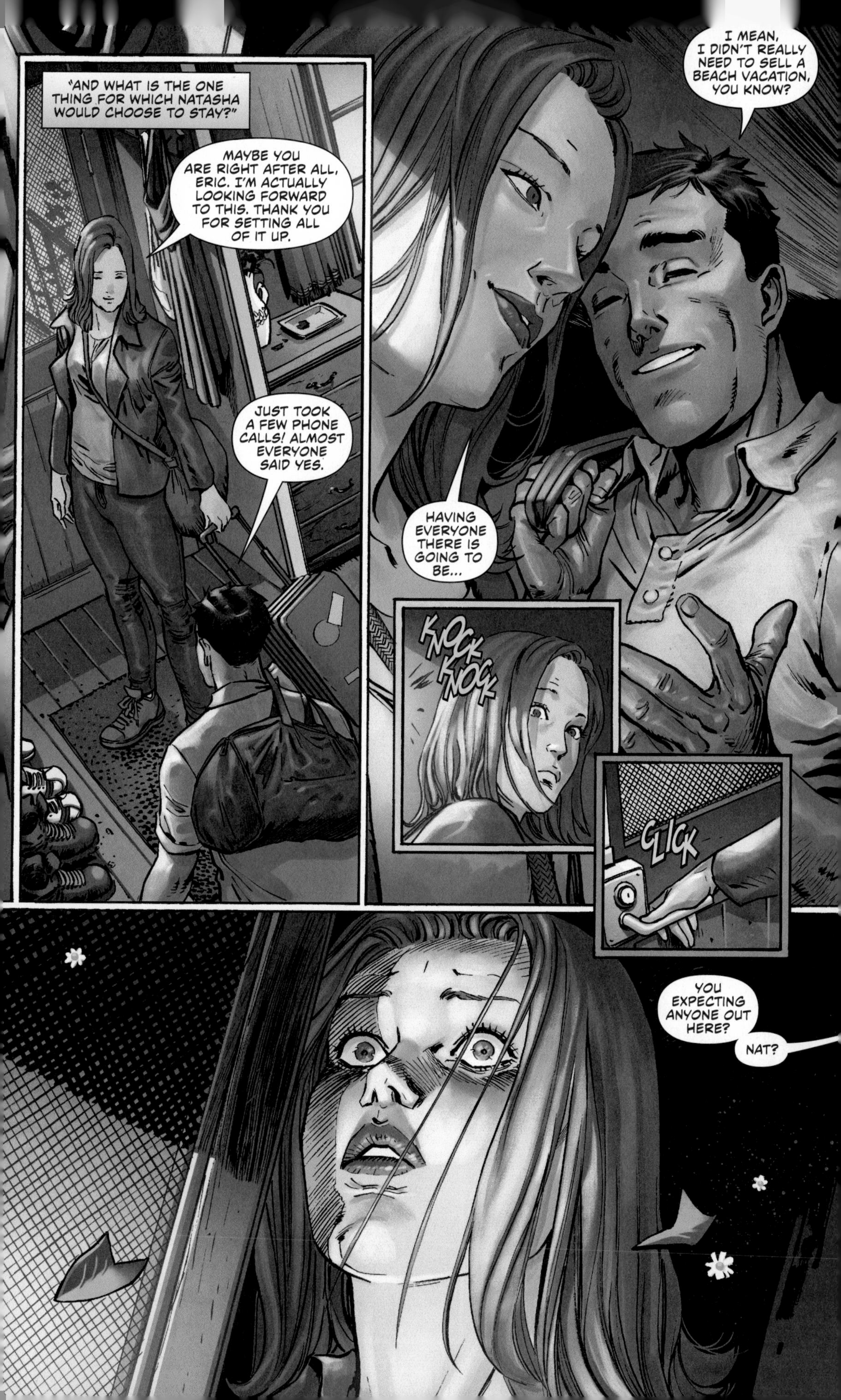
"AND WHAT IS THE ONE THING FOR WHICH NATASHA WOULD CHOOSE TO STAY?"
MAYBE YOU ARE RIGHT AFTER ALL, ERIC. I'M ACTUALLY LOOKING FORWARD TO THIS. THANK YOU FOR SETTING ALL OF IT UP.
JUST TOOK A FEW PHONE CALLS! ALMOST EVERYONE SAID YES.
HAVING EVERYONE THERE IS GOING TO BE...
I MEAN, I DIDN'T REALLY NEED TO SELL A BEACH VACATION, YOU KNOW?
KNOCK KNOCK
CLICK
YOU EXPECTING ANYONE OUT HERE?
NAT?

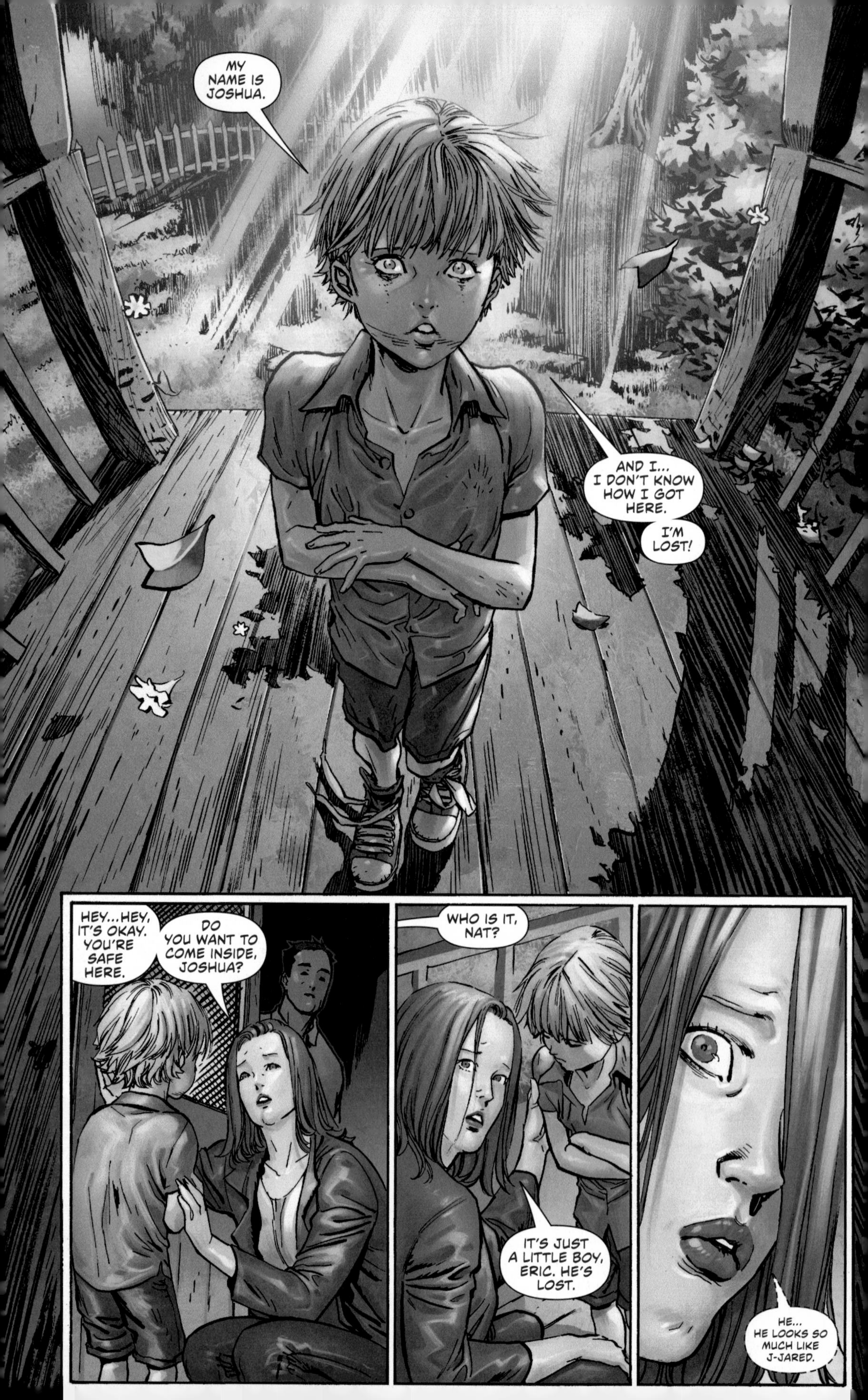
MY NAME IS JOSHUA.
AND I... I DON'T KNOW HOW I GOT HERE.
I'M LOST!
HEY...HEY, IT'S OKAY. YOU'RE SAFE HERE.
DO YOU WANT TO COME INSIDE, JOSHUA?
WHO IS IT, NAT?
IT'S JUST A LITTLE BOY, ERIC. HE'S LOST.
HE... HE LOOKS SO MUCH LIKE J-JARED.

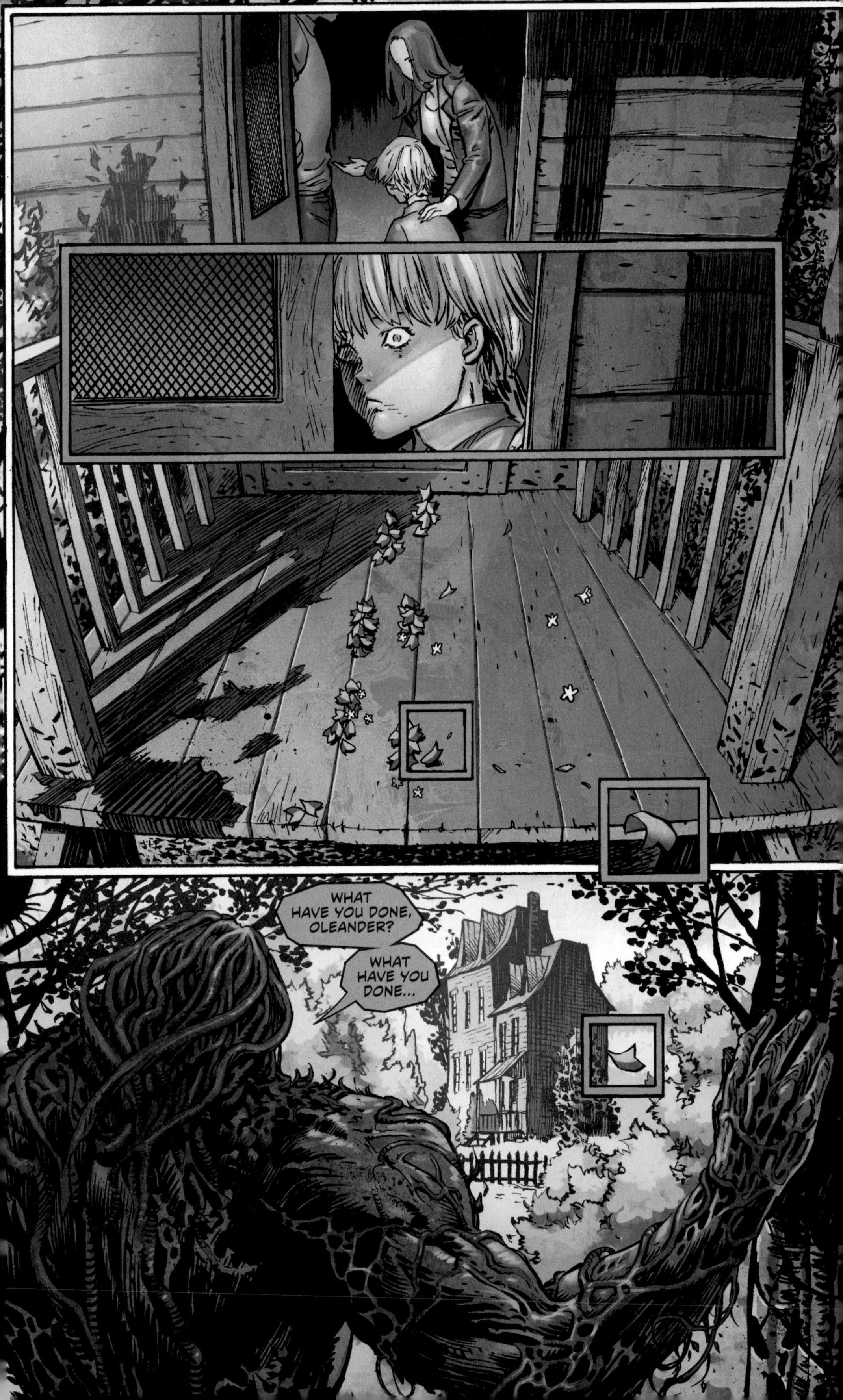
WHAT HAVE YOU DONE, OLEANDER?
WHAT HAVE YOU DONE...

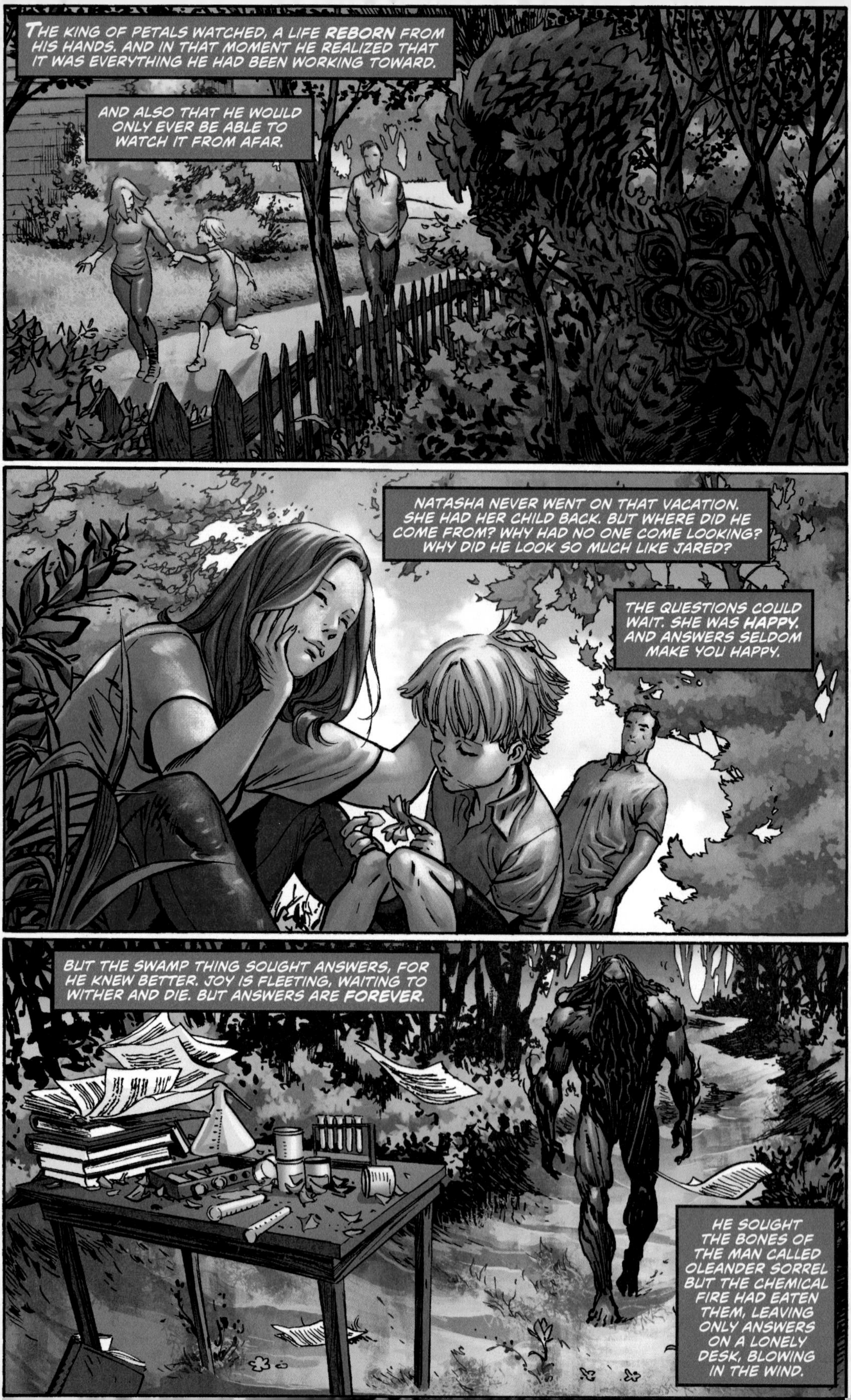
THE KING OF PETALS WATCHED, A LIFE REBORN FROM HIS HANDS. AND IN THAT MOMENT HE REALIZED THAT IT WAS EVERYTHING HE HAD BEEN WORKING TOWARD.
AND ALSO THAT HE WOULD ONLY EVER BE ABLE TO WATCH IT FROM AFAR.
NATASHA NEVER WENT ON THAT VACATION. SHE HAD HER CHILD BACK. BUT WHERE DID HE COME FROM? WHY HAD NO ONE COME LOOKING? WHY DID HE LOOK SO MUCH LIKE JARED?
THE QUESTIONS COULD WAIT. SHE WAS HAPPY. AND ANSWERS SELDOM MAKE YOU HAPPY.
BUT THE SWAMP THING SOUGHT ANSWERS, FOR HE KNEW BETTER. JOY IS FLEETING, WAITING TO WITHER AND DIE. BUT ANSWERS ARE FOREVER.
HE SOUGHT THE BONES OF THE MAN CALLED OLEANDER SORREL BUT THE CHEMICAL FIRE HAD EATEN THEM, LEAVING ONLY ANSWERS ON A LONELY DESK, BLOWING IN THE WIND.

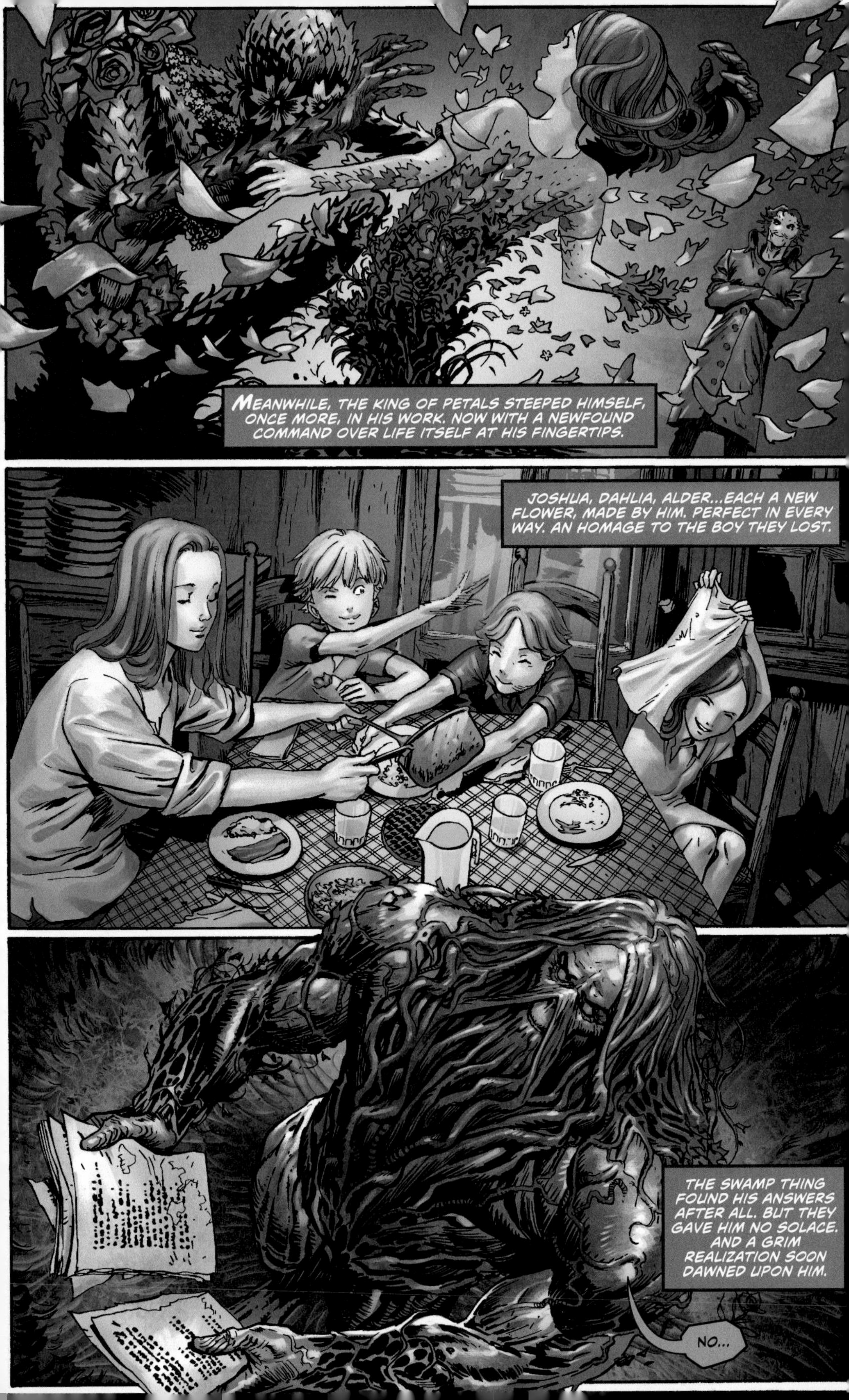
MEANWHILE, THE KING OF PETALS STEEPED HIMSELF, ONCE MORE, IN HIS WORK. NOW WITH A NEWFOUND COMMAND OVER LIFE ITSELF AT HIS FINGERTIPS.
JOSHUA, DAHLIA, ALDER...EACH A NEW FLOWER, MADE BY HIM. PERFECT IN EVERY WAY. AN HOMAGE TO THE BOY THEY LOST.
THE SWAMP THING FOUND HIS ANSWERS AFTER ALL. BUT THEY GAVE HIM NO SOLACE. AND A GRIM REALIZATION SOON DAWNED UPON HIM.
NO...

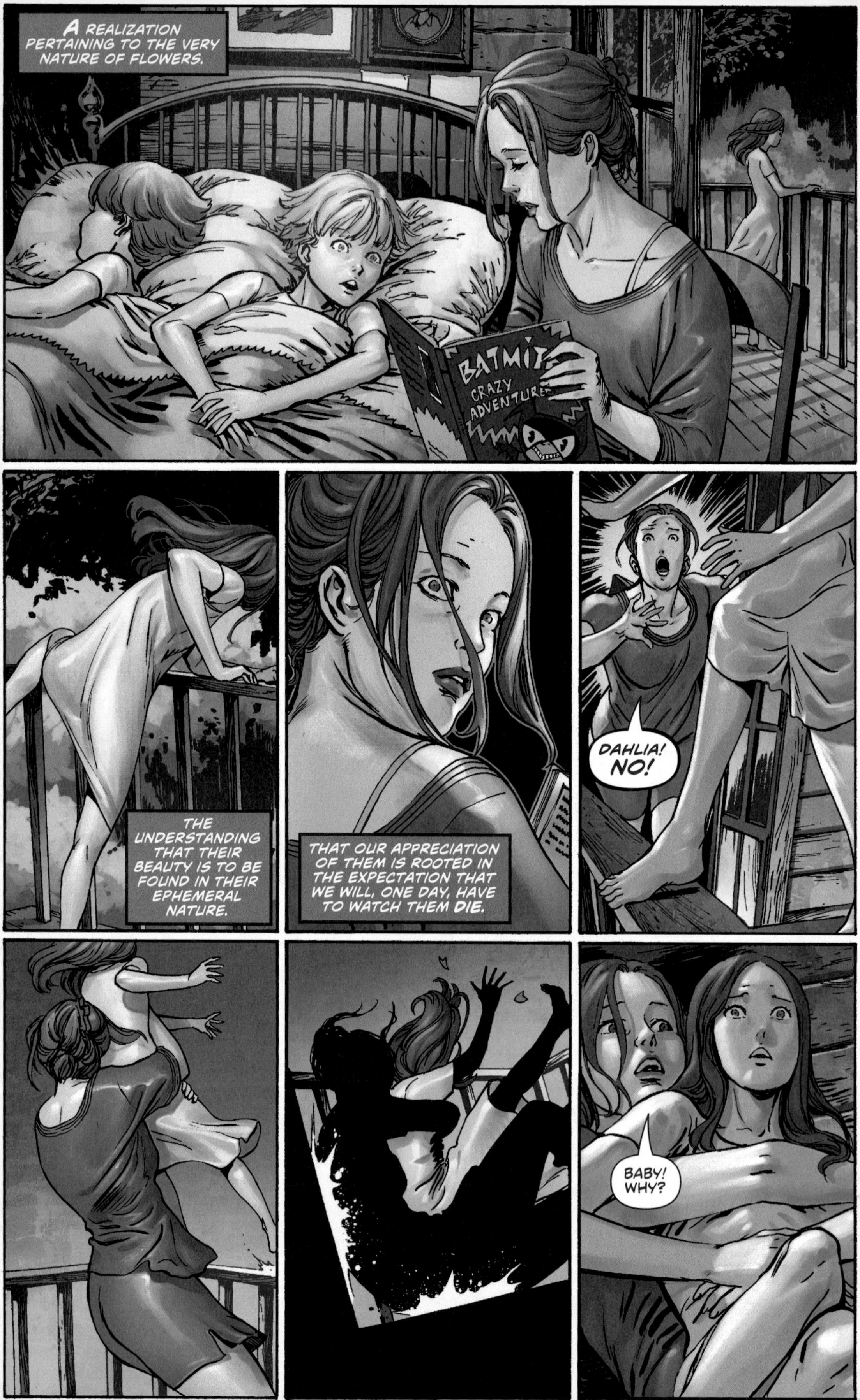
A REALIZATION PERTAINING TO THE VERY NATURE OF FLOWERS.
BATMITE CRAZY ADVENTURES
THE UNDERSTANDING THAT THEIR BEAUTY IS TO BE FOUND IN THEIR EPHEMERAL NATURE.
THAT OUR APPRECIATION OF THEM IS ROOTED IN THE EXPECTATION THAT WE WILL, ONE DAY, HAVE TO WATCH THEM DIE.
DAHLIA! NO!
BABY! WHY?

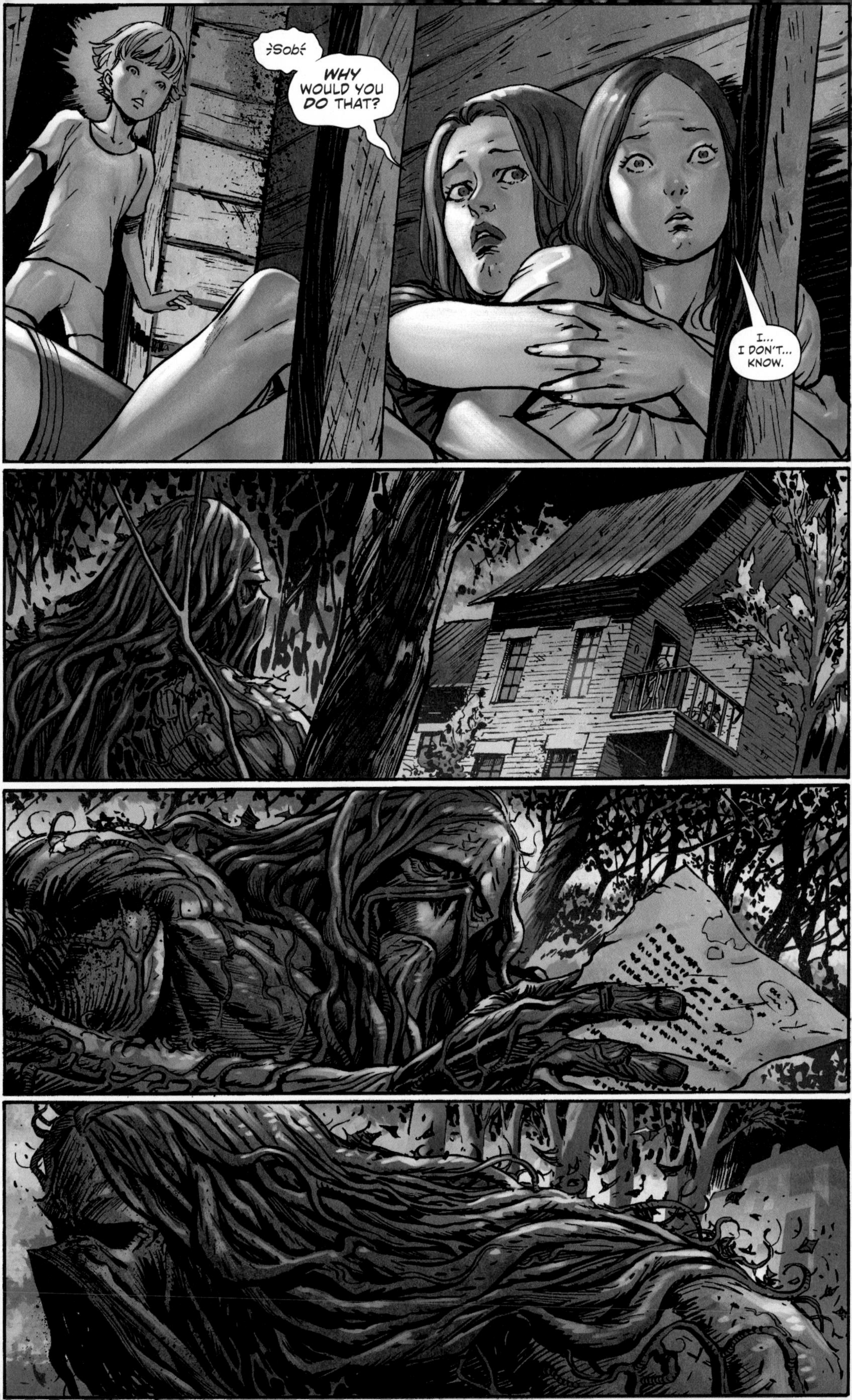

SOB
WHY WOULD YOU DO THAT?
I... I DON'T... KNOW.

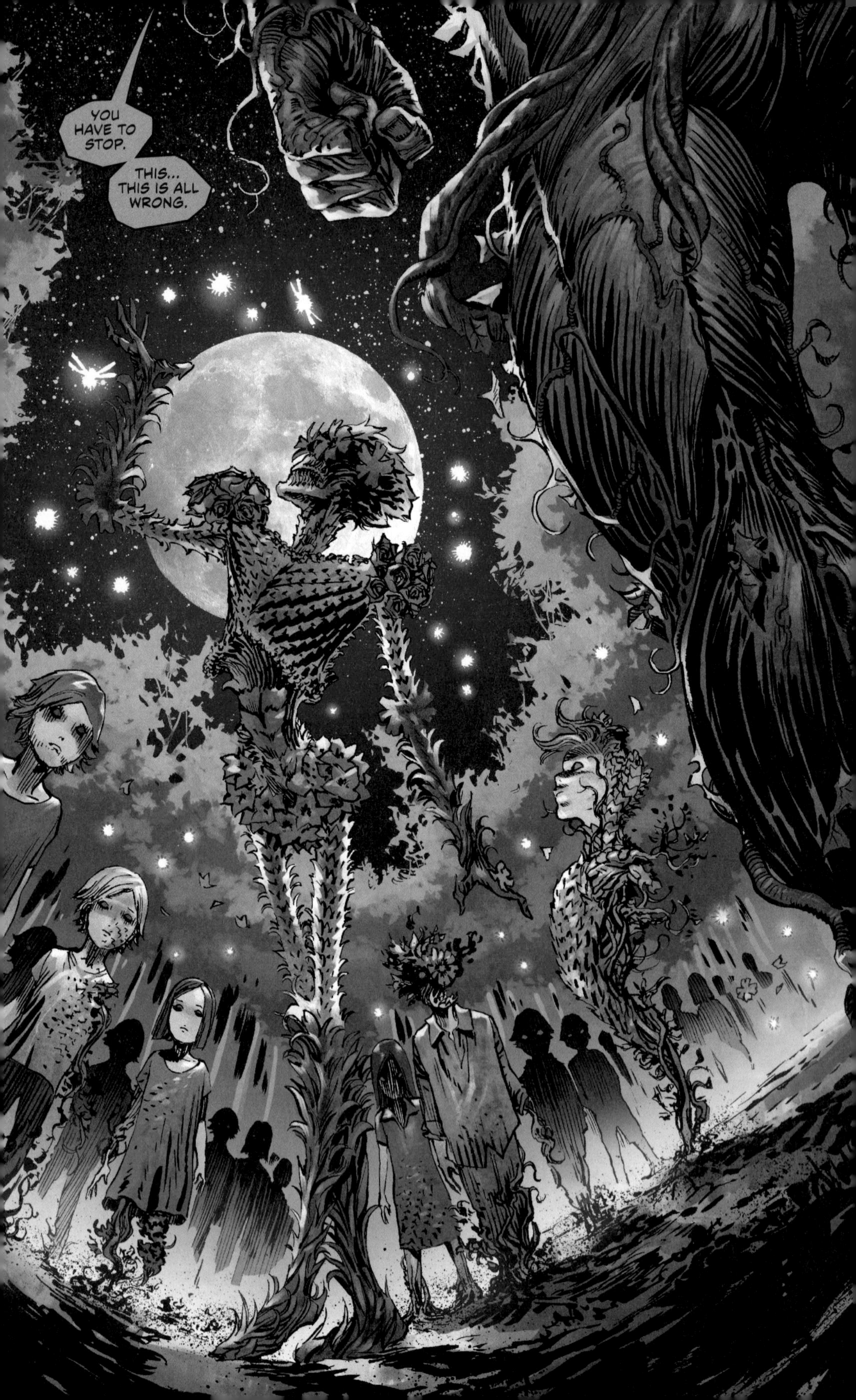
YOU HAVE TO STOP.
THIS... THIS IS ALL WRONG.

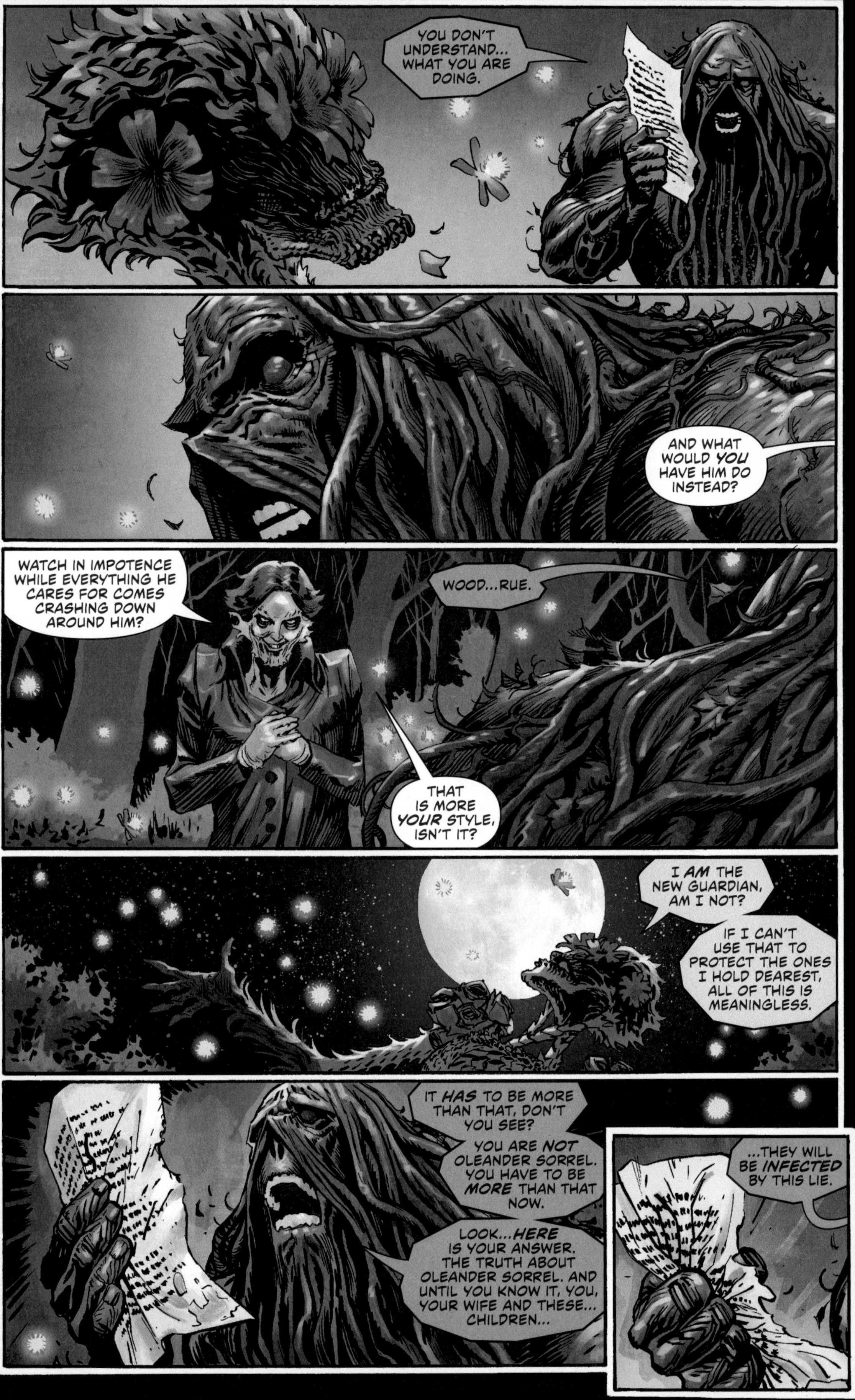
YOU DON'T UNDERSTAND... WHAT YOU ARE DOING.
AND WHAT WOULD *YOU* HAVE HIM DO INSTEAD?
WATCH IN IMPOTENCE WHILE EVERYTHING HE CARES FOR COMES CRASHING DOWN AROUND HIM?
WOOD...RUE.
THAT IS MORE *YOUR* STYLE, ISN'T IT?
I *AM* THE NEW GUARDIAN, AM I NOT?
IF I CAN'T USE THAT TO PROTECT THE ONES I HOLD DEAREST, ALL OF THIS IS MEANINGLESS.
IT *HAS* TO BE MORE THAN THAT, DON'T YOU SEE?
YOU ARE *NOT* OLEANDER SORREL. YOU HAVE TO BE *MORE* THAN THAT NOW.
LOOK...*HERE* IS YOUR ANSWER. THE TRUTH ABOUT OLEANDER SORREL. AND UNTIL YOU KNOW IT, YOU, YOUR WIFE AND THESE... CHILDREN...
...THEY WILL BE *INFECTED* BY THIS LIE.

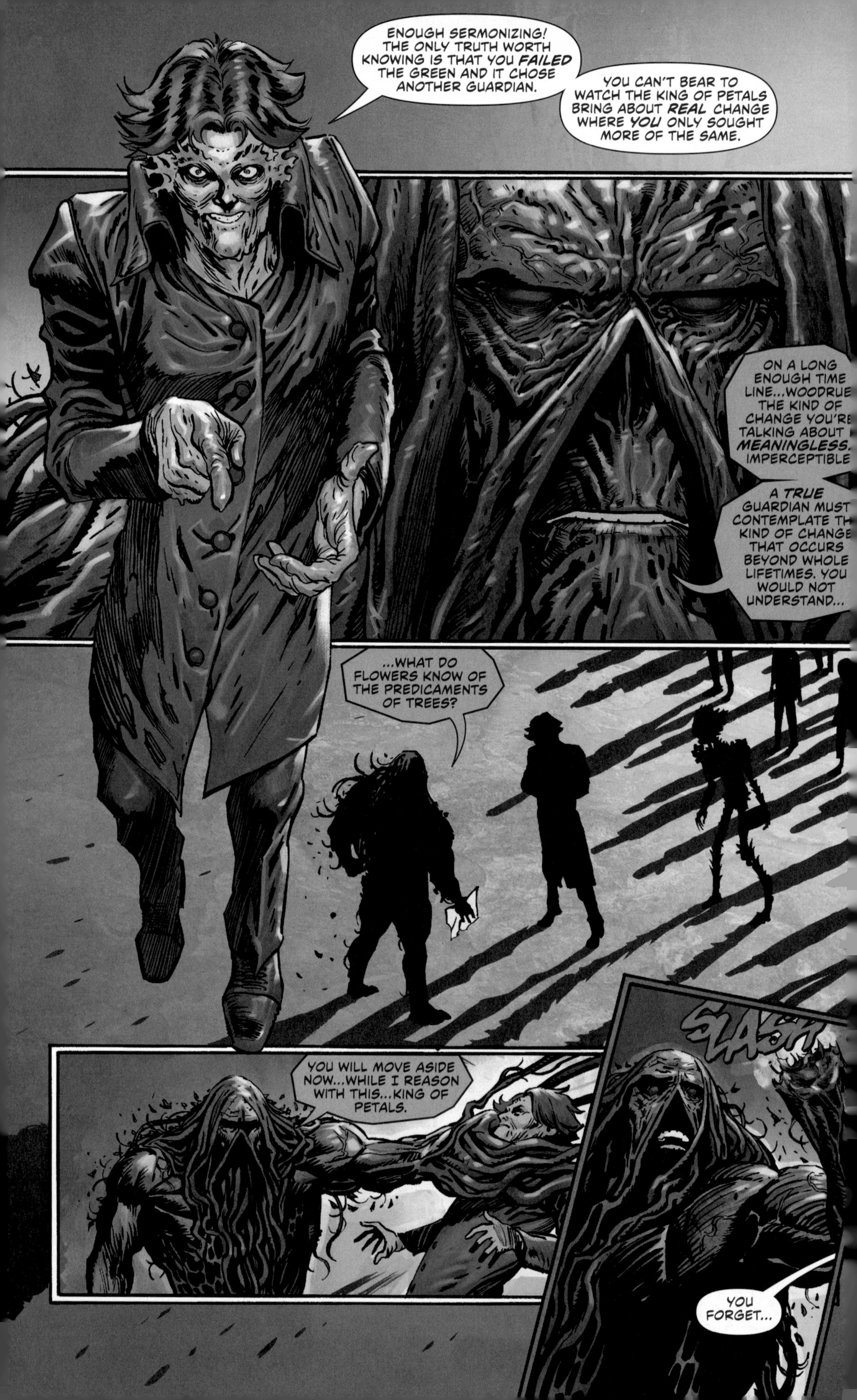
ENOUGH SERMONIZING! THE ONLY TRUTH WORTH KNOWING IS THAT YOU FAILED THE GREEN AND IT CHOSE ANOTHER GUARDIAN.
YOU CAN'T BEAR TO WATCH THE KING OF PETALS BRING ABOUT REAL CHANGE WHERE YOU ONLY SOUGHT MORE OF THE SAME.
ON A LONG ENOUGH TIME LINE...WOODRUE THE KIND OF CHANGE YOU'RE TALKING ABOUT MEANINGLESS. IMPERCEPTIBLE
A TRUE GUARDIAN MUST CONTEMPLATE THE KIND OF CHANGE THAT OCCURS BEYOND WHOLE LIFETIMES. YOU WOULD NOT UNDERSTAND...
...WHAT DO FLOWERS KNOW OF THE PREDICAMENTS OF TREES?
YOU WILL MOVE ASIDE NOW...WHILE I REASON WITH THIS...KING OF PETALS.
SLASH
YOU FORGET...

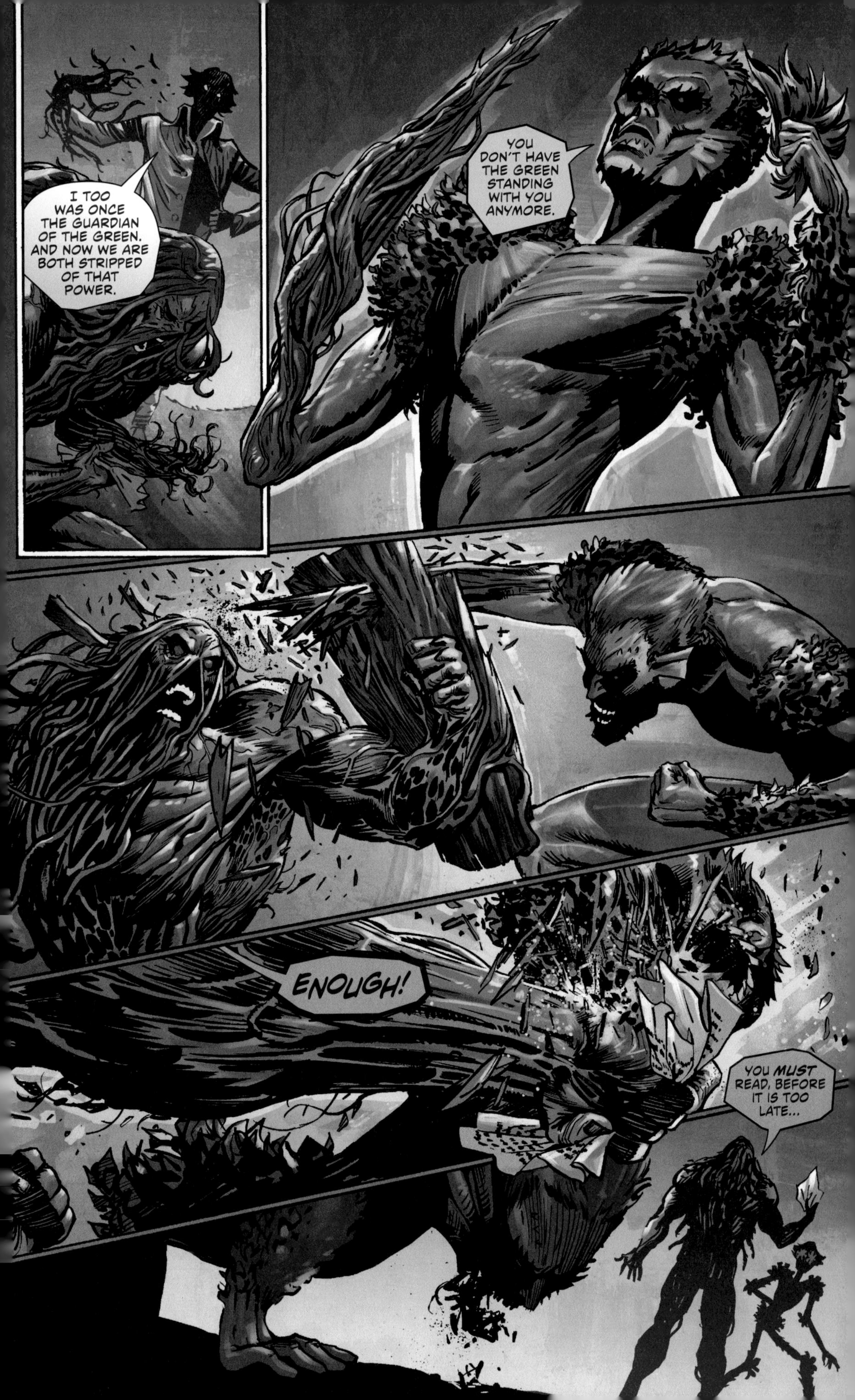
I TOO WAS ONCE THE GUARDIAN OF THE GREEN. AND NOW WE ARE BOTH STRIPPED OF THAT POWER.
YOU DON'T HAVE THE GREEN STANDING WITH YOU ANYMORE.
ENOUGH!
YOU MUST READ, BEFORE IT IS TOO LATE...

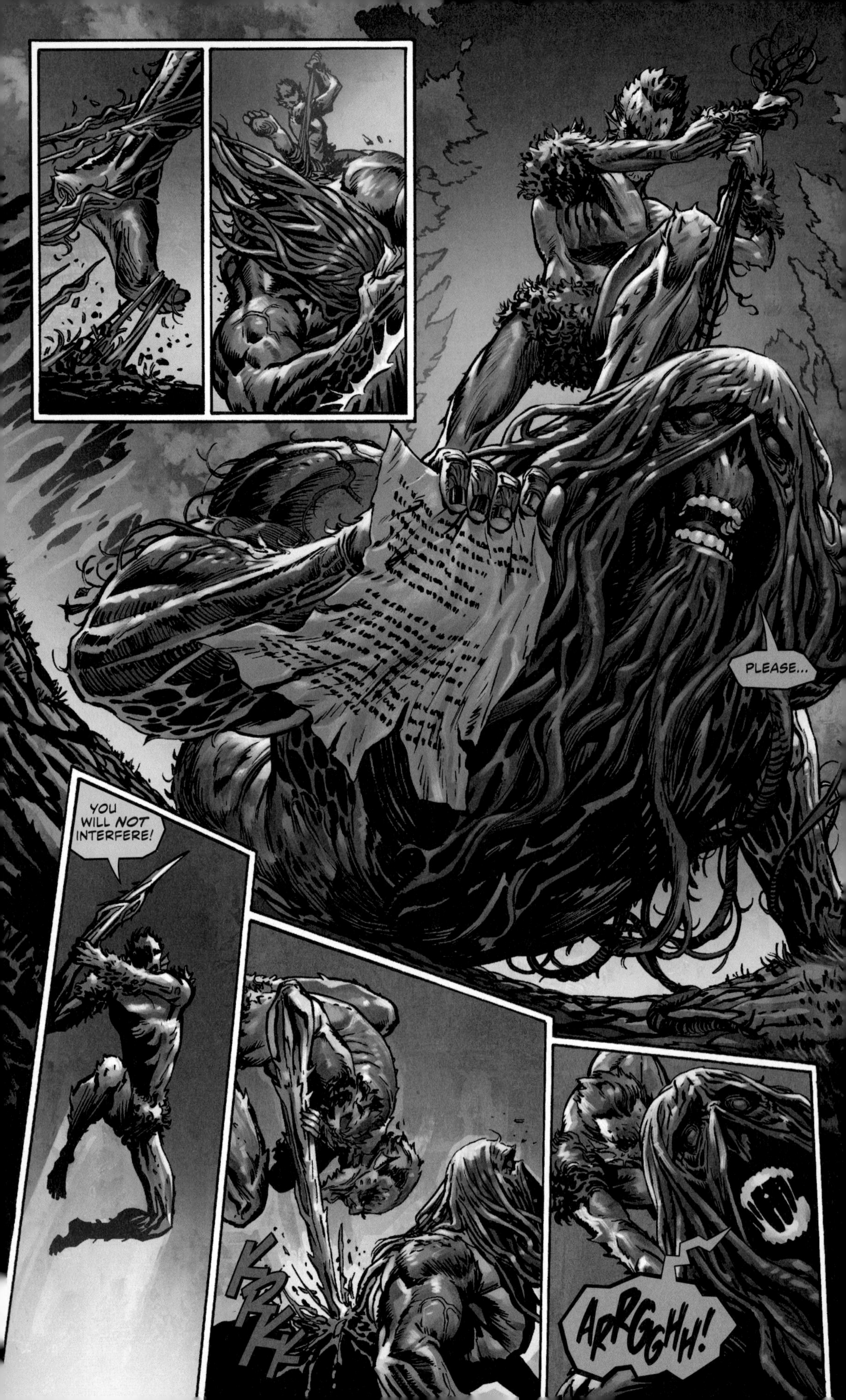
PLEASE...
YOU WILL NOT INTERFERE!
KRAK
ARRGGHH!

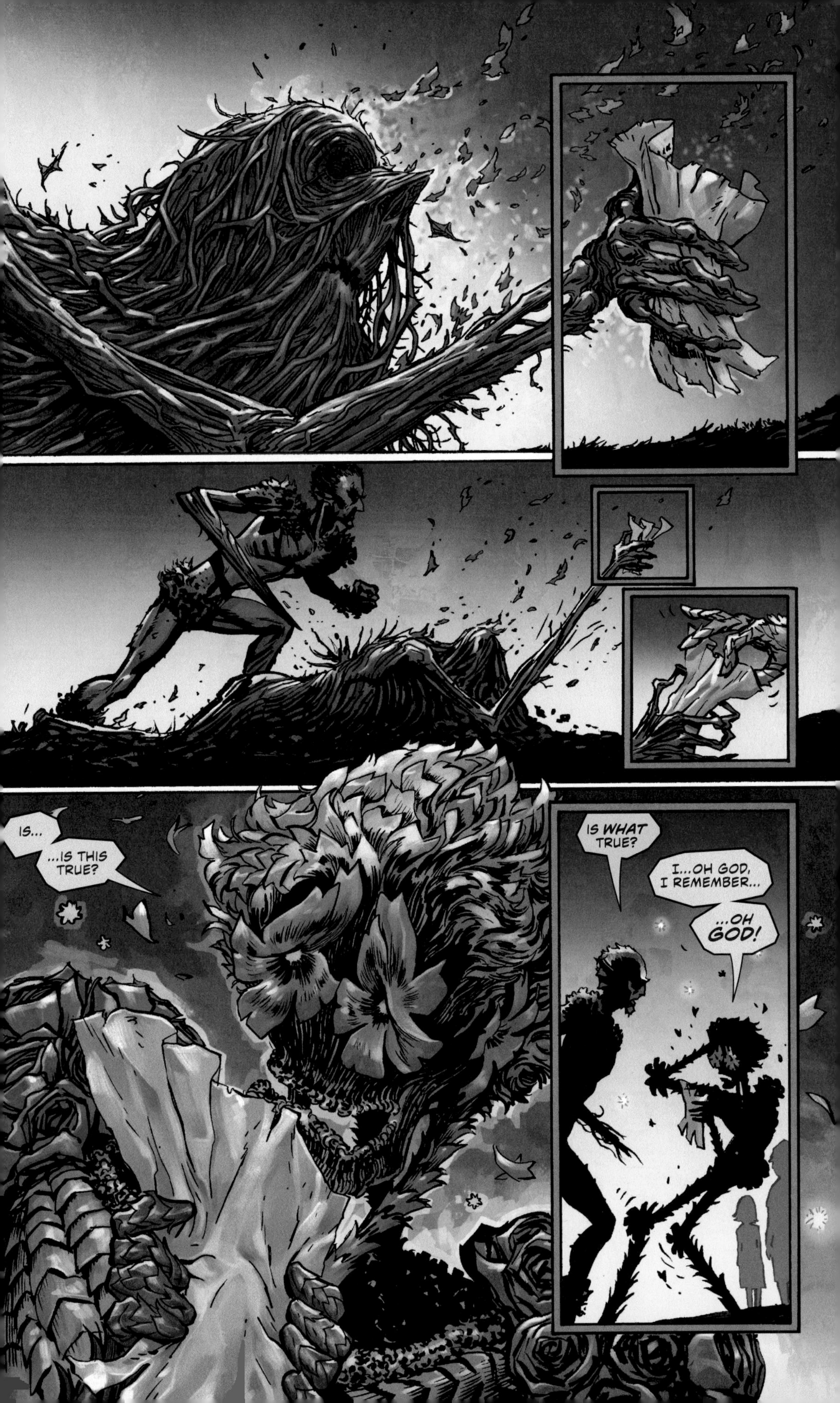

IS...
...IS THIS TRUE?
IS WHAT TRUE?
I...OH GOD, I REMEMBER...
...OH GOD!

I HAVE WORKED HERE FOR DAYS. NATASHA'S GONE AND I COULDN'T BRING MYSELF TO SET FOOT IN THAT HOUSE ANYMORE. HERE, IN THE MUD, I'VE SPENT DAYS SUBJECTING THESE SOLANACEAE TO ENDLESS TORTURES. IT WOULD SEEM THAT MY EXPERIMENT IS A SUCCESS.

I PLANT THESE FLOWERS IN THE COLD GROUND, STRIPPED OF NUTRIENTS, LACED WITH POISONS AND CHEMICALS. I LEAVE THEM TO THE ELEMENTS AND YET, THEY GROW SANGUINE. THESE PAST DAYS MY TESTS HAVE GROWN MORE EXTREME. I MASH THEM WITH MY INSTRUMENTS, STOMP THEM INTO THE MUD, I RIP THEIR PETALS AND SNAP THEIR STEMS. AND *STILL* THEY LIVE. NEEDING ONLY THE BAREST OF ENCOURAGEMENTS TO HOLD ON TO LIFE. THEY ARE MOCKING ME.

OLEANDER SORREL WHO WILTED AT THE FIRST HINT OF SORROW. JARED WAS GONE, FOR THAT I WAS NOT TO BLAME. BUT EVERYTHING SINCE... MY LIFE HAS CRUMBLED IN MY HANDS AS IF TURNED TO SAND. THE HARDER I TRY TO HOLD ON, THE EASIER IT SLIPS FROM MY FINGERS. AND YET THESE PETALS COME UNABATED IN A CARIOUS BLOOM.

I WILL SUBJECT THEM TODAY TO THE LAST TORTURE. BARRELS OF CAUSTIC, WHICH I WILL EMPTY INTO THE GROUND. WATCH IT EAT THROUGH EVERY LAST DAMN FLOWER. THEN I WILL SEED THE GROUND WITH MY OWN RANCID GRIEF. BY MORNING THERE WILL BE *NOTHING* LEFT OF ME. NOTHING AT ALL.

--FROM *THE JOURNAL OF DR. OLEANDER SORREL*

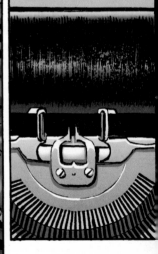

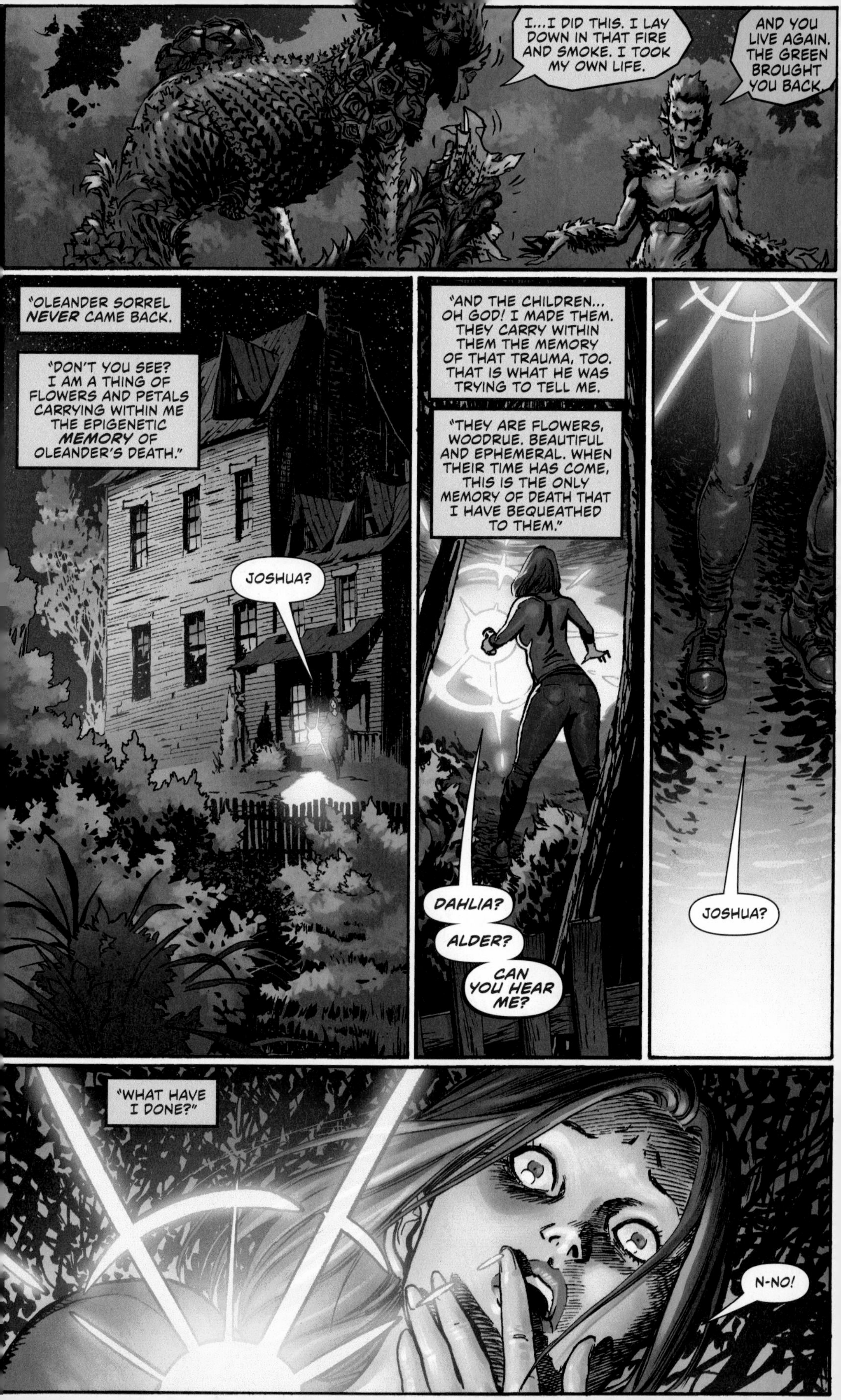
I...I DID THIS. I LAY DOWN IN THAT FIRE AND SMOKE. I TOOK MY OWN LIFE.
AND YOU LIVE AGAIN. THE GREEN BROUGHT YOU BACK.
"OLEANDER SORREL NEVER CAME BACK.
"DON'T YOU SEE? I AM A THING OF FLOWERS AND PETALS CARRYING WITHIN ME THE EPIGENETIC MEMORY OF OLEANDER'S DEATH."
JOSHUA?
"AND THE CHILDREN... OH GOD! I MADE THEM. THEY CARRY WITHIN THEM THE MEMORY OF THAT TRAUMA, TOO. THAT IS WHAT HE WAS TRYING TO TELL ME.
"THEY ARE FLOWERS, WOODRUE. BEAUTIFUL AND EPHEMERAL. WHEN THEIR TIME HAS COME, THIS IS THE ONLY MEMORY OF DEATH THAT I HAVE BEQUEATHED TO THEM."
DAHLIA?
ALDER?
CAN YOU HEAR ME?
JOSHUA?
"WHAT HAVE I DONE?"
N-NO!

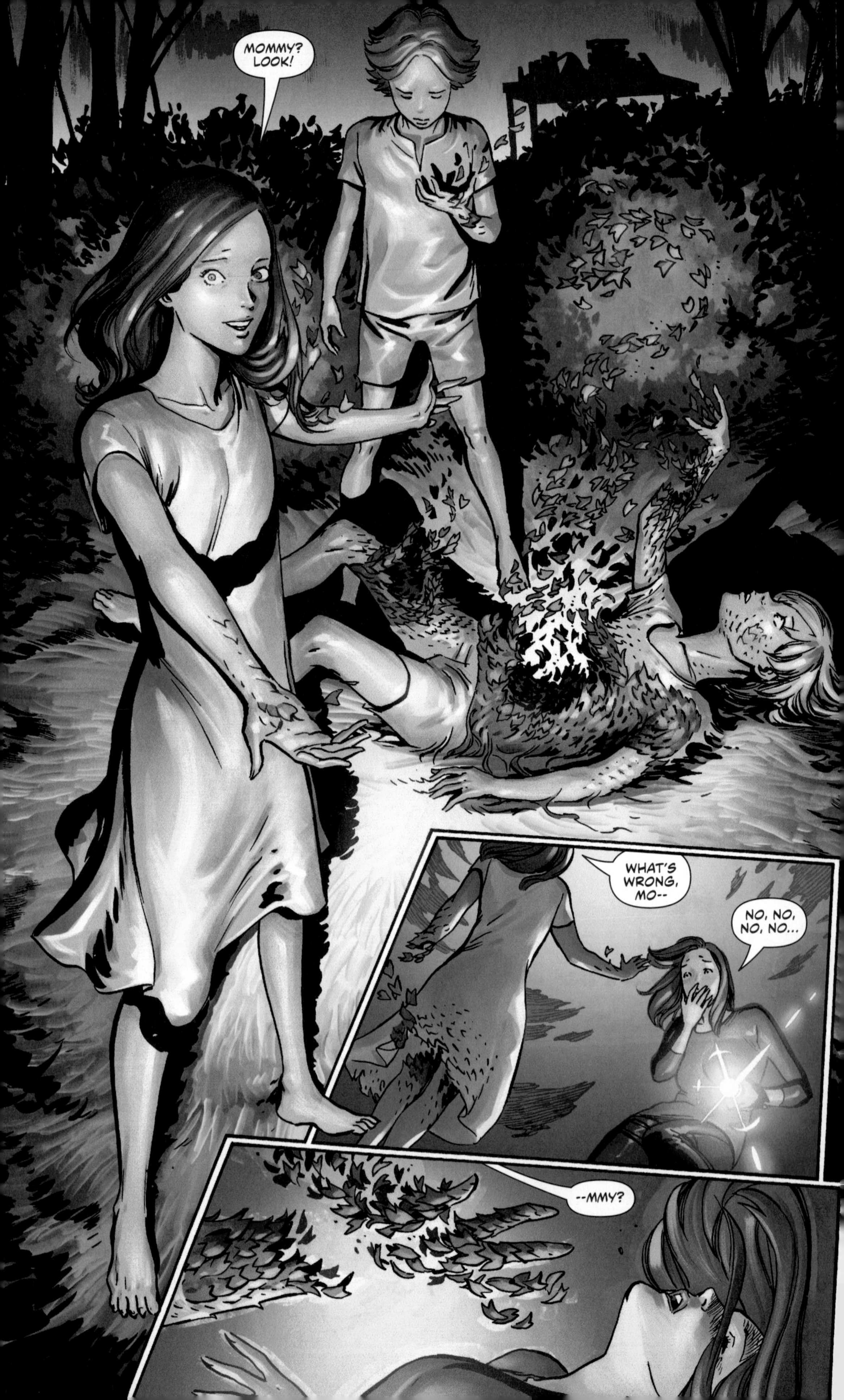
MOMMY? LOOK!
WHAT'S WRONG, MO--
NO, NO, NO, NO...
--MMY?

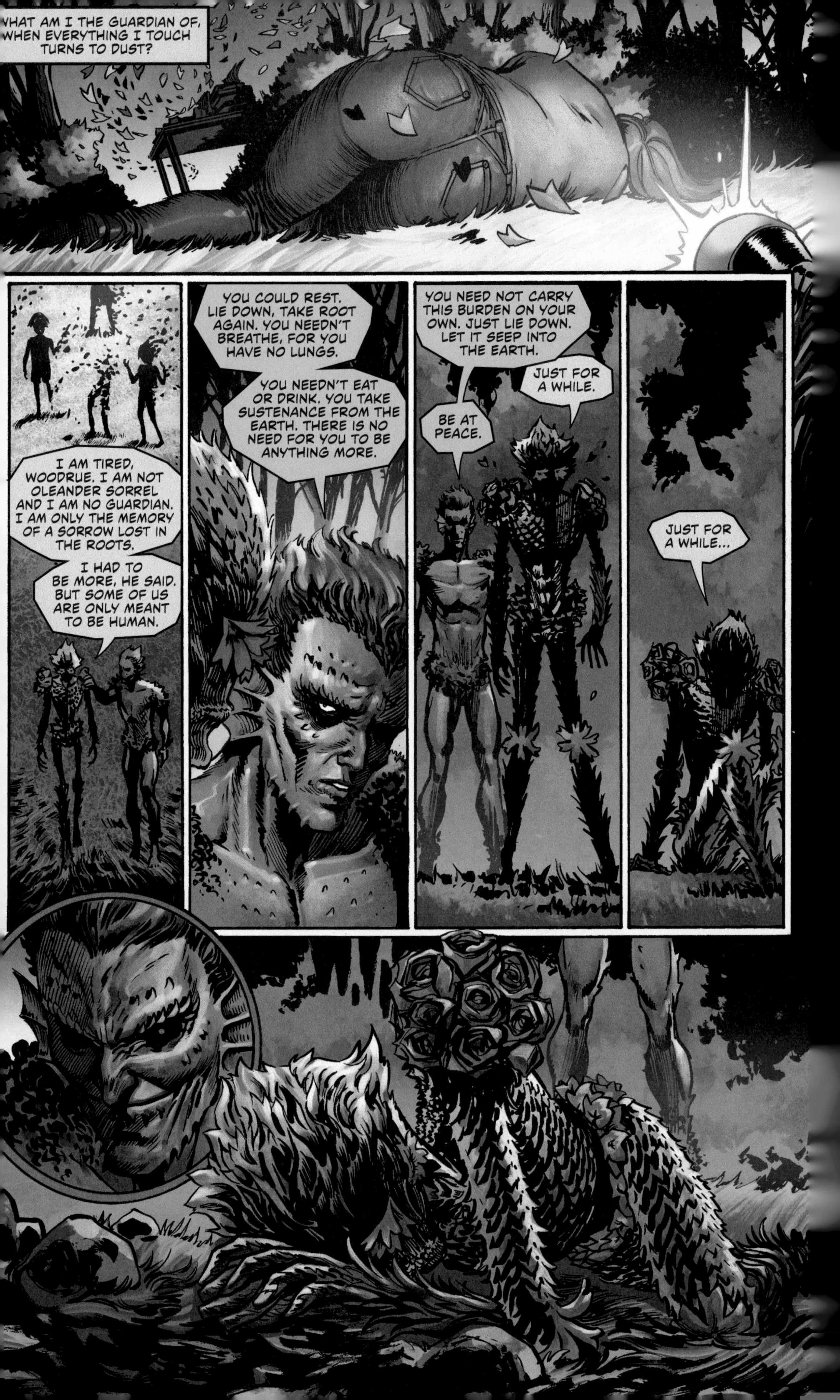
WHAT AM I THE GUARDIAN OF, WHEN EVERYTHING I TOUCH TURNS TO DUST?
I AM TIRED, WOODRUE. I AM NOT OLEANDER SORREL AND I AM NO GUARDIAN. I AM ONLY THE MEMORY OF A SORROW LOST IN THE ROOTS.
I HAD TO BE MORE, HE SAID. BUT SOME OF US ARE ONLY MEANT TO BE HUMAN.
YOU COULD REST. LIE DOWN, TAKE ROOT AGAIN. YOU NEEDN'T BREATHE, FOR YOU HAVE NO LUNGS.
YOU NEEDN'T EAT OR DRINK. YOU TAKE SUSTENANCE FROM THE EARTH. THERE IS NO NEED FOR YOU TO BE ANYTHING MORE.
YOU NEED NOT CARRY THIS BURDEN ON YOUR OWN. JUST LIE DOWN. LET IT SEEP INTO THE EARTH.
BE AT PEACE.
JUST FOR A WHILE.
JUST FOR A WHILE...

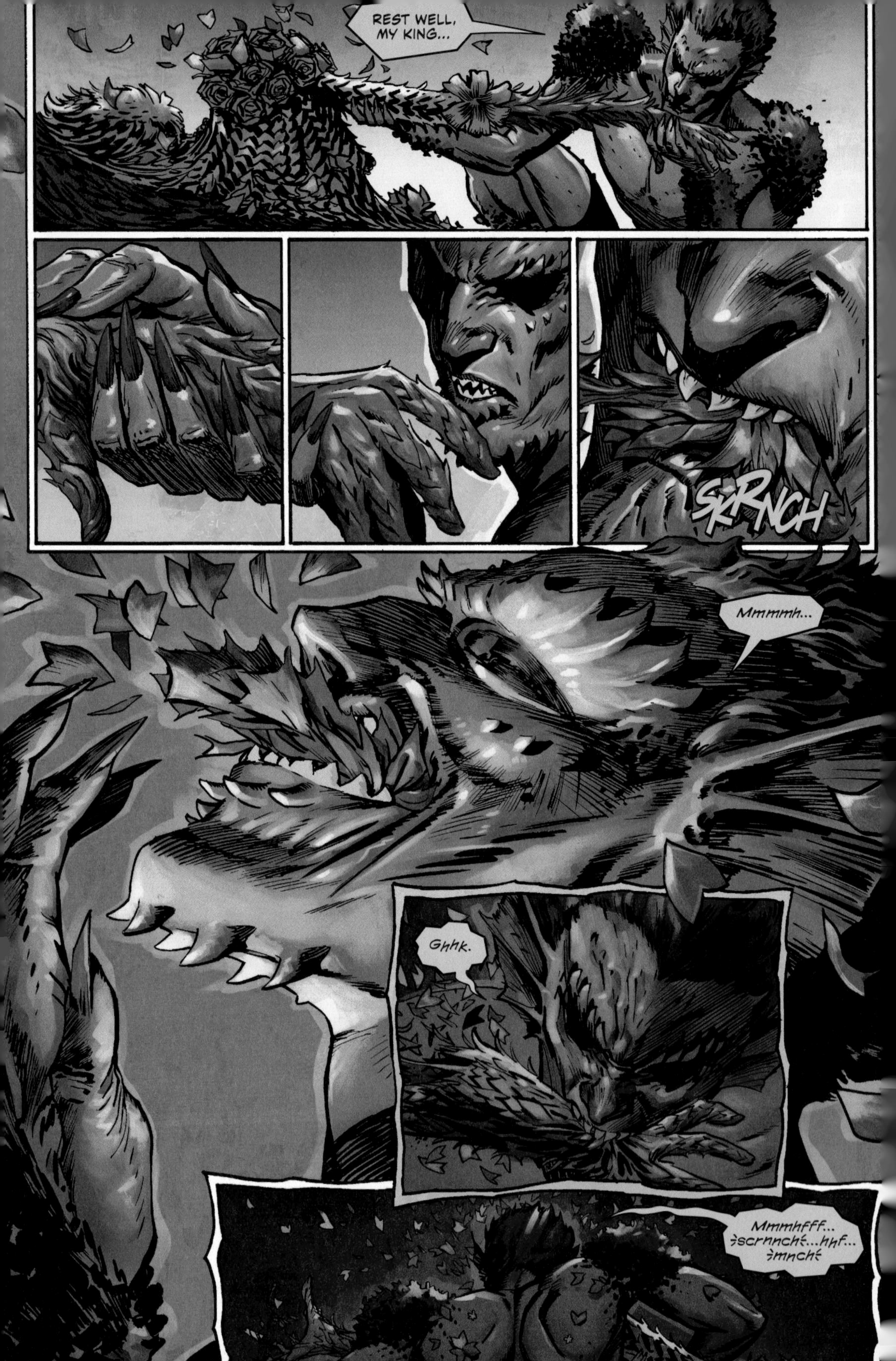
REST WELL, MY KING...
SKRNCH
Mmmmh...
Ghhk.
Mmmhfff... ⪢scrnnch⪡...hhf... ⪢mnch⪡

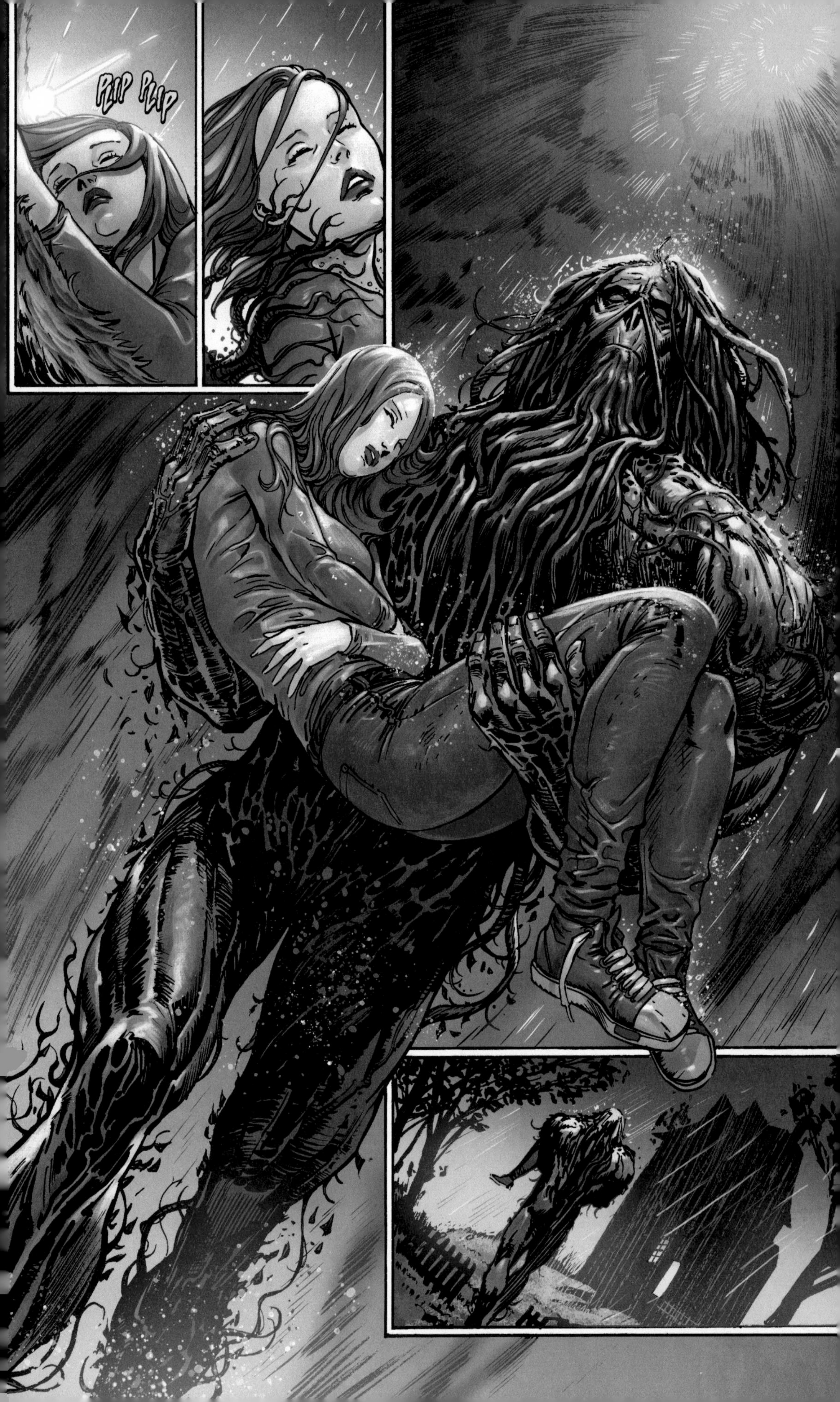
PLIP PLIP

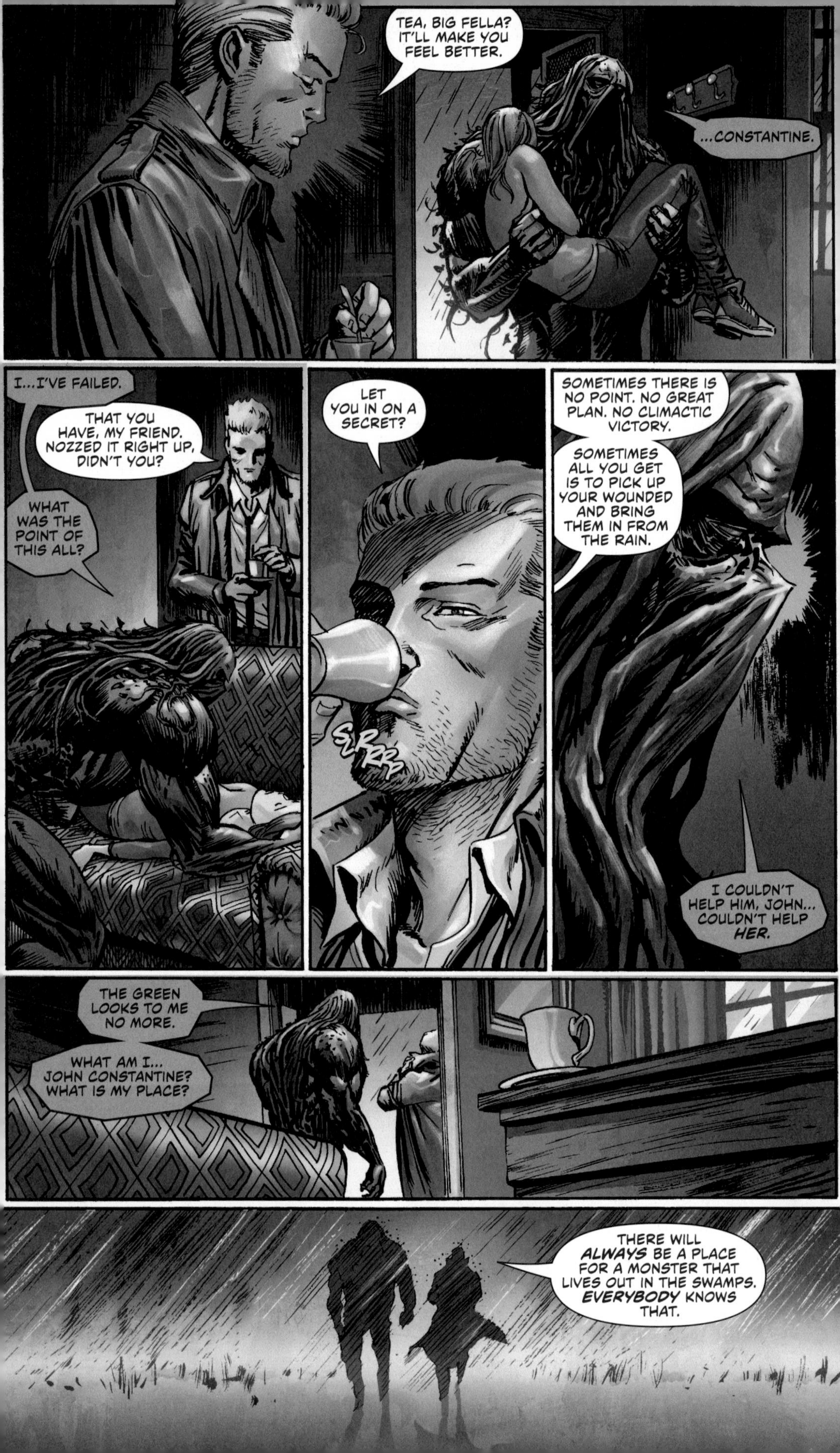

TEA, BIG FELLA? IT'LL MAKE YOU FEEL BETTER.
...CONSTANTINE.
I...I'VE FAILED.
THAT YOU HAVE, MY FRIEND. NOZZED IT RIGHT UP, DIDN'T YOU?
WHAT WAS THE POINT OF THIS ALL?
LET YOU IN ON A SECRET?
SLRRP
SOMETIMES THERE IS NO POINT. NO GREAT PLAN. NO CLIMACTIC VICTORY.
SOMETIMES ALL YOU GET IS TO PICK UP YOUR WOUNDED AND BRING THEM IN FROM THE RAIN.
I COULDN'T HELP HIM, JOHN... COULDN'T HELP HER.
THE GREEN LOOKS TO ME NO MORE.
WHAT AM I... JOHN CONSTANTINE? WHAT IS MY PLACE?
THERE WILL ALWAYS BE A PLACE FOR A MONSTER THAT LIVES OUT IN THE SWAMPS. EVERYBODY KNOWS THAT.

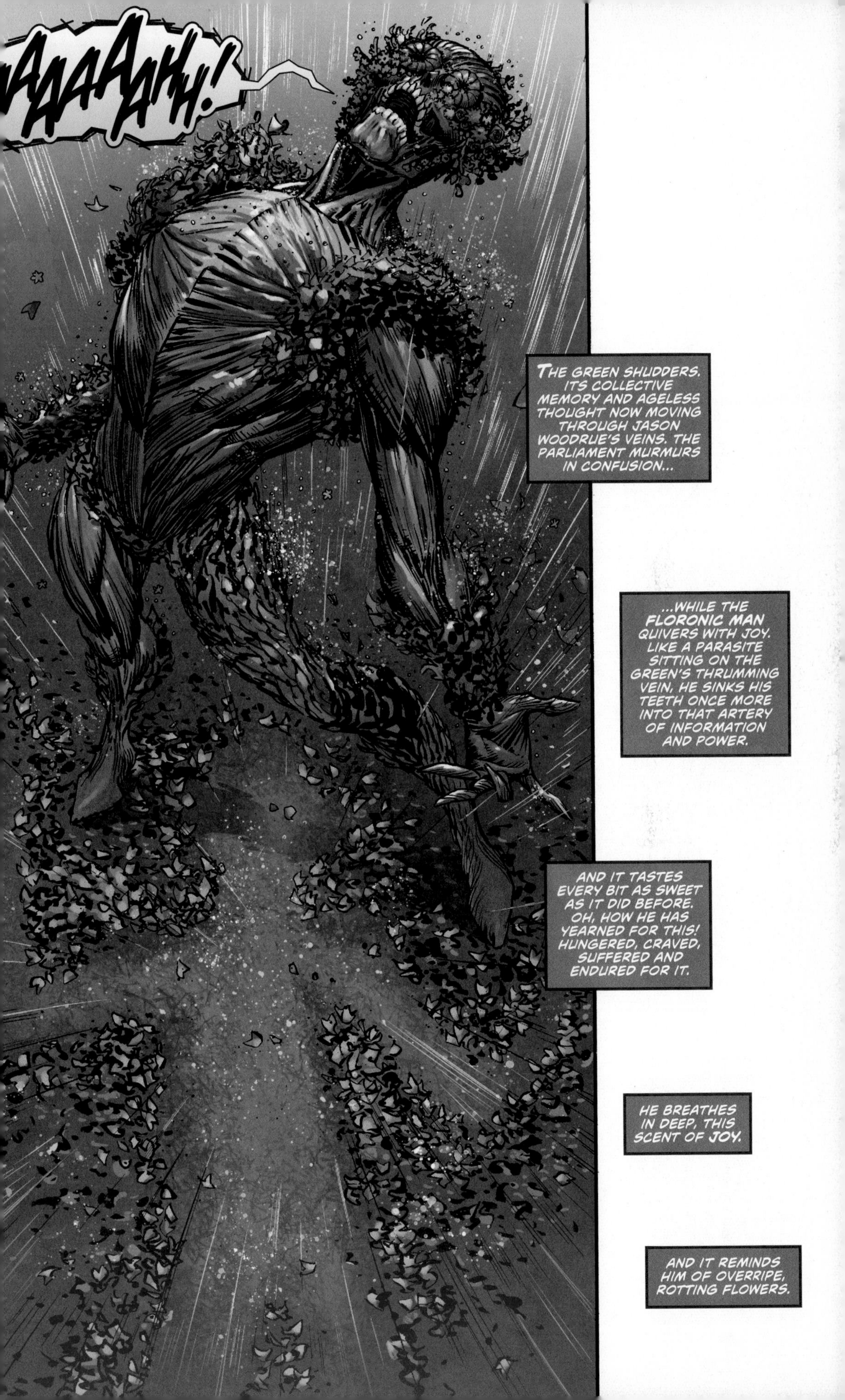

AAAAAAHH!
THE GREEN SHUDDERS. ITS COLLECTIVE MEMORY AND AGELESS THOUGHT NOW MOVING THROUGH JASON WOODRUE'S VEINS. THE PARLIAMENT MURMURS IN CONFUSION...
...WHILE THE FLORONIC MAN QUIVERS WITH JOY. LIKE A PARASITE SITTING ON THE GREEN'S THRUMMING VEIN, HE SINKS HIS TEETH ONCE MORE INTO THAT ARTERY OF INFORMATION AND POWER.
AND IT TASTES EVERY BIT AS SWEET AS IT DID BEFORE. OH, HOW HE HAS YEARNED FOR THIS! HUNGERED, CRAVED, SUFFERED AND ENDURED FOR IT.
HE BREATHES IN DEEP, THIS SCENT OF JOY.
AND IT REMINDS HIM OF OVERRIPE, ROTTING FLOWERS.

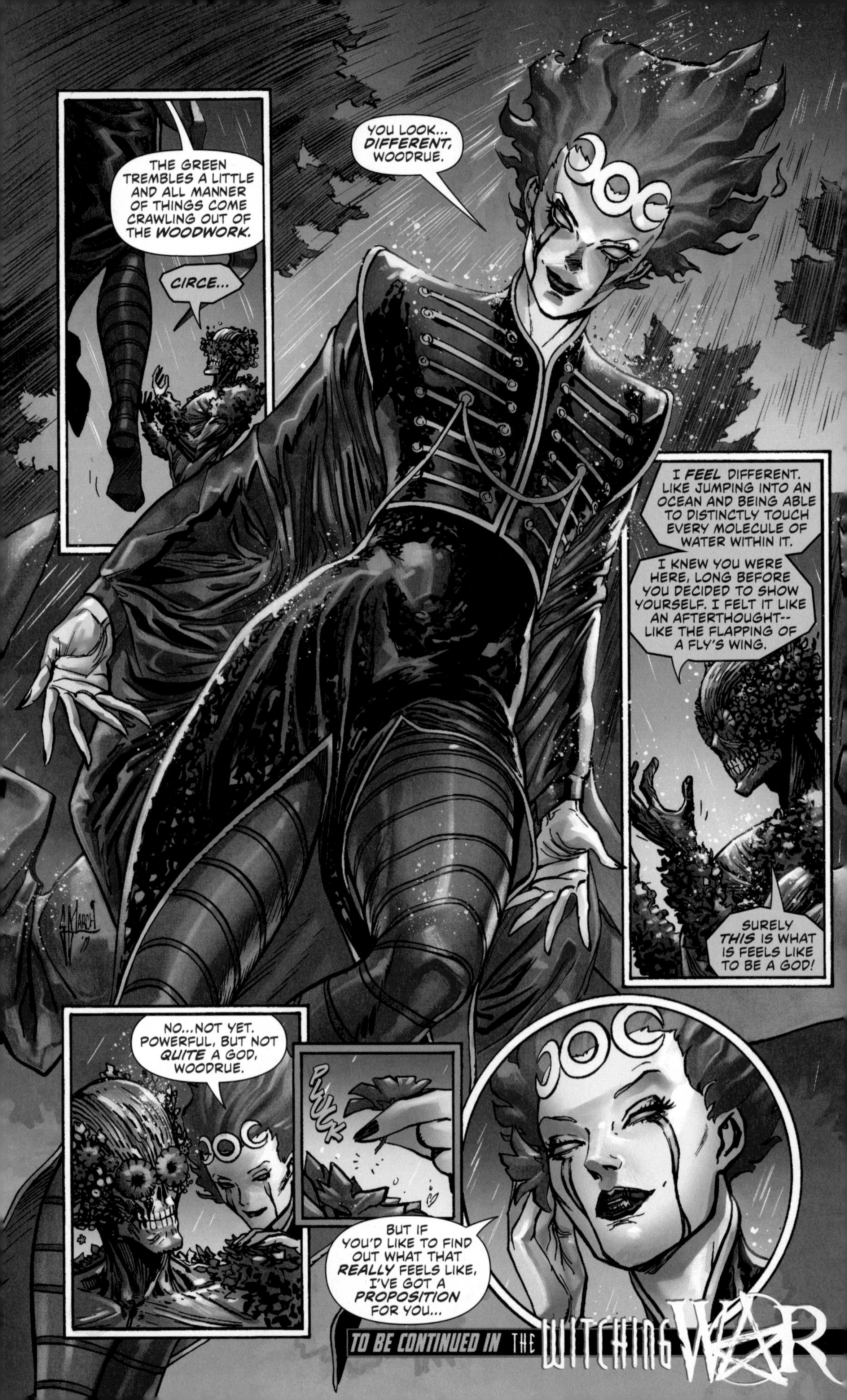
THE GREEN TREMBLES A LITTLE AND ALL MANNER OF THINGS COME CRAWLING OUT OF THE WOODWORK.
CIRCE...
YOU LOOK... DIFFERENT, WOODRUE.
I FEEL DIFFERENT. LIKE JUMPING INTO AN OCEAN AND BEING ABLE TO DISTINCTLY TOUCH EVERY MOLECULE OF WATER WITHIN IT.
I KNEW YOU WERE HERE, LONG BEFORE YOU DECIDED TO SHOW YOURSELF. I FELT IT LIKE AN AFTERTHOUGHT-- LIKE THE FLAPPING OF A FLY'S WING.
SURELY THIS IS WHAT IS FEELS LIKE TO BE A GOD!
NO...NOT YET. POWERFUL, BUT NOT QUITE A GOD, WOODRUE.
PLUCK
BUT IF YOU'D LIKE TO FIND OUT WHAT THAT REALLY FEELS LIKE, I'VE GOT A PROPOSITION FOR YOU...
TO BE CONTINUED IN THE WITCHING WAR

VARIANT COVER GALLERY

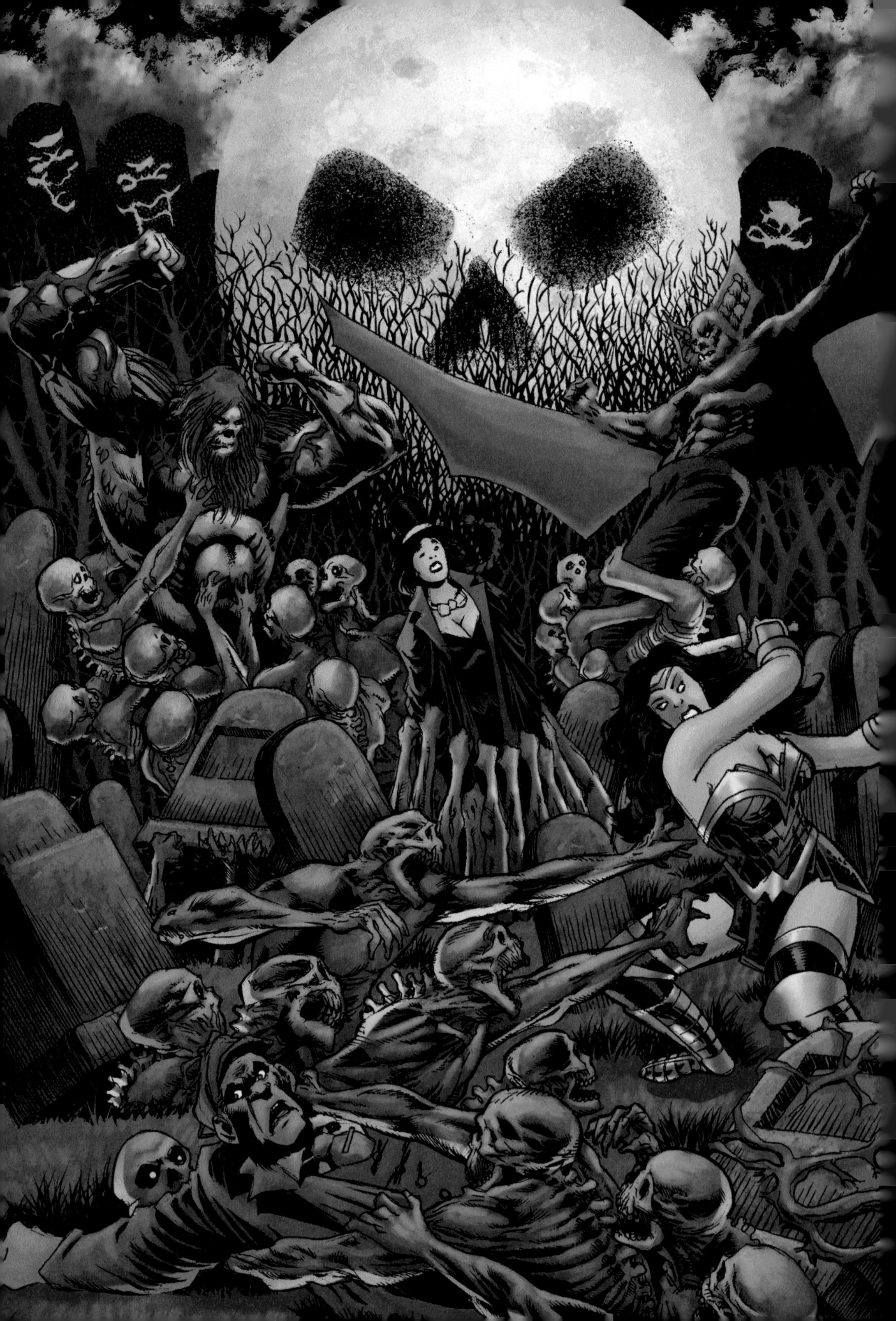

JUSTICE LEAGUE DARK #9 variant cover
by CLAYTON CRAIN

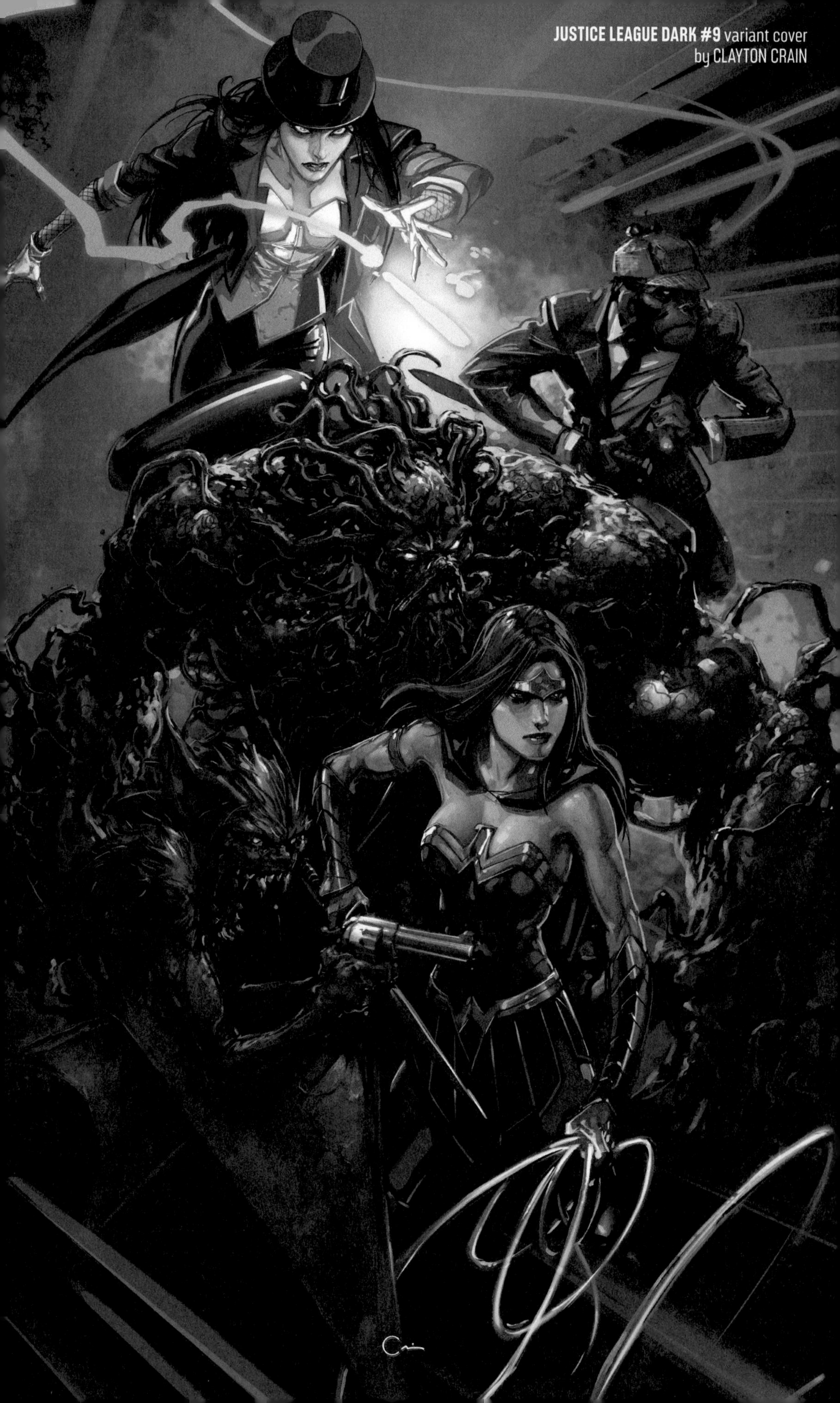

JUSTICE LEAGUE DARK #10 variant cover
by KELLEY JONES and MICHELLE MADSEN

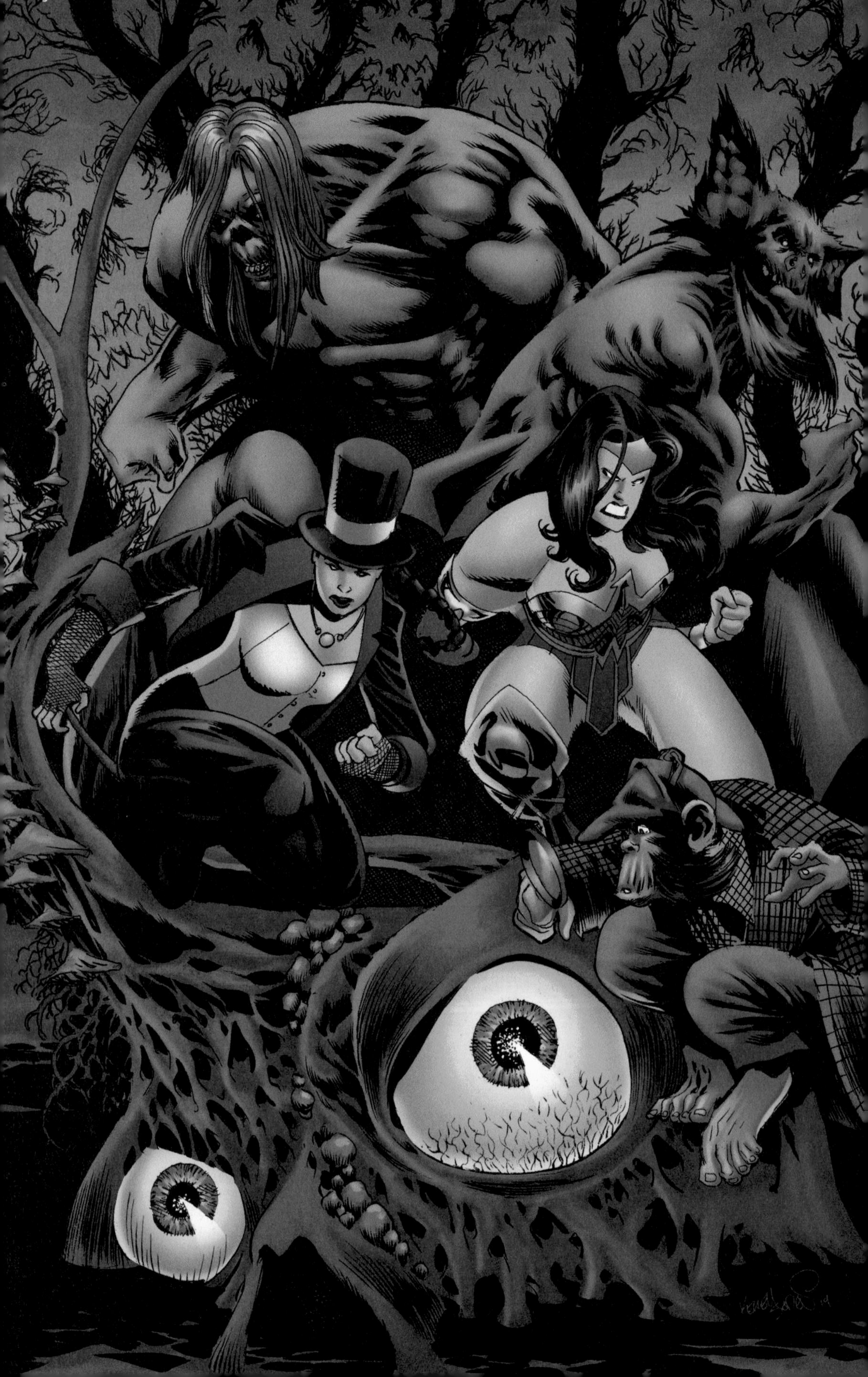

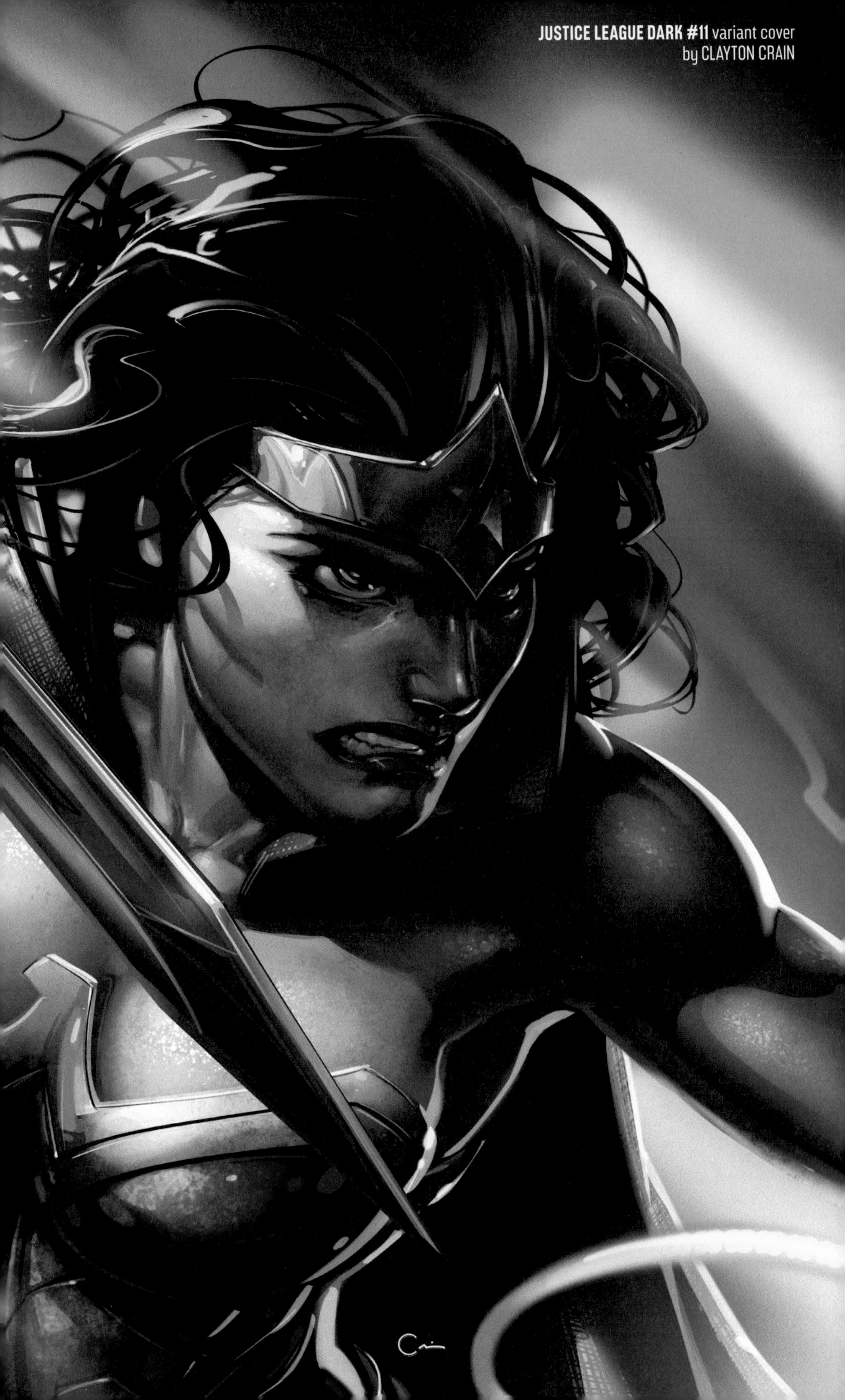

JUSTICE LEAGUE DARK #11 variant cover
by CLAYTON CRAIN

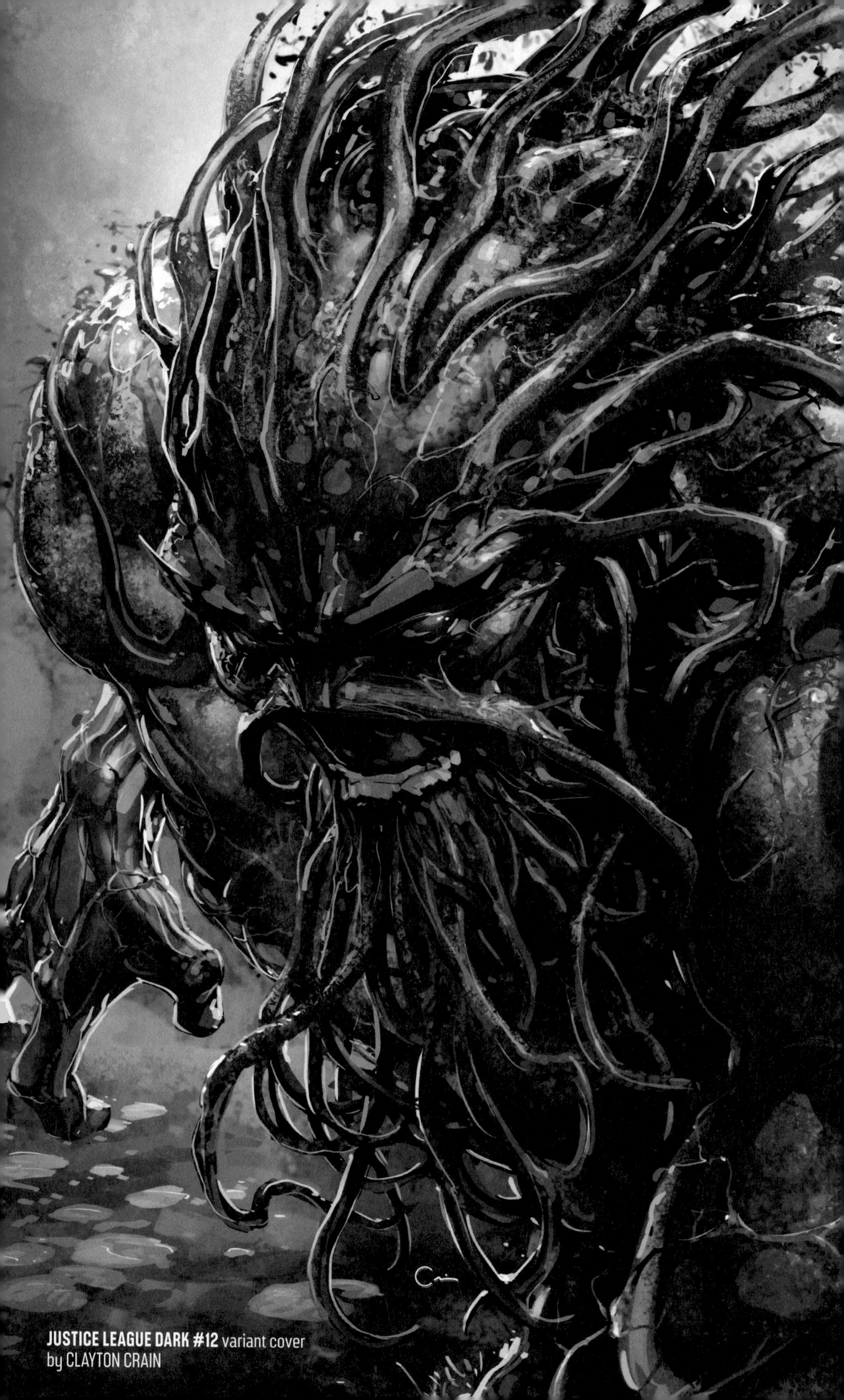

JUSTICE LEAGUE DARK #12 variant cover
by CLAYTON CRAIN

JUSTICE LEAGUE DARK #13 variant cover
by DAN QUINTANA

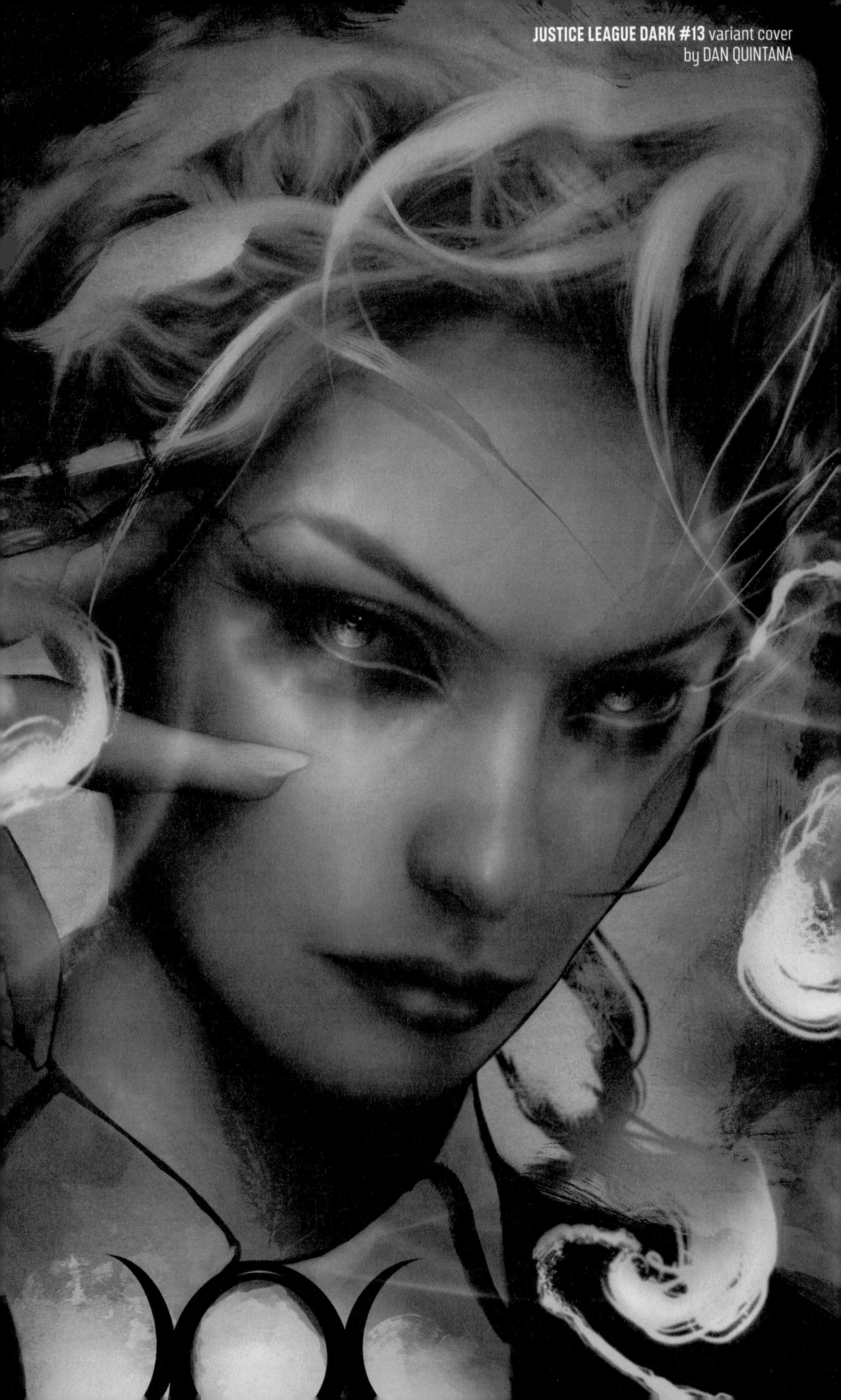